ACTING ON
ETHICS IN
CITY
PLANNING

ACTING ON ETHICS IN CITY PLANNING

ELIZABETH HOWE

CENTER
FOR URBAN
POLICY RESEARCH

Published by the Center for Urban Policy Research
New Brunswick, New Jersey 08903

Printed in the United States of America

Library of Congress Cataloging-in-Publication Data

Howe, Elizabeth, 1945–
    Acting on ethics in city planning / Elizabeth Howe.
        p.   cm.
    Includes bibliographical references (p.   ) and index.
    ISBN 0-88285-147-0

    1. City planning—Moral and ethical aspects. 2. City planners—
Professional ethics—United States. 3. Professional ethics—United
States. I. Title.
HT167.H695   1994
174'.971—dc20   93–28828
                                                  CIP

For Jerry Kaufman

Contents

Figures

Figures

Tables

Tables

Preface

This book has taken a long time. Two people particularly deserve thanks for its completion. One is my colleague Jerry Kaufman, who was an equal partner in the design of the study and in doing the interviews. Other commitments prevented him from being my coauthor, but he has been an active provider of ideas, a reader, and a critic. The other is Mac Passano, who also was actively involved from the beginning and who was pressed into service as an interviewer, a driver, a pilot, and a commentator. He arranged for a leave of absence, which allowed this book finally to be written.

Two sources of funds made this work possible. One was the Graduate School Research Committee of the University of Wisconsin—Madison, which provided support for the interviews themselves. The other was my mother, Sarah Tower, who posthumously supported the analysis and writing. I hope she would approve of the result. This project was also heavily subsidized by friends and family, who provided meals, lodging, cars, and pleasant relaxation as we careened around the country inter-viewing planners during the summer of 1982.

Three places have provided a conducive environment—meaning for me a view of a large body of salt water—for the years of transcribing tapes and then for the writing. The University of Washington's Friday Harbor Labs offered a beautiful view of Puget Sound and books that miraculously appeared weekly in the library from the Seattle campus. Next House, lent by Jack Churchill, provided an equally spectacular view of Buzzards Bay in Cape Cod, Massachusetts. Finally, Webb Cottage on Chebeague Island, Maine, looks out across Casco Bay to the Atlantic. Martha Hamilton of the Chebeague Island Library was helpful in getting exotic philosophical articles through interlibrary loan.

Other thanks go to Robert Lake, the editor, and to the reviewers for the Center for Urban Policy Research at Rutgers—The State University of New Jersey. Ken Pearlman, Marcia Caton Campbell, and a number of anonymous reviewers at *The Journal of Planning Literature* also commented very usefully on several articles written as background for this book. A similar debt is owed to reviewers from *The Journal of Planning Education and Research* for comments on an early draft of chapter 4 on the public interest. Material written as background for this book was previously published in the *Journal of Planning Literature* and is referenced here with permission of Sage Publications, Inc. Colleagues from the Department of Urban and Regional Planning at the University of Wisconsin—Madison, Roz Greenstein, Martin Wachs, Charlie Hoch, and Michael Teitz, were all supportive in different ways. I would also like to thank Kari Lavalli, who took time out from her research on lobsters to type fifteen of the interview transcripts. Judy Holmes was both precise and good-humored about all the rounds of correcting and of printing out the text.

Of course, the real and most fundamental thanks go to the ninety-nine planners who were interviewed during that summer of 1982. I assume many of them have gone on to other jobs and that many may have wondered if anything ever came of their interviews. I hope the results are useful to them and to other practicing planners.

1

Introduction

A city planner works in a conservative, middle-class suburb of a large city. The town's zoning ordinance has no provision for apartments, though demand in the local housing market is strong enough that he sees developers who would like to build them. The planner has taken several of these proposals to his city council, which would have to adopt apartment zoning to allow them to be constructed. The council members have always voted the proposals down.

It bothers the planner that the town discriminates against everyone who cannot afford a single-family house. When the most recent proposal came up, he quietly suggested to some council members that a slightly more diverse population would not harm and would in fact strengthen the town. The response he received was that if people really wanted to live there, they could save their money until they could afford a house. The planner feels strongly that these elected officials have the right to make such a decision but he wishes there were some way to make them see the issue in a different light. He says:

> Our zoning ordinance does not allow multifamily housing. People have the image that it will be of poor quality. I understand where they're coming from, but their image of who would live in the apartments isn't necessarily accurate. For certain segments of society—whether it's the elderly, the unmarried, or lower income people—housing is just not available. I tell them we need to have a balance of people . . . [but] we have a governing body with strong convictions and they're not going to do it. If you are a true believer in the idea of democracy, in what the majority says, that gets a lot of the guilt feelings out of it, but at the same time it is very difficult to accept.

1

He talks about this issue with a friend from planning school who he meets at a national professional conference. She works in another state but in a community that is not altogether unlike his—middle class, suburban, and fairly conservative. Because of a recent economic boom, "affordable housing" has become a fairly salient political issue. She says that she has encouraged the formation of an affordable housing coalition in her town and that she has worked closely with several developers to ensure that the affordable apartment units they have proposed are of high quality.

Rather than just taking the proposals directly to the city council, she has gone out to the neighborhoods and has held extensive meetings to familiarize residents with the proposals and to let the developers hear and address local concerns. It has been a slow process. One project was turned down by the council but another was approved. About her role she says:

> I suppose I have a general value that communities should attempt to be diverse in some way and that another need is that people should be able to live in housing that they can afford. I've been concerned with the incredible escalation of housing prices here. It's really reduced the diversity of the area, and it's something where the community can make some change. I've played something of a leadership role . . . but also our general plan, which I wrote [laughter], has very strong statements about that—social and economic mix—because that does happen to be something that I feel very strongly about.

These two cases typify a very difficult but also one of the most common issues of ethics in the planning profession. The planners are both faced with the issue of affordable housing, which they think would serve the public interest of their communities by improving social equity. Decision makers, however, do not see it as their job to serve people who do not presently live there, especially if this would get them into political hot water with the people who do. The planners work for their councils; neither has any authority to make a final decision on these apartment proposals. All they can do is try to convince their elected officials, but theirs are clearly not the only voices these officials are hearing.

The two planners have chosen different strategies for trying to make their arguments. The first one has taken it up quietly with council members. He feels that loyalty to his council, as well as political discretion, prevents him from doing more. The second planner has been actively involved in efforts to build public support for affordable housing proposals. She sees some political risk in this but feels that the issue of social justice has a higher priority.

Such fundamental issues of social justice do not come up daily in many local communities, but choices about how active a political role they should play and how much loyalty they owe to elected officials are fairly common for planners. All are issues of professional ethics and not of some distant, abstract ethics. These are not only issues that are dealt with in the professional organization's *Code of Ethics and Professional Conduct* (American Institute of Certified Planners 1981; a revised version was adopted in 1992. See page 214.) But also these are conflicts that arise in everyday practice because the planners themselves have value commitments about loyalty and social justice. Their values are not all the same nor are their images of the kind of role they should play as planners. So their answers to ethical issues such as apartments in the suburbs are likely to be different. This book is concerned with looking at why public planners make the ethical choices they do.

The Nature of Ethics

What is the purpose of ethics? Ethics involve rules or principles that regulate behavior, telling us what we ought or ought not do, but clearly they do not cover all such regulation. While there may be an overlap at either end of the spectrum of rules, ethics generally fill a gap between laws, which require or prohibit certain behaviors and which are backed by sanctions wielded by the state, and etiquette, which is concerned with the amenities of social interaction.

Ethics also involve codes of conduct that are not merely prudential or dictated by self-interest. In this sense, they impose serious obligations that may require people to undertake actions that are unpleasant or that involve personal sacrifices, such as the political risk of raising the issue of social justice. The reason for this is that moral obligations are obligations to others that are expected to be binding regardless of their personal consequences.

Ethics are a basic requirement of social life. They are concerned with aspects of behavior that allow us to live together, to experience a life in which we can rely on others and they can rely on us. They are concerned with truthfulness, keeping promises, loyalty, fairness, and a broader sense of justice and what is good.

Even though ethics are not legally mandated codes of conduct, they are enforced in part by social pressures among people who share the same organizational, professional, or cultural systems. Their effectiveness depends considerably on being embodied in an internalized sense of right and wrong and of good and bad. How well defined an ethical code of conduct is and how effectively it is enforced through external pressures and internalized norms may vary from one social group to another. On the one hand, we tend to think of small, traditional societies as having well-defined ethical codes that they can enforce effectively. A modern profession, on the other hand, takes in many people from diverse backgrounds and has only limited opportunities for socializing them to common norms before they go out to practice in diverse settings. In such a context, the problem of developing and enforcing a coherent code of ethics may be more difficult. A written code is just a beginning. Consider the multiplicity of social groups such as professions, each with its own particular mission and its own code of conduct, and the issue of whether it is possible for a broader society to have a common morality soon rears its head.

We accept quite easily the idea that different cultures have different moral standards and rules. People when challenged are often uneasy about saying that anything is right or wrong for anyone but themselves (Bellah et al. 1985). This sense of different but equal moral perspectives is supported by the bitterness of battles over such issues as abortion or capital punishment, but these controversies are only understandable because they draw on a common ethical system. They involve disagreements over the precedence of principles—the right to life or the right to privacy, for example—that are accepted as ethical by all participants.

The same issue of relativism could easily apply to professions as well. Descriptively, professions have quite different missions and values and the codes of ethics of various professions have different kinds of provisions. It may seem that each profession has its own values that cannot be evaluated or challenged by outsiders, such as clients or members of the public. While it may sometimes be in the interest of a profession to make such an argument, this is misleading. Within a common culture, such as that found in North America, the ethical standards of distinct subgroups such as professions are justified in part because they are supposed to serve the public. This means that these standards can fairly easily be judged by broader standards and certainly should be.

The Empirical Study of the Ethics of Planners

This book is a study of the profession of city planning. City planning is rather different from the traditional dominant consulting professions, such as law and medicine, which have been the focus of most discussions of professional ethics. The primary difference is that most though not all planners work as civil servants in public bureaucracies.[1] It is these public planners who are the subject of this study.

In this book, I have explored how some public planners defined ethical issues and how they thought about and acted on them. I have found considerable diversity among planners depending on how they thought about the role of planning in society and about the nature of ethics. Their ethical values were tied in many ways to broader societal ethical values, though the application of these values was, of course, shaped to meet the particular issues that were characteristic of planning. I have also evaluated their actions on these ethical issues using both the American Institute of Certified Planners' (AICP) *Code of Ethics and Professional Conduct* (1981) and a framework that I will discuss later in this chapter. On the whole, their values corresponded to those laid out in the code, though for a variety of reasons their actions sometimes did not. The disparity was greatest in relation to definitions of the public interest.

This is not a study of official corruption in public life. While there is often an assumption that such issues lie at the heart of public ethics, this is akin to equating issues of medical ethics with rape because physicians have intimate access to the bodies of patients. Rape can be an issue of medical ethics, just as corruption can be one of planning ethics, but professionals in each field face a range of other ethical issues as well. Such issues arise out of the varied aspects of professional activity and often pose choices much less clear-cut than those that are covered by law.

Urban planners have primarily been concerned with guiding the physical development of cities. Some have focused on the regulation of new land development using mechanisms such as zoning and subdivision controls. Others have been concerned with the revitalization of industrial or commercial areas, such as the central business district. Still others, often with a particular concern for low-income and minority groups, have worked to improve older residential neighborhoods. Much of this planning is concerned with the efficiency of urban infrastructure and services, but planners are often concerned with the aesthetics of urban design or the preservation of the historic fabric of a community. On a larger scale, some planners shape development by planning transportation systems, often at regional or state levels. While these activities have historically been and still remain the bread and butter of planning, the past twenty years have also seen some broadening out into related areas, such as economic development, rural land use, environmental planning, and even a short-lived effort in health planning.

Planning has been a relatively small profession, with perhaps about

30,000 members nationally in 1990 compared with 569,000 doctors and 655,000 lawyers. It has not been a very visible one either. Many people probably have a vague notion that planners are concerned with zoning, which is somehow related to protecting property values.

As civil servants, planners work in public bureaucracies and have input into but certainly not control over the outcomes of planning decisions. They are officially charged with serving the interests not of single individual clients but those of a whole community, whether it is a city, a region, or a state. Because of this, their role is played not in some one-to-one relationship but through the political process. Planners' own ideas of what would best serve the interests of the community are only one element in a complex process of determining public policy related to physical or economic development. Their expertise and professional charge relate to developing plans and recommending ways in which such plans can be carried out, but the process is also likely to involve considerable input by citizen groups and by those, such as developers or service providers, who have a direct financial stake in the plans and their implementation. The final decisions are ultimately in the hands of appointed officials, such as plan commissioners or members of executive boards, and then of elected officials, such as council members, mayors, and governors.

Professional ethics in planning are centrally concerned with the relationship between expert but not elected civil servants and the decision makers and citizens they are supposed to serve. When the ninety-six planners in this study talked about ethical dilemmas they had to deal with, they sometimes talked about obligations to professional colleagues or subordinates, but primarily they talked in a variety of ways about their obligations to the public. Some, for example, dealt with a procedural obligation to be fair to all applicants for planning permits or to see that the planning process itself was open to a broad range of interests. Some raised issues that grew out of their obligation to provide information to elected and appointed decision makers who were, in turn, chosen by and responsible to the public. Finally, some discussed substantive ethical obligations to the public—to provide more equitable or aesthetic development, to develop good transportation systems, or, in some other way, to serve the public interest.

While their responsibility to the public was the central ethical issue for the planners studied here, they differed substantially in the ways in which they thought about and acted on this issue. Planners have available to them three rather different images of the purpose and role of the profession. One has emphasized indirect responsibility to the public through loyal service to elected officials. Another has seen the planner as a more politically active and autonomous actor in the planning process. A third has stressed the role of the planner as a facilitator of the planning process. While the roles actually played by the planners in this sample were more diverse than these three basic models, all drew on one or another as a starting place.

In turn, each of these role models provides a different answer to the central ethical question of the relationship between the expert planner, elected officials, and the public at large. Indeed, each role is associated with a distinctively different approach to ethics. Planners who saw themselves as loyal servants of elected officials were content to leave the definition of the goals of planning to those decision makers. Their views of ethics focused substantially on procedural actions that they judged to be right or wrong in themselves. Conflicts between loyalty to superiors versus other ethical principles such as truthfulness or openness were especially central to them. Because of the basic assumptions of their role, however, these other principles were likely to be of secondary importance in comparison to loyalty.

Planners who saw themselves as more active, independent actors were much more likely to be motivated by a strong commitment to particular ideas of "the good," or the public interest, which they strove to see realized through the planning process. They worked to increase their own autonomy, and while they recognized the legitimate primacy of elected officials, they did not automatically defer to them. Some, though by no means all, were sometimes willing to neglect procedural ethical principles in the interests of achieving the goals they sought.

Finally, planners who saw themselves as facilitators of the planning process were centrally concerned with fairness and the openness of that process. They saw their role in relation to other actors as somewhat independent but responsive, bringing groups together to work out solutions to conflicts. While they tended not to have strong substantive ideas about the public interest, their focus on an open process made them sensitive to issues of social justice.

Normative Guidelines for Planners

While this is primarily a descriptive study of ethics, the description begs the question of evaluation, which is inherent in the idea of ethics. To say that members of a profession hold certain ethical values makes no judgment about whether those values are good for the profession or for the public. Indeed, a fairly substantial body of literature on professional ethics has developed in recent years (Bayles 1981; Freedman 1978;

Gewirth 1986; Goldman 1980; Kultgen 1988) because of public dissatisfaction with the ethical values held and the roles played by members of the powerful consulting professions (Freidson 1973; May 1976).

A study such as this cannot avoid the question of whether the ethical values held and acted on by planners serve the public well. A reasonable standard to use in evaluating their actions is the *Code of Ethics and Professional Conduct* of the professional organization, the AICP (1981).[2] It spells out planners' responsibilities to serve the public, to be accountable to clients and employers, to respect colleagues, and to contribute to the profession. The code in this case, though, is only a starting place in the framework for evaluating these planners' actions. In any study such as this one, the empirical data frame the analysis, but the values and perspectives of the author also shape both the empirical findings and the conclusions drawn from them.

The underlying framework for this study is a hierarchy of principles. These were drawn in part from the values used by many of the planners in the sample. In the end, however, the exact nature of the framework represents my judgment about the ethical values that planning should serve. At the top of this hierarchy is adherence to the law. Below that is adherence to basic ethical "duties of justice," which I define below. Below that are two coequal principles: accountability and service to the public interest.

The most basic principles are that planners should respect laws and what I have called "duties of justice." Such duties of justice are the most basic ethical norms that allow for predictability and trust among individuals. They include honesty, truthfulness, fairness, and promise-keeping. The way these issues arise in planning practice is, of course, somewhat different from the way they might come up between friends or family members or in a different professional context, but the planners in the sample saw them as continuous with their ordinary, nonprofessional ethics. These principles should take precedence over other, more characteristically professional ones.

The principles of respect for laws and for duties of justice are followed by two counterbalancing principles. One is the requirement that nonelected bureaucratic officials be responsible to the public, sometimes directly but more typically by being accountable to elected officials. The other is that they serve the public interest.

Accountability to the public through decision makers is a long-standing tenet of democratic administrative theory (Wilson 1887), and even though our understanding of the relationship between politics and administration has changed over the years and our acceptance of the absolute legitimacy of elected officials has been somewhat tempered, this is still a central tenet (Burke 1986).

Public servants such as planners work in public bureaucracies that institutionalize this relationship of responsibility. They have never been given the kind of autonomy that has been granted to consulting professionals such as doctors and lawyers (Baum 1983; Freidson 1973; Howe 1980b; Kultgen 1988; Larson 1977). They do not serve private citizens but provide policy advice and administrative support to public officials who retain control over the public bureaucracies in which they work.

Nevertheless, planners are not ciphers. They do have discretion in the way they develop and give policy advice and in the way they implement planning laws (Benveniste 1989). How much room they have for independent action will vary depending on the planner, the decision maker, the agency, and the larger political environment, but giving policy advice and implementing plans always provides some room for independent judgment and action. Planners do have their own independent, professional ideas of good policy, which can be quite different from those held by the public and by decision makers.

Much autonomous action is still grounded in processes that allow for oversight and accountability, but there are instances in this study where planners acted with radical autonomy, without the knowledge or sanction of elected officials and members of the public.

The problem with the ethical obligation to be responsible is that it can be interpreted as a requirement for unconditional personal loyalty to officials, regardless of the legitimacy of their demands. All bureaucracies seem to place a high value on institutional loyalty, but in the public sector, this claim is given further weight by the image of representative democracy.

The counterbalance that planners have to claims of loyalty is their professional judgment. They draw on bodies of technical knowledge and methods to suggest means for accomplishing ends set by elected officials. In addition, they have their own substantive values about what kinds of policy will best serve the public interest.

The usefulness or even the possibility of any idea of the public interest is something over which there has been substantial debate both in political philosophy and in planning (Howe 1992). Regardless of this academic controversy, however, practicing planners use the idea of the public interest as a common guide in their work. They generally mean by it one of two things that are not mutually exclusive. In some contexts, it has substantive content, such as a concern with social justice or the broad, long-run good of the community. In other cases, the planners saw it as the result of a process of negotiation or debate between their own ideas of the public interest and those held by elected officials and members of the public.

Both the AICP code and my hierarchy of ethical values place considerable emphasis not only on procedural ideas of the public interest but on substantive ones as well, such as working for social justice and for preservation of the natural environment. As chapter 13 will indicate, my own definition of the public interest would place substantial emphasis on working for social justice and for the preservation of the natural environment.

This framework or hierarchy of four principles will be developed throughout this book, beginning in chapter 2. I use it in part 3 as a set of normative principles for evaluating the planners' actions. The use of such a normative framework implies that planners should be held responsible for their actions as individual professionals. These planners worked in political and bureaucratic systems that limited their scope for autonomous action and their impact on ultimate policy decisions, but this lack of autonomy did not make them passive cogs in a machine. They made ethical choices about which issues to raise and how to raise them. Since ethics is a social institution, they also did not always think and act alone, but neither of these contingencies vitiates my judgment that in a book on ethics it was necessary to go beyond pure description to propose and apply a normative standard to the actions they took.

Others can easily pose other ethical frameworks for planning. As I have already indicated, I believe that within a common Western/liberal culture, other frameworks would share much with mine. I was amused, after working hard to develop a set of normative principles that balanced my own ethical values with those of the planners I interviewed, to discover that I had essentially reinvented the AICP's code of ethics.

Values and Action

If principles are necessary for ethics to be effective, so is action. Three steps seem to be necessary for effective ethical behavior. First, planners have to be able to see situations as posing ethical issues. There was a great deal of variability among the planners studied here in what they defined as ethical issues. Some had a quite narrow view of ethics, focusing mainly on the legality of actions. Others saw ethical challenges in a wide range of procedural and substantive issues.

Once an ethical issue has been identified, the planner next must be able to make a decision about what he or she should do about it. This should involve a process of rational analysis based both on the facts of the particular case and on impartial, generalizable principles.

Finally, the planner must have both the will and the freedom or leverage to act on his or her decision. Some planners had no trouble articulating perfectly acceptable ethical principles that they wished to live by but had difficulty putting these principles into practice. In some cases, they simply lacked the will or the skills to act on the issues they thought were important. Others were limited by being in organizational positions that gave them little leverage to act. Still others had difficulty acting because of corruption in the political systems in which they worked.

Some of the planners whose behavior I judged to be unethical worked in corrupt situations. Here the issue is not simply one of defining what behavior meets the test of being ethical. The real challenge is to support planners who try to do right and to discourage those who do wrong. In public professions whose members work in bureaucracies, professional organizations have a smaller role than they do in self-regulating, private professions, but some ideas about the supportive role that could be played by professional organizations in planning will be developed in chapter 13.

Before criteria for behavior and proposals for supporting ethical behavior can be discussed, it is necessary to understand how the planners in the sample thought about and acted on ethics. Before these findings can be presented, a bit should be said about the methods used to collect and analyze the data on which this study is based.

Methodology

This book is a largely qualitative study based on personal interviews with ninety-six planners working in public planning agencies. A more detailed description of the sample and methods is found in Appendix A. The sample included nineteen planners from each of four states—Maryland, New York, Tennessee, and Texas—and twenty from Northern California. The sample is not scientifically random, so generalizations from it are not justified. In the text, I refer to the planners in the past tense. This rhetorical device is intended to remind the reader that the findings refer to the specific group of ninety-six people who were interviewed and not to planners in general.

There are several reasons why the sample is not representative of all planners. First, with virtually equal numbers of respondents from each state, the states are not proportionately represented. Second, each state seems to have had a particular "culture of planning," which suggests that other states might be rather different as well. Third, the sample is biased toward senior-level planners. As we found once we began interviewing, the director of an agency often "subscribes" for the whole agency, so ethical issues that might have been raised by junior-level planners are poorly represented here.

The interviews were generally done in the planner's office by myself, Jerome Kaufman, and Mac Passano. This is why the text often refers to the planners "we" interviewed. Respondents were also given a survey questionnaire at the end of the interview to fill out and mail back. Copies of both the questionnaire and of the protocol for the interviews are reproduced in Appendix B. Thus, both qualitative and quantitative data were used in the analysis. In many cases, the quantitative data serve primarily as a check for the accuracy and balance of the qualitative data.

We expected that some ethical issues might be controversial, so we guaranteed the respondents' anonymity. Because of this, personal and place names in cases and quotes have been changed, and sometimes the facts have been altered so that a case could not be identified.

In writing up the analysis, I chose to adopt a theoretical framework that reflected the way these planners viewed their own professional work and the ethical issues it posed. These planners were liberals, both in a pluralist ideological and in a narrower "New Deal" political sense. Some of the current academic discussion of ethics and roles in planning draws on Marxist analysis (Beauregard 1978; Fainstein and Fainstein 1982; Kraushaar 1988; Marcuse 1976) or on the critical theory of the German philosopher Jurgen Habermas (Forester 1980; Innes 1990). These related but somewhat different perspectives were not shared by the planners in this sample, in part simply because they were too recent to have had widespread impact. In addition, though, these approaches require planners essentially to reject the legitimacy of the political systems in which they work. However compelling the analysis is that leads to such a conclusion, the tension and contradiction this implies for any practicing planner make its adoption difficult.

Since I have tried to use normative guidelines grounded at least in part in these planners' own ideas, a liberal framework drawing on the classical philosophy of the Utilitarians (Bentham 1948; Mill 1985) and of Kant (1964) seemed most appropriate. The AICP code, written by planners from within this liberal framework, can provide a standard for evaluating their behavior that does not reject the basic premises on which they were acting.

An Introduction to the Sample

Definitions of professional ethics and responses to ethical issues were shaped both by the identity of the individual planners and by the social, political, and organizational environments in which they worked. These various influences will be explored in succeeding chapters. Here it may be useful to begin to provide some description of the planners as a starting place for this exploration of their ethics.

Who were these ninety-six planners? The planners came from a wide array of places and agencies. As we have just seen, they came in virtually equal numbers from each of five states. The states themselves were quite different, and this seemed to rub off onto or to attract somewhat different kinds of planners. Planning was most accepted and, apparently, most powerful in northern California. All communities were required to have plans, and consistency between plans and implementation regulations was required by most communities. California also seemed to be characterized by a fairly pluralistic, open, participatory style of politics. With a few exceptions, its planners did not have to deal with problems of corruption.

At the other extreme were Texas and Tennessee. The former was on the verge of a tremendous growth boom, but it was also the state in which planning and its related institutions, such as zoning, were least accepted, even in quite large cities. Several communities were actively engaged in fairly participatory efforts to develop their first comprehensive plans. The day-to-day politics of planning in most places was characterized by a development-oriented, old-boy network style of politics, though corruption did not seem to be an issue.

Tennessee had a longer and a somewhat stronger tradition of planning, particularly of state-level, local-assistance planning, but, as in Texas, public attitudes seemed to be strongly prodevelopment and politics was characterized by old-boy networks. TVA—the Tennessee Valley Authority—played a large, powerful, and unique role in the state's planning. Corruption was an issue in some communities.

Maryland had a reputation for corruption in the days of Spiro Agnew who served as County Executive in Baltimore County and went on to become Governor. As Vice President in 1973 he was charged with bribery, extortion and tax fraud for activities in Maryland and was forced out of office when he pleaded guilty to the latter charge. However, the pattern of corruption he represented seemed largely to be in the past by the 1980s except in a few localities. Politics appeared to be hard-hitting and a fairly closed activity in some parts of the state. Since most governmental activity took place at the county rather than the municipal level, planning agencies were fairly large, and many, especially in Baltimore and in the Washington, D.C., metropolitan area, were highly professionalized and engaged in sometimes innovative practice.

Finally, New York State, as in everything, would have to be divided into New York City and "upstate." In New York City, the most obvious aspect of planning practice was its extremely bureaucratic character. Virtually everyone worked in very large city, state, quasi-independent, or federal agencies. This created a particular culture of planning in which people often seemed either to be crushed by the impossibility of having an impact or challenged to get things done despite the bureaucracy. There was a general sense that the politics was not only hardball but sometimes corrupt. Upstate, in smaller suburban communities and cities, acceptance of planning seemed mixed.

Planners were interviewed at the state level in California, Maryland, New York, and Texas. The first two gave the impression of having particularly activist state agencies engaged in planning. However, in these cases, the small numbers of people interviewed might produce a misleading impression.

Overall in the sample, planning at the local level was by far the most common kind. Almost one-fifth of the planners worked in large central cities, ranging from New York City, Houston, and Dallas to Baltimore, San Francisco, and Memphis. A quarter worked in suburban areas of those same cities. Another 19 percent worked in smaller, freestanding cities—in the Central Valley of California, in upstate New York, and in west Texas, for example. Of the rest, the largest group (23 percent) worked at the regional level. Altogether, two-thirds worked in local agencies—59 percent in general purpose planning agencies and 9 percent in specialized ones, such as redevelopment agencies or housing authorities.

As already noted, the sample was strongly weighted toward senior-level planners: 42 percent were directors and another 9 percent were assistant or deputy directors. Division heads made up 15 percent of the sample while virtually everyone else (34 percent) worked in the middle ranges of their agencies. To suggest that most departments had all of these levels, though, is a bit misleading. Slightly more than a quarter of the planners worked in departments that were quite small, with only the director and up to four professional staff. At the other extreme, another third worked in large and bureaucratic agencies with more than fifty professional employees.

Largely because of the number of directors in the sample, fully 50 percent of the planners had jobs that primarily involved administration and political liaison. Still, some of these were not directors; a few held jobs as assistant directors in which they specialized in internal administration. Several others specialized as lobbyists for their agencies. Most of the planners in very small agencies did a mix of general planning tasks. In larger agencies that could afford more specialization, the most common specializations were project planning (15 percent) and regulatory administration (10 percent). Only 3 percent of the sample focused primarily on comprehensive planning.

The average age of the planners was forty-four, with a range from twenty-eight to sixty-four. They had been in planning, on the average, for seventeen years. Virtually all their experience was as public planners, with the average sixteen years. Some had begun their careers with a short stint in consulting or had tried it somewhere along the way, but all had spent most of their working lives, which ranged from four to thirty-five years, in public agencies.

The planners were predominantly white men. Only 12 percent were women. In a profession dominated by men, the women who made it to the top of planning agencies were a savvy group. Of these women, three had raised families and then had gone into planning later in life. Thus, while there was no statistical difference in age between the men and the women, the men had significantly more years of experience as planners than did the women, 18 and 12 years, respectively. Even so, women were directors in almost the same proportions as men, 42 and 39 percent, respectively. Unfortunately, the number of minority planners in the sample was too small for any analysis. One was black and four were of Asian descent.

The Structure of This Book

Acting on Ethics in City Planning is divided into three parts. Each includes an introductory, somewhat theoretical chapter and several primarily empirical ones. Beginning with chapter 2, the first part explores the nature of ethical issues and describes the specific ethical issues the planners talked about. Chapter 3 examines the many issues that arose out of the day-to-day procedures of planning—issues of how to treat others, how to do analysis, or what accountability meant in practice. Chapter 4 explores the diverse ways they thought about the public interest.

The second part, introduced in chapter 5, focuses on the planners as individuals. Chapter 6 looks at the professional roles they played. Chapter 7 examines the way the planners thought about ethical issues. Each of these chapters develops a typology of different kinds of planners. Since ideas about professional roles implied particular ethical commitments, these two typologies are closely interrelated. Chapter 8, in turn, explores factors that shaped the ethical values and role choices of these planners.

The third part presents a framework in chapter 9 to evaluate the actions the planners took on the issues they raised in part 1. Chapter 10 looks at the relationship between their choice of actions, AICP's code of ethics, and my hierarchy of values. Chapter 11 explores how planners with different approaches to role and to thinking about ethics acted in characteristically different ways and faced characteristically different ethical problems. Chapter 12 looks at the factors other than planners' own values that shaped the actions they took. The concluding chapter 13 explores ways in which ethical action might be encouraged by the profession.

PART 1

Issues

2

The Nature of Ethical Issues

Ethics are concerned with duties and obligations. Obligations imply some object. They are owed to someone. The planners in this sample held rather varied images of the role that planning should play in society. These images had embedded within them ideas about the moral obligations of the planner. What did these obligations mean in practice? Who were they owed to? What ethical issues did they raise? What ethical principles were implicit in the issues they raised?

Asking about Ethics

Before we began the interviews, we had no clear idea of what kind of issues planners might consider to be ethical in nature. We also thought that ethics might be a difficult topic to get planners to talk about. On the one hand, it suggested an inquiry into their personal probity. On the other, it could seem to be a rather abstract topic.

As a result, in order to get the planners to talk concretely, we asked them to speak about their own experience with ethical issues (however they defined ethics) in their professional lives. Sometimes they were not quite sure that the issues they thought of were really ethical issues at all, but we left this decision largely to them. In the end, the planners talked about a wide variety of issues and situations that they, or people they had worked with, had faced, as well as some issues that they had no direct experience with but still thought were important.

The issues the planners raised seemed to be shaped by two factors. One was an abstract image they held of ethics. The other was their experience. These seemed, in many respects, to be independent of each other, though in part 2 I will explore how planners' experience seemed to shape the way they thought about ethics. Still, in the interviews, it was

19

apparent that when the planners were asked about ethical issues, they often consulted their image of the realm of ethics and then searched their experience to come up with examples. If they had not had any experience that illustrated some aspect of ethics they thought was important, they talked about it in hypothetical terms instead.[1]

A Framework for Describing Ethical Issues

In order to understand and, ultimately, to evaluate the choices the planners made, it is necessary to explore how they defined the realm of ethics. What issues were included and excluded, what kind of principles did they use, and what kind of obligations did this entail?

To talk about ethics, the planners did not explicitly use a framework based on the idea of obligations to various groups, but in the ethical issues they raised, this was implicitly what many of them were doing. As civil servants, they talked about obligations that were primarily owed either directly to the public or indirectly to the public through elected decision makers. A few also did discuss obligations to professional colleagues, but these issues ran a distant third. The nature of the obligations were primarily to meet a minimum standard of honesty, to provide independent professional advice on planning issues, to be responsive to the public and its elected representatives, and to serve the public interest.

While many planners thought in terms of all or at least many of these obligations, they did not all define the realm of ethics in the same way. Some focused largely on procedural obligations to the public and the officials they worked for. Others were more concerned with the idea of the public interest and the ends that planning should serve. This is not surprising since a similar distinction pervades Western philosophy where a "deontological" approach to ethics has vied for centuries with a "consequentialist" one, and these differing perspectives have found their way out of the realm of philosophy and into our everyday patterns of thought. (Both of these approaches will be discussed at length later in this chapter.)

This chapter will lay out a framework for describing and organizing the ethical issues the planners raised. It will be based on the distinction between deontological and consequentialist ways of thinking about ethics. Following an introduction to these two overarching approaches, the kinds of principles used in each will be explored. In the initial stages of the analysis, the issues raised by the planners were grouped into nineteen categories[2] based on the ethical principle (or principles) raised in the cases. These principles are listed in Table 2.1.

TABLE 2.1

Ethical Principles Used by Planners[a]

Honesty

    Conflicts of interest
    Bribery
    Doing political favors
    Violation of law, rules, or contract
    Accepting small gifts and lunches
    Theft

Duties of Justice

  To Provide Independent Professional Advice

    Freedom from political pressure on technical judgments
    Truthfulness
    Quality of work
    Freedom of speech

  To Be Responsive to the Public

    Fairness
    Procedural openness

Accountability

    Loyalty
    Keeping confidences

Serving the Public Interest

    Equity
    Process
    Natural environment
    Transportation
    Urban design

Note:

[a]The term "principle" is used rather loosely here. This initially was a list of issues raised by the planners, but as it grew it became apparent that the underlying organization was primarily a list of principles. Thus, some of the items, such as those under "honesty," remain as issues or problems.

This initial set of principles, in turn, has been organized into four groups that focus attention on the kinds of obligations they entail. The four overarching principles are: honesty, in the legal sense; "duties of justice," including the obligations to provide independent professional advice and to be responsive to the public; the duty to be accountable to elected officials; and the duty to serve the public interest. The first three obligations are characteristic of a deontological approach to ethics. They are not irrelevant to a consequentialist view of ethics, but in a consequentialist approach, they become subsumed under the central moral principle that all actions should serve the public good.

These four general kinds of principles will be used as an organizing framework throughout this book. Here in part 1, they will first be explained and will then structure the description of the issues the planners raised. In part 2, the patterns of issues raised by the planners will be used to divide the planners themselves into those who took a primarily deontological approach to ethics and those who took a primarily consequentialist one. Finally, in part 3, the four principles will be used as the basis for a normative framework for evaluating the actions the planners took on the issues they discussed.

Because these four kinds of principles are central to the analysis, they will be introduced in some detail here. The nature and general philosophical rationale of each will be explored. The primary point of this brief foray into philosophy is that some of these obligations can be thought of as more binding than others. This is why, in part 3, they can be used as a hierarchy for evaluating actions.

Ethical Approaches: Deontological and Consequentialist

Ethics are concerned with questions of what is right and wrong and what is good and bad. These are not by any means the same thing. The answer to the question of whether an action is good or bad depends on the consequences of the action. Take the question of whether the construction of subsidized, low-income housing in a suburban area would be in the public interest. An analysis of the consequences might look at the financial soundness of the project, the costs of extra services that it might require, or its impact on the local property tax. It might also try to measure in some way the benefit or cost to the community from having a more diverse population. The end result would be a summary of the costs and benefits or perhaps a more qualitative statement of the pros and cons of the project for the community.

An analysis framed in terms of right and wrong, however, would focus on the rights of the various parties and on the process used to arrive at a decision. The idea that low-income people should be able to live in the same kind of good neighborhoods as more affluent people might be balanced against the idea that existing local residents have a right to participate in the process of determining the nature of their community. These very different kinds of arguments may sound familiar to many planners. Both are examples of ethical reasoning.

Normative moral philosophy is characterized by a variety of fundamentally different ways of thinking about ethics. One distinction is particularly relevant for describing how the planners in this study thought about ethics. As Taylor (1972, p. 197) explains:

> All normative ethical systems can be divided into two groups depending on how they define the relation between right action and intrinsic value. . . . The basic principle of deontological ethics is that the right (what we ought to do) does not entirely depend on the good (what we judge to be intrinsically valuable), and this is the exact contradictory of the basic principle of teleological ethics.

A teleological view of ethics is concerned with the goodness of the consequences of action. As a result, it is often referred to as a consequentialist perspective. A deontological view of ethics, conversely, is concerned not with the consequences of action but with the rightness of an act itself.

Utilitarianism is probably the best-known version of consequentialism. It determines the "right" action by calculating the good to be produced, measured in terms of the balance of pleasure over pain. Early utilitarians in the eighteenth and nineteenth centuries were very much concerned with issues of public policy, and in this larger policy context, utilitarianism was concerned with trying to achieve "the greatest happiness of the greatest number." This approach has had a wide intellectual influence through classical "liberalism," which, throughout the nineteenth century, shaped the way Americans thought about economic and political institutions. Its influence has been even more direct in planning since it is the theoretical foundation for economic analysis and for such evaluation techniques as cost/benefit analysis.

As an approach to ethical thinking, consequentialism would involve trying to evaluate possible actions according to how much good they would bring about. If an action would have some good and some bad consequences, the evaluation would be concerned with the balance of good over bad.

Deontological approaches to ethics focus on the rightness of actions themselves, regardless of their consequences. More than consequentialist approaches, they are concerned with moral duties and rights.

The most common deontological approach relies on rules as guides to behavior. The rules may be as specific as the Ten Commandments or as general as the Golden Rule: "Do unto others as you would have them do unto you," or Kant's principle of humanity: "Act in such a way that you always treat humanity, whether in your own person or in the person of any other, never simply as a means, but always at the same time as an end" (Kant 1964, p. 96).

Common sense suggests that conforming with deontological rules, such as being fair or telling the truth, would have good consequences in the long run. This is an argument made by philosophers who support a consequentialist approach called rule utilitarianism (Howe 1990). This is not the concern of a deontological approach, though, which is concerned with the rightness of actions in themselves. It is perfectly possible, for example, to imagine an honest planning analysis, such as a population projection, that might have bad consequences, such as frightening whites into taking their children out of the public schools. Despite these consequences, however, one may still accept the idea that an honest analysis is right and a dishonest one would be wrong.

If a deontological view of ethics tends in general to focus attention on procedural duties, a consequentialist one focuses in general on the consequences of action and especially on the public interest. A pure consequentialist would not be unconcerned about being fair or truthful, but these actions would be evaluated, like any others, according to the good and bad consequences they produced. Both means and ends would be weighed according to how they contributed to the overall end of happiness, welfare, or the public good.

Deontological and teleological approaches are ways of thinking about ethical reasoning, but because they ask quite different questions about what makes an action right or a policy good, they focus on very different kinds of issues. Deontologists look at actions that are right or wrong in themselves, such as being honest or fair or truthful. They focus on legal or moral rules that should not be broken. Consequentialists, for their part, focus on good ends.

Philosophers writing about public morality have tended to think of it as more consequentialist than private morality. A teleological view of the public interest as the balance of good over bad consequences for the whole society seems a natural approach to talking about public policy goals (Held 1984). The large, impersonal nature of many decisions made by city councils or state legislatures may contribute to this consequentialist bias (Acton 1946; Nagel 1978).

This perspective disregards the existence in public life of many issues related to the legitimacy of the process of decision making. Procedural planning issues concerned, for example, with the truthfulness of analysis or with fairness to zoning applicants would be of concern to someone with a deontological perspective on ethics. One deontological idea of the public interest would view it as an open, fair process of policy-making, regardless of its specific content.

The deontological perspective is not only concerned with process, though. It could be concerned with the content of policy, specifically, the protection of rights. Here consequences would matter, but they would not be thought of as the balance between good and bad. Rather, the deontologist would look to see whether the consequences of action preserved rights.

Deontological Ethical Principles

Deontological principles are commonly thought of as rules: "Honor thy father and thy mother" or "Love thy neighbor as thyself." Rules imply obligations or duties that are owed by someone to someone else, such as your parents or your neighbor. The planners we interviewed saw some obligations as applying primarily to individuals and others as applying primarily to collective groups. Not surprisingly, duties owed primarily to individuals were easier to see as binding compared to those owed to collective groups such as "the public." One rather indirect measure of how binding an obligation seemed to be was the amount of consensus in the sample over whether, in fact, it was an ethical obligation at all. We explored this through answers to the questionnaire, summarized in Table 2.2.[3]

Legal Rules

Laws are not simply moral obligations. They are defined by a legitimate process of public decision making as binding on everyone. In the area of governmental ethics, laws are primarily concerned with bribery, the improper use of public office or of influence, and conflicts of interest.

Public office is a public trust. Civil servants and elected officials alike are expected to work primarily for the good of the public as a whole. This precludes using public office for private gain for oneself or for other individuals unless such gain is achieved through an open process of public

TABLE 2.2

The Realm of Ethics

	Planners Classifying Items as:	
	Clearly an Ethical Issue (percent)	Clearly or Probably an Ethical Issue (percent)
Honesty		
Planner tries to sell services by implying an ability to influence decision by improper means.	94.4	98.9
Planner uses the power of her office to obtain special personal advantage not in the public interest.	93.3	97.3
Duties of Justice		
Planner inaccurately represents his professional qualifications, education, or affiliations.	92.1	96.6
Planner inaccurately represents the views or findings of colleagues.	68.5	87.6
Planner does not provide accurate information to citizens or decision makers.	67.4	74.2
Planner provides accurate but not complete information to citizens or decision makers.	22.5	46.1
Planner is not fair and considerate in reviewing the work of other professionals.	49.4	81.6
Duties of Accountability		
Planner reveals information that employer requested be held confidential.	67.4	78.7
The Public Interest		
Planner does not serve the public interest.	50.6	75.3
Planner is not concerned about the long-range consequences of present actions in his work.	32.6	65.2
Planner knowingly reduces choice and opportunity to disadvantaged groups and persons.	60.7	83.1
Planner through her actions knowingly harms the natural environment.	39.3	55.1
Planner does not work to increase the opportunities for women and minorities to become planners.	13.5	36.0

Note:

Only thirteen of the twenty-eight items from the questionnaire are used here. These illustrate best the principles being discussed in the text. Many of the ones not used were also items that many of the planners thought did not raise ethical issues, such as contributing time to the professional development of students and interns.

decision making. As a result, covert or dishonest use of public office for such gain is prohibited by law in most places.

Historically, the use of public office for personal gain has not always been considered unethical or illegal. In seventeenth-century England, the sale of offices by the Crown was a normal way of raising revenue (Scott 1972). The corruption of political machines in nineteenth-century American cities was officially illegal but fairly widely accepted.

One of the primary concerns of civil service reformers and then of the broader Progressive reform movement of the late nineteenth century was to eliminate this kind of corruption in the administration of the growing number of municipal regulatory and service functions. Civil servants should be concerned primarily about the efficient performance of their duties; they should be protected against being fired for partisan reasons and from having to contribute to the political machine. This protection and their identification as professionals in turn would make them less vulnerable to bribery and to temptations to use their public office for their own or others' private benefit (Schiesl 1977). Today's legal prohibitions on bribery and conflicts of interest are simply one obvious result of this effort.

Table 2.2 shows that virtually all the planners in the study saw such behavior as clearly involving issues of ethics. It was also quite clear from their discussions of the cases they raised that they saw laws as the most binding of rules; in conflicts with other, purely moral duties, legal rules took precedence.

Duties of Justice

Duties of justice arise out of individual moral rights. They are not defined by law but they are often considered to be the most binding of all ethical duties owed to all other individuals.

People have all kinds of rights: moral, legal, and political. Dworkin (1977), writing from a political point of view, identifies rights as political "trumps" held by individuals that outweigh considerations of collective good. They cannot be bargained away in the interests of benefiting the broad public. They are respected for their own sake, not because of some benefit they create (Held 1984). They give the holder autonomy and freedom within a particular area of action or they provide for the protection of important interests (Martin and Nickel 1980).

Duties of justice, however, cover only a very limited kind of rights. They are moral rather than political. They do not derive from legal rules but from moral principles. At a minimum, duties of justice include being honest, fair, and truthful, along with the duty to avoid doing needless harm.

These rights entail obligations to other people, which is not true of all rights (Martin and Nickel 1980). Indeed, it is the duty—to be fair or not to lie, for example—that is really the central focus. This emphasizes the strongly reciprocal nature of these rights. They are not vaguely directed at "any" second party but are owed by each person to all other people. This is the essence of what Kant (1964, p. 89fn) called "perfect duties," which "allow no exception in the interests of inclination."

Duties of justice involve obligations and rights that from the point of view of individuals require reversibility. A lie may be acceptable to the person who uses it but not to the person who is lied to. The "recipient" is taken advantage of, is used as a means to the other person's end, and is treated in a way that reduces his or her individual autonomy (Hill 1975).

From a societal point of view as well, these obligations and rights can be thought of as necessary to the existence of trust and stable social relationships. This is why they are not just individual values but are essentially common ones. The ideas of truthfulness, of keeping confidences and promises, and of openness only have meaning if they are widely accepted and adhered to. This is the basic point that lies behind the idea of duties of justice or of Kant's idea of perfect duties that are especially binding. Indeed, Kant's test (1964) of whether an action is moral is whether it can be generalized to everyone. Clearly, I can lie in order to achieve my own ends. I might, for instance, present a policy that I am committed to in a more favorable light than my analysis on its effectiveness would justify. I might even get away with it, but if everyone lied, no one would believe anything that anyone else said. If all planners manipulated their analysis to favor whatever they thought was good policy, decision makers would cease to accept any analysis as valid or worth paying attention to. Thus, by Kant's test (1964), a lie fails morally because it creates a logical contradiction; the individual action cannot logically be generalized to everyone.

These duties of justice and the behavior they encourage can be thought of as collective goods. A liar would be a free rider on other people's truthfulness. In a society in which lying is accepted, "truth" and all the relationships that require it lose their meaning. Ultimately, if such principles are widely violated, they cannot continue to exist.

The problem of free riders is the same, as Kant (1964) would also argue, as the problem of treating people instrumentally. A planner who was so driven by the desire to achieve goals that he treated others simply as means to his ends would deny them the essential humanity on which real trust could be founded. While it might serve the purpose to treat others well, it might just as easily be necessary to mislead them or to cause them harm. In any case, what happened to them would be something over which they themselves would have little or no control—and planners did have power to treat others as objects, as we will have an opportunity to see.

In planning, the idea of reciprocal duties of justice applies at both individual and institutional levels. As individuals, people, whether they are planners, citizens, or elected officials, expect to be told the truth and to be treated fairly (unless they are engaging in a structured process, such as a negotiating session, where they know that these rules do not apply).

As systems of social relations, bureaucracies and policy-making systems depend on these values just as other social systems do. As public bureaucracies have grown, these values have been codified as institutional principles. Again, the Progressive movement was important in pressing for the establishment of an independent, expert bureaucracy protected from corruption and inefficiency by civil service laws. Effective policy advice was to be based on expertise and truth, not just on political preference. Administration of the law, once enacted, was to be fair and neutral.

Generally, as Table 2.2 shows, the planners in the sample saw issues of lying and fairness as issues of ethics. Three-quarters saw all but one of these issues as clearly or probably involving an ethical issue. Agreement that these came within the realm of ethics was higher than on any of the twenty-eight issues posed except for the ones involving legality. The planners talked in their interviews about these as principles that should not be violated, but Table 2.2 also indicates that the planners set limits on what they defined as binding duties of justice. Thus, for many, providing accurate but not complete information in a policy context was apparently not seen as an example of lying.

Accountability

For public planners, the principles of loyalty and accountability are closely related. Loyalty to one's agency and to superiors becomes intertwined with the duty of the civil servant to be accountable to elected officials. Both were defined as ethical principles by planners we interviewed. However, philosophers seem to consider loyalty, at least, to be problematic in ways that are useful to understanding the dilemmas planners commonly faced over loyalty.

Baron (1984) argues that loyalty is suspect from a moral standpoint because it can lead to violations of the moral obligation to be impartial or fair. It involves an obligation whose only justification is that a special relationship exists: An action provides a benefit solely because the recipient is my cousin, my boss, or my agency. If moral reasoning consists of logical, universalizable arguments for actions, then the argument that I should, for example, recommend a zoning variance for my cousin simply because he is my cousin is not convincing to most other people. Is the argument any different when the issue is whether I should lie for my boss?

For public sector planners, however, there may sometimes be a difference. For civil servants, the obligation to an appointed or elected official is not just a personal one. It involves an obligation to the public through the mechanism of representative democracy. This can raise loyalty to elected officials to the status of a moral principle. The public has a right to responsive and accountable government.

In a public profession such as planning, the principle of accountability of bureaucrats to the public through elected officials is a central one. It has been a principle since public professions emerged in the nineteenth century and has been a mainstay of Progressive administrative theory (Finer 1941; Wilson 1887). It has recently been reaffirmed, though in a somewhat less rigid form, by Burke (1986), who places the principle of "democratic responsibility" at the heart of the ethics of bureaucrats.[4]

Burke, though, also argues that loyalty (which he does not differentiate from accountability) could be subject to limits. Strict adherence to rules, regulations, and the orders of superiors can sometimes run counter to or could undermine the achievement of democratically defined goals (Burke 1986). Thus, civil servants must have standards for evaluating such rules or orders.

A planner owes loyalty to an official because of that person's office, not just because he or she is the boss. An official may require the planner's loyalty, in effect, to the public, for instance, on policies that have been arrived at through a legitimate public process. Sometimes, however, officials may try to require loyalty when their action conflicts with their obligation to the public—they may be trying to mislead the public, for example. Here the planner's own judgment about what is owed to the public may conflict with and might legitimately take precedence over loyalty to the boss.

The Public Interest: Deontological and Consequentialist

All the principles discussed so far have been deontological in nature, that is, they have been concerned with rules governing actions that are seen as right or wrong in themselves. It is not necessary to know if the consequences of breaking a law or of being unfair are bad—they are considered to be wrong in and of themselves. In contrast, the principle of serving the public interest can be thought of either in deontological terms or in consequentialist ones. It focuses attention on both substantive ends and the consequences of action.

Like accountability, the principle of serving the public interest is one that is particularly relevant to public officials and civil servants, though they hardly hold a monopoly on defining or using it. More than any of the other kinds of principles, it is concerned not with duties to individuals but with some duty or obligation to the whole public.

The idea of the public interest has had ups and downs in political theory and in planning and has collected a variety of different meanings. It has been criticized (Altshuler 1965; Meyerson and Banfield 1955; Schubert 1957, 1960, 1967; Sorauf 1957, 1967; Vasu 1979) and rehabilitated (Howe 1992; Klosterman 1980) over the years, but throughout all the debates, its use, in several different versions, seems to have continued among practicing planners.

The central concern in a utilitarian version of ethics is to ensure the greatest good for the greatest number of people. This in itself is an image of the public interest. It suggests weighing the good consequences of action against the bad ones. The rational argument for or against some policy thus takes the form of evaluating the pros and cons and using this information to arrive at a policy recommendation. In its purest, utilitarian version, this could take the form of a formal cost/benefit analysis. However, many planners used a considerably looser idea of evaluating the benefit to a broad public over the long run.

A deontological view of the public interest could take either of two rather different forms, both of which draw substantially on values articulated by the social movements of the 1960s. Some planners focused on the legitimacy and openness of the process by which planning decisions were made. If the process was broadly participatory, then the outcome, whatever its substantive content, could be seen as being in the public interest.

Other deontologists defined the public interest in terms of rights. In particular, the principle of fairness is broadened out into the principle of social justice. All people have rights to be considered equally in the policy-making process, which characteristically is biased against those with few financial or political resources. Some environmentalists also extend the idea of rights in the political process to the inanimate natural environment.

Ideas of the public interest could not be thought of as binding obligations in the same way that duties of justice could. The public interest cannot be thought of in terms of reciprocal rights owed to each individual. Instead, it involves an obligation to a social collectivity. In a deontological context, this would seem to make the obligation to serve the public interest more like what Kant (1964; Baron 1984) defined as a "duty of benevolence" that would not involve correlative rights. Kant gave examples of duties to be kind or generous or to help people in need. These are general obligations, but one does not owe them to every person because to do so would simply be impractical. Thus, a planner may have a general obligation to serve the public interest, but exactly what form this would take and who the specific beneficiaries might be would be discretionary.

The planners in the sample were, on the whole, less certain that issues related to the public interest came within the realm of ethics at all. In Table 2.2, only half thought that not serving the public interest would clearly pose an issue of ethics, though three-quarters thought it probably would. Specific issues, such as being concerned about the long run or about social equity or the environment, drew still more limited responses. The planners were more certain about intentional harm, which suggests a duty of justice. When the issue of affirmative action was posed as a discretionary duty of benevolence (rather than a duty of justice), very few saw it as clearly posing an issue of ethics.

Professional or Ordinary Ethics?

Initially, I have laid out a framework for looking at the ethical issues raised by the planners in the sample. It suggests that they had obligations to be honest, fair, truthful, loyal (or, perhaps more properly, accountable), and, perhaps less certainly, to serve the public interest in a variety of ways. Put in these terms, these obligations sound like the Boy Scout Oath, but that is exactly the point. Shorn of their specific professional context and verbal trappings, these are basic ethical values that could apply in different variations to both personal and professional life. They draw, as the planners themselves did, on both deontological and consequentialist views of ethics. Exactly how the planners used these different perspectives and general principles to define ethical issues in their professional lives as planners will be the subject of the next two chapters. Chapter 3 will take up the procedural, deontological issues of legality, duties of justice, and accountability. Chapter 4 will describe their deontological and consequentialist ideas about the public interest.

3

Procedural Issues

The procedural issues raised by the planners we talked to were shaped both by their images of the realm of ethics and by their particular experiences as civil servants in public bureaucracies. General principles concerned with honesty, fairness, truthfulness, and loyalty were applied in the professional context, giving rise to specific kinds of issues and conflicts.

As indicated in chapter 2, there was widespread agreement among the planners that issues related to legality, to duties of justice, and to accountability were clearly ethical in nature. On the questionnaire, except for 4 percent who were not even sure that legal issues fell within the realm of ethics, everyone saw both legal and procedural issues as ethical in nature. To this base, 52 percent of the planners saw ethics as including the idea of the long-range, broad public interest, and an additional 25 percent added substantive ideas of the public interest, such as social equity, as well. However, legal and procedural principles still formed the core of most planners' images of ethics.

From a purely descriptive standpoint, the discussion here will try to provide a sense of the diversity of the issues the planners raised. It will also examine how often each of the various principles was raised, whether they were raised as hypothetical or real issues, alone or in conflicts with other principles, and how central they were to the planners' actual professional experience. Such a description can begin to give an idea of the overall importance of the various issues in the day-to-day practice of planning.

The central reality of that day-to-day practice was the bureaucratic and political nature of planning. Planners had only limited autonomy to act. This was no accident. Restrictions on the role of public bureaucrats were a product not only of the Progressives' image of the role of experts

in government but also of broader American values that distrust the idea
of power in general (McConnell 1966) and the power of bureaucrats in
particular. Thus, many of the ethical issues raised by the planners were
indicators of the constraints they faced, but the way they described these
ethical issues also begins to give some sense of the sources of leverage
they could bring to bear to deal with their bureaucratic roles and the
ethical challenges they produced.

How immediate these issues actually were to their working lives
depended somewhat on the nature of their particular situations. Some
had actual experiences with corruption, for example, but many without
such experience simply raised legal issues in hypothetical terms because
they thought of them automatically as an aspect of planning ethics. It is
hardly surprising to find that loyalty was the single issue most commonly
raised by the largest proportion of the planners (Table 3.1). It, as well as
the issues of political pressures, truthfulness, and fairness, arose out of
daily contacts with individual developers, citizens, agency superiors, and
elected officials. These were more likely to be raised as real issues than
as hypothetical ones. Moreover, these day-to-day contacts generated
direct ethical demands and conflicts. These were not issues where the
planner was under some general but discretionary obligation to act, as
was the case, for instance, with the issues involving openness of the
planning process.

Finally, these procedural issues could produce many situations
where ethical principles conflicted with each other. These often were
situations where it was difficult for the planner to know what was the
right thing to do. If someone offers you a bribe, you may be tempted to
take it, but the ethical issue would be straightforward to virtually all of
these planners. To take it would be illegal and wrong. In another scenario,
though, you have promised a developer to keep confidential his very
preliminary proposal for a prime site while he does initial financial and
design studies, but the city council member for that district, hearing
rumors about development, has just called to ask what you know. In such
a conflict between keeping a confidence or a promise and being accountable to an elected official, many planners we interviewed would have had
a struggle.

By and large, though, procedural principles rarely conflicted with
each other in the cases described by these planners. The one exception
was loyalty, which generated conflicts with everything from laws through
truth, fairness, and openness to the planners' ideas about the public
interest. This might, in itself, be an indicator of the somewhat problematic
status of loyalty. Planners were being asked in the name of loyalty to
violate a wide range of other ethical obligations, and they clearly strug-

TABLE 3.1

Procedural Ethical Principles in Cases Described by Planners[a]

	Issues Raised		Respondents
	Number	Percent[b]	Percent[c]
Honesty			
To Maintain Minimum Standards of Honesty	166	31	82
Conflicts of interest	55	10	42
Bribery	39	7	33
Doing political favors	24	4	21
Violation of law, rules, or contract	22	4	20
Accepting small gifts and lunches	18	3	16
Theft	8	1	7
Duties of Justice			
To Provide Independent Professional Advice	99	18	65
Freedom from political pressure on technical judgments	50	9	40
Truthfulness	29	5	25
Quality of work	13	2	9
Freedom of speech	7	1	5
To Be Responsive to the Public	82	15	51
Fairness	57	10	41
Procedural openness	25	5	20
Accountability			
To Be Accountable to Elected Officials	86	16	55
Loyalty	75	14	52
Keeping confidences	11	2	10
Total procedural issues	433	80	
Total issues	541	100	

Notes:

[a] These 433 procedural issues made up 80 percent of the total of 541 ethical issues described by the planners. The other 20 percent are discussed in chapter 4 and are shown in Table 4.1.

[b] The percent of all 541 ethical issues raised, including the 20 percent of issues shown in Table 4.1.

[c] This column does not add to 100 percent because most respondents raised more than one issue.

gled to determine in which cases these demands were legitimate. Indeed, it is impossible to understand the issues related to truth or to providing independent professional advice without first considering how the planners were using the idea of loyalty.

The sections that follow will initially examine legal issues and then issues related to accountability to decision makers. These will be followed by the issues related to the various duties of justice, such as truth and fairness. Issues related to what ends planning should serve will be taken up in chapter 4 on the public interest.

The Obligation to Maintain Minimum Standards of Honesty

The planners raised a substantial number of issues that they presented as posing problems of minimum standards of honesty. More than 80 percent of the planners talked about honesty as a basic ethical issue, and such cases made up the largest group of issues (31 percent in Table 3.1). These cases all involved actions that could be illegal or that they thought were clearly improper. Those most often mentioned, as indicated in Table 3.1, were conflicts of interest, bribery, and doing political favors for well-connected people. Some, like the issue of theft, were "plain" issues of honesty. A planner who fudged on his or her time sheets was cheating the public.

Most of these issues also shared a somewhat different common thread. They involved at least the possibility that public power would be used to benefit someone who would otherwise be ineligible. At heart, they raised an issue of fairness, of special attention to certain people regardless of merit. It might be the planner who benefited by fudging on time sheets, by investing in property that was then rezoned by the planning department to allow for more intense use, or by extorting bribes from applicants for development approvals or it might be a developer who would get favorable action, either by buying it or by exerting pressure through the political system. The planners were saying that the public had a right to expect fair and honest government. Indeed, these duties were so basic that they were not simply moral duties but also legal ones.

Many planners raised these issues as examples of things that would clearly pose ethical questions, but for many, these legal issues were not central to their actual practice. Thus, bribery was raised thirty-nine times, but only a third (31 percent) of these cases involved situations in which the planner was directly involved. Fully half (49 percent) were simply brought up hypothetically as examples of actions that would clearly be unethical. In relation to conflicts of interest, where only 17 percent of the fifty-five cases were hypothetical, many of the 39 percent that were actual cases involved planners who were scrupulously trying to avoid improprieties. Several planners, for instance, talked about being especially careful not to allow any appearance of impropriety in buying a house.

Only 4 percent of all the legal cases involved conflicts with other ethical principles. Generally, these infractions of the law were simply raised as ethical problems in and of themselves. It did not take a conflict with some other obligation to make them ethical issues.

The avoidance of legal impropriety was thought of as basic to professional ethics, a foundation for a wider reputation for honesty. As one planning director explained:

> You're talking about a whole range of little things. I have standards that I use in judging what I do. I find that the most important thing a planner can do is that he has got to be honest, he's got to be forthright, he's got to avoid at all costs any form of conflict of interest that may tend to compromise your ability to make value judgments. By that, I mean the planner cannot get involved in any kind of development, he can't own any property as far as I'm concerned, anywhere. Just the mere fact that you own more than the house that you live in is going to place you in a compromising position. You don't associate with people on a personal or social basis who are involved in the development of your community. Whether you do it consciously or unconsciously, you're going to be placed in a compromising position. I take a very hard line on these kinds of things, and I don't like any of my staff being involved in these kinds of things. To be a conscientious, forthright professional planner, and do the job that's expected of you in a community, you got to be as squeaky clean as you can be. And I mean it. I'm not the purest guy in the world, but I do command enough respect in the community where, when the department is reorganized, people will come forth and say, ''George is the guy you ought to put in that position. Not that he agrees with us on everything, but at least he's honest and he will tell you the way he thinks it is. His word is his bond, and he will follow through on that commitment. He won't double-deal you.''

These legal rules marked out the things that planners should clearly not do, not what they should be doing in a positive sense. For at least the two-thirds of the planners who saw themselves as working in communities with clean, open politics, abiding by these rules was fairly unproblematic, requiring little thought or effort on their part.[1]

These legal issues were not always dead letters to be held up as obvious but unrealistic examples of ethical problems, though. There were certainly planners who portrayed their communities as either corrupt or governed by old-boy networks that encouraged favoritism. Planners in smaller communities in rural areas of Tennessee and Texas were more likely than others to raise issues of favoritism. In some large cities, planners had to deal with patterns of corruption held over from the days of machine politics. All told, seven communities were portrayed as very corrupt and another eighteen as moderately so.

In these communities, the issues of minimum honesty were often central to the planners. A planner in a large city described the case of a friend of a departmental project manager who was hired as a consultant by a neighborhood project in return for lenient monitoring of their performance:

> One [issue] is graft, the other is a conflict, and so we brought up the conflict question. We ignored the graft question, like it didn't exist, though we know it does. Our head of contract compliance said, "Well, you know, he's really consulting . . . not to us but directly to the neighborhood and therefore it's not that bad," except that we know that the way the conflict law reads it's the same damn thing. So we pretended to look the other way, but we did report it to management, and management told us to shut up about it. "Don't make waves." So we didn't make waves, but discreetly, all of us are letting the word out that this guy is on the take. Let him stew in his own juice.

For this planner, working in a system pervaded with this kind of corruption engendered a kind of ruthlessness born of disrespect and cynicism.

In a somewhat different vein, the planners in smaller Texas cities often described the political systems as clean in the sense of being free of things such as bribery, but in such small and fairly closed systems, avoiding favoritism was an issue that many of them talked about. One was worried about his relations with the downtown businessmen's association, which was pressing for his active involvement in a downtown revitalization program:

> Recently, there have been moves, particularly with the economic development activities that are being encouraged, to place planning directors more into a broker role, and I think that's something that needs to be pursued with a great deal of caution. I think that if planning directors are placed in the role of being urban renewal

directors, there's a propensity to see a lot of potential for abuse. Suppose [a program] has been designed so that they submit their applications to me and I can approve those applications. I can say, "Hey, Joe, why don't you send your application in." And that's one reason why I try to divorce myself as much as possible from any organizations that might be involved there. I don't sit on Downtown's executive board—I don't want to sit on their executive board. I will sit ex officio and I explained what we can do. However, [I told them] if you want to pursue [a project] you need to prepare a proposal that will go to the city council.

The kinds of legal issues discussed ranged from the obvious to the more subtle. Direct political pressure to violate the zoning ordinance was mentioned by several people:

We've been hit with [pressure] quite a bit. It's one of the routine kind of things you get: "I know the mayor" and all that kind of crap. . . . [With a recent change in the city council] the pressure isn't direct, but they call, saying, "We know you've got to approve it, but how come it's taking so long?" or "Is that really important?" The old council would have just said "Do it."

In a less obvious issue, several planners worried about compliance of local jurisdictions with contractual state planning requirements. In one case, a state official was quite sure that the requirements were not being met, but he felt torn about what he should do since the only recourse he had if a community did not plan adequately was to cut their funding, in which case they would not plan at all.

Thus, legal standards provided a foundation for ethics in planning. They set minimum standards specifying what actions must not, under any circumstances, be taken. In this sense, their scope was narrow. In some communities, this basic standard was not met, and legal issues were central to the ethical concerns of their planners, but for the majority of the sample, these issues formed a taken-for-granted backdrop to the major business of planning.

Obligations to Be Responsive to Decision Makers

Two kinds of issues seemed to bear directly on planners' obligations to be accountable to decision makers. One was the basic issue of loyalty. The other was the closely related obligation to keep certain kinds of information confidential.

Loyalty

The most commonly mentioned issue in the interviews was loyalty (see Table 3.1). Its pressure could be very strong in both personal and organizational relationships. This was why it gave rise to many conflicts with other ethical principles.

Bureaucracies, whether public or private, depend for their efficient functioning on the compliance of their members. By instilling the idea of loyalty to the organization, they can counterbalance some nonconforming tendencies among individual members. The practical dependence of lower level employees on higher level ones for approval, for a sense of effectiveness, for promotions, and for job security all increase the pressure for conformance defined as loyalty.

In public agencies, the idea of responsibility to the public through elected officials only strengthens the pressures. Normally, the planners in the sample gathered facts about a particular situation or issue and developed recommendations to be acted on by an agency head, an appointed plan commission, and/or some body of elected officials. Traditional Progressive administrative theory has always made a sharp distinction between the planning staff work and the actual policy decision. Though many planners in this study recognized that they did shape decisions by the information and recommendations they provided, they nevertheless accepted this distinction and the final authority it gave to official decision makers. Elected officials were the representatives of the people and as such expected loyalty and responsiveness from their nonelected staffs.

Usually, this loyalty was implicit and unproblematic. Often it became an explicit issue only if it conflicted with other ethical principles, as it did in more than a third (35 percent) of the cases. The planners themselves often did not explicitly frame this as an issue of loyalty. The expectation of accountability to superiors was simply the taken-for-granted background against which ethical issues were posed. However, the conflicts were real. Organizational loyalty produced conflicts with the law, with duties of justice, such as truth, fairness, or keeping promises, and with planners' ideas of the public interest.

A planner struggled with the issue of whether to blow the whistle on her boss. She described the issue as one of legality; the conflicting principle of loyalty was simply left implicit:

> Two or three years ago, I was having many disputes with our executive director, and so were many people on the board, and he was doing many things, some of which I think were illegal in terms

of accounting for funds and things—and having an affair with someone in the agency. It got to the point that we were going toward some sort of a showdown, and the board officers changed and people came in who were more or less against him. It came down to the board doing an evaluation of him and asking, "What do you think of him?" So I talked to the officers of the board, and even shared papers—internal papers—which was an ethical dilemma for me to do. I thought the board is running the agency, but if they don't know what's happening and if their conduit is just him, they just don't see it, they don't have the information. I think for the good of the agency as a whole, I just became convinced that he should no longer be the executive director.

Among duties of justice, the most common conflict was between loyalty and truth, which was often posed as the problem of political pressure on technical judgments, which will be examined below. Other cases of conflict with duties of justice included a conflict between loyalty and promise-keeping. A neighborhood planner was pressured by his superiors to provide information about the contents of a set of neighborhood housing recommendations that he had promised a citizens' committee he would keep confidential. Another planner refused to hire a council member's job candidate on the grounds that it was unfair to other candidates.

Most common of all were conflicts between what the planners thought would best serve the public interest and their organizations' or superiors' policies. These disagreements occurred over such issues as downtown revitalization, bike paths, a marina, a mixed-use development, and the locations of a landfill and several industrial facilities. A planning director who was in the early stages of such a conflict with his mayor played out the possible alternative scenarios. The issue was the location of a large industrial facility that was proposed for an area that was not close to the city's good transit system:

I have told the developer that I think that's wrong and I may oppose it if they propose to do such a thing. We went in to see the mayor together. The mayor took a much softer line than I did about whether it was desirable for the city to locate it off the transit line. Presumably, the mayor and I don't see eye-to-eye on that. Now we're in the very early stages of this. It seems to me that it's incumbent on me now, as a professional planner, to convince him that the planning factors surrounding this case are overriding and that the public is not going to be well served. Particularly, the people who use transit are not going to be well served if this facility is away from the public transit line. I've got a job to do there. Let's spell it out all the way. Let's say the mayor continues to disagree with me and so he thinks that it's okay if Consolidated Technologies goes down there. I continue to say "no." Two choices: I disagree with him in public. I'm overt and I instruct the planning commission that they ought to vote it down and we have a public disagreement with the mayor. Or I go along with the mayor, I relent and say, "Oh, well, I won't oppose it. I'll go along with it." Or, three, I could resign over it.

His approach to such a conflict was both matter-of-fact and vigorous. He did not really expect either to give in or to resign.

Others with less leverage and autonomy felt more pressed by the weight of the authority of the officials they had to deal with. A planner in an unusually hostile political situation was questioning the design of a new personnel classification system. He too was considering his options, but he said:

We're being put under pressure on that account to toe the line, to don't question—do what you're told, and this is where it is really getting into a very definite conflict. The other problem is: What are my options? Right now, they're not very good. There are not many at all.

Even many of these conflicts were settled routinely. As one planner said about conflicts between what he thought should be done and the judgment of his city manager:

If it conflicts, I voice it. If the decision is still made, then I proceed with the decision that's made. The only obligation that I feel is voicing it and making it understood as best as I can, and once the decision is made, I will carry it out.
Q: So perhaps loyalty is a principle?
Well, I guess that's it. I don't know if I would use those terms, though. I think all that falls under the primacy of local elected officials, which is what this institution is composed of.

Planners often recommended actions that were not adopted or were accepted only in part, a circumstance that reminded them forcefully of their obligation to be team players. Thus, a planner who very much wanted to see the adoption of a system of bike paths in his community was disappointed that his department would not push for them because they raised some potentially controversial issues and did not have a strong constituency. He spelled out what he saw as the trade-off for this loyalty:

> You are being trusted by your superiors to methodically and fairly apply the regulations. [You have a responsibility] to keep the office operating smoothly, and therefore you don't want to generate a problem or controversy over something that you believe strongly in if it's going to bog down the flow of work, and so you tend do go along with what the policy has been in the office.

More difficult still was the problem of several planners who struggled with the issue of loyalty to decision makers who clearly did not care about planning. One, at the time of the interview, was contemplating the propriety of campaigning, either overtly or covertly, against an antiplanning official up for reelection. Another accepted the obligation but was dissatisfied:

> When you're in school you're very idealistic, and you don't really think about these conflicts that can arise. You think affordable housing is good, protect the environment is good, and I'm going to go out in the world and do this, but then when you get out in your job situation, you find out that it's also important to be accountable to those you work for. You have a tendency to think that when you get out you're going to have the authority to make these decisions, but in reality, it's the elected and appointed officials who have that authority, and you're just providing them with information and making recommendations. It's somewhat frustrating at times.

On these issues where the planner's idea of good policy conflicted with that of superiors, the assumption was generally that if the policy they opposed was adopted through a legitimate decision-making process, team loyalty would take precedence over personal judgment.

There were some planners, though, who did not accept the idea that disagreements within the bureaucracy should not be taken outside. Several said they had some obligation to be accountable to the position of their superior but that loyalty to a particular individual had to be earned:

> When you get to the ethical behavior, you start talking about how far are you going to go, you know, are you going to kill for your boss, so to speak—and if you don't, you're not loyal. The current city manager and the previous city manager were, I believe, the

kind of people who believed you should be loyal to the position, no matter who it is, to the office, no matter who's in it. I have a certain loyalty to the office, I think, as a general rule. It's a general guideline in my behavioral thing, but I don't have any built-in magical loyalty to persons, necessarily. Loyalty has to be earned, it has to be nurtured, has to be built, and it needs to be a mutual kind of a trust situation, which probably creates one of the greatest challenges to ethical behavior that I face on a daily basis, and that is the question of how do you bridge this gap between doing your professional job, which you consider to be in a particular direction but which may not be the same philosophical direction that the city manager may want to take. You've got a city council that's kind of split on the issue, some are with you, some are with him. You know in your own professional mind what you think is best for the city, and I keep going back to that, very honestly, as a major driver in my own behavior.

The upshot of this was that he sometimes did end runs around his city manager to sympathetic members of the council.

Another planner worked in a highly politicized and corrupt environment that undermined traditional ideas of loyalty. She was actively promoting a project, on which her agency was officially neutral, by quietly providing information to a neighborhood group, a council person, and another agency that supported it. The project was opposed by powerful interests close to her agency:

Ethically, I should not be working behind the scenes. Ethically, my position should be, I think, probably the same as my agency's: that I have no position on it, but my own personal ethics dictate that if I see a dirty deal, and if I see something such as [this project] that works, that can be a tremendous benefit to the city, I think it is something that should be adopted. Due to my position, though, I cannot do that publicly. I cannot work for it publicly.

Keeping Confidences

Confidentiality of information was not nearly as important an issue in planning as it generally is in consulting professions where information provided by clients or patients is considered to be inviolate. It came up in only 2 percent of the cases discussed by the planners (see Table 3.1). Public meetings, documents, and decisions are usually required by law to be open to the public. This is one structural support for a fair planning process. It involves notifying citizens who might be affected by a decision, making information in files available, and holding public hearings.

Even so, as in all government agencies, planning departments had information that was confidential and that staff were expected to keep quiet about. Keeping confidences in planning was generally tied closely to loyalty to one's agency. One planner talked bluntly about this:

> As a planner, you sometimes have access to certain privileged, confidential information. For example, particularly at the higher levels, you deal with local politicians, and sometimes they will share with you some confidential information which if you release or talk to someone, it can cause some potential practical problems, and I think one of the important things as a planner is that you have to be able to keep your mouth shut.

Information was most often considered to be confidential if it bore on a decision that was still in the process of being discussed within the bureaucracy. Once a final plan or proposal was developed, it would become public. The point at which this occurred, however, was often not entirely specified. A planner who worked in a large and powerful development agency that was criticized by several others in the sample for being secretive said that planning should be aboveboard and went on to explain what he meant by that:

> I recognize that everything can't be done open and publicly to begin with. There's privileged information in almost any activity, and you've got to protect your interests from those who would steal the marbles if you're looking the other way. If you are making a decision about some activity, some development or something, you need a chance to do your homework and get your ducks in a row, legally and legitimately. Then there comes a time when it's supposed to become public and you have to declare what you're doing. There may be a time then, following that, when it's open to scrutiny, and then presumably beyond that there's some sort of approval or ratification. So I would define a procedure like that as open and aboveboard, [but] I'm not so naive as to say that there are no backroom deals, and even if there necessarily shouldn't be.

This kind of discretion before a formal proposal had been made was also extended to applicants for regulatory actions. A number of planners noted that they felt they had an obligation to developers to keep proposals confidential while they were still in the preliminary, preapplication stage and the department was negotiating over their final content. As one said:

> I have a rule that if a property owner or a prospective property owner walks into this office and says, "What I really want to do on the corner of so-and-so and so-and-so is the following but I haven't gotten the property yet or I haven't sought out an architect," I have a rule that those types of conversations are confidential.

This was an incentive to get prospective developers to come in early for discussions.

Finally, several planners described their somewhat uneasy relationship with an active, inquiring press. In one case, a reporter asked to look at the public file of a controversial land-use decision:

> The issue was a major issue, and I was told to keep the "good stuff" in my personal files out of view because the guy who would be coming up to see me in five minutes had already written a scurrilous article about the planning department's role and we didn't want to give the "good stuff" again unless we had to. The "good stuff" was current cost estimates and current analysis that I as a staff person had done that had not even been put in memorandum form and given to the director, so that, you know, this was stuff before the director even saw it. I think that was a major rationale for holding back the material, and the person in the office that told me was the counsel to the director. He said that, you know, "You don't have to show them everything, and you don't want to show him key things in your personal files."

Another planner whose girlfriend was an investigative reporter felt he was always watched with some suspicion by people higher in the department in case he had leaked information.

Duties of Justice

Duties of justice in general include principles such as being fair, telling the truth, keeping promises, and not doing harm. In planning, fairness and truth were the most often mentioned of these values, and each of these was a central value in a particular aspect of professional life. Fairness, on the one hand, could easily be an issue both within the bureaucracy—toward colleagues—and outside—in relation to members of the public. Truthfulness, on the other hand, was the central principle in a complex of values related to providing independent professional advice to decision makers. Here the planner was seen as having obligations to be truthful and to do high-quality technical analysis. In return, this implied that decision makers should encourage accurate analysis and should listen to and take seriously the findings provided by their staffs.

Obligations to Be Responsive to the Public

Two kinds of issues of fairness were raised by the planners. One might be thought of as fairness to individuals, or procedural fairness. The other was the issue of the fairness of the political structure within which planning took place. The planners generally talked about this latter notion as an issue of the openness of the planning process.

Procedural Fairness

One of the most commonly raised issues was fairness to individuals or, as some called it, objectivity. This was primarily an obligation to the public imposed by the nature of bureaucratic decision making.

Max Weber was the founder of the systematic study of bureaucracy. In his image of the ideal-type bureaucracy (Weber 1947), a central characteristic was the reliance on general rules that would be applied objectively, "without regard for persons" (Gerth and Mills 1946): All those in the same situation should be treated the same way. Procedural fairness was an issue that permeated all regulatory activity, and regulation—the application of general planning criteria to specific development applications—was the heart of plan implementation for most of these planners, whether of land-use, environmental, or health systems plans. It was often raised as an affirmative obligation.

The most commonly raised issue (by twenty people) was that of not playing favorites between developers, consultants, or, sometimes, between jurisdictions when a planner worked for more than one. A planner might be tempted to favor a developer because he was easy to deal with or did particularly nice work or—moving into even more questionable territory—because he was a friend or an influential person. In many communities, the same developers worked on many different projects and became quite familiar to the planning staff so that maintaining bureaucratic objectivity was more difficult. As one planner put it:

> There are individuals who you encounter in this job who you really do dislike. I may say I like everyone, but there are certain people in

my job that just rub me the wrong way. I could really like them on the street, but in this particular job, because of the way they treat the staff, the way they treat you, you just don't create a tremendous liking for them, and you've got to put that aside when you evaluate their projects.

This planner went on to clearly articulate the relationship between being fair and not doing harm:

It would be very easy, I mean, you could really ruin someone so quickly. You could delay their projects, you could put so many roadblocks in their way that they'd lose their financing. It's just there, and I think that you have to look at that.

The same issue of bias applied to relations with the broader public as well. One state planner talked about citizens who complained about and to governmental officials:

If you ignore [the people who complain] in total, I think that would be unethical, and you really have to watch out for the situation where one of these folks is a habitual moaner and groaner because if you tune him out just once, he can burn you bad because it could be the one time where the guy's really got a legitimate complaint or a point where you really should go out of your way to take a look at what he's saying. It's the crying wolf syndrome. I'm a public official, I should listen. If you start tuning out even sections of the public, no matter how off-the-wall you think they are at any point, then I think that's unethical.

Openness of the Planning Process

The other side of the issue of fairness was the "squeaky wheel" problem, which was more an issue of structural fairness. Several planners argued that it was basically unfair for a planning decision to be based not on the technical merits of the case but on how many people came to the public hearing on it. In this case, vocal groups got benefits that less vocal but perhaps equally affected groups did not.

Here the issue was that of open, fair access to the planning process and responsiveness to community wishes. Some planners who raised this issue were concerned in general about the lack of opportunity for public input into particular decisions. One such case involved a regional development agency that accepted a proposal for industrial development without holding any hearings or notifying surrounding residents. Only a challenge from a local planning agency, and some unrelated political developments, finally forced the regional agency to hold hearings, which indicated that the project was not appropriate to the site.

Another planner who worked in an office similar to the regional development agency thought it should be opened up to more public scrutiny:

> It is a public agency but it sees itself as an agency that must do things that are for the good of the agency and will not necessarily do things that are necessary for the good of the region. [It is] an example of the kind of bureaucracy that I as a planner and other planners work in where we see things occurring that we have little or no control over and where there are important public policy issues being decided for several reasons but not for a whole broad litany of reasons that ought to be brought to bear. I guess that the problem that I see with the more secretive aspects of our work is that, sure, there are things that every agency has to do in a secretive way—secretive meaning kept under control so that people in the agency understand what is being looked into—but I think there is a point in examining a specific issue or project or program where you want to bring others in to focus on what it is you are looking at, and you want to bring them in early enough to be able to get their input. In past instances, this agency has not done that, in my view, early enough.

In this powerful agency, a closed process was seen as politically advantageous.

In contrast, a number of planners who were engaged in trying to get controversial projects adopted by their communities stressed the importance of encouraging widespread participation so that issues could be dealt with openly. Several raised small issues about the need for proper notice of hearings that were symptomatic of this concern. One dealt directly with the underlying issue:

> Everybody ought to get to participate in this process I talk about. It's very important here that everybody gets a whack at it. That's part of the process. Also, it's time-consuming, and developers complain about it because of the money involved in it, but as long as you have controversy—and no major project here is without controversy—it's a way of life around here. The process is going to

take time and I'm not going to speed up the process for the sake of seeing to it that somebody saves money because that's not what I'm serving. I've got to make sure that everyone has had a chance to say what they want to say and we've taken everything into account.

Another indicated that in her community, both ethics and practicality supported openness:

I found that definitely the best way to operate is as openly as possible, not that you go out leading with your chin, but . . . things here are very open. I don't think [a closed process] would work even if it was right, [and] it is a matter of principle, too.

People should have access to public information. These planners did not work in especially powerful agencies, but many did work in California. Indeed, in these cases, the planners themselves, along with others in their communities, sometimes acted as advocates for the interests of poorly represented, disadvantaged groups or for alternatives that otherwise did not have a constituency. Such planners sometimes raised the issue of whether their own active role could, in effect, reduce the access or influence of other groups or perspectives. One said:

As a community planner, I'm always concerned about the extent to which I should lead and the extent to which I ought to listen, both in the review of development plans and in the formulation of studies and in setting my own priorities. It's a case of not imposing my values, but at the same time, if the values aren't articulated, I feel I'm not performing my job adequately. I not only bring a point of view to the community but I also let the community know that point of view. [I'm] also willing to respond to concerns that they raise, and I adjust my own expectations or my own working attitudes accordingly.

For some planners who wanted to get things done, however, the obligation to be fully open was not always an absolute one. More than a third (36 percent) of the cases involving openness raised conflicts with other principles or obligations. Sometimes it was loyalty, but several planners did pose conflicts between citizen participation and other ethical obligations, usually related to substantive ideas of the public interest that did not draw strong public support, such as getting developers to adopt a better design or the need for mass transit. One designer said that he would like more public participation in the process of design review:

We have no process here of citizen participation in any of this. Our version of being involved with our real clients is not really alive. We think we're doing good things for them, but I think there's a big gap between the public understanding and what site planning review is all about—what they're getting from it.

When asked to choose between participation and design, given the reluctance of developers and decision makers to make the process more complex than it already was, he said:.

I don't think they can coexist. I don't think they ever will. That may be pessimism, but . . . that's reality.

Obligations to Provide Independent Professional Advice

In a profession whose primary function was to do policy research and to provide advice to decision makers, truth played a central ethical role. The obligation to be truthful applied both within the bureaucracy and to the public. In a political system, though, pressures to be less than truthful were common. They might come from decision makers who found the information the planners gave them politically unacceptable or they might come from the planners themselves who could sometimes see strategic advantage in being less than truthful.

Since truth in analysis obviously seemed to be a central ethical issue, in many cases if planners did not bring it up themselves we asked about it. Two-thirds of the sample were queried in one way or another, and, perhaps not surprisingly, only three people came anywhere close to saying that they had lied in some kind of analysis.

A number of the planners stressed, in different ways, the importance of good, truthful analysis. Two planning directors gave examples of having to fire employees who simply made up findings for reports. In neither case did the employee do it because of an ideological commitment to a particular outcome: both were simply described as incompetent.

Being open and truthful with decision makers was especially important. As a practical matter, planners had to be honest in order to retain credibility with decision makers, though for many this was not the primary reason why they thought they should be honest. One planner talked about the problems he saw with the city manager in a neighboring community:

. . . not keeping the council informed and, in many instances, only telling them what they wanted to hear and not the whole story. I think you have to bring up both sides here. Ethics in itself is to me straight and aboveboard. I've always considered ethics honesty. If I can't tell the truth, I'm not going to say it.

The planners who raised this issue were generally trying to get things done and so had to think about both the ethics and the long-run effectiveness of selling their ideas. The open approach was one that could generate conflict and controversy, which not all planners were comfortable with, but it also was the basis for a reputation for honesty that, they argued, was a necessary ingredient for getting things done in the long run.

In any case, lying was really not the important issue. In much of planning analysis, facts are often complex, lending support to a variety of possible interpretations. Planners often recognized that their recommendations were based on judgment rather than certainty and that this left them vulnerable to pressure or temptation. This was especially clear to planners who had strong ideas about what they thought was good policy. As one planner said:

I think if you make figures lie, it's unethical, [but] frequently you have preconceived notions and you're really looking at the data to verify that you're right. Well, data won't tell you you're right, but they don't tell you you're wrong, and if you just plain old say "These numbers mean thus and so" when they clearly don't, that's just lying. In any of these things, you take everything into account and you can express this caveat, you can say, "I think we ought to do thus and so but the data say this."

The most common issue that planners raised about truthful analysis was political pressure from superiors on their technical judgments. Most of the instances of pressure in Table 3.1 did not involve lying, but 14 percent did. When planners raised these issues, they were saying, in effect, that they had an obligation not only to officials and to the public but also to themselves to perform accurate and informed technical analysis and to make recommendations based on it. Several public planners were scornful of private consultants who they thought were willing to come up with any conclusions wanted by their clients. A planner in Texas said:

When you get into the private field, you've got to start doing work for utility companies, oil companies, developers, and you've got to help them figure out ways to plunder, to get what they want at the expense of—well, in some cases, they are using public lands and it becomes the role of planners to prepare the EISs and the social assessment papers and all the things to get the project through.

In their relations with public officials, however, the issues became less black and white. Planning is by nature a political process, and decision makers sometimes wanted planners to justify decisions already taken.

Sometimes the planners were in a strong position to argue that such a request was unreasonable. Having legality or hard data on their side gave them strength. Pressure to change technical judgments or to lower technical standards could easily result from illegal commitments made by superiors. Cases of this kind were not uncommon. One planner described the case of a councilman who wanted the department to approve the subdivision plan of his friend without the normal requirements for utilities, curbs, gutters, and other infrastructure.

If data were "hard," that is, factual rather than judgmental, then the planners not only felt the pressure was more illegitimate but they also seemed better able to resist. A planner who was fairly typical of a number of others talked about pressure to fudge data:

> [Changing numbers] drives me crazy. I've had battles with those folks over reports that I've done where the numbers don't justify the preconceived conclusion and they say, "I think this is high, blah, blah, blah." Sometimes I guess I'm willing to compromise to the point where, if I don't have full faith in the numbers and they really aren't hard numbers, we can round off and we can guesstimate. But hard-core factual results being changed, I won't tolerate that.

Sometimes decision makers found more judgmental information or recommendations personally or politically unpalatable for perfectly legal but largely political reasons. Take the case of an industry trying to locate in an undeveloped area that had been zoned for industrial use for many years. Past planning decisions, a draft EIS, and other agencies all supported the developer. However, influential nearby residents were able to mobilize political supporters who pressed the agency to modify its environmental impact statement to oppose the project on environmental grounds, an argument that could be made technically though it was not strongly supported by the evidence. The planner felt torn between his belief that the elected officials had the right to make such a choice and his feelings that the EIS should not be changed to justify it.

Other cases of such ex post facto justification were discussed by the planners. One had been told to justify the choice of one of three neighborhoods for a housing program. Another planner had produced a social impact assessment of changes in bus fares that supported decision makers' preconceived ideas. A third was told to justify the predetermined location of certain industrial projects. All three thought these studies were ethically questionable.

Planners differed in their tolerance for such pressures. What might seem to one planner to be unethical pressure or suppression of the truth might appear to another to be simply the normal workings of the political process. However, there also seemed to be real differences in the environments faced by these planners. Tennessee, for example, produced 30 percent of all of the cases of such pressure and 44 percent of the ones involving firsthand experience.

If planners did not like to be put in the position of having to lie or to justify decisions after they had been made, they were nonetheless aware of temptations to be less than fully honest. Eighteen percent said they would put the best face they could on their preferred alternative in making a recommendation. One planner echoed a number of others in making a distinction between the way he dealt with data in the early and later stages of a project analysis:

> Earlier in the process, the more completely open you have to be in your presentations and the more you focus on the technical parameters that will contribute essentially to the decision-making process. Filling out the pros and cons of the factors, you bring out all these factors in a technical report. When the decision has been made to do something, like a decision on Route 111, I'm very similar to an attorney before the state legislature: I'd argue for that particular case. Obviously, when you write a report favoring a particular project, you write it in such a fashion that you bring out the factors that favor what you're doing.

Many of the planners who said they put the best face on their recommendations seemed to be talking about the second part of the process.

Several planners said that they had an obligation to provide accurate information but that they did not feel they always had to volunteer everything they knew on an issue. On the questionnaire, 93 percent said that providing inaccurate information would pose an ethical issue, but only 71 percent felt the same about providing accurate but incomplete information.

Projections of various sorts were a particular source of temptation since they were especially "soft" (Wachs 1982). They were likely to shape expectations about the future and could sometimes be thought of as self-fulfilling prophecies. Alternatively, since they underlay many planning analyses, such as environmental impact reviews, grant applications, or capital improvement programs, the possibility of strengthening the justification for more sewers, a new highway, or some form of grant money led decision makers and planners alike to want "hopeful" estimates. One planner talked about the idea of the self-fulfilling prophecy:

> I wrote a report in 1969 projecting the future retail sales downtown. It was a lot to do with straight-line projections. These projections are always drawn in such a way that they would give you an opportunity to add more of a certain quantity to whatever you were building, and a lot of the things that I made, they were certainly ex post facto rationalizations.
> Q: Did that bother you at the time?
> Well, no . . . no, it didn't bother me. I was aware of it but I was thinking that I was trying to create a self-fulfilling prophecy—after all, anything that's a projection—you know. . . .

Constraint and Leverage

The procedural issues raised by the planners reflected the tensions and pressures of work in a setting that was both political and bureaucratic. The planners' roles involved providing policy advice to decision makers and carrying out policies that had been enacted into law. In both instances, they might have influence on the outcomes of their actions, but they did not control those outcomes. Many other participants were involved: other bureaucrats from higher levels or from other agencies, citizens, developers, representatives of interest groups, and elected and appointed officials whose job it was to make the formal decisions. These various groups would have their own values, goals, and concerns on any given policy issue. The give-and-take of this political process could fairly easily pose challenges to a planner's ethical values concerning the nature of the decision-making process. How difficult such a challenge was depended both on how basic and binding the ethical obligations were and on how much leverage the planner had in the context in which the issue was raised.

Ethically, laws were the basic foundation for the substance of planning policy and for the procedures through which policy would be adopted and carried out. A view of ethics limited only to laws would be an impoverished one, but the planners who worked in corrupt systems provided ample evidence of the importance of this legal foundation to the

maintenance of trust and a sense of fairness and to the effective performance of planning tasks. Characteristically, planners in corrupt communities had relatively little leverage. The law itself was their strongest tool,
and it was not a sure one. Some accepted this weakness passively; others
fought to gain some control.

Planners and Bureaucratic Constraints

Basic honesty was not an issue in most communities. Even so, within the
bureaucracy, both politics and bureaucratic expectations could raise
ethical issues. Planners pointed out the politically flexible nature of truth
in a policy profession. While they might feel that they had been improperly pressured by superiors to bend the truth, they could sometimes also
see that they, too, could be tempted by the same kinds of policy
commitments that influenced their superiors.

The central ethical issue within the bureaucracy was loyalty and
what could legitimately be required in its name. Confusion over the
difference between loyalty and legitimate responsibility to elected officials
lay behind many conflicts between, for example, loyalty and truth or
between loyalty and openness to the public. There could certainly be
cases where it would be possible to argue that elected officials would be
proper in telling a civil servant to lie or to withhold information from the
public. Such actions are taken, for instance, to protect national security
in times of crisis, but the many instances of the misuse of official secrecy
suggest that this rationale is overworked (Bok 1983). How often would it
really be a legitimate argument in local land-use planning?

The discomfort of the planner who was told to take the "good stuff"
out of his file before he gave it to the reporter reflected his belief that the
order, and the way it was given, were not legitimate. Of his own action in
removing material from the file, he said:

> I think it probably was [pause] unethical, but I'm not sure. I can
> think of a good reason to have kept material out of the central file. I
> removed things that had not been reviewed by others, and there
> might have been errors in them, [but] I think I probably removed
> some stuff for reasons other than the one I just mentioned, and I
> think I was responding to what I felt was a message from counsel
> that said, "Look, this guy, he's coming up. He ought not to be
> shown everything. He's distorted things by his article before." So I
> probably removed other things that I thought would just be
> controversial.

He felt he had been rushed by the authority of his superior into an action that was not ethically defensible.

It was sometimes difficult for the planners to see that accountability was not the only principle that they should use. Their acceptance of the principle of loyalty, and the organizational pressures and incentives in their agencies, seemed for some at least to inhibit the development of a well-defined, independent sense of professional purpose that could serve as a counterweight to loyalty.

It would not be easy for notably independent professional standards to thrive in a bureaucratized profession. It appeared from the sample that most planners did not find their professional values or work standards at variance with those of the bureaucracies in which they worked. Indeed, some were quick to say how highly professionalized their agencies were:

> [This agency] has a tremendous technical resource staff that are paid darn good salaries to weigh and balance and come up with whatever staff recommendations we're talking about. There are very few decisions that are made that aren't shored up by very comprehensive assessment work on the staff's part.

This description, though, led up to an example of how the ideas of the technical staff were not always accepted by the agency's policy board. In this case and in the other cases of political pressure on technical judgments, it was apparent that agency standards could conflict with personal or professional ones.

The planners seemed to have fewer sources of leverage against pressures to be loyal than they had in relation to many other ethical challenges. Many took the position that they could argue for their position within the bureaucracy but that once a final decision had been made, they should be loyal team players. Those who were not willing to accept this position were, in effect, left with little except end runs and covert opposition.

A few planners went beyond individual cases to raise the general problem of a clash between professional and organizational standards. Talking about the need for more analysis of alternatives on a transportation project, one said:

> I see [the lack of more analysis] as an ethical issue in terms of the professional responsibilities of a planner. I see that as being an ethical question, but in terms of the characteristics of the bureaucracy that we live within, the bureaucracy permitted the professional planner a way out because the bureaucracy said, "We don't

require this." The profession said, "You should do it," but the bureaucracy said it was not necessary at this time.

The same organizational pressures that prevented planners from playing highly autonomous professional roles could also serve to reduce a general sense of professional identity and lead to co-optation into the values of decision makers, developers, or other influential groups in the community. This was not an issue that was raised by many of the planners, but one who was concerned about it thought that planners were often open to co-optation of various kinds:

> I'm very concerned about planners being better able to articulate their concerns in society both within the profession and vis-à-vis the other professions. Inasmuch as a planner is required to deal with such a variety of actions in real estate and government, unless the expectations and the tasks of planners are understood among all those professionals, I think the planner is open to co-optation by various forces to explicit or implicit acts of rationalization. [In] approaching his job, [he] may become a partner in a particular development process without regard to larger issues, or, on the other hand, the planner may simply function in a purely technical and mechanical capacity in the organization and really not realize the potential.

For the planner functioning in a purely technical capacity, the idea of loyalty to decision makers would substitute identification with the organization for identification with the profession.

Finally, while planners did talk about direct obligations to the public, as everyday duties these were somewhat abstract. Obligations within the bureaucracy were more real for most planners since decision makers were immediate employers while the public was not only more distant but also more divided into often competing interest groups.

Take fairness, for instance. The individual obligation to be fair was central to a bureaucratic role and, in that sense, perhaps not a strong indicator of direct obligation to the public. Many of the examples of fairness related to treatment of developers rather than of citizens. These were people the planners had to deal with on a day-to-day basis. In worrying about fairness to them as individuals, though, the planners seemed to lose sight of larger, structural issues of procedural fairness. The more difficult, discretionary, and potentially more controversial external obligation to maintain an open planning process was brought up much less often, and when it did come up, it often conflicted with other obligations, especially loyalty or confidentiality.

The best source of leverage for planners who wanted to promote a more open policy process was an already fairly open political system. Such communities could accept the idea that a planner could play an active role in encouraging broad participation in controversial issues. In some cases, such roles might be institutionalized in a neighborhood planning staff, for example, but in other cases, planners simply took on this role. In communities and larger agencies with fairly closed political systems, where the need for participation would be greater, this kind of role was much less accepted or supported in the bureaucratic and political systems.

Ethics and Conflict

These cases were the product of an interaction between what planners defined as ethical issues and the pressures imposed on them by the real world in which they worked. Hoch's (1988) national survey of threatening conflicts experienced by planners produced a similar list of issues, suggesting that many of the most difficult and conflictual issues planners face are ethical ones.

Hoch emphasized how the conflicts his planners reported suggested a limited acceptance of planning by external, powerful groups, such as elected officials and developers. In this study, these limits were especially evident in Texas and Tennessee, where planning was least accepted. Not all planners faced constraints that placed them constantly on the defensive, though. As chapter 4 will show, many had commitments to ideas about the public interest. As part 2 will further show, at least some were active in their efforts to see these commitments realized. Like all planners, they worked in a complex and constraining political structure, and they accepted the conflicts it produced as part of the job.

Indeed, this chapter has begun to suggest the sources of leverage planners might use in dealing with specific ethical challenges. These include strategies such as appeals to the law, reliance on the "hardness" of data, active organization of support, or covert action. In some situations, as chapter 4 will indicate, an independent idea of the public interest could be used as a balancing force against procedural pressures. Most fundamentally, however, as we will see in part 3, the way the planners responded to or managed ethical challenges depended on the kinds of roles they chose to play in the bureaucratic and political decision-making process.

4

The Public Interest

Procedural principles and issues of means formed the core of ethics for most planners, but this did not mean that they had no concern with ends. Quite the contrary. Most of the planners in the sample used some idea of the public interest, though only 20 percent of the cases they talked about turned on issues related to the public interest (Table 4.1). There were some who never used this concept in their interviews, but for most, having some idea of what would serve the public interest was probably almost indispensable. After all, planning is concerned with making recommendations to elected officials on public policy issues. Some of these are purely concerned with the most efficient means for carrying out goals that have already been set. Others, inevitably, are concerned with what ends a community should be trying to achieve. In either case, the central question is what actions would best serve the public interest. Professionally informed judgment on such issues lies at the heart of a planner's role.

The planners did not all define the public interest in the same way. In this they were no different from philosophers and political theorists (Held 1970; Howe 1992; Meyerson and Banfield 1955). All their definitions had at their core the obligation to serve the public, but, not surprisingly, how knowledge of the "interest" or the "good" of the public might be arrived at was open to different interpretations.

However, running like a thread through these diverse definitions of the public interest was the idea of it as a balance between planners' own professional definitions and those of decision makers and the public. Thus, it was seen as a process, but one in which the substantive views of each of the parties were also important. This image again reflected in a different way the need to balance the various, sometimes competing, procedural obligations to provide independent professional advice, to be responsive to the public, and to be accountable to decision makers.

TABLE 4.1

Public Interest Issues Raised by Planners[a]

| | *Issues Raised* | | *Respondents* |
	Number	*Percent*[b]	*Percent*[c]
Deontological Issues	34	6	28
Rights			
Equity	23	4	19
Natural environment	4	1	3
Process	7	1	6
Consequentialist Issues	74	14	49
The public interest	67	12	44
Natural environment	3	1	2
Transportation	2	d	2
Urban design	2	d	1
Total public interest issues	108	20	
Total issues	541	100	

Notes:

[a] These 108 issues related to the public interest make up only 20 percent of the 541 ethical issues described by the planners. The other 80 percent are shown in Table 3.1 and were discussed in chapter 3.

[b] The percent of all 541 ethical issues raised, including the 80 percent of issues shown in Table 3.1.

[c] This column does not add up to 100 percent because most respondents raised more than one issue.

[d] Less than 1 percent.

If the primary ethical problem posed by procedural issues was the balance between loyalty and other obligations, a clear idea of the public interest could give a planner an independent professional standard of the goodness or rightness of policy that could help to identify when loyalty was not legitimate. Three rather different ideas of the public interest were used by the planners in the sample. Two of these—the idea of the public interest as rights and the public interest as a process—framed the decision about what would serve the public as a deontological issue of right and wrong actions. The third idea, the consequentialist view, was concerned with good and bad policies. Overall, 84 percent of the planners used one or another of these ideas.

Use of the idea of the public interest raised its own problems, too. The issue here was the balance between a planner's own idea of the public interest and other ethical principles, including ideas of the public interest held by others in the planning process. On the one hand, the planner's concept of the public interest could serve as a useful balance to pressures for loyalty from superiors. On the other, just as excessive emphasis on loyalty potentially might lead to the co-optation of planners, so a strong commitment to specific ideas of the public interest could lead planners to autonomous actions that could place them beyond accountability. Burke (1986), for example, who places responsibility to decision makers at the center of his idea of bureaucratic ethics, rejects the idea of the public interest on these grounds.

Planners' Definitions of the Public Interest

When the planners introduced the idea of the public interest or raised ethical issues in which it figured, they were primarily talking about their own ideas about the public interest. The consequentialist idea was the one they used most commonly; in some form, it figured in 14 percent of all the cases the planners discussed (see Table 4.1). The most natural way to think about the public good was as a balance between the good and bad consequences of policies. The definition of the public interest as the protection of rights was the second most common approach, used in 5 percent of the cases. The idea of the public interest as process was used by a small group.

Part 2 will show that these different ways of thinking about the public interest were indicative of quite different ways of thinking about ethics generally and of thinking about the role that planners should play in the political process. Consequentialist approaches to defining the public interest were often associated with a more overtly politicized view of planning; this active role also characterized some of the planners who identified the public interest with the idea of social justice. Moreover, the planners who had a procedural view of the public interest formed the core of a fairly distinctive group who saw the role of the planner in strongly procedural terms.

The actual patterns were somewhat more complex than these sketches suggest, but the quite different ways in which the planners saw their professional roles can begin to be seen in the way they thought about the balance between their own ideas about the public interest and those of decision makers and members of the public. Some, for instance, primarily deferred to elected officials while others saw planning as a process of active involvement by all parties in which they could press for their own ideas about what would best serve the public.

Thus, understanding the way the planners defined the public interest involves looking both at their own ideas of what this was and then at how they viewed the role of others in the process of arriving at a definitive, legitimate decision. Here the exploration of the planners' own ideas of the public interest begins with the two deontological approaches—one concerned with rights and the other with process. Then I will take up the consequentialist one.

The Public Interest as Rights

A deontological view of ethics is very much, though not entirely, concerned with rights. The duties of justice, for example, all involve correlative rights, which is why they are considered to be especially binding. Those particular duties happen to be ethical ones enforced by moral sanctions, not by law, but rights can be created legally as well. A decision is made through the public policy process that the public interest would be served by the protection of some group or aspect of life. Such legally guaranteed rights often arise out of the idea that certain needs are basic and must be met, such as needs for minimum levels of food, clothing, shelter, and health care or, more broadly, rights to freedom or to the exercise of political opinions or rights to self-determination in a variety of other ways. Others involve collective goods, such as security, which includes systems of law and justice, or things such as clean air and water, which would be difficult for individuals to provide for themselves in a complex urban society (Barry 1964; Benditt 1973; Held 1970; Klosterman 1980; Meyer 1975).

The definition and enforcement of these rights are important aspects of governmental activity. One planner articulated the need to have public planning to protect important, collective environmental values by reducing the externalities resulting from shortsighted, individual actions:

> I think in looking at just the land-use planning part of your job that the public interest is the course of action that will assure the protection of environmental values and productive resources over a long-range period at the possible expense of limiting profit-making activities. I really see the planning field as deliberately put in place to counterbalance the American profit motive. That's the reason we're here. I do not buy the idea that somehow the private market knows best and if all the bureaucrats would just stand aside and stop

overregulating everything would be fine. When it comes to land use, if there's anything that this year's bottom line is certainly not an adequate measure of whether you're doing the right thing, it's land use because there's just so much of it and when it's gone it's gone.

Planners could be concerned both with creating and with enforcing rights, though they were more routinely involved in the latter, including the implementation of efforts to protect rights to health and safety, to adequate housing, or to equal access to essential services, for example.

Some of the ethical issues the planners raised in relation to the public interest were concerned with just this kind of protection of the right to health and safety. Several in Texas were concerned about developments that might harm underground aquifers that supplied the region's water. One of these planners talked about pressure on his agency from the developer of a large subdivision above an aquifer. As he saw his director getting "a little too cozy" with the developer,

> I pulled him aside and said, "You know this is bad, I know this is bad. You know that certain comments and certain precautionary measures have to be taken on that project"—because it was being built in a very sensitive area: Right across this bottom area of the map [pointing to the map] is a large underground aquifer that supplies all the water for the city, and when you build on top of that—and Mira Linda Acres sits right on top of that—it's very porous and oil from cars, fertilizer, or whatever can go through it and can penetrate into the aquifer if you're not careful. Certain precautionary measures have to be taken when any development takes place down there.

The most commonly raised deontological issue was the much broader one of social justice. This expands the right to be treated fairly from an obligation owed primarily to individuals to one that applies to groups at the societal level. It was brought up both as a general, hypothetical issue and as a very real, practical one. The few people who raised it as a hypothetical issue talked in broad terms about the need to eliminate poverty and racism and about the responsiveness of planners to other, more powerful interests.

The planners who raised the issue of social justice in a practical way were working in a variety of ways to try to achieve it. Some were trying to get their communities to accept low-income or at least "affordable" housing. Several planners worked directly with tenant or low-income neighborhood groups. These planners almost took the overarching issue of social justice for granted and tended to raise more detailed ethical issues of tactics or priorities in relation to the question of how to achieve it, but the underlying outrage that motivated them can be seen in this planner's outburst:

> Every day our agency is aware of unfairness in what's coming down the pike. I mean, I don't know if this is an ethical decision or not, to decide to say, "Oh, well, you can't solve all these problems." A lot of people are paying 40, 50, 60 percent of their gross income for rent. According to the figures I've seen, 15 percent of the people are paying more than 60 percent of their income for rent. In some of the projects, we have people who are eligible for Section 8 who are paying 160 bucks a month and in the same building there are people who pay $300, both of them with the same income. That is grossly unfair—inequitable—which should be considered a form of ethics.

The issue of social justice was potentially relevant to many planners faced with obvious racial and class disparities in most metropolitan areas. Even so, the issue seems largely to have been raised as an ethical one only by planners with an existing ideological commitment to equity who were willing, as one planner said, to do some "boat rocking." One planner said:

> I have a strong personal concern about housing. It was something I was interested in before I had this job, and I've been interested since I came. I suppose I see a real community need for it.

Because of this commitment, she had been able to get some movement:

> When I first came here, the idea of high density was really anathema to people, and although technically as a planner in a lot of cases I didn't really think it was so bad, it would have been, I suppose, political suicide at the time to have advocated higher density developments. Over time that's changed, and I've—the commission—we view the housing market and so forth and I've been able to push them to agree to more small units.

Besides housing, other issues that planners raised in relation to equity included public transportation fare structure and strategies for economic development that might best serve low-income people.

Process Ideas of the Public Interest

Six planners raised as an ethical issue the question of how the public
interest was defined in procedural terms. They were primarily concerned
that the planning process be open because they saw its outcome as the
definition of the public interest. The most enthusiastic proponent of this
idea of defining the public interest talked about working on a major issue
with many conflicting groups:

> How do you orchestrate that—take all those differing points of view
> and emerge with what is the correct thing for the city in the long run
> in that area? It is up to the professional planner to bring about some
> sort of balance in all of that. The planning function needs to
> orchestrate that, needs to emerge from that process with what is the
> public interest. [You collect information, but] information isn't going
> to make the decision. You try to provide leadership [in the planning
> process] with what you yourself and what [the planning] department
> thinks is the correct approach, and with always the sense that what
> you're proposing has enough in it so that all interests can see their
> interest in it. That's an art! That's what separates us from an
> engineer, from an architect, or whatever. It is the planner saying: I
> see this piece of ground. I sense what's needed here from my own
> training and so forth. I know what all the interests are. I've got all
> the information I can get. Now, how do I provide the leadership so
> that there's enough of that interest in there for everybody to be
> [satisfied]?

This image of the public interest as a process could be either a
deontological or a utilitarian one, but among these planners it was
primarily the former. The planners discussed in chapter 3 who were
particularly concerned about fair access to the process, especially for
disadvantaged groups, were essentially taking a deontological approach
that worked outward both from the principle of openness and from the
principle of fairness.

Several planners were concerned about the balance they should give
to their own professional values compared with those of other participants
in the process, such as citizens or elected officials:

> Planners in general face the ethical problem of pursuit of their own
> objectives. In situations where the community has different objec-
> tives from your own, how do you wrestle with that one? Do you end
> up carrying out the community's direction, even though you may

strongly disagree with it? My own feeling on that one is that I've carried out policies that I was in personal disagreement with but I felt comfortable with that as long as those policies were derived through a very public, open planning commission/city council process, and I've had my opportunity to get my own recommendations and feelings into that process.

Unlike the idea of the public interest as social justice, this extension of the principle of fairness was substantively contentless. As long as a wide variety of groups had access to the planning process, these planners were willing to accept whatever outcome resulted from the process.

Consequentialist Ideas of the Public Interest

Consequentialist ideas of the public interest focused on analysis by the planner of the good and bad consequences of policies or projects. They were not some vague generality. Planners raised seventy-four issues in which this idea of the public interest was used, and these were virtually all real issues for the planners. They involved real conflicts, either with someone else's idea of the public interest or with other ethical principles, such as loyalty or fairness.

For many of the planners, the institutional role of planning was systematically to consider the long-run consequences of action for the community as a whole and to make this analysis available to decision makers. Many planners agreed with this one, who said:

I'm serving not just one interest group or a few but I'm trying to give recommendations for community development that, in my opinion, are serving the best interests of everybody, including future populations.

When planners like this one who used the idea of the public interest were asked what they meant by it, 45 percent said they were concerned with a broad view of the community while 35 percent particularly mentioned a concern with long-run consequences.

By using the idea of the long-term, broad interest of the community, planners often wanted to focus attention on collective interests that were shared by many or all people but that did not produce well-organized or vocal interest groups. Recreational access to the waterfront was an example raised by one planner. Another talked about a chronic problem of transportation planning:

> Dealing with the neighborhoods versus transportation, which is a constant conflict, building arteries through now resurging neighborhoods—trying to get the council and the neighborhoods to understand the larger context: You can't just draw up the drawbridge completely, you're still part of the whole city. We've been losing those [battles] of late.

These were NIMBY problems, with people saying "not in my backyard" to some socially necessary but locally undesirable project. They resulted from individuals or local groups—neighborhoods in a city or independent jurisdictions in a region—trying to be free riders on everyone else. If some other area would provide shore access or would be forced to accept a highway or a landfill, they could reap the advantages without paying the costs.

Environmental planners saw this as an issue of "the tragedy of the commons." Asked why he had become a planner, one local planner described the deterioration of a lake where he had summered as a child as a metaphor for other planning problems:

> The reason it was becoming [polluted] was because of a lot of the development around the lake. A lot of it was runoff problems that were caused by landowners just kind of looking out for their own parcel and not caring about this public amenity out there.

Here it was in each owner's interest to take advantage of the collective resource without accepting any responsibility for the collective harm their use created.

While most planners expressed their professional perspective in terms of this kind of general commitment to a long-range, broad view of the public good, some defined the teleological public interest in more specific, substantive terms. Transportation planners saw the long-range public good in terms of a transportation system that provided flexible options for personal mobility. One planner said that the public interest involved

> ensuring that there's mobility, accessibility, so that community members can circulate and move about and do the things they wish with as much freedom as is practically possible.

Environmental planners saw protecting the environment as serving the long-range, broad public interest. One talked about the importance of the "conservation ethic":

That, I think, is very much a part of what we need. The whole idea of conserving the natural resources—land, water, air, forest, wildlife—should be, I think, a sort of unwritten principle, an underlying guiding objective. Therein lies the concept of husbandry—manage those resources so they will serve us in future generations rather than abuse them unnecessarily.

Urban designers thought the public benefited from more aesthetic development in somewhat the same way.

The institutional role of representing the long-term, broad view of the public interest could lead to small, routine conflicts or to large-scale, politicized ones, and at both ends of the spectrum planners raised such conflicts as ethical issues. One Texas planner, echoed by several from other states, talked about his constant struggle with engineers and developers who provided inadequate utilities for subdivisions. He criticized them as

> just wanting to make a buck and knowing that's not adequate, that's not long-range planning that will really meet the community's needs down the road.

At the other end of the policy spectrum, another planner highlighted the clash of different ideas of the public interest, giving the example of a proposed rezoning of an old, downtown manufacturing district. This area was beginning to see the incursion of residential uses. Rezoning to residential was supported by developers and was seen by many as a sign of the upgrading of the area, but the planner worried about the effect of making the existing industrial uses into nonconforming ones. Once they were the exception rather than the rule, and once the price of property began to rise, he thought that they would soon be driven out. What was the trade-off between the benefits of residential development and the cost to the city in jobs and economic activity?

Another planner who worked for a regional agency, trying to balance environmental conservation and development in local communities, described the conflicts this generated:

> We frequently find ourselves in the middle of two extreme views. There used to be a good deal of frustration between planners and the clients at the community level, which tended to be chambers of commerce and local industrial government committees, that . . . the main mission in life—and their principle objective—was to do whatever it takes to get an industry to either come in or expand and

create jobs. Some of the decisions that were ultimately made and some of the maneuvering to get those decisions made frequently shortchanged the environmental quality in the interest of satisfying and almost rolling over and spreading your legs for some big industry that sorta acted like it might come to your town if you would do everything. I felt that you didn't have to submit to that. You might miss the immediate catch, but if you did a good job of balancing the resource, you at least protect it—and we've always tried to work on how you could still have your cake and eat it too. I got equally frustrated at times with the environmentalists, who are some of the most difficult people to ever deal with, because if there's anybody who's got a one-track mind, it's them. They would save the world for the sake of saving the world and people be damned. So we frequently find ourselves between these two extreme views, trying to somehow achieve the better of both.

In the first case, the conflict was between the planner's idea of the public interest and the self-interest of the developers. In the other two, it was a disagreement over different views of the public interest. Some planners presented disputes that they saw simply as disagreements between people with different institutional roles or different ideas of the public interest, but many of the cases raised issues of responsiveness, political pressure, and loyalty, which showed the potential for conflicts between consequentialist ideas of the public interest and deontological principles.

Conflicts

These planners' ideas about the public interest were largely concerned with the ends that planning should strive for in the policy-making process. The only group for whom this was not the case were the six planners who used the image of the public interest as process (and, of course, there were fifteen who seemed not to use any idea of the public interest, at least in these interviews). For most, their sense of the public interest gave substantive direction that was stronger than just a tendency or an inclination. It involved a moral commitment that was strong enough to produce conflicts with other moral principles.

The most common conflicts were those between planners' ideas of the public interest and accountability to their superiors and those between a consequentialist idea of the public interest and duties of justice. Each of these conflicts posed characteristic problems, but the former, at least, could have advantages as well.

Conflicts: The Public Interest and Accountability

Planners not uncommonly had ideas about the public interest that were not shared by the officials they served. They experienced these as issues on which they were expected or pressed to accept policies or to take actions that professionally they thought were not "good." One planner described the problem he had testifying for his community on a proposed landfill:

> We're going through a process where we have a municipal utility district and they are in the process of building or trying to get permits to build a regional landfill, and a remote little town adjacent to that facility is trying to fight it. We've been going through the permit process and the hearing process and, as planner for one of the major cities within the district, I had to testify and things like that. I certainly was aware of what position my testimony was to reinforce, and I think that as a planner you can certainly sit back and say, "Well, there may have been another locale where they could have located this." It's not close to a lot of the cities and it's going to require a lot of hauling and there are certainly conflicting points or values that come into that. If they'd asked me, "If you were designing the waste disposal system, is this where you would put it?" I probably would have said "no," but I think there are some loyalties there and I don't know what's right in a situation like that.
>
> Q: I guess what I'm trying to clarify is what was the conflict here between . . .
>
> Well, I think the conflict to me was—I'm a paid staff person to represent the interests of the city, not only in zoning issues but also in court issues and in other things, yet as a professional, as a planner who is trained in a lot of development matters, I can certainly take a look at the interests of those people and the wider environmental interests of where that leachate is going to wind up and say, "Hey, this probably is not or very possibly is not one of the best places you could put this landfill."

Sometimes conflicts over accountability were framed as tactical choices, especially when planners had become committed to specific positions. One explained the situation these planners faced:

> There's been one project in particular, a lakefront park project, that I've been involved with where I felt very strongly that the design

that was being promoted by the landscape architect group was not the best plan, [and] I guess the problem for me was how far to push denial for something that I felt was very important.

In these cases, their ideas about the public interest enabled them to do just what they were supposed to do as professionals, make judgments about whether some policy would benefit their community. It gave them a criterion, independent of the dictates of their superiors, for accepting or rejecting some course of action. As was shown in chapter 3, many of these choices were settled routinely without much overt conflict, but some were not so simple. A planner who was active in the local APA (American Planning Association) chapter found himself caught by conflicting demands of loyalty to several different organizations with different views of the public interest from his own:

> The one that's been most troublesome for me was the convention center. I just didn't think it was a good policy. The agency, particularly the director, was very firmly in favor, and he was an extremely powerful person. I think the chapter membership was perhaps a fifty-fifty split. I had the problem of being identified with the agency. My own personal beliefs on it—trying to represent the professional chapter, who finally supported it—that's probably been the most troublesome.

In these cases, the planners were walking a tightrope between their own views of the public interest, the expectations of their superiors, and the views of others to whom they owed institutional loyalty, trying to maintain a balance between what they thought would be good policy and their own willingness to take risks. Still, it was their own ideas of the public interest that made them struggle with these conflicts.

While having a clear idea of the public interest was useful in balancing claims for loyalty, some planners were sufficiently driven by their consequentialist ideas of the public interest that they challenged the idea that they should primarily be accountable to the public through elected officials. If their views of the public interest did not coincide with those of their officials, some considered undertaking not just open persuasion but even covert opposition. They argued that the end justified the means.

A planner described a situation he had been involved in several years before. His description, given, of course, after the fact, builds to the inevitable conclusion that the only option he had was covert action in opposition to the policies of members of his city council:

We had a very volatile political happening where a five-member coalition on the city council got together and—very much supported by the home-building industry—it ended up in the city manager being fired over, principally, the issue of the plan. The city manager was a very strong planning and growth-management-oriented person. So he was here; he had been here for six years, was very instrumental in supporting planning and our contemporary general plan, and so forth. I was the chief of planning, and I was very visibly involved in the long-range planning policies of the city, and during that period one of the things that happened was that there was a fear that this five-member coalition on the council was going to throw out the city's general plan and growth policy [and allow] wide-open development in the community. I felt this alternative direction that the city would have been taken in was bad. Developing the future plans for this city and seeing to it that they get implemented has been such a major part of my professional career that it [the covert action] was kind of a natural follow-up to what I had been working on.

Conflicts: Dirty Hands

In a consequentialist view of ethics, actions are evaluated according to the goodness of their consequences. Generally, lying or breaking promises may be considered to have bad consequences and so would fail this test, but it is possible to imagine situations where telling a lie or doing harm to some small group of people would be necessary in order to achieve a substantial benefit for a large group. In a purely consequentialist framework, this would be ethically acceptable.

This perspective, however, poses a direct challenge to the deontological idea that some actions, such as lying or doing harm, are wrong in and of themselves. In a deontological framework, this would be an obvious case of treating some people as means to the ends of others, not as "ends" or individuals with worth in themselves. This conflict has come to be known as "the problem of dirty hands" (Walzer 1973).

The sense of violation and outrage that this could produce is seen in one planner's discussion of his own early experience as a target of planning. His family's business had been located in an urban renewal area and was taken for the greater good of the city. His sense of his family having been used as a means to others' ends was still strong many years later:

When I was brought up, my dad ran a grocery store, sort of the neighborhood one-man, one-and-a-half-man store, and when I was in high school, that grocery store got earmarked to be taken in an urban renewal area. Of course, I didn't know anything about planning or urban renewal or anything. Heck, I was just a fourteen-, fifteen-, sixteen-year-old kid—I didn't know anything from Adam about stuff that I now call my profession. I just knew it was a very traumatic thing. The store ultimately was taken and was cleared, and my dad went through a lot of trauma and developed a heart illness, and, I don't know, my mother blames it all on the fact that the store was probably . . . This was in the early fifties, mid-fifties, and for two years, we thought that the store was going to be taken, but nobody could tell you anything. The housing authority, which was the urban renewal agency, would say almost nothing, but meanwhile, for two years, the word was all over town that, "Hey, this was going to be cleared." Little by little, people started leaving this neighborhood, which was a slummy neighborhood, low rent, a lot of transients, and here my dad's in a store—his source of livelihood, sitting there on the curb with rumor driving business away. Finally, after two years of just steadily defending it—and, you know, he might have during that time improved the place or done some expansion or done something to keep things going. But you couldn't. The only thing they told us was, "Don't spend any money on your building because anything you spend we won't pay you for." Well, that had the effect of just, you know, holding you dead in your tracks. Meanwhile, the damn building was deteriorating and you don't know if you should go out there and nail the board back up or not, you know. There was no such thing as relocation assistance payments, and when they finally got around to coming and making him an offer, it was absurdly, ridiculously low. So, yeah, all those two years of agony then here comes the day and it's a total insult. So he has to go then and hire a lawyer. It was condemned, you know, but just before trial, it was settled out of court, and they, as I recall, offered him five or six thousand dollars more than they did the first time, one thousand of which he had to pay the lawyer.

A planner with dirty hands would be one who ignored such individual costs and acted on a purely consequentialist idea of the public interest, violating duties of justice or accountability in order to do good. There were a variety of cases raised by the planners that pitted a consequentialist idea of the public interest not only against loyalty but also against openness, fairness, and even against the law. An environmental planner, for example, who was working with a number of conservative communities in an environmentally sensitive area, said:

> There isn't much enthusiasm for planning. I would say there's some problems with planning in the more rural communities that center around ethical issues, mainly because the people in power—the city council members—don't want very much to do with land-use [planning].

He struggled to find ways to encourage or push them to plan and ended up being faced with choices of overlooking violations of contracts, doing favors to win support, and awarding grants unfairly. Another planner was negotiating with a developer over modifications he planned to make to a housing complex he owned. Her own ideas of the public interest not only came up against community pressure for a solution but also against her sense of fairness toward the developer:

> [I wished] I had a better sense of his real financial situation. I thought he was crying poor about a lot of this, but I also thought that his architect had led him down the path and that the improvements were costing him more money than he had expected. So it was very hard. It would have been tempting to stick by your guns, but something else you have to watch out for is not getting in a position where you just want to go power play with a guy, where you want to have your own recommendations approved regardless.

Conflicts: Justice

Finally, the issue of dirty hands also raises a related but slightly different kind of conflict that was discussed by a few of the planners. It concerned conflicts between the deontological idea of the public interest as justice and a consequentialist idea of the public interest.

Take a case that involved the business district of a minority neighborhood. It had been designated as a historic district to encourage revitalization, but the planner thought that there was more concern with property values than with the rights of the people who were likely to be displaced by the revitalization, if it worked. A more extreme example involved a planner who had worked in the city of Yonkers's urban renewal program in its most active days. He spoke proudly of its achievements, making no mention of the increased racial discrimination it had produced, which later made it the target of a successful civil rights suit. In both cases, the benefits of revitalization to the wider community were considered to justify costs imposed on one largely powerless segment of the community.

Both of these cases were quite similar to the earlier case of the condemned grocery store, but in these, the issues being raised by the planners were not just ones of unfairness to individuals. There were also structural issues about systematic discrimination against blacks and low-income people.

Defining the Public Interest: Balancing Obligations

All of these examples of conflicts between the public interest and other kinds of ethical principles involved efforts to balance conflicting obligations. One was the obligation to provide independent professional advice on policy issues, and some idea of the public interest was virtually indispensable to this. Others involved obligations to decision makers and to the public. In their own discussions of the public interest, many of the planners recognized that they were facing conflicting obligations—to their own professional ideas of the public interest and to those held by decision makers and members of the public. In effect, many of them posed an idea of the public interest as a balance among these responsibilities. An activist planning director spelled this out at some length:

> I tell the people who work for me that they're most fortunate in that at the end, their own responsibility is to do what's in the public interest. There aren't very many people, there aren't very many professions, vocations, that afford the employee that opportunity. . . . So how do you determine the public interest? I think that it is listening to all segments and where they're coming from, but I think there's a responsibility to introduce new ways of thinking. Who is the public? I serve at the pleasure of the council, and my philosophy is that if I lose their confidence, then I really don't belong there. If [the community is] dissatisfied with the job the city council is doing with the city, then they can vote the rascals out, and they have that opportunity every two years. Therefore, I have to believe, because someone has to pin your understanding of what the community consciousness is, that those seven individuals on the city council do indeed represent the attitudes of the city. Okay, but having said that, I believe the public interest can be garnered from many angles. A lot of it is just doing a lot of listening, recognizing that it's a pluralistic society, recognizing that there are a number of vested

interest groups, and, you know, I see it on both extremes. To me, a developer who sees dollar signs as a goal is no better and no worse than neighborhood property owners who just moved into town and would prefer to see no further development because of either their perception that the value of their home is going to increase with no further subdivision activity or simply because they like the idea of having this open space as a kind of de facto park even though it's private property, not public property. And so, I mean, goals and objectives of various and sundry segments of the community all kind of intermesh.

In terms of my advocacy, I might say this. We had a situation [about ten years ago] where financial institutions would not give any construction loans to developers to build attached town house/ condominium–type units. Why? Because the marketplace was such that individuals wanted a single-family home. They were salable; why fool around with anything else? Well, in my opinion, the public was not given a choice, and, therefore, someone, someplace had to draw upon his or her experiences and say, "Hey, you know, people do live in life-styles other than single-family homes, and the condominium approach, cluster development may indeed preserve more open space land, so from an environmental standpoint, higher density on select locations may be better than sprawl." I guess what I'm saying is ten years ago, you could have surveyed residents and said, "What is your first choice in terms of housing?" and I would presume the vast majority would have said the single-family home. If you said that today, because we have good examples of cluster developments, it may be a much different percentage because people have been exposed to different habitations than the standard single-family home.

Here he started with the relationship between the people and the council and his responsibility, first to the council and then to interest groups. Then he added his responsibility to provide advice about other alternatives, based on his own ideas of the public interest. He represented many other planners who talked about balancing three elements—their own ideas about the public interest and those of members of the public and of elected officials—in order to arrive at a real definition of the public interest.

In this balance, where the emphasis of any particular planner revealed both the planner's ethics and his or her approach to planning, more than half (54 percent) of the sample talked about all three elements. For clarity's sake, I will focus on them, but they were apparently not atypical. Remember than 16 percent of the planners did not use any idea of the public interest and so are irrelevant here, but an additional 15 percent talked about two of the three elements.

Among the planners who discussed balancing all three elements, their own ideas of the public interest have already been described. Some thought of it as rights, many as a consequentialist idea of the broad, long-term good of the community. Some used a formal definition of the pubic interest embodied in existing laws and plans. Others had an idea of the public interest as a process of open negotiation. It was also quite possible to include several of these definitions in one's own concept—formal ideas of the public interest were a more specific version of a concern with the broad, long-range good, for example. Many planners who primarily thought of the public interest as rights also cared about a more teleological, broad, long-run view.

No planner was under the illusion that his or her own idea of the public interest was the last word, that he or she alone could define the interests of the community. So the need for balance with ideas held by the public and decision makers was almost self-evident. A planner who worked in a rather unstable political environment, using a formal idea of the public interest, discussed the limits of that definition:

> We have both a policy plan and we have a zoning code, and when I'm dealing with particular projects, I feel that it's within the public interest to operate within those codes—and that's very simple. When it comes to changing those codes, I also have a role to play, and then I'm still in a position of listening to what the public is saying and which part of the public is the part that is in power, and trying to respond to that. I think that a lot of times, in writing reports, what I try to do is to take all of the different things that I've heard and shape a consensus out of that.

"Those in power" were her elected officials, but they might change at the next election, and it was important to try to be more broadly responsive.

Despite the difficulty of her political situation, this planner essentially took an optimistic view of the role played by both decision makers and the public. Not all planners agreed. Generally, their views about the role of the public were more complex than those about decision makers (Table 4.2).

Of the fifty-two planners who talked about the role they thought the public should play, half (52 percent) saw the public as important participants in an open planning process. One planner simply said:

> The best part [of the job] is working with the public, even if I'm in the wrong, or not so much if I'm in the wrong but if I disagree with them. I enjoy the give-and-take.

TABLE 4.2

Planners' Views of Decision Makers and the Public

Images of Decision-Makers' Roles	Images of the Public's Role (percents)			
	Optimistic	Limited Public Contact	Pessimistic	Total
Positive	40	15	11	66
Mixed	8	4	8	20
Negative	4	6	4	14
Total	52	25	23	100

Note:
n = 52; see text for definitions.

A director whose department encouraged extensive, systematic citizen participation in major policy-making efforts explained how this had evolved and how their comprehensive planning process had worked:

> There was a general shift that occurred in the late 1960s. Prior to that time, no one really cared, no one ever showed up at public hearings, there was just an absolute apathy. Community development was controlled by developers and realtors and so on—you know the story. In the late 1960s, the Sierra Club began to send representatives to public hearings and board and commission meetings and council meetings, and for about four years, that activity increased, it brought in more people from the neighborhoods. It brought in more special interests—generated a whole lot of interest. As I was watching that happen, I felt that it was very timely to get into a new comprehensive planning program, that the activity, the interest was there.

On the other side, however, almost a quarter of the planners saw citizen groups as primarily parochial, self-interested, and not concerned with the good of the whole community. Since their own ideas of the public interest made them especially concerned with the long-range, broad view, they did not want such groups to play a dominant role in the planning process. One planner said bluntly:

> I have never run into organized public groups that had a grasp of the picture larger than their own narrow interest. They can't weigh that big a picture. I think that's the planner's job to do.

For some, it was more a matter of pride than of unease that their views differed. It did not bother them that they were saying what was "best" for the community, regardless of what preferences organized groups expressed:

> I feel that the public's perception of the needs of the community generally lags several years behind what the planner knows from his observance of socioeconomic and market trends, and therefore I don't feel that badly in trying to push a planner's solution. Often the public is not that informed. Specialized committees that represent very specific issue groups, I respect their opinions, but when it comes to the sample survey of Joe Blow, who doesn't want a bike trail, I don't have much identification with that.

Not all were so confident, but they could not escape the logic that their institutional role and the way they defined their roles could easily place them at loggerheads with the public.

Finally, a third group (25 percent) had a rather disembodied view of "the public" taken as a whole. Many of these planners worked in jobs—in state or regional agencies, in research offices, or in internal administrative jobs—in which they just did not have much contact with members of the public. A few were teleologists, referring to the whole public in the sense of "the greatest good for the greatest number."

While some planners used several images of the public in their interviews, many seemed to have either a generally positive or a generally negative view. This was reflected in their scores on a scale on the questionnaire measuring attitudes about citizen participation.[1] Optimists had scores most favorable to participation (3.86 on a six-point scale), followed by those with a disembodied view (3.48) while those with a pessimistic view brought up the rear (2.90). Differences between each of the groups were statistically significant.

Attitudes about decision makers involved the same kind of range but were more straightforward. Of the fifty-two planners who expressed a view, two-thirds not only said that officials did, in fact, make the final decisions about the public interest but that as planners, they were content that they should do so. As one county planner said of her planning board, county board of supervisors, and county executive:

> It's really their responsibility. They are the ones that really have to live with it and they're the ones who make a decision. Because for us as planners, you know, we don't really make the final decisions.

It's the board, the planning board—they're the voted people who have the power to do that.

Many worked with elected and appointed officials whose judgment they respected. A few talked about "guiding" officials to better decisions by a series of incremental steps. Some others just tried loyally to trust them to decide for the best, sometimes despite evidence to the contrary.

However, a minority of 14 percent were quite skeptical about the devotion of their decision makers to any concept of the public interest that would find favor with a planner. A regional planner struggling with this problem said:

A planner has as his ultimate client the public, as opposed to the officials, who are maybe on his board or commission. Where a local official may be putting some political pressure to do something the planner feels is not in the public interest, that raises some ethical questions, but it's a fuzzy gray line because, you know, especially elected officials do represent the public, but not always in the public's best interest.

Sometimes decision makers were corrupt or favoristic in the way decisions were made. The planning board in one city sued the city council for blatantly violating the zoning ordinance. One planner who worked in a state agency described the pressure exerted by members of his state legislature:

The politicians are always lobbying for their particular [cause] . . . and they put pressure on us. You know, we serve—supposedly the department serves at the discretion of the governor, but they've also written into our enabling legislation that we also serve at the pleasure of the legislature to do special studies and this, that, and the other. They phone us and they want this and they want that— there's a local project, a road project, that might be having problems and it's kind of unusual or not quite really eligible. They'll get on the phone and they'll put pressure on, and, I mean, it really gets down to the point where, professionally, you know that something really shouldn't go, but politically the pressure is there and the political pressure is too much.

Some officials didn't believe in planning as a useful governmental function while some were simply described by the planners involved as narrow or expedient in their approach to planning issues. If some of these planners seemed to have good factual reasons for their lack of faith in their decision makers, there were a few others who simply set a high standard for what elected officials should do and felt that theirs did not measure up. An additional 20 percent of the planners were not quite so negative (see Table 4.2). They said that they accepted elected officials' right to make the final decisions but were skeptical about the quality of the decisions that would result.

The fifty-two planners who discussed balancing all three views of the public interest arrived at rather different conclusions about the weight to be given to their own ideas relative to those of decision makers and members of the public. For convenience, I have clustered them into five groups (Table 4.3). The twenty-two planners who were optimistic about the roles of both decision makers and the public were likely to be engaged in the political process themselves. Some used a process idea of the public interest while others held a more goal-directed, either consequentialist or rights-based, idea.

TABLE 4.3

Approaches to Defining the Public Interest

Images of Decision-Makers' Roles	Images of the Public's Role		
	Optimistic		Pessimistic
Positive	Optimistic (22)		Technicians[a] (16)
		Vague[b] (4)	
Negative	Blind Faith[c] (5)		Cynics (5)

Notes:

n = 52.

[a] Technicians had a positive or mixed view of the role of decision makers and a pessimistic or disembodied view of the role of the public in making decisions.

[b] Vague planners had a disembodied view of the role of the public and mixed feelings about the role of decision makers.

[c] Planners with blind faith included planners who were negative about decision makers and had an optimistic or disembodied view of the role of the public.

The other large group was the sixteen technicians. They ultimately were content for elected officials to make the final decisions on the public interest. Two-thirds saw themselves as representing a broad, long-range view of the public interest in the planning process, contrary to the short-range, parochial views of citizens groups.

There were, finally, two smaller groups (besides the four people who launched into discussions of the public interest but were hopelessly vague about what they really meant by it). Both of the smaller groups rejected the legitimacy of decision makers at least for defining the public interest. One group was composed of true cynics. They believed that neither the public nor elected officials would do very well at defining the public interest. Thus, they were thrown back largely on their own definitions, which were quite varied. One health planner seemed skeptical about both the public and the Congress that passed the legislation under which his agency operated. He was equally skeptical about the members of his local board:

> I think we know what they [the public] want, but I don't know if we should be following that either. The public may want a hospital on every corner, but they don't know who's going to pay for it. We have the presumed guidelines of our act. Congress is representing them, but they don't have any more idea of what the public wants than we do. Our plan does go . . . we have a number of hearings on it. People scream and yell, but that's mostly [health care] providers. If the public comes at all, they say they want "more, more, more," but part of our role, defined by Congress, is to go against this; to make these technical decisions about the costs and benefits of health services.

Those with blind faith were not negative about the possible role that citizens might play. However, this was more because they had not lost faith completely and wanted some force to counterbalance what they saw as the lack of concern about the public interest among elected officials. One planner who worked in a fairly closed and corrupt community had little faith in his officials. There was not much direct citizen involvement in planning, but there were some active citizens providing support for it. He was essentially not a cynic, so having faith in the role that citizens could play helped to give him a sense that it was possible to achieve planning goals. Both the cynics and those with blind faith had strong commitments to their own ideas of the public interest and did not hesitate to reject others' definitions.

Thinking in terms of the balance between planners, citizens, and decision makers, optimists held to the idea of a fairly even balance. They saw citizens and decision makers engaged in an open policy-making process in which they, too, would have an active role. On one side of them were the technicians, whose balance was weighted toward a dominant role for elected officials. On the other side were the cynics and those with blind faith in the public as supporters for planning. Some may have hoped that a process with more citizen involvement would produce better planning results, but this was more a wish than a reality. In the end, both of these groups were thrown back primarily on their own ideas of the public interest.

Conclusion

The procedural obligations that the planners brought up in their ethics cases were primarily concerned with honest government or with internal bureaucratic relationships. These issues were largely deontological in nature. Cases that turned on the idea of the public interest as rights or on a consequentialist idea of the public interest were more substantive. They raised issues of encouraging the construction of low-income housing, of reducing transit fares to better serve low-income people, of protecting public water supplies, of working for better urban design, of balancing the demand for new "upscale" development against the need to protect older industrial land uses, or of balancing environmental protection and industrial development. These policy issues were of concern to planners. They raised ethical issues because they involved the questions of what would best serve the right and the good. Only the process idea of the public interest had no particular substantive content.

A theorist such as Burke (1986) worries about bureaucrats imposing their own personal preferences on policy choices. He rejects the use of ideas such as justice and the public interest on these grounds. Among public planners, the lack of institutional autonomy makes these concerns seem overblown. In real life, though, the planners in this sample certainly did have values that inevitably shaped their work. This was almost necessary in order for them to play effective roles as policy professionals. It also helped to balance the demands of loyalty made on them by bureaucratic and political superiors. A strong commitment to particular ideas of the public interest, however, could lead some consequentialists into arguing that good ends justified the use of means that deontologists, at least, would have considered wrong or that could put them beyond accountability to decision makers.

In describing the cases, however, and in talking more generally about their ideas of the public interest, the planners often framed the issues in terms of balancing their own ideas of the public interest with the obligation to be responsive to decision makers and to the public. The optimists were the ones who seemed most concerned about making an even balance among obligations to their own professional judgment and their responsibility to elected officials and the public. The others tended to give priority either to decision makers or to their own ideas of the public interest. The actual balance each planner struck varied a great deal depending on the way each person thought about what role he or she should play as a planner. So this is what we will turn to next.

PART 2

Planners

5

Planners: An Introduction

The issues raised by the planners we interviewed give a clear idea of how they defined the realm of ethics and of the kind of issues that seemed most pressing to them. The discussion of the issues related to the public interest also begins to give a sense of the people themselves—of who raised which issues and why and what this meant about the way they thought about ethics and about planning. More broadly, on all the issues, not just those related to the public interest, the ethical values the planners brought to their work and the ways in which they structured their working roles both shaped the way they defined issues of ethics. This meant that what one person might see as an ethical dilemma might never arise for another or might not be seen as raising an ethical issue at all by a third.

Part 2 will introduce these planners. Why were some planners committed to achieving specific goals in the planning process that they saw as having moral worth? Why were some frustrated in their effort to do this? Why did some planners eschew this active role altogether, choosing as their central moral commitment service to the elected representatives they were officially responsible to in the hierarchy of government? Alternately, why should some planners be trying to work out a role in which their central moral commitment was to the openness of the planning process itself? The three following chapters in part 2 will look at how these individuals saw their roles as planners, how they thought about ethics, and what seemed to shape these values.

This description of the planners will use two overlapping typologies, one for roles and the other for approaches to ethics. These try to cluster the members of the sample into fairly distinct but internally homogeneous groups to allow for some generalization, at least within the sample, but because people are so variable, there are six groups in each typology. Each typology can be thought of as a continuum, but even so, this is bound to be cumbersome to some extent. What is the relationship between them: Does six categories times six categories mean that we have to think about thirty-six types of planners?

The answer to this is no. Planners chose roles, consciously or unconsciously, in part because a role suggested an image of what planning should be doing in the world. The values that underlay each role were in part moral values, and each role grew out of either a primarily deontological or a primarily consequentialist way of thinking about moral obligations. In this analysis, the two variables of role and approach to ethics are not by any means the same thing, but they are closely intertwined. These planners brought an ethical approach to the profession; some were even attracted to it by the possibility of acting on their moral convictions. Ethics shaped the choice and performance of role, and experience, in turn, sharpened ethical values.

Because of the close relationship between the six roles and the six approaches to ethics, the next two chapters will essentially develop descriptions of eight kinds of planners. Rather than giving them a third set of descriptive names, I have chosen instead to embody them as characters—individual planners who "characterize" the planners in each group with a particular combination of role and approach to ethics.[1] This not only avoids another typology but also provides a little of the personal vividness of the real members of the sample. These planners are introduced in Figure 5.1.

The rest of this introduction will discuss briefly how the two typologies were developed and what the groups, such as the "passive hybrids" or the "rule utilitarians," are. The remaining three chapters in part 2 will explore them in more depth.

FIGURE 5.1
Approaches to Ethics and Role

Role	Character	Approach to Ethics
Traditional Technician	Edward Smith, Jr.	Narrow Deontologist
Passive Hybrid	George Walters	Public Interest Planner
Technician Activist	Richard Breitman	Public Interest Planner
Process Planner	Rebecca Giulini	Process Deontologist
Closet Politician	Sam French	Substantive Deontologist
Active Planner	Grace Sumner	Substantive Deontologist
Active Planner	Tom Stuart	Rule Utilitarian
Active Planner	Paul Michaud	Act Utilitarian

Role

The planners in the sample essentially drew on three different ideas of the role that their profession should play in a democratic society. One was the image of the profession as a force for social change. Another was the image of the profession as a servant to elected officials. The third saw planners as coordinators and facilitators of the planning process.

Each of these images provided a normative framework for defining the kind of role that an individual planner should play in a political process in which they might have influence but could have little real autonomy or control. Each image also represented a view of ethical planning practice—of what professional actions were good or bad, right or wrong.

The Empirical Definition of Planners' Roles

As it is defined here, the idea of a planner's role has two dimensions. It includes both what a person wanted to do as a planner and what he or she could do in practice. It was the interaction between these two forces that produced the role each planner actually played.

Role here is represented as a typology with six categories: traditional technicians, passive hybrids, technician activists, active planners, process planners, and closet politicians. The typology was developed by sorting the planners into groups using four variables: the ideal role they thought a planner should play; the actual role they seemed to play in practice; how much they cared about the implementation of their plans; and how proactive they were in trying to get their plans carried out. What they wanted to do is captured in their ideal role and their concern for implementation; what they could do is captured by their actual role and their degree of proactivity.

Arriving at this typology of roles involved an interaction between what the planners said about their approaches to planning and the substantial body of theoretical, normative, and empirical thinking about the roles planners play (Baum 1983; Beckman 1964; Benveniste 1989; Bolan 1969; Davidoff 1965; deNeufville 1986; Hoch 1988; Howe 1980a; Howe and Kaufman 1979; Kaufman 1978; Rabinovitz 1967, 1969; Vasu 1979; Walker 1950). To say that the typology of roles simply emerged out of the interviews themselves would be untrue, but while the analysis was influenced and guided by theories about planners' roles, it was exploratory, trying to reflect the diversity of approaches taken by the planners themselves. It did not simply test the applicability of typologies developed previously by myself or others.

Even so, the six roles can be thought of as lying along a continuum, somewhat similar to the one developed by Rabinovitz (1969) in her study of planners in New Jersey. Three of the roles—the traditional technicians, passive hybrids, and technician activists—are technical in nature; the active planners and closet politicians were political in nature; and the process planners played a negotiating or mediating role that seemed to lie in between.

Ideal and Reality

Role was defined by the interaction between what the sample thought planners ought, ideally, to do and what they were actually able to do in their own practice. This was an important issue among these public planners because, as civil servants, they could not play autonomous professional roles but were dependent for results on a complex process that they did not control. The various roles reflected different approaches to dealing with this lack of control over the end products of their work.

The planners in the sample had varied ideas about what they were trying to accomplish. Some had fairly ambitious images of the role planning should play, others had more modest ones. However, one thread that ran through many of the interviews was the question of how effective they were at achieving their images and the possible disparity between ideal or intent and achievement.

The public planners in the sample did many different kinds of work. Some developed broad, long-range plans while others developed plans for smaller, shorter range projects. Still others reviewed projects proposed by private developers for their conformance with a community's plans or other policies. In some cases, such as long-range, comprehensive planning, the process of getting from a plan to actual physical reality was long and indirect. Development and adoption of a plan and compatible regulatory mechanisms, such as a zoning ordinance, could involve a lengthy political process, sometimes involving large numbers of citizens as well as appointed and elected officials. One planner who had recently been through such a process described its complexities:

> We just had a good time to do it, and I felt that the plan ought to begin with citizen participation and that would provide the base for the plan that would follow. We were able to convince the planning commission and the city council and the manager that that was a

good approach. About thirty-five hundred people participated over two years. [Then they spent about three years revising the zoning ordinance.] We spent about a year with citizen groups before we ever went to the commission, and it was to discover from neighborhood meetings and special groups, such as AIA [American Institute of Architects] and the chamber of commerce and attorneys and so on, the problems that they saw with the existing ordinance and the existing procedures. The consultant then wrote a position paper that tried to identify all of those problems. He then went back to the same groups and asked, "Did I reflect your concerns accurately?" Six months later, he delivered his draft to the staff. The planning department, the building inspection department, and the legal department met with the consultant for a week to go over the text, and he redrafted what he had to do and then came back a month later and presented it to the planning commission. They presented it to the council a couple of months later. The council accepted it and referred it to the planning commission, and now we have been at it for fifteen months in neighborhood meetings and workshops—seven public hearings, 118,000 notices out in the mail—and the commission finished its work at the end of July. They are making their final set of recommendations that are now available to the public before it goes to the council in October.

Once adopted, the implementation of a plan would depend on many, often small actions by both the public and the private sectors. Planners concerned with regulatory review were one actor in this process, taking proposals made by private parties and examining their conformance with the comprehensive plan. Here one would have a measure of whether one's recommendation for approval or disapproval of a particular proposal was being heeded by decision makers, but a clear sense of accomplishing the goals of the plan would be harder to sustain, especially in the face of many pressures to neglect it in day-to-day decisions. A planner talked about an earlier plan adopted by her community and the difficulty of applying it:

We had an old plan that was adopted in 1965. It was a very watered-down plan, but it was the first one that was really adopted by the city. It was a land-use plan and it had the arterial system and it had parks and recreation—it was a plan. The arterial system—many times people would say, "We don't want that to happen." I'd say, "It's in the plan, and if we ever want the plan to mean anything, we have to uphold it. If it's wrong, let's change the plan, but let's not be selective about which part we wanted to follow''—we just couldn't be because then we would gut the whole thing.

Project plans might lead to more direct results in a shorter period of time. However, the process of getting to those results could prove to be quite political so that the planner's idea of what should happen was only one of many. One project planner who was very negative about comprehensive planning said:

> I particularly enjoy working with developers, working on projects that are a large-enough scale that they'll have some sort of impact, be involved with projects that have a chance of moving forward. I don't like . . . and don't just sit down and do prepared plans or fix documents strictly for their own sake. Our approach here has been that planning is—can only be—a successful process if the people who are going to be implementing the plan and who have a stake in the outcome of the plan are involved from the start.

He went on to discuss at least one case in which his most strenuous efforts were not able to produce a result that corresponded to what he thought the project should be like.

In all of these kinds of planning, the planner could play only a limited role. He or she could do analysis, make recommendations, even lobby for them, but final decisions rested with others and were likely to involve input by a range of political groups. Indeed, the more central a planning issue was to a community's politics, the more complex the political process would probably be and the more the planner would have to share the stage with other actors. Planners could have influence but they could not have direct power to make things happen. One planner who presented himself as a cynic about his own role in this process said:

> Somebody else sets the parameters—I just play with them. I think it's absolutely essential that local planners recognize the fact that they can't set these parameters themselves and that they have some constructive advice along these lines.

While the political nature of planning was one reason why planners might have only limited control over what they could accomplish, it was not the only one. Some planners with ambitious goals might find, as their careers unfolded, that they did not have the personal capacity to achieve them. This might be a function of the particular political system they worked in or their position in it, but sometimes it was a matter of their particular personality.

Besides having a commitment to a certain role, a planner had to have the skills and personal capacity to carry it out. Needleman and Needleman (1974), in their study of neighborhood planners, identified some people as having "role incapacity." They wished to be neighborhood planners but simply did not have the skills and personal presentation to play the role well. Similarly, in this sample, there were planners who did not have the personality to play the role they were committed to. This was more common for planners choosing value-committed, political roles, but it was not unheard of among technicians as well.

Thus, in their careers, most planners had to deal in one way or another with their limited autonomy, power, or capacity to accomplish planning goals. Several previous studies have shown that planners feel considerable frustration over this limitation. Mayo (1982), using a mail survey of a national sample of planners drawn from members of the National Association of Regional Councils, found that planners felt that their ability to play more politicized roles, such as those of public leader, vetoer, coalition builder, mediator, and judge,[2] were constrained by the organizations they worked for. This feeling of role dissonance, in turn, was one of the most powerful predictors of job dissatisfaction.

In a very different kind of study of a sample of fifty planners in Maryland, Baum (1983) found that many of the planners were attracted to planning by the hope of accomplishing ambitious goals but, in actual practice, could see few results from their work. Only a third of them entered the profession for pragmatic reasons, such as salary or professional status. The rest were interested in large-scale design, in trying to achieve social change, and/or in acquiring influence and power (Baum 1983). In the bureaucratic and political world of planning, achievement of these goals was exceedingly difficult at best.

In this study, about a quarter of the planners experienced some frustration over their limited autonomy. However, for more than a third, this lack of power posed the challenge of creating the capacity for action in a political setting. Either way, though, a tension could exist between what planners wanted to do and what they could get done. How they adapted to this tension fundamentally shaped their professional roles and whether they felt a sense of harmony or dissonance, of success or of failure, in their work.

In the typology of roles that is developed here, two related sources of tension have been identified. One was between the goals the planners wanted to accomplish and their actual achievement of those goals. This relationship seems to have been the one that troubled Baum's planners.

The other was between the ideal role they thought a planner should play and the role they actually played in reality. This seems similar to the role dissonance measured by Mayo (1982).

On the first of these two sources of tension, I looked at how much the planners talked in their interviews about trying to accomplish particular goals or about being interested in the implementation of their plans. I also looked at whether they described themselves as playing an active or a passive role in the political process.

For 34 percent of the sample, a concern about implementation was central to the planners, pervading all they talked about and shaping their behavior. One spoke of how this emphasis on implementation represented a change in the profession and of how it affected his personal behavior:

> The profession, in my opinion, certainly has changed from the days twenty years ago when the planners saw their role as purely a technician who wrote the technical report and then threw it out there and hoped something happens. I personally, as an individual and as a professional planner, don't see me wasting my time preparing plans or ideas that just sit on shelves. So I believe in carrying it the next step, that is, seeing to it that it gets into place. Clearly, that creates some real challenges in defining what role you play in doing that. It's my philosophy that when we propose something to the city council, we do what we can to attempt to get that implemented.

At the other extreme from these planners with a concern for implementation were 41 percent of the sample who did not mention it at all. An additional 12 percent mentioned it only in passing, and, finally, another 12 percent, in between, considered it important but for a variety of reasons it did not seem to affect their actual behavior.

The second variable related to role tried to get more directly at behavior. It measured how proactive or reactive the planners seemed to be in their present work. Did they try to anticipate reactions and take initiative on issues? Did they actively seek to promote the plans they worked on by organizing and lobbying for their adoption and implementation? One-third of the planners seemed by their very nature not to be proactive. Another 17 percent were prevented by the nature of their work from being proactive. For example, planners in regulatory jobs largely reacted to proposals by developers or a planner might work in a political situation that precluded an active role. One such planner, who worked in a community whose council was strongly divided, described her role:

I don't always go to the last breath in trying to defend something because I don't see that as being constructive. We're staff people, we give the recommendation. It's either accepted or rejected, and then we go from there, and there is a limit as to how far you can go in terms of advocating one position or another.

Almost half the sample did play proactive roles; 37 percent were judged to be "somewhat" proactive while the other 13 percent were "very" proactive. For those who were only somewhat proactive, this was often because their jobs involved a mix of both reactive and proactive issues. As one planning director said:

When I came, it was a very divided community, but one that was really looking for some good planning, so there were a lot of opportunities for me. I think they were looking for a planning director to give a certain amount of leadership in controlling development. [On one issue], I think it was not really appropriate for me to take a very hard position initially, either for or against. I really considered it a policy question that they [the planning commission and the city council] had to make up their minds on. [On another, a housing issue], I thought it was important [to act], so I talked to the housing committee, we worked through them and then made suggestions for changes we thought were needed; I talked to the planning commission and council about it [and after workshops and committee meetings] they reached a general agreement about changes, and they were pretty much in the direction I had urged.

Another planner, in describing her job as a project manager, ran through the range of activities it involved that required a strongly proactive role:

Our field here is economic development, and basically it is real estate development that promotes economic development. What I do is I coordinate and manage projects from the time they come in the door to the time that the first spade of earth is turned and even beyond that point. Quite frankly, since our organization takes a financing in these projects, we act afterward like a mortgage banker servicing a project. So there's still a project management role. I deal with government officials on the outside because very often the projects that come in here do come from state legislators, municipal and county officials, congressmen in some cases. I deal with planning personnel, community development directors, economic development directors, that sort of person. Sometimes with community groups but very often not. Most of our stuff is involved with government, other people in government rather than with the public at large.

These two variables of implementation and proactivity were clearly related to a broader idea of planning effectiveness. Generally, a concern with implementation indicated that planners cared about whether their plans were having an impact, and a proactive stance indicated that they were working to see that this happened.

The theoretical relationship between these two variables is shown in Figure 5.2. If a planner had no clear goals or had little or no interest in the implementation of plans, then a passive role would involve no tension, but the more important goals or implementation were to a planner, the more necessary it was to try to achieve them—to be proactive—in order to maintain a sense of accomplishment. Thus, a planner with ambitious goals but a passive role might feel dissonance while a planner who was active but had no goals to guide his or her action might also have a feeling of dissonance.

The other source of tension was less obvious but actually proved to be more interesting for exploring ways of adapting to the political nature of planning. It was the relationship between a planner's ideal role choice and the role he or she was actually able to play (Table 5.1). Here, both roles were originally thought of as ranging from technical to political in nature, with a "hybrid" role in between.[3]

A planner's ideal role was determined from his or her response on the written questionnaire that accompanied the interview. The questions on role measured respondents' attitudes about the roles that planners should play in general. That is, it was a measure of ideal role, not of the role the respondent actually played in practice.

The planners' actual roles were determined from what they said in the interview about the technical and political dimensions of their day-to-

FIGURE 5.2

Dissonance Between Goals and Achievement

Proactivity	Goals	
	Not Interested in Implementation	Very Interested in Implementation
Passive	Harmony	Dissonance
Active	Dissonance	Harmony

TABLE 5.1

Initial Typology of Planners' Roles Based on Harmony and
Dissonance Between Ideal and Actual Roles

Actual	*Ideal Role*		
Role	*Technical*	*Hybrid*	*Political*
Technical	Traditional Technician (13)	Passive Hybrid (13)	Closet Politician (7)
Hybrid	Technician Activist (11)	Active? (35)	Active? (6)
Political	—	—	Active Planner (2)

Note:

n = 87. The number of planners in each category is indicated in parentheses.
Ninety (90) planners filled out the questionnaire that was used to determine ideal
role. Of these 90 planners, 3 were classified as low/low on ideal role and were
excluded from this table (see note 3 for chapter 5). "Low/low" means they scored
low on two attitude scales, one measuring the importance of technical and the
other of political activity.

day work, using the same theoretical framework as was used in the
questionnaire. How did they feel about the political context in which their
work took place? Did they engage in political behavior, such as lobbying
or mobilizing citizens groups? Did they see technical analysis as their
primary source of influence or as one of several? In somewhat simplified
terms, technicians were those who saw analysis as their central tool and
disapproved of playing an active political role. Politicians (of which there
were very few in terms of actual role) approved of acting politically and
discounted the importance of technical analysis. Hybrid planners used
both technical analysis and active lobbying to achieve planning goals.

The harmony or dissonance between planners' ideal and actual roles
is summarized in Table 5.1. The possible combinations of ideal and actual
role could potentially produce nine roles. For 57 percent of the planners
in the sample, actual and ideal roles were the same. For the rest, the roles
the planners actually played differed from what they thought planners in
general ought to do, and the possibilities for tension and dissonance were
obvious. The chance of harmony was greatest where the ideal matched
the actual, along the diagonal from top left to bottom right in Table 5.1.

The first rough assignment of planners to role categories suggested that there actually were only seven role possibilities (see Table 5.1). The thirteen *traditional technicians* and the two most *active planners* stood at opposite ends of the spectrum of role choices. These planners had the clearest ideologies to be committed to, and their actual performance reflected their ideals. Between the two ends of this continuum were at least four and maybe as many as six other roles. Toward the technical end were thirteen planners tentatively categorized as *passive hybrids* and eleven classified as *technician activists*. Toward the political end were seven people identified as possible *closet politicians*. Finally, two other groups, with forty-one members, were candidates for adding to the active role.

In some of the cases where ideal and actuality were not the same, this difference was a source of dissonance. This was true for the closet politicians who identified with politicized roles in theory but actually played more technical ones. The dissonance was the defining characteristic of this group. The seven planners shown as initial candidates for this category were joined by two others whose interviews revealed that they wished to be politicized planners but could not play the proactive role necessary. The eleven technician activists were an equally clearly defined group who identified themselves as technicians but actually played more active roles. However, the difference between their technical ideal role and their hybrid actual one was not a source of dissonance for this group.

Among the forty-three planners tentatively categorized as active planners, the question remained how many actually were. In particular, one distinct cluster emerged within this group when attitudes about implementation and proactivity were examined in the interviews. Nine of the planners who were hybrids on both ideal and actual role were unusual in not having much interest in seeing their plans implemented, although they were fairly proactive in their work. This pattern suggested that they might experience a feeling of dissonance, but their interviews indicated that they did not. They were more concerned with the planning process itself than with its outcomes. This group comprised nine of the eleven planners termed *process planners* in the final typology of roles (Table 5.2).

These four variables of ideal and actual role, and attitude toward implementation and proactivity, provided the framework for defining the categories in a typology of roles that captures some of the complexity of actual practice. The final assignment of the planners to roles used the two sets of tensions as a starting place, but each person was also considered individually, based on their interview; to see if the tensions suggested by certain cells in the classifications really applied to them or whether they

TABLE 5.2

Final Typology of Planners' Roles Based on Harmony and
Dissonance Between Ideal and Actual Roles

Actual Role	Ideal Role		
	Technical	*Hybrid*	*Political*
Technical	Traditional Technician (26)	Passive Hybrid (14)	Closet Politician (9)
Hybrid	Technician Activist (10)	Process Planner (11)	Active Planner[a] (26)
Political	—	—	—

Notes:

n = 96. The number of planners in each category is indicated in parentheses.

[a] It would be theoretically neater if the active planners were political for both ideal and active role. However, they were not. Some did choose the political role as their ideal but virtually all played hybrid actual roles (Table 5.1).

might fit better in some other category instead. The small groups of technician activists, closet politicians, and process planners were easily and clearly identified. So were the twenty-six active planners remaining once the process planners and closet politicians had been assigned their own categories along with six other people who were reclassified as passive hybrids. Virtually all of these twenty-six active planners were proactive hybrids, and all had an interest in implementation of their plans.

Some people did not seem to fit any category easily or seemed to straddle two. Particularly among the technical planners, I did a good deal of shifting people back and forth between the traditional technician and the passive hybrid categories. There initially were thirteen people (increased to eighteen when those who had not filled out questionnaires were included) who not only thought planners should play a neutral, technical role giving advice to decision makers but also did exactly this. They made up the core of the final group of twenty-six traditional technicians. They were joined by an additional eight planners who shared either their actual or their ideal role orientation as well as their lack of interest in implementation or in being proactive. The fourteen passive hybrids accepted a more active role for planners in theory but not in their own practice.

In sum, this exploration of the relationship between what planners wanted to do and what they were actually doing in practice produced six roles (see Table 5.2). Three were essentially technical in nature. The twenty-six traditional technicians seemed to be the ones with the best initial match between intent and action. The fourteen passive hybrids and ten technician activists potentially seemed to face some dissonance in their roles, although as chapter 6 will show in more detail, this proved not to be the case. They kept the ideal commitment of technicians to serving elected officials and adapted their actual roles to the real world in which they found themselves.

Among more political, value-committed planners, the twenty-six active planners more closely matched ideal and actual roles while the nine closet politicians did not. The eleven process planners found their own adaptation to often difficult political environments in which they actively worked to ensure an open planning process.

In all of these cases, the values that underlay the image of the ideal role of a planner were moral values. These values provided guidelines about what planners should and should not do. For some, these obligations seemed to be an incentive to work actively to see that they were met, even in a complex and political world where their autonomy was significantly limited. When these obligations did not match what the planners were able to achieve, this was sometimes a source of feelings of frustration and even guilt. This was a problem for about a quarter of the sample.

Approaches to Ethics

Exactly how the planners defined these moral obligations that underlay their ideas of professional role depended in part on the way they approached ethical issues in general. Some focused on good ends—environmental quality, social justice, or a broader idea of the public interest, for example. Others emphasized right actions—it was important to be fair, truthful, and responsible to legitimately elected officials.

This indicates that the two basic approaches to ethics already discussed in connection with issues also applied to people. Planners as individuals took characteristically deontological or consequentialist approaches to ethics, and these paralleled differences between active, process, and technical approaches to planning. For people rather than for issues, however, the distinction between consequentialist and deontological approaches is somewhat oversimplified. While it corresponds to common usage in moral philosophy, in real life, many planners thought about ethical issues in ways that combined elements of both approaches, primarily because they thought about ends and means in different ways. It may be more useful to think about approaches to ethics as being spread along a continuum from purely deontological to purely teleological. At one end were deontological planners who were concerned primarily with process issues while at the other end were pure consequentialists who took a very ends-oriented view of ethics. In between, the planners used approaches that combined both deontological and teleological elements.

Few planners are trained in philosophy, so the planners in this sample could not simply say what kind of approach to ethics they were using. Their ideas about ethics were often not very clearly formulated, and the interview involved an exploration for them as well as for the interviewer.

In the end, by looking at the whole interview and using the elements of the various philosophical theories as criteria, most of the planners were tentatively characterized as either consequentialists (21 percent) or deontologists (66 percent). Indeed, the difference between the two groups was fairly well defined. In addition to these two large groups, there was a small group of nine planners whose way of thinking about ethics was so vague and unformed that it was not useful to try to categorize them at all. Finally, there was an even smaller group of four people whose interviews suggested that they were aethical or perhaps even fundamentally unethical.

Table 5.3 suggests possible combinations of ways of thinking about the ethics of ends and means. The planners' approaches to thinking about ends or about the public interest are described using the categories from chapter 4. In much the same manner, process or means can also be thought of in deontological and consequentialist ways. Thus, some planners thought about both ends and means in deontological terms while others thought about both in consequentialist terms. These might be considered "pure" approaches compared with the mixed deontological and consequentialist approaches used by the rest of the planners.

This table suggests that there were three groups of planners who might be thought of as pure deontologists—those with an ethical concern only for means, here called *narrow deontologists;* those using an idea of the public interest as rights, called *substantive deontologists;* and those with an idea of the public interest as a fair process, called *process deontologists.* At the other end of the spectrum, there was a group of pure consequentialists or *act utilitarians* who thought of both ends and means in terms of the balance between good and bad consequences.

Finally, between these various "pure" groups, there were two groups of planners who used consequentialist ideas of the public interest but accepted a deontological view of means. One group, called the *public*

TABLE 5.3

Typology of Approaches to Thinking about Ethics

Approach to Ends or Public Interest	Approach to Process or Means	
	Deontological	Consequentialist
None	Narrow Deontologist (11)	—
Deontological		
Public interest as process	Process Deontologist (12)	—
Public interest as rights	Substantive Deontologist (14)	—
Consequentialist	Public Interest Planners (26)	Rule Utilitarian (8) / Act Utilitarian (12)

Notes:
n = 83.

This table does not include 9 planners who had such unformed ideas about ethics that they could not be classified. It also does not include the 4 aethical planners.

interest planners, was predominantly deontological in orientation; the other, *rule utilitarians,* was primarily consequentialist. The distinction will be more fully developed when the groups are described in more detail.

What did it mean for a planner to be a deontologist or a consequentialist? Descriptions of issues belonging in either category do not necessarily convey what it means for a person to take one kind of perspective or the other. These two basic approaches will be described briefly here, but a fuller discussion of the six different categories can really only be understood in relation to the roles that the planners played. So after the discussion of roles in chapter 6, it will be possible in chapter 7 to look at the variations and combinations that provide a more accurate picture of what kinds of issues were raised by each group and how they thought about these issues. These patterns, in turn, begin to suggest the characteristic ethical problems faced by each group, which will be the focus of part 3.

Deontologists

A deontological approach to ethics focuses on the rightness of actions regardless of their consequences. What is right may commonly be defined by an overarching rule, such as the Golden Rule, or by a set of more specific ones. The rules may either be explicitly written or they may be internalized in a person's conscience.

This approach seems to correspond to the way many people think about ethics. In the sample of planners, there were far more deontologists than teleologists. This is similar to findings by Lang and Hendler (1986). In a survey of forty-seven planners in Ontario, they found that 84 percent identified with a deontological view of ethics. Indeed, the deontological approach was more of a "default" category than the consequentialist one. Planners who had rather undeveloped ideas about ethics were more likely to talk about right and wrong, rules and conscience, all of which suggested a kind of vague deontology rather than a teleological calculus. (The most vague of these planners were simply classified as ethically unaware.)

There were many deontologists who were quite clear about what this approach involved for them. One said crisply:

> It's very simple with me. I think I have a very strong set of personal moral values—a lot of it is from my family. If something conflicts with my moral values, then I think it's unethical. Quite simple.

He then went on to give a series of examples of these values:

> I mentioned equality, and I guess I would give sort of the Christian or Judeo-Christian value of the importance of the individual, but on the other hand, I guess there is a certain conflict. I give an important role to the institution—the planning commission in this sense—that probably goes back to my planning training. I support a nonviolent approach to problem solving [as well as] honesty and candor.

Another was almost outraged that anyone would even ask what constituted right and wrong and reeled off in quick succession a catalog of principles that were very characteristic of many of these deontological planners:

> It's pretty damn obvious what's right or wrong! Being honest in relationships with others; knowing you're working for a public agency—we're responsible to elected officials and they're responsible to the general public; treating everyone fairly; doing unto others as you would have others do unto you—putting yourself in the other person's shoes, trying to see where they're coming from; not owning property in town; and keeping confidences on proposed developments.

A list of the principles used by members of the sample is certainly weighted toward the duties of justice, such as fairness and honesty, as well as to the principle of loyalty (Table 5.4).

The principles that these deontological planners relied on most often were procedural in nature. This is hardly surprising in light of the deontological focus on actions that are right or wrong in and of themselves regardless of consequences, but deontological planners also raised issues of ends, thinking of them as rights giving rise to corresponding duties. Justice was the prime example since it has traditionally been a central deontological right in philosophy as well. The right to health and safety was one used by some planners. An environmental or land ethic also seemed to be used in a similar way by a few.

All deontological planners relied on principles to tell them what actions were right. Where these principles "resided" did vary. Some talked about relying on external rules—four actually said that they used professional codes of ethics, though it was clear from the interviews that they had other, internalized ethical values as well. Most talked about relying on intuition or conscience as a guide, suggesting a less structured, internalized set of principles.

In fact, rules and conscience seemed simply to be two sides of the same coin. The rules seemed to be a more explicit or conscious rendering of what their conscience told them was right; they also knew that many or most of the dictates of conscience had been shaped by rules that they had been taught early in life. One planner described the relationship between his clearly articulated moral code and the actual process of decision:

> I just find it sort of an ethereal kind of thing. You just do it instinctively most of the time. You don't think about "Is this the moral code and is this what I should do?"

TABLE 5.4
Principles Used by Deontologists and Consequentialists

	Deontologists (n = 63)		Consequentialists (n = 20)	
	Number	*Percent*	*Number*	*Percent*
Means				
Honesty	39	62	14	70
Loyalty	42	67	6	30
Fairness	32	51	8	40
Openness	20	32	5	25
Keeping confidences	1	2	2	10
Objectivity	9	14	2	10
Technical quality of work	6	9	2	10
Freedom	7	11	0	0
Golden Rule	3	5	1	5
Ends				
Public interest	31	49	14	70
Equity/justice	14	22	5	25
Environment	5	8	2	10
Health/safety	3	5	1	5
Aesthetics	1	2	2	10
Transportation	—	—	1	5

Note:
Vague and aethical planners are not included here.

Thus, the basic deontological planner was a person with internalized moral principles about duties of justice and loyalty. For some, the realm of ethics extended further to justice or even to rights for the inanimate natural environment. These principles all imposed duties that were to be acted on because they were right in and of themselves. They were the rules.

Consequentialists

In a consequentialist approach to ethics, the right is defined by the goodness of the consequences of action, usually thought of as the balance between good and bad effects. The "good" here is not a moral quality in itself. It is just something that is considered to be of value. For a universal system of moral evaluation such as utilitarianism, it must be a value that is general, like pleasure or happiness. Less universal evaluation schemes have used monetary measures of value, and some planners in this study used quite specific values, such as aesthetic enjoyment or personal mobility, assuming that these, like money, had some connection to general happiness. The bottom line with all of these values is that an act would be considered right if the happiness or good created by it would exceed the pain or bad consequences.

Planners who were consequentialists were no more aware of their approach to ethics than deontologists were of their ethical perspective. Even so, consequentialists were fairly obvious in practice both because they talked about the goodness or badness of policies, plans, or projects as ethical issues and because the process of calculating consequences was done consciously.

Consequentialists were much more likely to bring up the goodness of a policy as an ethical issue than were deontologists. As one might expect, 70 percent talked about issues that involved the public interest compared with only 49 percent of the deontologists (see Table 5.4). Half of the public interest issues raised by consequentialist planners were described primarily in terms of substantive disagreements over what would be good policies or projects compared with only a quarter for the deontologists. One planner, when asked about ethical issues he had faced, started right in although initially he was a bit unsure if this counted as ethics:

> What we are always confronted with—I don't know if I'd describe them as ethical choices—is whether it's the right thing to do in terms of planning for the city.
> Q: Would you describe that as an ethical choice?
> Sure, in many ways it is. I mean, I'm confronted with that issue right now . . . one could describe it as an ethical question. I see them as "What is the right planning—what is the professional thing to do?" Like one of the choices that I face right now is, we've had a mammoth amount of office building in the city and we get to the question of the degree to which the city can absorb that amount of space and services directly and understand that we are actively making life better in Sunbelt City. What is the correct posture for the planners? Do I take what could be a very dramatic position, which is we ought to have some limitation on downtown building until we understand better what the traffic requirement is and whether we can absorb it? All we know right now is that rush hour is pretty tough around here. It raises the question of whether it is

really the correct thing for the city. If I called for some limitation and it actually happened, what effect would that have on the economy in this city? What long-term effect would that have? Would that then dry up the energy in that industry in the future?

This planner was talking about the public interest for his city, and for these planners, the public interest was central to their view of ethics. It was a public interest defined in terms of benefits and costs, of calculation about what would serve the public. One put it this way:

I try to do what I feel is best for the city, and I guess my interpretation of what is best has to do with—particularly since I'm very involved with projects—how a project can function most efficiently that is to accommodate the largest number of people. [M]any of the projects produce revenue or tax benefits or other economic benefits to the city, and we have to weigh the advantages of producing the maximum benefits there against the aesthetic considerations and social benefits.

A concern for the goodness of results made these planners focus on the importance of analysis in determining what would be the best policy and in arguing for it. Perhaps it is not surprising to see that not only did they use the principle of the public interest more, they actually used the principle of honesty more frequently than did deontologists (see Table 5.4). This would be essential in order for analysis to be credible to its consumers. A transportation planner who favored extension of a subway line still wanted to see as objective an analysis as possible of a number of alternatives:

People knew I was generally supportive at that point. Let me go on to say that the alternatives analysis as I saw it at the time, if it was done well—effectively, rationally, professionally—it might have showed that there were other ways to transport through that territory, and it might conceivably have shown that some of the other ways might have saved some dollars, but it would not have negated the subway extension. It might still have concluded that among the alternatives the subway extension was one reasonable way to go in that corridor, but it would have at least given the decision makers— the community, the county, and the state—the opportunity to understand the impacts of the rail extension versus a bus or other transportation mode in that corridor.

As these examples indicate, these planners' concerns about the goodness of consequences easily led them into commitments to particular goals. Sometimes the judgment would be made on individual policies or projects as they came up, but some planners had strong commitments to the goals or approaches to planning that were served by the agencies they worked for.

These consequentialists were not asserting that these values were "rights" that should be protected against utilitarian calculation or against trade-offs with other benefits, such as economic development. They believed that planning for transportation systems, protecting the environment, or working for more aesthetically attractive development provided benefits for the public. The head of an urban design review staff who struggled constantly with the unmeasurable nature of the "benefits" of design relative to its costs said:

> People react to good design but they can't always tell you why. I think we have to go on the premise that we do have something good to say [and] I believe that good design doesn't necessarily have to cost more.

These planners saw it as their role to be advocates for these particular benefits. If this planning produced costs as well, the outcome would be determined by elected officials in the political process.

This strong commitment to the public interest, combined with their consequentialist ethics, also led at least act utilitarians to have somewhat different ideas from deontologists about the process of planning. While they clearly used procedural principles in many cases, these rules did seem to have more the quality of rules of thumb. The planners were less absolutist about the rightness or wrongness of such things as lying or being loyal or fair. They not only referred to the public interest much more but they also mentioned loyalty, fairness, and openness as principles less often than the deontologists (see Table 5.4). They were more likely to think that such judgments depended somewhat on the situation, that the end might justify the means. One planner, talking about tactics used to get a project through, said:

> I guess I believe in contextual ethics or something, but in the context that they were done, I felt like I was doing the right thing.

Since consequentialist calculation balances the harm created by an action against the good, it does not preclude doing harm in order to achieve good. If a large number of people could be benefited at the expense of a lie or a broken promise to a small group, for example, that action might be a "right" action. Some planners felt that in some situations, at least, a good end might justify the use of questionable means. This is what is called "the problem of dirty hands."

Role, Ethics, and Professional Identity

What was the relationship between planners' roles and the ways they thought about ethics? While there certainly were exceptions, technicians of all kinds tended to take a predominantly deontological approach to planning. It was no accident that they emphasized the deontological, if somewhat problematic, principles of accountability and loyalty. The planners who used a consequentialist approach to ethics were predominantly ones who also accepted the idea of planning as an active force for social change.

A planner's role had an ethical perspective embedded in it. The ethical approach shaped, in part, the choice of the role and playing out the role reinforced that approach. Ethics were shaped mostly in childhood and youth, but in professional practice, both experience and the political and organizational setting also shaped ethical values and action. The next three chapters will explore these various elements of professional identity as well as the planners' views of what had shaped their values.

6

Planners' Roles

One of the challenges of doing planning in a democratic society is to try to balance a long-range view of the interests of a community, sometimes contrary to preferences of its individual members, with being responsive to those same members. This balancing act takes place in a political system in which planners, as I have argued already, can have influence but not control. The roles that the planners in this sample played, described in this chapter, represent different ways in which they responded to this challenge. Each role involved an element of choice and of commitment to central moral values. Technicians emphasized responsiveness to decision makers though they also hoped to be farsighted. Process planners emphasized responsiveness but to a broader image of the whole community. Active planners were more committed to achieving particular goals that they saw as beneficial for their communities in the long run.

Many planners' roles were also in some respects a response to their political and organizational environments. They could keep their ideal and actual roles from diverging either by adapting to the setting they found themselves in, by choosing particular jobs, or by working to shape their political environments. As long as planners were able to achieve the moral commitments implied by their ideal roles, they would experience some sense of harmony. Divergence seemed to be the result of the interaction between particular moral commitments, personality, and organizational settings that discouraged or prevented a planner from keeping his or her ideal and actual role in synchrony.

What were these moral commitments that were strong enough to affect the choice of a job or to be held to even if they produced a sense of frustration? Exactly what these commitments were will be discussed in more detail in chapter 7, but the kind of issues characteristically raised by people in each of the roles will be described here and will begin to suggest the rather different ways planners in different roles thought about ethics.

The essence of all the technician roles was a repudiation of autonomy for planners in the policy-making process and a commitment to loyally serve those who were officially designated policymakers. The essence of the more politicized roles was to work for social change or human betterment, whether through better urban design, a more equitable distribution of resources, more environmentally sound development, or whatever. Achievement of ambitious goals requires substantial power. This commitment required planners to look for ways to increase their influence and autonomy in the planning process.

The six roles can be thought of as lying along a continuum. The three technical roles range from the traditional technicians at the technical extreme through the passive hybrids to the technician activists. The process planners seemed in a number of respects to lie in the middle, between the various technicians and the two politicized roles—the active planners and the closet politicians. However, in this discussion, the order will be somewhat different. The presentation of the three technical roles will be balanced by looking next at the opposite extreme—the active planners. The process planners and closet politicians can be more easily understood in contrast to the other roles. The ethical issues raised by each of the different groups will be discussed at the end to highlight the differences between the various roles.

Traditional Technicians

Among the technicians we interviewed, twenty-six were called traditional technicians because they were most like the image of the technical planner common in the planning literature (Baum 1983; Beckman 1964; Rabinovitz 1967, 1969; Vasu 1979). This was also the image used in developing the ideal technician role in this study's questionnaire (Howe and Kaufman 1979). As Table 6.1 indicates, among the traditional technicians, 69 percent were actually technicians and 71 percent chose that as their ideal role as well. Most (69 percent) had little or no concern for implementation and 77 percent were not proactive. These patterns, taken together, suggest that for most of these planners, their role should be harmonious in the sense that they were doing what they believed planners should do.

Edward Smith, Jr.,[1] worked in a smallish Texas city, the market center for a substantial rural area. Most of his day-to-day work was

TABLE 6.1
Components of Role: Traditional Technicians

	Low/Low	Technician	Politician	Hybrid
Ideal Role (n)	3	15	1	2
Percent	14	71	5	9
Actual Role (n)	0	18	0	8
Percent	0	69	0	31

	None	Some	Not Important to Behavior	Important to Behavior
Interest in Implementation (n)	16	2	5	3
Percent	61	8	19	11

	No	Situation Prevents	Somewhat	Very
Proactive? (n)	12	8	6	0
Percent	46	31	17	0

Note:

n = 26 planners, except for ideal role, which is based on items from the questionnaire that were not filled out by everyone.

regulatory, administering the zoning and subdivision ordinances, although he also did some comprehensive planning. He called himself a "strict constructionist" and said that he tried to remain uninvolved, that is, neutral, objective, and fair, in relation to the people served by the planning department. In relation to his elected and appointed officials, Smith saw his role as simply providing advice rather than as lobbying for his recommendations. In making these recommendations, he relied primarily for justification on research and technical analysis. If the officials rejected his advice, Smith could still feel he had given them the best information he had and that it was their right to decide. As he said:

> I try to keep the emotional tones out of [the recommendations] and I try to let the chips fall where they may after the recommendation is made. I've done my job at that point, and I back off and they make the decisions and sometimes they're favorable and sometimes they're not to whatever position I've taken.

He did not mention implementation or spell out any image of what he was trying to accomplish. The city was growing, a trend strongly supported by local officials. Smith saw his job as trying to make sure that the growth would be orderly and efficient from the point of view of city services. Generally, he took each development as a separate matter as it came up, although he did say that the comprehensive plan provided the overall framework for his recommendations. He did not particularly like the role that organized political groups such as neighborhood associations played in planning because he considered them to be too parochial, but Smith accepted as inevitable their right to be involved in planning decisions.

Traditional technicians were found everywhere—in all states, in all sizes of agencies, and at all levels. This role was also a perennial. Traditional technicians were not significantly older than more politicized planners, and proportionately just as many came out of planning schools in the politicized period between 1965 and 1975 as before and after.

The role represented a coherent approach to planning practice, and all but a couple of the traditional technicians seemed to be ideologically as well as practically committed to it. Although there was no single characteristic that applied to all traditional technicians, there was a complex of about eight things that together made up this role. Each individual planner generally talked about at least two or three and sometimes more. The two central themes in this approach were the importance of technical analysis and the planners' deference to elected officials.

Traditional technicians believed in the separation of planning from politics. They saw their power, such as it was, flowing from the information they provided, not from their advocacy on issues:

> I think that we're in an information business, and any compromising with information is just wrong. Let me say that I don't proceed necessarily on *my* concerns as an administrator. I take other people's issues, from the public, from the staff, or from the elected officials themselves, and would carry those to the hilt, but I don't feel like I'm . . . the issues are not mine. Once I have those issues from those sources, there is no compromise on that as far as exploring them.

They had faith in the influence of good technical analysis; almost a third (31 percent) mentioned this in their interviews. An additional 11 percent talked about how they enjoyed doing this kind of work. This planner contrasted the technical work with his experience with politics:

It's been very frustrating, and I've appreciated the technical side much more, which is my basic orientation: real estate analysis, economic analysis.

Traditional technicians emphasized providing objective information. Again, almost a third (31 percent) mentioned it in their interviews. Some (15 percent) stressed giving both the pros and cons on any issue. They were the most likely of all the groups to believe that planners should be value neutral in their work. Indeed, they were significantly different from active planners on their rating on this scale in the questionnaire.[2] In their interviews, they were the least likely to use or give any indication of being influenced by substantive values, such as a commitment to social justice, to environmental protection, or even to good land use. Several who did have fairly strong personal values talked about how they tried not to let them influence their planning recommendations:

> One thing is absolutely imperative and that is that you divorce your personal feelings from your professional feelings. There are things that I don't like to have happen that I would recommend because I feel as though it is for the good of the community and the best that I see at the time.

They did not believe in crossing the line between planning and politics to actively use their information to lobby or make a case. They were not trying to increase their autonomy from decision makers.

Some traditional technicians (15 percent) objected to the particular nature of the politics in their communities. Others (27 percent) simply felt that politics in general were inappropriate in planning:

> I fully recognize that planning's a political process, and I'd be naive if I didn't say that, but on the other hand, my general approach is to try to stay out of the political process as much as possible and try to maintain a very professional attitude about how we deal with things. So my feeling has always been that the general plan represents the basic policy document that is adopted by the city council and that we need to couch our recommendations in terms of the basic policy document and to remain professional about that and be consistent about that and not try to, if you will, go with the political winds. Some planners will become very political in working with councilmen on a one-to-one basis, but I do not do that.

Traditional technicians seem to have chosen this stance primarily because of a commitment to the role as "public servant" to elected officials. Fully 50 percent talked explicitly about this in their interviews. They were not always enthusiastic about the elected officials they worked with, though many had high respect for them, but whatever their specific evaluation, they accepted the right of these officials to make the final decisions even if they were different from the planner's recommendations. One rather cynical traditional technician said:

> You've got to accept it—they [the politicians] are the people who make the decisions, right or wrong, as long as they don't make an illegal decision, a blatantly illegal decision. As long as I tell *them* the best that I know, if they want to screw it up after that, to me, I've done my job. I think I could be successful at it [lobbying], but I don't think it's good form. It's very unprofessional to go lurking around trying to make deals, no better than the others. I hope we're somewhat above mucking around with backroom deals. If they want to do that, that's fine—well, not fine, but it happens. I would hope that we don't do that.

Another who worked in a community with cleaner politics talked about the public interest:

> I think there's a public good, but I think that is done through the political process and, you know, until planners are elected by the people, I just don't think that it's in the best interests of anyone that they can appoint someone like me and I say "This is the public good and we need to do this, this, and this." I think that those decisions are best made by the elected people, and that's democracy.

Many of these planners have already been described in chapter 4 as those with a technical approach to defining the public interest. These planners thought it was primarily up to elected officials to determine what would be in the public interest for their communities.

While this deference to elected officials lay at the heart of the moral commitment of this role, some traditional technicians also seem to have ended up in this role in part because of their personal style. Thus, 15 percent said explicitly that they did not like conflict or had few political skills. One planner said that what he liked least about his job was that:

> I guess that I'm forced to make decisions that affect people and it doesn't make all people happy and I'm real sensitive. It's an emotional drain when I have to make decisions, that I can't have

winners all over the place—there are winners and losers—and that takes an emotional toll.

Others were not so explicit but seemed to have similar reactions.

Traditional technicians seemed committed to the role for both moral and practical reasons. Since they were not trying to find or create room for discretionary action on their own part, they could be found in all kinds of agencies and jobs. They were spread more evenly across different sizes of agencies, from very small to highly bureaucratic, than were planners in other roles. Similarly, they were spread more evenly than people in other roles between top positions (35 percent) and middle-level ones (31 percent). Sometimes the political liaison that came with being a director made a traditional technician uncomfortable. When asked what he liked least and most about his job, one said:

> This may sound strange, but the most interesting part of the work is the people contact, day-to-day, and the interest on the part of the people. Probably the worst thing about the job is the people [laughter]. I've been at this thing for more than twenty years, and in the early 1960s you had planning in a vacuum. The planning commission and the city council did whatever they wanted to do, whatever they thought was right for the community. Now it seems in the last eight or ten years is it's everybody's right to voice an objection. They may not know anything about it, but they're going to get up there and say it—and you can't reason with them. They become emotional about it and it's just a free-for-all, it's just a gripe session. I like the part, you know, when citizens are concerned and they get involved and get to what I think is the proper and logical solution to the problem.

On the whole, however, the conventions about the giving and receiving of advice were clear enough, at least among both planners and elected officials, to make the politics manageable.

While traditional technicians did not seem to deliberately search for particular kinds of political settings, there were some situations where this role seemed especially to fit. They were more likely than other planners to work in the kinds of communities that have probably always been the bread and butter of planning practice. Thus, 73 percent worked in local agencies in communities smaller than 500,000 in population— suburban areas and smaller cities—many of which (76 percent) were growing. Officials who were progrowth saw planning as a means of ensuring that it would be orderly and appropriate to their social aspirations. By and large, traditional technicians were content to accept the values and goals set by these officials, though some wished they could get them to look at that growth in a more regional or longer term perspective.

Fairly often, there was a kind of fit between the expectations of officials and the technical role of the planner. In addition, this role was especially appropriate for planners who specialized in regulatory review, such as zoning administration or Certificate of Need review in health planning, since these involved the fair, neutral application of existing laws and policies. Seven of the ten planners in the sample who specialized in this kind of work were traditional technicians. As one described her approach:

> I think that you have to evaluate things professionally. We're here to implement the zoning code, and it's very specific. We do things and we make our recommendations in accordance with what's in the ordinance; also what's in accordance with the master plan. I think it's obvious that we have to recognize that anyone we're dealing with is selling a product, and I think we do recognize that and we try to look behind what they're saying. [It's] a matter of analyzing what is the best solution to whatever the problem is and looking at what will meet the criteria in our plans and will meet the criteria in the zoning laws.

This overall description, however, does not give a sense of the variations among these traditional technicians. While most were technicians by inclination or personality, there were five who deliberately chose this role as particularly appropriate to their situations—zoning administration, for example—although they had previously played other, more politicized roles. A few were somewhat proactive—more so than the "take it or leave it" approach articulated by pure technicians like Smith would suggest—but in conservative communities such as those in which most of these planners worked, being somewhat proactive was a delicate matter in which it was necessary to have political support and to tread carefully.

In a somewhat similar vein, about a quarter of the traditional technicians also cared about the implementation of their plans. This was especially the case for planners who had previously held jobs in which they could see direct results but who had now moved into administration or regulation where results were not so immediate.

In theory, the role of the traditional technician ought to have been one of harmony, with a match between ideal and actual roles and between their low level of political activism and their lack of concern about goals. Was this actually the case? The answer is a qualified yes.

More than half (58 percent) of these planners gave no sign in their interviews that they had hesitations about the role they played or that they were frustrated about what they were able to accomplish. Of course, though, this leaves a substantial 42 percent who did.

What was the difference between these two groups? The notable difference was that half of the planners (seven people) who had a sense of harmony in their roles were either the ones who deliberately chose them as appropriate to their situations (five people) and/or who were, in fact, more proactive than the standard technician image would call for (five people). These were planners who took action to ensure harmony. The other half were simply satisfied traditional technicians.

Among those who expressed some sense of dissatisfaction, it had less to do with their role than with their sense of not seeing accomplishment. All were passive, either by nature or because of the nature of their jobs. Three clearly did care about implementation, so for them, the source of the feeling of disparity was fairly obvious. One planner who had worked in the field for about ten years said:

> The thing I like least about it [my job] is not getting anything accomplished, not seeing things implemented. You do a comprehensive plan, but it's so long before you see the projects in it develop. I have seen some projects develop, but the results are a long time in coming.

Several others probably had cared about implementation in the past but had, in effect, given up. One planner, for example, had worked in his department for twenty years. He had originally been fired up by a designer's desire to have his community adopt design review, but he was unable to convince them, and gradually over the years he seemed to have adapted his approach to a more technical one that simply accepted the values of the community. However, this lack of success made him somewhat cynical; not bitter but rather distant emotionally from his community and his work.

Passive Hybrids

The fourteen passive hybrids chose the hybrid as their ideal role but played actual roles that were like traditional technicians. This suggested that they might have wanted to play a more politicized role but, for some reason, did not. In fact, they were primarily notable for being even more uniformly passive than the traditional technicians. Thus, two-thirds were classified as technicians in terms of their actual roles, but fully 92 percent were not proactive and none cared about implementation (Table 6.2). Why did they adopt such an apparently passive stance? Some seem to have chosen it, either deliberately or unconsciously, as suitable to the political systems they worked in. The others seem to have been pushed into it.

George Walters was a planning director who had worked in the same small city for more than thirty years. In the interview, he primarily talked about substantive issues and the managerial and technical aspects of planning. He was such a fixture in the city that he apparently had influence within its fairly closed political system but hardly had to think of this as "being political." In the abstract, Walters thought of politics as mostly the influence of narrow pressure groups. He did not approve of

TABLE 6.2

Components of Role: Passive Hybrids

	Low/Low	*Technician*	*Politician*	*Hybrid*
Ideal Role (n)	0	0	0	14
Percent	0	0	0	100
Actual Role (n)	0	9	0	5
Percent	0	64	0	36

	None	*Some*	*Not Important to Behavior*	*Important to Behavior*
Interest in Implementation (n)	9	5	0	0
Percent	64	36	0	0

	No	*Situation Prevents*	*Somewhat*	*Very*
Proactive? (n)	9	2	1	0
Percent	75	17	8	0

Note:

n = 14 planners, except for proactivity, where 2 planners could not be classified.

this and thought that planners should be above it. In practice, what this meant was that he thought the most effective strategy for planning was simply to present the best technical case for any proposal. He clearly understood and could operate in the politics of his community. In fact, Walters was a bureaucratic survivor who kept a fairly low profile but who had been able to adapt to the changing political and planning winds over the years. He talked about the gradual process of establishing credibility for his agency. While he had apparently built a base of support, he could not articulate the strategy, though Walters could describe its elements when asked:

> I've personally worked a lot of years to establish credibility for myself and for the profession. I knew in the early days, back in the 1950s, that planners didn't have much stature, they didn't have much credibility, they were pretty generally ignored, and their recommendations didn't have much weight.
> Q: What did you do to establish that credibility?
> I don't know. Maybe through the preparation of reports and the way they were presented and the way I would make a presentation to the council, how I make that presentation, the background I use, establishing and identifying the issues, and how we approached the final recommendation.
> Q: Did you at that time also give any attention to building a support system in the community for planning?
> No. Only in the sense that individuals and groups began to recognize that the planning director and his staff were to be trusted, could give you valid data and information that you could rely on. That's how we developed the trust of the people in the community, and not go out and solicit it. We don't have a cadre of people or friends that supports us by merely giving them a phone call or something like that. . . . One thing that we happen to have as a very strong ally is the newspaper. They are very supportive of the planning process, and if we screw up they'll make it known to the community, but they will publicize what's happening, they will get our report when the agenda is distributed to council, and they will publish that in the newspaper. They will write stories about it.
> Q: From what you were saying before about the neighborhood planning activities, it sounds like there must be considerable awareness at the neighborhood level.
> Yes, there is. It does help greatly to know that there are people out in the community who understand what the process is all about and the implication of land-use changes or zoning changes or what have

you. The community has discovered over the years that you gain an influence in the final decision by being present and making presentations.

Here his own initial version sounded like the response of a traditional technician—they had provided good technical analysis—but overall, through the activities of the entire department, Walters seemed to have established a solid role for planning in the community. Given this support and his lack of ambitious goals for the community, he did not have to take a proactive role.

Walters captures the most common type of passive hybrid—survivors who fit into a political system so that, at least for some, they rarely presented themselves as overtly political and appeared to hardly think of themselves this way. Their descriptions of their roles were quite similar to those given by traditional technicians. More than half (57 percent) emphasized the importance of good technical analysis. More than a third (36 percent) said that they tried to keep this analysis as neutral and objective as possible.

Passive hybrids seem to have worked in situations where action would have been difficult either because of a lack of support for planning or because of the weight of bureaucracy. Nearly half (43 percent) worked in Tennessee, where support for planning was not strong. They were also somewhat more likely to work in regional agencies that often had tenuous power bases or in large state bureaucracies.

They were also significantly older than most of the planners who played more overtly politicized roles. Two-thirds had come out of planning school in the 1950s and early 1960s, at a time when the technical role was dominant. None came from personal backgrounds that would have encouraged them to challenge this passive image of the planner's role.

A majority of the passive hybrids accepted and, in effect, melted into the political structures within which they worked. These political systems did not encourage them to play proactive roles. However, a minority (36 percent) were quite critical of the political systems within which they worked. They would have liked to play a more political role but either did not know how or were simply too cautious or too discouraged to do so. For example, one regional planner whose agency had just undergone major budget cuts talked about the problem of getting political support and of implementing plans:

I think the follow-through in many cases is outside of the control of the planner. As a matter of fact, we're into that now. We're completing extensive investigation into regional implementation strategies, and we found in our research that if we are to carry out our plans—we found more than 230 entities from the international level to the local level, and they're the people who have the actual power to implement the plans and that's where the funding becomes involved, the political process is involved, and the professional planner can't deal with it. It's really the political organization—this region needs more of a unity and it's even apparent in partisan politics—there's a lot of fragmentation within the parties.

Faced with what he saw as a hostile and fragmented political system and a fragmented system for implementation, this rather mild-mannered planner reacted passively.

Clearly, this planner presented a disparity between what he wished he could accomplish and what he could do. He was joined by two others. The others, however, had little or no apparent sense of dissonance. While they saw a somewhat political role as appropriate for planners in general, they had no strong reasons to play it themselves. Their own personal sense of mission was not strong, and the passive role seemed to fit fairly easily into the political contexts in which they worked.

Technician Activists

If the passive hybrids seemed somewhat colorless, the ten technician activists stood out as a well-defined and opinionated group. All presented themselves essentially as traditional technicians, but as they talked about their planning experience, they showed themselves to be politically so-phisticated, activist planners. In line with this presentation of self, Table 6.3 shows that on ideal role, two-thirds supported the technician role, but on actual role, 80 percent seemed to be hybrids.

Richard Breitman was director of his agency and a man with long experience in planning. He had worked for many years in his community and was a member of its small inner circle of political influence. He came into planning in the 1950s when the technician role was the dominant one and when planning was not familiar to or well accepted by decision makers. This was a role that they could relate to, like that of an engineer. Over the years as his authority became established, Breitman developed something of the image of an outspoken curmudgeon—honest, straight, and forthright. It gave him a little extra independence in the bargaining over planning issues, and bargaining had clearly occurred as the community moved beyond pure land-use regulation to undertake downtown

TABLE 6.3

Components of Role: Technician Activists

	Low/Low	*Technician*	*Politician*	*Hybrid*
Ideal Role (n)	0	6	0	3
Percent	0	67	0	33
Actual Role (n)	0	2	0	8
Percent	0	20	0	80
	None	*Some*	*Not Important to Behavior*	*Important to Behavior*
Interest in				
Implementation (n)	2	0	0	8
Percent	20	0	0	80
	No	*Situation Prevents*	*Somewhat*	*Very*
Proactive? (n)	0	0	8	2
Percent	0	0	80	20

Note:

n = 10 planners, except for ideal role, which is based on items from the questionnaire that were not filled out by everyone.

revitalization and a variety of other more proactive policies. He did not mind conflict and was willing to go to bat for policies he thought were in the community's best interest, but once the decision was made—whether it went with him or against him—Breitman was a loyal team player. He gave the example of his relationship to the mayor on the capital budget:

> We present all the projects that we propose, that we reviewed, with the planning commission and with the other city departments. The mayor goes down the projects and says, "I don't like this project— take it out," or, on the other hand, he says, "No, I think we ought to do this project this way rather than that way." We make a case for the way we think, of course, in our presentation, but he may reach a conclusion by virtue of certain political considerations, you know, in the most fundamental sense . . . and, of course, my feelings are that he's the person who was elected by the populace and he

has the last word on these things. He has made it very clear to all of us in city government that up unto a point—and he says this very openly—up to the point he makes a final decision on something, we're free to do anything we want—anyway we can convince him or anybody else—but once there's an agreed-upon decision, we either have to go along with him or resign.

Breitman represents most of these technician activists. The maintenance of the technical facade and its apparent incongruity with the reality of their style does not seem to have been an effort to hide anything. They simply thought of themselves as technicians. In talking about their roles, 40 percent emphasized the importance of good technical analysis to getting results, and 40 percent also said that their primary strategy was simply to provide objective information to decision-makers. Moreover, other people in their communities expected planners to be technicians. In effect, they took advantage of the "straight" and "competent" associations with the technical image to build a more activist role, but they did not like to be too explicit about it.

They were one of the oldest groups among all the planners, with an average age of 49.7 years, so 60 percent had come into the field when the primary role was the technical one. They were all men; it was hard to imagine how a woman could play quite this role of the gruff curmudgeon.

Their effectiveness came from long experience working in the same community and from a thorough knowledge of and long involvement in its political system, which they tended to describe as a fairly closed power structure. All but one worked at the local level; 80 percent worked in cities that were large enough to be doing fairly complex planning (between 100,000 and one million population) but small enough to be controlled by a mayor-centered power structure or by an old-boy network. There were no technician activists in the open, participatory politics of northern California. All but one were agency directors or assistant directors. The one exception was the development coordinator in the office of a mayor. While they were involved in working with a wide range of external, political groups, their primary focus was on elected officials. One planner described the requirements and possible pitfalls of this approach:

A great deal of the planner's time needs to be spent in seeking out the so-called "power structure" in the community, and once identifying it, to try to get within it and guide them in the broader public interest, away from their narrow interest—to sell them. But you have to be very careful in doing it because you can suddenly find yourself espousing their narrow viewpoints because you want to be one of the good old boys.

Two of these planners had recently been centrally involved in organizing highly participatory efforts to develop comprehensive plans. Nevertheless, even given this highly proactive behavior, which was reflected in other aspects of their work as well, both presented themselves simply as traditional technicians. As one said of his department:

> Now, one can get into [trouble] if one takes a very strong advocacy position or a strong lobbying position on any issue because then one starts to alienate those that you don't advocate for or don't lobby for, so our department is not an advocacy department. It is not a lobby department. We take the position that the boards and commissions that we staff, the manager and the council that we staff, make the decisions. Our responsibility is to provide them with all the information necessary to make that decision and the options that are possible, and, if asked, we will recommend one that we feel would be appropriate.

Ultimately, however, almost all of the technician activists were motivated by a strong concern about getting results. A concern with implementation was important to their behavior for 80 percent, and all were somewhat or very proactive (see Table 6.3):

> I don't like to see plans lying on shelves. I want them to be used and fortunately I've had some pretty good experiences where they got used. [That's why] you need to be there [close to decision makers] because they have a great deal to do with what happens— in reality, in fact, what eventually happens.

Another reflected the mayor-centered nature of the political system he worked in:

> I believe that a planning agency must be useful to the processes of government. It must be useful to the mayor since the mayor's the chief executive; if your agency isn't *useful* on a day-to-day basis, it's not very useful at all.

Unlike other technicians, they all also seemed to like "the action"— the contact with people, the give-and-take of mediation and bargaining, the involvement in real decisions, but they also had a kind of caution, a reticence about being too open about their political role. They could retreat into the technician role as a way of indicating that, in the final analysis, they did not make the decisions, they only gave advice. As one said:

> I don't like to use the word "power" because I'm not a powerful person. I try very hard not to be that. I do try to influence and I do try to use my judgment where I think I need to, but I don't consider myself to be a powerful person. I'm here to tell you that I'm not.

Despite the apparent contradiction in being an active technician, these technician activists definitely did not experience any sense of dissonance. Their concern for implementation, their proactive behavior, and their actual roles as hybrids were all logically interrelated. Indeed, most seemed to have a real sense of competence and pleasure in their work. They continued to believe in the traditional technical role, not as some kind of contrived cover but simply as part of their identity as planners. Their central tenet seemed to be that ultimately they answered to and were loyal to their elected officials. As long as this condition was met, the role was sufficiently flexible to allow for a fairly wide range of professional action.

Technicians: One Role or Three?

There was a substantial difference in approach between traditional technicians, taken as a group, and technician activists. The latter seemed to be much further along the continuum toward a politicized role. (This is why they were identified as a separate subgroup.) The distinction between passive hybrids and traditional technicians, however, exists more in theory or ideal role than in actual fact. Even so, all the technicians shared common central values: an emphasis on the importance of technical analysis in planning and an acceptance of the idea that they primarily served elected officials.

Movement along this continuum and within this value set seemed to be quite easy, at least for some planners. Probably all the technician activists had done it. Some people for ideological or strategic reasons moved back and forth during their careers. A technician zoning analyst could be an activist when assigned to work on projects on housing; or take the planning director in a community that had been transformed, over his thirty-year tenure, from a corrupt rural county seat to a rapidly growing suburban area in which planning was a central political issue—

he still held to many of the tenets of the passive, technical role, particularly accepting the principle that elected officials set the goals, but he was also a survivor and over the years not only had become more political but seemed to enjoy it. He talked with gusto, for example, about a recent battle over agricultural land preservation.

While some traditional technicians seemed to have an almost naively apolitical quality, at least some of the ones who had a sense of harmony in their work were exactly those who had moved somewhat beyond the usual political confines of the role. In both the technician activist role and in the passive hybrid role, the technical approach allowed the planner to blend into the background in communities where more obviously politicized roles might have been considered to be out of place. Moreover, they all seemed, still, to accept the basic normative premise that they were there to provide the best information they could to decision makers whose role it was to make the final decision. Thus, there were both similarities and important differences among these three technician categories, and in the analysis that follows, depending on which perspective provides the most insight, the technicians will sometimes be presented as a single group and sometimes as a set of three.

The Active Planners

The group that is most directly and overtly politicized has been called simply the active planners. It is the same size (twenty-six people) as the traditional technicians and represents the other dominant group in the sample. These planners by and large saw planning as a tool for accomplishing particular goals to which they were committed. They had begun as idealistic young planners, often but not always in the 1960s. Experience had given them more realism, but essentially they had turned their considerable energies to creating enough autonomy and to amassing enough influence to contribute actively to achieving the goals they valued.

Tom Stuart was a policy analyst for a state environmental agency. He was involved in preparing the department's budget and program bills for the state legislature and was actively involved in lobbying for them. He was used to the ideological politics, the logrolling, and the pressure brought by legislators, and Stuart sometimes engaged in political tactics that took advantage of political divisions or played on symbolic themes to enhance the department's bargaining position. He talked about how he felt that this was in some respects unprofessional for a planner, who ought to make the case for a policy on its merits, but he was strongly committed to the environmental goals of his department, and particularly

to some programs he had been involved in developing, and he knew that
he had become an effective lobbyist. Stuart satisfied his professional side
by doing careful analysis of bills, even if he thought it would largely be
ignored. Sometimes it turned up important issues or problems that would
otherwise have produced problems later.

Most of the active planners (85 percent) were very much concerned
with goal achievement or implementation (Table 6.4). As one experienced
director said:

> In this day and age, planning now has become instrumental in the
> city process. I mean, you and I can remember twenty years ago,
> you had to jump up and down to be *heard* in government, but that's
> not true today. Today planning is an important bureaucracy in the
> city. What I say makes a difference. My role here is not just a
> planner-observer. I am in a position of authority, and one of these

TABLE 6.4

Components of Role: Active Planners

	Low/Low	Technician	Politician	Hybrid
Ideal Role (n)	0	0	7	17
Percent	0	0	29	71
Actual Role (n)	0	0	2	24
Percent	0	0	8	92
	None	Some	Not Important to Behavior	Important to Behavior
Interest in Implementation (n)	3	1	0	22
Percent	11	4	0	85
	No	Situation Prevents	Somewhat	Very
Proactive? (n)	0	4	12	10
Percent	0	15	46	38

Note:
n = 26 planners, except for ideal role, which is based on items from the
questionnaire that were not filled out by everyone.

authorities is to say "The conclusion is correct, and here's what step we ought to take to rectify the problem." The job of someone in my area is to take the technical machine that is represented in the planning department and blend it into the political process some way so you can affect what *happens*.

Some were strongly committed to the implementation of plans they had been involved in developing. Many had well-defined, substantive values that they strove to see realized. These values included central city revitalization, protecting the environment, social equity, and good urban design. In many cases, these values were not necessarily shared by the residents of the communities where the planners worked. However, several did stress that they believed it was important to be responsive to the values of their communities.

While not all these planners played the role of advocate for particular substantive issues, all but four (that is, 84 percent) of the active planners were somewhat or very proactive. They held jobs that involved political liaison or lobbying; three of the four Davidoff-type, equity-oriented advocate planners in the sample were in this group.[3] Many simply seemed to enjoy the political side of the work, and the rest certainly accepted it as a normal part of their jobs. One spelled out the kind of actions he took on planning issues:

We lobby council members, we work with their aides to find out what interests their council members in terms of the kinds of initiatives we take. In terms of timing and moving on particular issues, we will choose those that we think have a better chance of flying—so that there are some conscious decisions going on in our minds in terms of when we make a move that may well be timed around political things.

Some thought the most effective way to get things done in their communities was through an open and participatory process, but some of the active planners were either more driven or were less trusting of the outcomes of a purely open process. Among the most aggressively proactive planners was one who, behind the scenes, helped a citizen group to oppose the city council's effort to decimate the plan he had been involved in developing; another provided information behind the scenes to community and industry groups opposed to a major rezoning backed by large, powerful, and well-connected interests. One talked about quietly developing a diverse and independent political base among various interest groups and politicians.

Among those who were only "somewhat" proactive was a planning director in a high-income, low-density suburban area who advocated, and finally got through her commission and council, a proposal for allowing the division of single-family houses for granny flats. Another in an equally high-income suburban county lobbied through an inclusionary zoning ordinance in the face of opposition from real estate interests.

Active planners developed political support and mobilized it on particular issues, accumulated and called in political debts, and generally lobbied actively. In addition, they used information strategically. Sometimes it was provided covertly; often it was provided openly in the traditional planning manner. On the inclusionary zoning plan, for example, the planner said that

> in addition to doing a lot of information gathering, we hired a consultant who analyzed what the impact of inclusionary policy had been elsewhere. We talked to each board member about that and answered their questions and really lobbied them and got other people to also.

This was the essence of the hybrid role: Not only did 71 percent of these planners choose that as their ideal role but 92 percent were classified as hybrids on their actual role (see Table 6.4). They did technical analysis, and some made the point that this was an aspect of the work that they enjoyed. A neighborhood planner, in describing certain aspects of his role, indicated that he did

> work with the city council and the planning commission, the transit board, a number of political groups. Part of our role is as a lobbyist, making sure that [the neighborhood] gets its fair share of whatever pie is being divided up.

Still, when asked about what he liked best about the work, he said:

> The things that I've worked with—the demographics, the social problems that you work with are fun for me.

In some cases, these planners behaved essentially like traditional technicians but did so strategically:

> [On proposals from private developers] it works best to have us be really objective and professional about the recommendations that we make and then if the board members like it, that's fine. If they

don't, then okay, they've not bought into what we recommend. They can stand off from us and disagree, and usually we know it's going to happen and they don't Mau Mau the staff, they just make it clear that they disagree and that's fine. I mean, they're the politicians, we're the planners, and there's a definite difference.

This planner, though, said she would use this approach only for proposals by private developers. On issues of public policy, such as plan amendments or public projects, the department would be more active.

The 29 percent of this group (see Table 6.4) who classified themselves as politicians were especially skeptical about the power of information alone to persuade. None was negative about the need for, or the importance of, good technical analysis in planning. They did not believe, in a cynical way, that analysis was just done to support decisions already made, but they certainly did not see it as some absolute, value-neutral "truth." It was just that, for them, technical analysis took a definite second place to the need for active and strategic political action in order to get plans adopted and implemented.

Finally, these generally were planners who accepted conflict and could deal with it in their lives. Some even seemed to see it as a creative element in the political process. As one planner said contemptuously of other planners she dealt with:

Most that I have seen, particularly on the public level, what they basically know is how to duck. [There's] no controversy, no controversy! No issue! There's no right, no wrong. I think that we tend to be more timid than we really should be or have to be. We just don't know how to have a point of view. You have to think about it and be prepared to back it up and risk having it attacked and defending it, which requires a little thinking and a little preparation.

However, one of those other planners that she criticized said proudly:

I am able to do battle and walk away with some wounds sometimes but, quite candidly, I have not lost many battles in fifteen years. I wouldn't be here if I did. I don't seek conflict per se, but I'm not afraid of it or don't tend to walk around it. Usually you sort of like to deal with it head-on and sometimes turn conflict into some positive kind of a result, which can be done, but it's kind of again a strategic thing.

Active planners were quite different from technicians in the way they came to play this role and in the way they approached their professional

careers in order to be able to do so. More than two-thirds talked about
how they had deliberately chosen a political role. Active planners were
significantly younger than technicians, with an average age of forty.
Ninety percent of the twenty-one who had planning degrees had come
into the field since 1965, so they were more likely to have been exposed
in school to more political role models, though only one person talked
explicitly about this. Perhaps in part because of their younger age, half of
the women in the sample were active planners.

More important, though, more than half (54 percent) of all active
planners talked about how they had been influenced by the social and
environmental movements of the 1960s. These younger planners joined
the small number of older active planners who had been influenced by
earlier union-oriented social radicalism. An older one, describing the pull
between social commitment and ambition that he had dealt with in his
career, talked about where the commitment had come from:

> I think I got it from the neighborhood that we lived in—that liberal-
> socialistic milieu. When I was a young man, a high school student,
> I was very radical. I mean, I went to City College in New York,
> which was radical compared to the rest of the country. When I was
> sixteen or seventeen, I knew what a Trotskyite was. I can say this—
> I'm old enough to remember when they used to lynch black people
> in the South by the hundreds and I remember that kind of social
> awareness, so it must have hit me at that point. I was much more
> attuned to it when I was a teenager because I remember now that I
> was a science major in college and the reason I gave to people when
> they asked you why you had done this silly thing [of going into
> planning] was because I thought the social problems of the world
> were very important and key things.

Another who had come into planning later said:

> I was, you know, in school in the sixties, in college, the late sixties
> and the whole concept of trying to straighten out this mess that
> we'd been in, you know, the dissatisfied generation there was
> undoubtedly influential. Idealism.

Some said they had been socialists. Many more, including some activists
who had not been influenced by social movements, said how idealistic
they had been as young planners. Some saw it as a useful beginning;
others were not so positive:

> For a number of years, when I got out of undergraduate school, I was pretty idealistic and went to work for the metropolitan planning commission here. They prepared plans, and because the planning commission was never really involved with implementation and was very careful to stay out of politics, [it] meant that on most tough issues that were up, often they wouldn't take a position. I had a very idealistic view of what planning was and what it could achieve.

Active planners like this one who were not influenced by social movements were more likely to talk about how they had come to play an activist role as a result of their professional experience. These were planners who wanted to see results and who found that they had a talent for the political side of planning. A planner who talked about how he liked the challenge of the politics, the "people work" in his job, said:

> I think it's a function of the experience here in the last eight or nine years, but it probably taps something in me that was dormant, you know, probably I think it's the ability to really deal with a spectrum of people on problems. I said I enjoy the fights. I guess I put up with them, but I think it's a very goal-oriented thing. The more scraps you get in and you can stick with your functions, I don't think that's a bad experience.

The decision to be an active planner brought with it the need to find or create a niche that would allow this to be done. Thirty-eight percent gained some degree of autonomy by rising to the position of agency director, but clearly this left more than half who had to acquire their ability to act in other ways. Some gravitated to specialized agencies that represented their values. This meant that 40 percent worked in very large bureaucracies, for example, at the state level. While such bureaucracies could stifle autonomous action, these active planners tended to work in jobs as lobbyists or project planners, which made use of their political skills and value commitments. At the other extreme, 35 percent worked in quite small local planning agencies (fewer than ten professionals) where they seemed to have considerable discretion. Three followed Davidoff's (1965) original model of the politicized planner and worked as neighborhood planners.

Effective activism also required many of these planners to make some compromises with the ideals they had originally brought to the field without losing the motivation for action that the ideals had given them. Some found that they were sufficiently politically effective to see "enough" results to keep going. As one said:

Professionally, the goal of the planner is to get from A to B. An idealist wants to go directly, but you can't do it directly. After several years on the job, this began to sink in. In terms of what you can achieve on a large or small scale in that kind of [incremental] approach—you smack your head against the wall so many times that you realize that wall is not going to move or maybe you find out that the wall is moving a little at a time. You are pushing for the ultimate, but you do realize that you are making some progress and it's not all in vain. I'm just beginning to see results of things I worked on eight years ago.

Another, who worked at a fairly high level in a powerful and highly political agency, also used the image of the brick wall, saying:

I decided a long time ago that I wanted to spend my energies and years doing something that I liked, that I could contribute to, and I wasn't going to ram my head against a brick wall. So I . . . those are the brick walls. I found them and I go around them if I can. If I can't, then we deal with the situation and climb over it or something. I'm just not big enough to take on all the brick walls in the world.

These planners and others like them kept their ideals alive by working, as one of them said, "as adults in the real world" to achieve them.

A few others, for various reasons, became somewhat cynical but kept working anyway. One who said it had taken him a long time to learn this lesson said:

I don't feel that this is an ideal world nor would this necessarily be the social system that I would pick if I had my choice completely, but I understand the fact that I don't, and I get some sense of accomplishment out of accepting these things and cultivating them and still achieving things. If this were an ideal world, perhaps development on Lawford Hill would not occur, but it is not an ideal world. I couldn't change the basic framework that made it impossible for me to make people decide to stop living in single-family houses and start moving into apartments downtown. I accept those things, and I work within the confines of what is possible for me to work in as an administrator in a local government.

Overall, the active planners were characterized by a sense of energy and satisfaction in their work. This was a role in which harmony ought to have existed. Ideal and actual role corresponded, as did the desire to see implementation and the activism required to see it happen. In the case of the active planners, it generally did. The three active planners who were cynics were responding to the difference between what they had originally wanted to achieve and what they could do, but rather than making them passive, the disparity made them search for ways that they could have some impact. One thoughtful activist raised as an ethical issue the difference between this active role and the traditional image of the technician planner, but there was no real indication that any of the active planners were unhappy with the choice they had made.

Process Planners

As their name suggests, these eleven planners had an overriding concern with the legitimacy of the planning process and a concern with keeping it open and responsive to input from a wide variety of groups. They were moderately political. Some presented themselves as more negative about politics than others, but in all cases, they had to deal with it. Most (82 percent) chose the hybrid role as the ideal one, and 73 percent seemed to use it as their actual role as well (Table 6.5). Almost two-thirds were moderately proactive, but none were extremely so. However, fully 81 percent had little or no concern with implementation. This indicated fairly clearly that their primary focus was not on the goals or ends of planning but on the process itself.

Rebecca Giulini was the assistant director of a local planning agency. The community was in the middle of a development boom at its fringes while older, downtown neighborhoods that had been in decline were reviving. It had fairly active neighborhood groups and a growing growth management movement. These groups were active in contesting a substantial number of large development proposals. This situation cast Giulini as mediator or facilitator in resolving at least some of these conflicts. She had faith that mutually acceptable solutions could be arrived at by bringing groups together to ensure that everyone had accurate information about projects and to encourage an open exchange of viewpoints. While she was sometimes frustrated by what she saw as the narrow stubbornness of some groups, Giulini was sustained by a moral commitment to an open and participatory process. As she said:

> I see it as looking for that middle ground in a community like this—mediation, balancing competing objectives, trying to make the best out of sometimes a difficult situation for which there is no immediate solution or no solution that we can provide by ourselves. So that principle—balancing competing objectives—is one.

TABLE 6.5

Components of Role: Process Planners

	Low/Low	Technician	Politician	Hybrid
Ideal Role (n)	0	1	1	9
Percent	0	9	9	82
Actual Role (n)	0	3	0	8
Percent	0	27	0	73
	None	Some	Not Important to Behavior	Important to Behavior
Interest in Implementation (n)	6	3	2	0
Percent	54	27	18	0
	No	Situation Prevents	Somewhat	Very
Proactive? (n)	2	2	7	0
Percent	18	18	64	0

Note:
n = 11.

The process role did not seem to be one that planners chose deliberately or explicitly. If passive hybrids and technician activists could be thought of as adaptations on the basic technician role, so the process role might be thought of as a variant on the active role. Process planners worked in situations that were quite political. Most (73 percent) worked at the local level, about half (54 percent) in declining communities where problems might be more likely to take the form of zero-sum conflicts. In growing communities as well, they seemed to face divisive conflicts. Their response, rather than playing an activist role, was to play the role of a coordinator, a facilitator, or a mediator. Whether this was a matter primarily of personality or of something about the situations themselves is difficult to determine, but they all talked about their focus on the process. The director of a small planning department said:

> Probably the biggest function I see for myself as a director is mainly just playing the role of mediator and problem solver.

A health planner, dealing all the time with the conflict between the interests of well-organized health providers and poorly organized consumers, struggled to accept the fundamental and unresolvable nature of the conflict:

> I may get annoyed at people that we're dealing with, and on the board, and sometimes they do out-and-out lie or really misrepresent facts, but I ascribe a lot of that—and I don't mind it—to people defending their own or talking forthrightly for their own. We have on our planning committee and on our board the president of the hospital association, so I would like to think that because he has been on the committee, you know, then he supports what we're doing. But I think that's an unfair—I mean, he is there to protect his interests, and he's got to, and he does do it, and so I can't get annoyed when he does.

It was not surprising that most of these planners talked about the need for fairness and for objective information or analysis. One who worked in a region with significant disparities of income and power was concerned, over a series of several issues, that the interests of poorly represented "underdogs" should be fairly represented. A neighborhood planner first laid out the situations where an effort was needed

> in trying to strike a balance between serving the objectives of the community and the case that is being offered by a developer to advance a certain project. It occurs a lot [sigh]: development proposals, zoning variances . . .

Then he talked about the role he played:

> Where I can be most useful is in creating the opportunity for the issues to be aired and to just see that the information is presented as fully and as accurately as possible. I know a number of planners, probably not an uncommon position to take, who, you know, feel that their responsibility and accountability go beyond simply making good information available, offering a point of view when required and a helping hand all the time, and they take on an advocacy role within their communities. I guess I can admire that commitment, whether it's a general stand they've taken or whether it's on special issues, but when the advocacy role becomes overwhelming, then I think you begin to undermine the unique effectiveness that you can bring to the job as a community planner, that effectiveness being

that you can be trusted and relied upon in terms of consistency by all of the actors involved. A councilman can call me up and, you know, tell me what he wants to do. He can know who he's talking to and he can be reasonably certain what my response is going to be—and that the information he offers me on the face of it has no more or no less value than what any number of other people are offering, and, again, to take the points of view and to take the information and both to synthesize it in my own mind and somehow use it.

As with the active planners, the process planners were younger (the average age was thirty-nine), coming into the field as more politicized role models were gaining acceptance. They were politically more liberal than the technicians, and 29 percent were women. Like the active planners, too, almost half talked about being influenced by idealism and/ or the social movements of the 1960s, and some talked in a similar way about coming to terms with that idealism in the real world. A planner working in a very conflictual situation who had, nevertheless, presented it almost as a comedy of errors, said:

> I had more idealistic notions as a younger person. I don't really feel that those ideals are no longer there, but I think I understand a little better [sigh] the limitations of any one person in changing the world—maybe that's where I've developed my sense of humor [laughter].

Unlike the active planners, though, the process planners did not seem to feel that it was appropriate to press their own agendas or ideals on their communities. Instead, they used their somewhat more politicized style to try to deal with the issues and conflicts they found.

The process planners as a group almost uniformly seemed to have experienced role harmony. The apparent dissonance between being proactive and not caring about implementation was just that—apparent rather than real. The role presented difficulties, but this was not one of them. The one person who did seem to have some sense of dissonance was one who was not proactive and was, in effect, being pushed by circumstances and his own concern for the process into a role in which he did not feel entirely comfortable.

Closet Politicians

This last and smallest group (nine people) was also a distinctly different one. These planners were a kind of alter ego of the active planners and the polar opposite of the technician activists. They all felt that planners should be highly political, so that on ideal role 78 percent chose the politician role and the rest chose the hybrid one (Table 6.6). However, more than three-quarters were technicians on actual role.

These planners really were, in differing degrees, "closet" politicians—people whose idea of what a planner should do was quite at variance with their own performance. They were apparently quite willing, indeed often anxious, to talk about this disparity. In some of these interviews, there was a feeling of suppressed energy, of pressing issues that needed to be brought out, almost of confession. These were planners who had a strong moral commitment to liberal values and felt frustrated or guilty not to be acting on them. Many seemed to suffer acutely from a sense of dissonance.

Sam French was research director in a medium-sized planning agency. He had originally worked in housing but moved into this area by mutual agreement with his agency as one more suitable to his strengths

TABLE 6.6

Components of Role: Closet Politicians

	Low/Low	*Technician*	*Politician*	*Hybrid*
Ideal Role (n)	0	0	7	2
Percent	0	0	78	22
Actual Role[a] (n)	0	7	0	1
Percent	0	78	0	11

	None	*Some*	*Not Important to Behavior*	*Important to Behavior*
Interest in Implementation (n)	3	1	5	0
Percent	33	11	56	0

	No	*Situation Prevents*	*Somewhat*	*Very*
Proactive?[a] (n)	8	0	0	0
Percent	89	0	0	0

Notes:

n = 9.

[a] On each of these variables, one person could not be classified.

and weaknesses. Not only did his job shelter him from involvement in immediate planning issues but he said himself that he did not like conflict. However, French had strong proequity and proenvironmental values and was critical of both his agency and of planning in general for being too wishy-washy. He belonged to several citizen organizations, such as the local chapter of the Sierra Club and a housing advocacy group, and was sometimes active as a private citizen on these issues. Despite this activity, the interview was pervaded by a combined sense of impotence, self-blame, and a bit of bravado as he tried to justify behavior that he fundamentally felt was unjustifiable.

Clearly, these planners made a fairly deliberate choice of their ideal role. They talked about the same kind of idealistic motivations for becoming planners that active planners did. They were politically the most liberal group and had a stronger commitment to substantive issues than even the active planners. They had not lost that commitment over the years, though they were the oldest of the groups (the average age was 50.5). It was simply that a combination of structural factors and personality prevented them from acting on their commitments. Structurally, all worked in highly bureaucratic agencies, at the state or regional levels, or in large agencies in which raising controversial issues was difficult for anyone. Though they were the oldest group, only one had a job near the top of his agency.

French perhaps represents the gloomiest side of this role. Three of these planners did not suffer from such apparent, chronic dissonance. While a few were spinning out the last years of their careers sidelined in dead-end jobs, there were others who were making useful contributions in the niches they had found in the planning system.

Nevertheless, there was certainly a pattern of withdrawal from active jobs that would have directly called upon the value commitments they held so important. A planner who had worked in the New York metropolitan area for many years was quite explicit about this:

> I made a very clear and conscious decision some time ago to try to avoid the planning policy area because I found it full of conflicts with my moral values, and I have become much more involved in sort of basic information and graphics, maps, you know, it's sort of neutral—it's neutral aspects of planning. Every time I see Paul Davidoff, of course, he's getting me all involved in the moral issues, so there's all this tug.

Several clearly felt frustrated. The person who was perhaps the most neurotic of anyone in the sample expressed this feeling and some of the reasons why he thought he had been ineffective:

I feel frustrated about not having achieved more as a planner due to my psychological problems. I didn't enjoy meeting with neighborhood groups or going to meetings and I hate to give presentations.

Others expressed a pervasive cynicism about the environment in which they worked and their ability to have an impact on it. A regulatory planner was deeply cynical about the commitment of government to honest regulation:

I believe the thing that's being used by government now at various levels is what is called a partnership. And I say partnership? That's the last thing in the world I want. I don't want a partnership with the traffic cop on the corner—there's no partnership between me and him. He's protecting my life in what he is doing, but if I do something wrong, I don't want him partnershipping around here. I want him to enforce the law that he is supposed to enforce. Now we're getting back to things about the agency in general, and what I said early on about the failure of agencies to carry out their assigned role—not just from a professional or an ethical standpoint, they are not even meeting the requirements of the law! This is the pits!

Another, who worked in the middle level of a large state agency, explained his basic ideological framework and went on to his frustration about what he could actually do:

In college, as I started to read a little more deeply, I became committed to some form of socialism as a political philosophy, which I have maintained to date, and there's no adequate political expression of it in our country. I've certainly become more cynical about the possibility of having a concrete, tangible, positive impact through the narrow activities of my job. I've become more cynical about that. Back in the [1960s], we all thought that we were working on the New Jerusalem, we were going to create a better society for all. I'm much more realistic, both in terms of what can be accomplished through the present political structure in the country but also through the bureaucratic structures that we have to live with in our jobs. Cynical may be a bad word. Realistic might be a more appropriate word. I'm much more realistic about what can and can't be accomplished. So to some extent, one way in which I can still look at myself in the mirror after the job is to say, "Well, it may not go anywhere but at least I've done what was appropriate or right."

> I've got a file of memos, this whole thing of memos here. . . . Where
> have they gone? I don't know.

Among active planners, experience and the active exercise of their values
showed them that they could have an impact and reinforced their value
commitments. Among closet politicians, experience seemed to produce
frustration at how much needed to be done and passivity in the face of
such an enormous task.

Harmony and Dissonance in Planning Practice

As ideals, the roles used by the planners in this sample embodied rather
different values and goals. Each of these images represented a simplified
ideal, not a practical reality. Each involved particular moral commitments
on the part of its adherents. Each could evoke considerable commitment,
sometimes even in the face of a reality that made achievement of the ideal
difficult or frustrating. Some planners were clearer than others about
what these ideal commitments were. Some were flexible about interpret-
ing their meaning and boundaries, keeping one foot, as it were, in their
ideal but modifying their actual behavior to be effective in their particular
setting. Others interpreted and held to their ideals more rigidly. This
flexibility or rigidity was one explanation for the pattern of tension within
each role.

Traditional technicians hardly needed to articulate their ideal since
their actual behavior conformed to it. Technician activists seemed to
articulate the technical ideal more clearly, in part because in many
respects their behavior did not conform, but the technician role for them
was not simply a useful fiction. It did seem to be part of their own
professional identity, not something to be discarded lightly as their actual
behavior diverged from the ideal image.

This may have been partly because the role did embody a moral
commitment. However politically savvy and active they were, the technician activists still saw themselves as loyal servants to elected officials
who made the final decisions on planning issues. As long as they held to
this central principle, their divergence from other elements of the ideal
gave them little cause to experience a sense of dissonance.

A somewhat similar pattern could be seen among planners committed
to the ideal of active, goal-oriented planning. Active planners were
perhaps more likely to be articulate about their ideal simply because it
was still considered to be fairly new and not altogether accepted. For the
active planners, commitment to the image was also reinforced by their

ability to translate it into something that could be acted on in the real world.

For closet politicians, however, the moral commitment to achieve good ends, such as social justice or environmental preservation, could not be translated into effective action. Unlike the technician activists, who could still hold in practice to their central moral tenet, the closet politicians could not. A sense of dissonance and frustration was the result.

The passive hybrids were the one group for whom ideal role did not seem to have moral significance. They chose the hybrid role on their questionnaires but did not articulate it otherwise. They accepted it as legitimate, but an active, politicized stance did not have a great deal of relevance to their day-to-day planning activities. Still, there was a minority within this group who would have liked to see more results and who shared some of the frustration of the closet politicians.

Finally, the process planners were mapping out a fairly new image of the planner's role, largely by playing it in practice. It involved a commitment to facilitating an open planning process. This involved being responsive to, but still independent of, the various groups involved—elected officials, developers, and citizens. The process planners were morally committed to the idea that the public interest was most likely to emerge from a fair and participatory process. Not surprisingly, they were the group in the sample with the highest score on the scale measuring positive attitudes about citizen participation in planning. Perhaps because it was a role that seemed to emerge out of practical need, it was one that involved little sense of dissonance.

It is largely the emphasis in this study on the relationship between espoused theory and actual performance, between what planners wanted to do and what they could do, that produces the somewhat unwieldy typology of six roles. In essence, however, the roles portrayed here are quite similar to Rabinovitz's (1969) typology of technicians, brokers, and mobilizers. Our larger sample produced more variation among the technicians. While Rabinovitz had no closet politicians, Baum (1983) and Mayo (1982) seem to have found many. Our process and active planners bear a general resemblance to Rabinovitz's brokers and mobilizers.

Baum (1983), for his part, emphasized the way in which both personal role orientations and the politically and bureaucratically complex nature of planning made it difficult for planners to see results from their work—to make what they wanted to do match what they could do. He found that "most" of a sample of fifty planners in Maryland suffered from a sense of dissonance (Baum 1983) between what they had hoped to achieve as planners and what they could see in reality.

In this study, with a somewhat different kind of sample,[4] only 27 percent of the planners (twenty-six people) experienced dissonance of some kind (Table 6.7).[5] Those who experienced a sense of harmony in their work were largely planners whose ideal and actual roles matched. More important, they were also much more likely to be those who actually played politicized roles. These planners developed a variety of rather different styles of active planning that suited different personalities and political and organizational settings. However, all these politicized roles seem to have given the planners in them a sense of accomplishment.

Among the quarter of the sample who did experience feelings of frustration, the two sources of dissonance were similar if apparently not as important as those found by Baum (1983). A fairly small group of nine planners struggled with dissonance between their ideal and their actual roles. This included six closet politicians and three other planners who identified with the technical role but ended up playing a more value-committed and political one.

The greater source of dissonance, though, was the disparity between what planners wanted to see done and the constraints of the roles they chose to play. This was a conflict that also troubled two-thirds of the closet politicians, but it was also an issue for 42 percent of the traditional

TABLE 6.7

Tension within Roles

	Sources of Dissonance (percents)		
	Ideal Versus Actual Role	Seeing Results	Total Feeling Dissonance[a]
Technicians			
Traditional Technicians	4	42	42
Passive Hybrids	0	21	21
Technician Activists	0	0	0
More Active Planners			
Active Planners[b]	4	15	19
Process Planners	9	0	9
Closet Politicians	67	67	67
Total	10	23	27

Notes:
[a] Planners could feel dissonance from more than one source.

[b] This coding includes three planners who were somewhat cynical about their ideals but acted on them anyway.

technicians and 21 percent of the passive hybrids. The reasons these planners were unable to achieve the results they wanted turned on the interaction between two factors. One was their own personalities. The closet politicians and, to a lesser extent, the passive hybrids ideally wanted to play active, politicized roles, but in reality they chose to play reactive, technical ones. They were, in Needleman and Needleman's terms (1974), role incapacitated.

In addition, Baum (1983) suggests that planners feel isolated and lacking in influence over the use of their analysis because of the highly bureaucratic nature of planning. This clearly contributed to the sense of frustration of some of the planners in this sample, but it did not always have this effect. As one planner in New York said of the bureaucracy there:

> It tends to either break you and make you part of the system or it tends to make you try to evade it even more. It produces greater extremes of behavior—the greater level of frustration [or the feeling that] it's all right to be a little anarchistic.

Closet politicians overwhelmingly held middle- and lower-level positions in large bureaucracies. Others who were frustrated also tended to hold similar positions or were directors of regional agencies that seemed to have weak political support. More than half of the active planners, however, also worked at middle and lower levels and 40 percent worked in large bureaucracies. Only one of these planners struggled with a strong sense of frustration. The difference was that part of what made the activist planners active was their ability and will to search out or to create niches in the bureaucracy in which they had some autonomy to press for the issues to which they were committed. As we will see, only a few who had become cynics "became anarchistic" in revolt against the bureaucracy.

That a few planners held to images of the role that planning should play but which they could not act on suggests the power of moral commitments. That many did act on the values they held, with apparent results, was perhaps an even clearer measure of that power. In acting, and even in choosing not to act, though, all planners faced dilemmas—challenges from others to the moral values that underlay their images of their roles or conflicts between competing principles that were implicit in those images. It was these dilemmas that they discussed as issues of professional ethics.

7

Planners' Approaches to Ethics

The planners in the sample differed among themselves both in the way they thought about the role a planner should play in the policy process and in the roles they actually played. These roles drew, in turn, on rather different moral commitments and led the planners to raise rather different ethical issues. More fundamentally, the planners used somewhat different ways of thinking about ethics. These suggested that certain kinds of issues were within the realm of ethics while others were outside. These approaches also gave them principles for making ethical decisions.

Chapter 5 has already indicated that some of the planners in the sample took a characteristically deontological view of ethics while others used a more consequentialist one. This chapter explores the issues that were raised by the planners and how they reflected different ways of thinking about ethics. It also examines the relationship between roles and approaches to ethics and lays out the kind of ethical dilemmas that were particularly problematic for planners in various roles, taking various approaches to ethics.

The Typology of Approaches to Ethics

As chapter 5 explained, the planners were initially divided into three groups: those who took a primarily deontological approach; those who took a primarily consequentialist one; and a small group who seemed to be aethical. This set of distinctions, like the separation between technicians and the other roles, which it parallels, is sufficient to give some sense of how the planners approached ethical judgments; sometimes comparisons will simply be made between the sixty-three deontologists and the twenty consequentialists. (Of the remaining planners, nine had such unformed ideas about ethics that they could not be classified and four were considered aethical.)

Within each of these broad categories, not all the planners seemed to think alike about ethics. Different ways of thinking about both ends and means separated one group from another. Several distinct deontological approaches seemed to be in use. "Narrow deontologists" focused only on process and did not seem to consider ends to be within the realm of ethics at all. "Process deontologists" used an idea of the public interest as a process while "substantive deontologists" defined the public interest in terms of rights. At the other extreme, some consequentialist planners were more consumed with the idea of achieving the greatest good for the greatest number than others were. In between, there were two groups of planners who appeared to be essentially deontological in their approach to issues of means but nevertheless, as planners concerned with evaluating policy options, needed to have a consequentialist idea of the public interest as well. All these variations resulted in the typology of six approaches, plus the aethical planners.

Even though the planners had some difficulty articulating their ideas about ethics, most did seem to have a solid internal core of ideas that they drew on. Chapter 8 will make the argument that ethical values were in many cases acquired in childhood and adolescence and were brought with them into the field. Professional experience might modify or sharpen these moral values, but they were not just the sum of this experience. When they were asked what situations they had been involved in that raised ethical issues, the planners seemed to summon up their image of the realm of ethics and searched their experience for situations that seemed to fit. If they had none, they talked about the issues they thought were important in hypothetical terms instead. Over a series of such issues, a pattern of what lay inside and outside this realm could be determined, as could the way they described and analyzed these issues.

Ethics and Role

The relationship between approaches to ethics and role was very close. Moral values informed the choice of a role and shaped the planner's behavior in it. Experience in a role could also modify how a planner defined, thought about, or acted on ethical issues as well.

The relationship between the typology of roles and approaches to ethics is shown in Table 7.1. The fit between the two is hardly perfect. They did not measure the same thing, but the patterns are clearly understandable.

TABLE 7.1

Typology of Roles and Approaches to Ethics: Focus on Roles

Approach to Ethics	Roles (percents)					
	Traditional Technicians	Passive Hybrids	Technician Activists	Process Planners	Active Planners	Closet Politicians
Deontological						
Narrow Deontologists	19	21	20	9	0	0
Process Planners	8	0	0	64	11	0
Substantive Deontologists	0	14	10	9	15	67
Mixed Approaches						
Public Interest	46	36	60	10	0	22
Rule Utilitarians	0	7	0	0	27	0
Consequentialist						
Act Utilitarians	0	0	10	9	35	11
Aethical Planners	4	14	0	0	4	0
Vague Planners	23	7	0	0	8	0
Total	100	100	100	100	100	100
Number	26	14	10	11	26	9

150

Technicians did tend to take a predominantly deontological approach to planning, though not all deontologists were technicians by any means. More than 50 percent of each of the three groups of technicians used a narrow or a public interest perspective on ethics, with an additional sprinkling of people with the process or substantive perspectives. They focused on a concern with basic honesty, with responsibility to decision makers, and with the independence of the process of providing technical advice.

The predominant approach to ethics (62 percent) among active planners was a consequentialist or utilitarian one, though not all active planners were consequentialists. This way of thinking about ethics, which focuses on the evaluation of policies and of their benefits to society, seems appropriate to a more overtly political role by going beyond process to look at outcomes. However, it was also the process planners and active planners and closet politicians who took a substantive deonto-logical approach concerned with a commitment to rights (Table 7.2). Together they made up 79 percent of the substantive deontologists and shared a concern with citizen participation and with achieving social justice and environmental balance.

This discussion of planners' approaches to ethics begins with the three deontological approaches. As with the discussion of roles, the opposite, consequentialist extreme—the act utilitarian approach—is discussed next. This provides a clear background for understanding the two mixed approaches: rule utilitarianism and the public interest approach. These sections are followed by an examination of the aethical planners. All of these approaches posed characteristic ethical dilemmas, but these are simply raised here and will be explored in more detail in part 3, on actions.

Pure Deontologists

The pure deontologists made up 39 percent of the sample and included three rather different groups: narrow deontologists, process planners, and substantive planners. The narrow deontologists had the most restrictive view of ethics of any group in the sample while the substantive planners had the most inclusive one.

Narrow Deontologists

The eleven planners with a narrow deontological view of ethics defined only the legal and procedural issues, such as fairness, truth, and loyalty, as within the boundaries of ethics. As a result, they raised purely legal

TABLE 7.2
Typology of Roles and Approaches to Ethics: Focus on Approach to Ethics

Approach to Ethics	Roles (percents)						Total	
	Traditional Technicians	Passive Hybrids	Technician Activists	Process Planners	Active Planners	Closet Politicians	Number	Percent
Deontological								
Narrow Deontologists	46	27	18	9	0	0	11	100
Process Planners	17	0	0	58	25	0	12	100
Substantive								
Deontologists	0	14	7	7	29	43	14	100
Mixed Approaches								
Public Interest	46	19	23	4	0	8	26	100
Rule Utilitarians	0	12	0	0	88	0	8	100
Consequentialist								
Act Utilitarians	0	0	8	8	75	8	12	100
Aethical Planners	25	50	0	0	25	0	4	100

issues more than any other group (Table 7.3). Bribery, conflicts of interest, accepting kickbacks, and doing favors for influential people figured largely in their cases. Some had actual experience with illegal actions. One practical planner, not apparently given to fancies, thought she had probably been offered a bribe:

> I had an instance where a major commercial project wanted to occupy a building, and, you know, the contractor jokingly says to you, "Listen, it would be cheaper if I just sent you to Bermuda." And you know, you respond . . . the problem is you can't joke about things like that.

Like other planners as well, these planners did not define the boundaries of ethics by what experiences they had had but rather by what they thought of as central to professional ethics. Their first definition of professional ethics was that it was primarily related to legal problems. If they had no firsthand experience with such problems, they raised the issues hypothetically instead.

In effect, they worked out from there but generally only as far as the procedural issues that involved obligations within the bureaucratic and governmental system. Of all the procedural principles these planners raised, accountability was by far the most important (22 percent of all issues they discussed), followed by fairness and truthfulness. Often the examples they gave of procedural issues were also tinged with legal overtones.

On the central principle of loyalty, they accepted as basic the principle that a planner should be loyal to his or her agency and to decision makers as long as it did not entail illegal actions. Several described issues, not involving violations of law, in which decision makers' disregard of their analyses and recommendations had made them question this loyalty, but they all agreed with this planner, who said:

> You try to educate them, and if you lose, go back and go back and keep trying to convince them to accept your view.

These planners were certainly not raising as ethical issues large questions such as the purposes of planning. They rarely talked about what might be thought of as broader procedural issues—how open should the planning process be, for example. They did not use the idea of the public interest, and only one raised an issue of equity, and that in a rather equivocal way. These planners saw ethics as concerned with being loyal while at the same time keeping to the "straight and narrow," avoiding

TABLE 7.3

Relative Importance of Ethical Issues by Approach to Ethics

Approach to Ethics	Ethical Issues (percents)					Total	
	Legal	Duties of Justice	Account-ability	Public Interest	Substantive	Number	Percent
Deontological							
Narrow Deontologists	44	32	22	0	2	55	100
Process Planners	22	40	19	13	6	63	100
Substantive Deontologists	23	39	11	10	17	88	100
Mixed Approaches							
Public Interest	36	36	17	11	0	150	100
Rule Utilitarians	22	45	5	18	10	40	100
Consequentialist							
Act Utilitarians	26	25	20	21	8	80	100

154

the violation of minimum standards of honesty, fairness, and technical integrity.

The very narrowness of their view of ethics was their characteristic dilemma, though it was not really one that they could see or raise themselves. Loyalty, especially, bulked large among their principles, and with few other principles to balance it, they were sometimes asked by superiors to act in ways that a broader view of ethics might have found problematic.

As the planners with the narrowest view of ethics, it is perhaps not surprising to find that 46 percent were traditional technicians and an almost equal number (45 percent) were passive hybrids (27 percent) or technician activists (18 percent). For a few, both their narrow role and their narrow approach to ethics seemed to be associated with either extreme caution or some frustration in their work; the others were just ordinary technicians trying to do a job.

"Strict constructionist" Edward Smith, Jr., began his discussion of ethics by saying that bribery was the most obvious problem of ethics. Luckily it was not an issue in his city, and humorously he told of a misunderstanding created by an outside developer who had asked who he should pay for a zoning change. He was concerned, though, about the problem of possible favoritism in a fairly small community with what he called "buddy-buddy" networks. In particular, downtown businessmen had good access to elected officials and expected Smith to be an active participant in their revitalization efforts. This made him uncomfortable, feeling not only that it pushed him too much into the policy-making role but also that it placed him in a position to favor their interests more than was proper. Smith felt that he should not be an advocate for any single group—it would be unfair, in his mind, unethical—and he tried to limit his role to simply advising them about possible funding options. He said he did not socialize with people who were involved in development, and he did not accept lunches from developers.

Smith also explained that before he had come to the community, enforcement of the subdivision ordinance had been rather lax. This meant that his prodevelopment plan commission sometimes pressured him to recommend approval of inappropriate projects. He said that he usually could take the obvious way out and simply tell them that he could not do it under the city's ordinances. Indeed, Smith's major overriding ethical rule was to comply with the law and with officially enacted policies. If he did not have a law or policy on which to rely, he tried to get his plan commission to adopt one.

He was quick to add that where the issue was not one of an obvious legal violation, it was within the authority of the city manager, the plan commission, or the council to reject his recommendations. He said he was a loyal team player:

> In this town garage study, the manager and I have disagreed on some of the points of view in the proposal, but I've always kept our disagreements between us, and we are still arguing over it. When we get out in public—thank God he's usually been there to defend it himself, but if he wasn't, I would say, "The point of view here is . . . what we're trying to do is . . ." It would be inappropriate for me to stand up and say, "The report may say so and so but I think it's wrong." That sort of thing would be unethical.

Process Deontologists

The second group of pure deontologists were those who saw the public interest in terms of a fair planning process. These twelve planners saw their ethical duty as facilitating the process of determining policy by providing good information, trying to see that various groups were fairly represented, and keeping communication open. The result of the process was defined as being in the public interest, regardless of its specific content or consequences.

As might be expected, 58 percent of these planners played process-oriented roles (see Table 7.2). They were joined by two traditional technicians (17 percent) and three active planners (25 percent). Because of this range of roles, there were some differences in their images of how the process should work. In their view of ethics, they all included both loyalty to decision makers and a commitment to an open process, though in somewhat different proportions. Four, including the two technicians, particularly stressed that elected decision makers were the ones who made the definitive decision about the public interest. The others, including the three active planners, had images that emphasized an open political process in which the public interest would be determined through bargaining among interest groups and elected officials and in which planners would play an active role.

The pattern in Table 7.3 highlights their procedural orientation. They were among those with the least concern about legal issues and were among the most likely to raise all kinds of procedural issues, related both to duties of justice and to accountability. While they talked about cases related to the full range of procedural issues, they were more likely than any other group to have experience with dilemmas that turned on the openness of the planning process. One issue raised by several was a concern about the balance between their own ideas about the public interest and those of various other participants in the process.

For four of these planners, the concern with fairness also took the form of a secondary substantive commitment to social justice. This did not seem to be as central to their ethics as it was for substantive deontologists. It was more of a procedural concern for the underdog. They wanted disadvantaged groups to be represented in an open process.

Rebecca Giulini was one of the more active process planners. In talking about the ethical dilemmas raised by her work, openness and fairness were the central principles. She stressed the importance of giving honest and full information to participants in a planning process even if it would create controversy. She gave an example about trying to gain leverage to open up the process begun by the local school district that would lead to the closing of schools in areas where the number of children had declined. Knowing that such decisions were bound to create opposition, the district administration was keeping the process closed, not informing neighborhood groups of the criteria the district would be using. Indeed, it was not even clear whether they had developed criteria that could be justified on substantive grounds. Even if they had criteria, it was primarily the exclusion of groups with legitimate concerns that Giulini thought was unethical. She also stressed the importance, in dealing with developers, of being fair in evaluating their proposals and said that it was important in the early stages of discussion to guarantee that their plans would remain confidential even from the inquiries of elected officials. Otherwise, they would not be as willing to come in and talk openly.

However, she also could see the other side. Giulini talked about fairness to a community group, anxious to have development, which she thought was vulnerable to being taken advantage of by a developer with a proposal for a large mixed-use development. In this case, she did have opinions about what she thought would be a good outcome, but she was careful not to push her own opinions too far and did her best to bring all the parties to the table and to facilitate a compromise solution. The worst thing, Giulini thought, would be to try to close the planning process on such an issue prematurely. She felt that the nature of the process

> has ethical implications. I do seek a certain consistency in planning, as well as compromise and accommodation of legitimate interests in the community, and just how I steer a proposal through this process without attempting to color the course of events too much by my personal opinion, but still bring some intuition or skills to the task, poses at least potential dilemmas.

These process planners all took a purely deontological approach to ethics, focusing on the process and the procedural principles that would ensure its legitimacy. If they had a problem, this was it. The goodness of the consequences was not an issue they brought up as an ethical one. Implicitly they seemed to have faith that an open process would produce equitable results for the groups involved. This was not something that they focused on explicitly, although several of these planners did talk about their concern that in their communities it did not produce equitable results.

Substantive Deontologists

There were fourteen pure deontologists who did have a concern about the substantive content of policy. Table 7.3 shows that 17 percent of the ethical dilemmas they raised involved substantive planning issues, more than any other group. They were not primarily interested in whether the benefits of a policy outweighed its costs but rather whether it protected certain kinds of rights. As indicated in Table 7.2, this was a very diverse group, much more so than most of the others. The reason for this was that protecting these rights was not a simple matter of waving the flag and being in favor of apple pie. While most planners saw protecting rights as simply a duty of benevolence, not binding in all cases, these planners seem to have thought of this as involving serious, binding duties. This implied a requirement to act on them, but actually acting for these rights was controversial, and planners who cared about them had to face fairly directly their capacity and willingness to act politically. This was their central potential problem.

Six of these planners were committed to the idea of social justice, meaning that they believed in policies that would help low-income and disadvantaged groups get benefits, such as affordable housing in middle-income areas, tenants rights, or programs for the low-income elderly.

Five others were concerned primarily about environmental issues, though three expressed this as a concern for the rights of people to such things as clean water or air while the others were asserting the "rights" of nature to be preserved from development. A longtime state environmental planner reflected on the projects in which he had been involved and on how his own environmental values had changed over the years. He thought in retrospect that some of the projects had led to unjustifiable damage to the natural environment:

> We've done some things that in hindsight we shouldn't have—resort parks with golf courses, lodges, and restaurants. I never questioned

it at the time, but as I get older, I've come to have more sensitivity to the landscape and I think that golf courses are not a good use for the land. We were criticized at the time, but I didn't support the idea of doing harm intentionally. Now I think we should have considered more alternatives. In the end, I'd argue for the land over the people—you shouldn't harm the land.

The final three planners in this group were concerned about both equity and the environment and argued that, despite common perceptions to the contrary, the two were not in conflict:

I don't perceive that the environmental values are at odds with the social values. I know that's a common argument that is used by developers and people who are on that side of it—"all these crazy environmentalists who are keeping housing from being built." Well, I think that's not really true. The people who are keeping housing from being built are, well, the financial institutions and also the neighborhood groups—that's a real deterrent and that's where I can see some ethical problems that could affect us.

Moreover, as deontologists, their commitment to duties of justice, such as fairness, truth, and openness, was also strong. The claims of rights could, and sometimes did, conflict with other deontological principles, but for them, ends, however important, did not outweigh wrong means. The planner who said that environmental and equity values did not conflict was actually raising the conflict between equity values and the right of residents to control the development of their communities:

On the one hand, you know that neighbors do have a right to say what happens in their community. They're affected by it more than anybody else and our laws are set up to make sure they know what's going on. They can attend public hearings, and that's good, but on the other hand, there is this very strong parochial interest in keeping things just like they are. That's understandable, but you're certainly not going to get housing built if you have that kind of a situation.

These examples give a sufficient sense of the controversial nature of these substantive issues. The responses of the planners to the possibility of controversy took two very different forms. Four of the planners were active planners (29 percent in Table 7.2) and one was a technician activist (7 percent). These were all people who took on their issues fairly directly. They were the 63 percent who were optimists about the ability to balance

competing definitions of the public interest (Table 7.4). Two were advocate planners, working at the neighborhood level to organize low-income
residents and to help them voice their political demands effectively. Two
others worked to place affordable housing in high-cost, middle-class
suburban areas.

At the other extreme were the six closet politicians who made up 43
percent of the substantive deontologists in Table 7.2. They cared about
"justice" and "the environment." They seemed pressed by their active
consciences, which would not allow them to ignore problems that most
other planners were quite willing to leave alone. Sometimes this seemed
to come from a moral meticulousness, reflecting a kind of general obses-
sion with detail, but they did not or could not act on their convictions.
This was described by one of them as a "passive nonethical" approach:

> I know a little about passive resistance and I know about passive
> aggression, having read about it, and I think there is sort of maybe
> an area there that I haven't given much thought to 'til today, where
> there are some of these same sorts of reactions to situations that
> people who work in large, powerful bureaucracies, who have fairly
> high-level positions of responsibility, they just turn off certain
> situations. I guess I would call that as the passive nonethical.

The more actively a planner worked for rights, the more likely it was
that the ethical issues he or she raised would be concerned primarily with
tactics rather than with the ultimate goal. Only closet politicians were
likely to talk in broad terms about the need for more equitable social
policy or environmental sensitivity.

Tom Stuart was not a planner motivated by a commitment to rights,
so a new planner, Grace Sumner, also an active planner, will give a sense
of this approach. She was the planning director in Denton, an affluent
suburb in a sprawling metropolitan area. Personally, in addition to her
administrative duties, she was especially involved in the department's
efforts to encourage the town to diversify its housing stock and population
by allowing for higher density, lower cost housing. Sumner justified it as
being for the benefit of the community:

> From a social-equity standpoint, I think there is a public interest in
> making housing opportunities available to a range of people. Partic-
> ularly in a place like Denton that is increasingly wealthy, the more
> stratified you become, the less well the society operates.

TABLE 7.4

Approach to the Public Interest by Approach to Ethics

Approach to Ethics	Approach to the Public Interest (percents)					Total	
	Optimist	Blind Faith	Technician	Cynic	Vague	Number	Percent
Deontological							
Narrow Deontologists	0	0	0	0	0	0	—
Process Planners	44	11	33	0	11	9	100
Substantive Deontologists	63	12	0	12	12	8	100
Mixed Approaches							
Public Interest	28	6	56	11	0	18	100
Rule Utilitarians	50	0	25	25	0	4	100
Consequentialist							
Act Utilitarians	50	25	12	12	0	8	100
Aethical Planners	0	0	100	0	0	1	100

This sounds like a consequentialist rationale, but fundamentally her concern was with the rights of people to live where they choose and not to be closed out by discriminatory housing and zoning practices.

Knowing that this was a volatile issue, Sumner had gradually built legitimacy with her elected officials and local citizen groups. In raising the topic of higher density, affordable housing, she was committed to the idea of an open process in which real exchange and movement could take place on both sides. Since her motivation came largely from an internal commitment to social justice, Sumner also worried somewhat about co-optation, recognizing that it was difficult to work against the political grain and easy to let up or slide into acceptance of the dominant community values:

> I think probably when you work for any government, and you're part of a rather small group of decision makers, that you probably come to think of things as open when maybe if you were looking at it from the outside you would think that they weren't. Not that you're doing something wrong, as much as maybe you should be pushing more for something, advocating rather than sort of softening things and making compromises. I can see how that process does go on, and it's not so much being confronted with yes-or-no decisions and you say yes when you know you should say no, it's just that you work with people over time and you find that you're not quite as high-minded as you were when you first got out of school. What could happen is that you could get sort of seduced into thinking that you're doing the right thing when maybe you're not.

In her ethics cases, Sumner raised not only issues related to social equity but also procedural ones about being evenhanded about information given out to different groups, the need to be careful about open notice of meetings, and about fairness to developers and employees.

Closet politician Sam French, with his equity and environmental values and his sense of frustration, could hardly have been a greater contrast. He started right in by talking about the difficulty of raising equity issues, giving an example of a housing plan he had worked on in his previous position. He talked in general terms about the distribution of political power and the mobilization of bias that made it difficult for many people to see this as a really pressing issue of justice. Essentially, though, raising the housing issue in these terms had upset his superiors, and, not liking the conflict, French had ultimately switched into the research job. Still, he thought that not raising the housing issue would have been a sin of omission, and almost because he had found a bureaucratic niche where he could avoid such conflicts, his conscience would not be stilled. French justified his passive role by arguing that people who could have a greater impact had a stronger obligation to act, saying:

> If you feel you have an impact, yes, then you have a moral obligation. If you can honestly say that what you do will have no impact, then probably there's less of a—strictly speaking—moral obligation to fight the good fight.

He never actually said that he did not take action, talking in general terms instead, but during the course of the interview he gave no examples other than the initial housing case where he had acted on the issues of justice and environmental preservation, which he raised as central to planning ethics.

Consequentialists

The most common form of consequentialism is utilitarianism. It is concerned with producing, in Bentham's (1948) formulation: "the greatest happiness for the greatest number." As this suggests, the public good was classically thought of in terms of pleasure or pain, though this has more recently been interpreted in terms of benefits and costs, either in general or in monetary terms.

Utilitarian approaches take two forms. In the original, more radical version, generally known as "act utilitarianism," each action is supposed to be assessed according to its consequences. While this sounds tremendously cumbersome for the conduct of day-to-day life, John Stuart Mill ([1865] 1985) thought that experience would provide rules of thumb that people would use in an everyday way. However, these would not take on the character of hard-and-fast rules. Any action could be assessed according to the pleasure and pain it would produce. In planning terms, for example, routine decisions could be made using the guidance provided by ordinances and plans. Day-to-day interactions with others could rely on rules of thumb, such as being fair and open. Full-dress analysis of benefits and costs would be reserved for new plans, policies, large projects, or significant interpersonal conflicts. In any such analysis, the pros and cons of both means and ends would be on the table.

The other form of utilitarianism, "rule utilitarianism," as its name suggests, takes a more moderate approach that accepts the use of stable rules about such things as telling the truth or being fair. It developed as a response to criticisms that act utilitarianism could not adequately deal with the need to ensure some basic moral rights. Thus, the general nature of a practice such as telling the truth would be evaluated in terms of its consequences. If it was determined that, in general, telling the truth produced more benefits than costs for society, then it would become a rule that should always be obeyed even if, in an individual case, it could be shown that the bad consequences would outweigh the good ones (Rawls 1955; Urmson 1953).

The idea of establishing such rules in some formal way seems rather absurd, but people often seemed to think loosely in rule utilitarian terms when they gave reasons why moral rules were good for a society or a profession: "You shouldn't lie because lying is bad for the credibility of the profession, and, besides, it's wrong." The first argument would be a utilitarian one, the second a deontological one, but there was nothing unnatural about using them together.

Act Utilitarians

The twelve planners who were act utilitarians stood at the opposite end of the spectrum of approaches from the pure deontologists. Most had a general, consequentialist idea of the public interest as the greatest good for the greatest number, though two had more specific substantive goals that they accepted as serving the public good. All but three of these planners, that is, 75 percent, were active planners, and this group included many of the most energetic, some might say the most driven, people in the sample (see Table 7.2). Half were optimists about balancing everyone's ideas of the public interest (see Table 7.4).

Consequentialism was an ethical approach that could give form and legitimacy to these planners' activism. Indeed, it highlighted some of the characteristic aspects of their role. Much of what they actually did to pursue their goals was to make technical arguments that their proposals would serve the long-run benefit of the community, so analysis was important to them.

The importance of analysis was most clearly revealed in this study when some situation arose where they thought analysis had been inadequate or dishonest. As politicized planners, they accepted the possibility that analysis could be made to prove a point or to avoid one, and they certainly put the best face they could on proposals they favored. They themselves, though, still seemed to value honest analysis. Having a reputation for honesty was a necessity, and one described in some detail the ins and outs of a disagreement she was having with another agency over the analysis of a controversial project, concluding:

> I don't think that they can adequately challenge the veracity of my information. I think mine is good information. I think they know it, and I know that the stuff that they're peddling is just bullshit, and I don't think they're that stupid that they don't know that. But when the pieces of information that you trip over and ignore are the ones that portray the developer's proposal in a bad light, and the ones that you analyze and put forward to the decision makers are the ones that put the developer's proposal in a good light, you have to question that it really is a random pattern.

If analysis was important, though, so was political strategy. These planners did not appear to view deontological principles, such as loyalty, fairness, openness to public input, or even truthfulness, as inherent duties, at least in a professional context. Issues related to duties of justice made up a smaller proportion of their ethical cases than they did for any other group (see Table 7.3). This rather narrow view of procedural ethics would be compatible with an act utilitarian perspective that would emphasize calculating the benefits and costs of action whether it involved means or ends.

A major premise of act utilitarian ethics is that it ought, in general, to produce the same ethical behavior as deontological ethics because being truthful or fair could be shown to produce the best consequences in the long run. One neighborhood planner provocatively put it this way in relation to his own behavior. Talking about a situation where he had to choose between being loyal to city officials and keeping a promise to a neighborhood group, he showed how he had considered the relative consequences of each option:

> I thought that if the neighborhood leaders would have ever found out about me that I'd have no more support from the neighborhood—they would say, "Joe Blow—holy cow." At the same time, even if the city got sore now, they were bound to hold me in higher regard or respect as a guy who can't be bought. I knew that you can't really hurt yourself that much by being ethical—doing the right thing. You can look at those very qualities Machiavellianly, too—that is, that people who people think are honest, trustworthy, and reliable—they like it! Don't you? Those are commodities which are pretty much well-thought-of.

These planners' consequentialist approach did not mean that they lied, capriciously favored one developer over another, or gave out confidential information. Generally, they did not, but they did seem to think strategically about how the process could be used to achieve the results they thought were good.

This view of procedural principles was the seed of their characteristic ethical problem, the problem of dirty hands. Since they had strong commitments to achieving ends they defined as good, and a more strategic view of means than deontological planners, they could convince themselves that a good end could sometimes justify a means that harmed others.

Pure consequentialists talked about ethics in a very different way from the way deontologists did. Most important, they talked primarily about good policies and how to achieve or preserve them and only secondarily about procedural principles such as loyalty or truthfulness. To get an idea of what these planners were like, we must have another new character since activist Tom Stuart was not an act utilitarian either.

Paul Michaud was the assistant director for project planning in the planning department in the large city of New Bristol. He had previously worked in a somewhat similar capacity for a state development agency in another state. His previous experience in that powerful and somewhat corrupt agency had given him a rather cynical view of politics and the role of both development interests and the citizens in it. However, the more open but highly competitive politics of New Bristol somewhat modified his view. The excitement and challenge of working in the political process fascinated him. Michaud believed that citizens and decision makers would act out of their own self-interest but that their approach might be shaped in part by his own driving commitment to work for what he defined as good planning in general and as good projects in particular.

Michaud got into talking about ethics by way of talking about how much he had liked working for an agency that had real power and could undertake large projects. With a certain amount of enthusiasm, he talked about how developers had courted the staff in his previous agency because they did have influence. One had even offered to split the syndication fee for setting up a project if Michaud would use his influence to get it approved. He said that it was impossible not to at least consider an offer of tens of thousands of dollars:

> For a second I may have thought, "My God! Here's my chance to make a bundle—and my chance to wreck myself professionally," because I must have only been about thirty-five or thirty-six when the offer was made. I still had a lot of years to go, and there was also the chance of being caught.

In his present job, the open and very contentious politics of New Bristol was the major challenge. Michaud talked about several projects that he had been involved in getting off the ground, projects he clearly felt were in the public interest. How did he know? It was a combination of doing analysis, making professional judgments, and dealing with affected interests:

> I think I come to what's best for the city from my own professional background and training. I have to evaluate my planning goals, my city's other goals, and come up with a solution which is a balanced proposal for the area. [It also comes] from my knowledge of the issues in the city, from my communications with people in the city—groups, individuals, and so forth. All that weaves into some knowledge of or sense of what is best for the city, and that's probably what the greatest kind of a challenge is. I will, if I think it's best for the city, push a program that I believe is right as far as I can push.

One such project, to encourage the construction of a large industrial facility, was raising a current problem. Michaud thought that the site, chosen in negotiations between the developer and the mayor, was not a good one because it was too far from the city's mass transit system. His staff was busy producing analysis to convince the mayor that another site would be a better one.

This issue, he said, didn't really raise a question of loyalty since the process was still in its early stages, but it did lead Michaud to talk about another case in which his department, under considerable political pressure from powerful interests in the city, had backed a project that he was sure was misguided. He finally had become so frustrated that he had ended up questioning his loyalty to the department and the mayor in light of his idea of the public interest.

Indeed, his interview was full of talk about good and bad policies and calculations about the risk and usefulness of tactics, and toward the end Michaud said:

> I hardly ever think of right and wrong. Going over this ethics, you know, ethical implies not doing certain things because they are *wrong* and doing certain things because they are *right*—quotes around right and wrong. I don't ever think I . . . I think I may put that in the equation, but it's not really up in my head when I make the calculation.

His ethics, about which he had strong feelings that he could articulate, were more concerned with good and bad than with right and wrong.

Mixed Approaches

In the middle, between the pure deontologists and the pure or act utilitarians, there were two groups who used approaches to ethics that seemed to combine elements of both deontological and consequentialist thinking. One group was the rule utilitarians, whose basic approach was consequentialist but who, perhaps for the kind of utilitarian reasons described earlier, accepted procedural ethical limits that were rather deontological in nature. The other group was the public interest planners. They took a basically deontological approach to ethics except that they had a consequentialist view of the public interest.

Rule Utilitarians

The eight rule utilitarians were, on the whole, quite similar to the act utilitarians except that they drew back somewhat from the implication that means had no ethical standing except as they contributed to good consequences. These "mixed" consequentialists accepted a basic core of absolute rules that should not be violated, just like a deontologist. Beyond this basic level, they were utilitarians, calculating what they thought was in the public interest and flexible in the tactics they were willing to use to achieve it.

Like the act utilitarians, all but one of these planners, that is, 88 percent, were active planners (see Table 7.2). They worked as lobbyists, as state bureaucrats, and as local planners. Most were committed to substantive values, urban, environmental, design, or mobility, and they saw these values as serving the broad long-run interest of the community. Also like the act utilitarians, more than a quarter (28 percent) of the ethical issues they raised were concerned with substantive values or the public interest (see Table 7.3).

The nature of their work and their strong value commitments exposed them to the same pressures as the act utilitarians to argue that the end justified the means, even if the means might be problematic. However, these planners were not willing to do everything and anything to achieve what they thought were good policies. The procedural principles that they said they thought were basic and should not be violated were primarily duties of justice, including legal constraints, truthfulness, fairness, and maintaining an open planning process. A lobbyist took as his image of the quintessential consequentialist community organizer Saul Alinsky (1946):

> I admire Saul Alinsky and agree with him up to a point, but I wouldn't go so far as to say that the end would justify all means. I wouldn't lie, and I don't think I would stab someone in the back.

Another started to say that he would use any means to achieve an important end but then reconsidered:

> I'm pragmatic. When the end isn't that important to me, then I go through the ethical process. If the end was really important . . . I don't think . . . I've never really thought of anything being so important that the end product would justify *anything*. I do draw lines.

There was no way to know whether the planners who adopted this mixed strategy would justify the rules on consequentialist grounds, but the end result looked like rule utilitarianism.

Activist Tom Stuart was such a rule utilitarian. He saw the public interest as concrete results:

> I think it's realizing or seeing, on the ground or in law, some tangible item—a building or a park or a piece of legislation. Something that serves (I know this sounds hokey) to help the citizens of the state more than they were before. It benefits them in a positive fashion.

Like Michaud, he talked about the good projects he had been involved in developing or lobbying for and about bad ones he had helped to kill or modify. Most of Stuart's cases involved tactical issues as well. The central focus was on what principles were inviolate in the face of either pressures or temptations to "cut corners" in order to get things through the legislature.

In the case of a wetlands bill, he had fought a series first of substantive and then of budgetary battles, presenting the technical case but also calling in some political obligations owed to the department and drumming up support by environmental groups. These actions, Stuart said, presented only tactical and not ethical issues. Another case was not so clear:

> There were a couple of proposals to modify the recreation areas program, one of which I was absolutely convinced would have

destroyed the program. We—the department—figured out a strategy to scuttle this plan, and, I mean, we really did a number on it. I guess we sort of snuck around the back door and we played the politicians' game, and we basically killed it in committee. It never even saw the light of day. [On the other bill] there was a Senate version that we didn't like and there was a House version that we didn't like, and we went through the process of being neutral on the outside, to everybody involved, but behind the scenes we just played on the natural hatred of the Senate against the House. We got the Senate to kill the House version and the House to kill the Senate version. Whether that was unethical, I don't know. The traditional planning approach would be to go ahead and convince them and show why philosophically they were bad. However, we knew that would have been time consuming, it might not have worked, and at that point, I guess, we did feel that the end result justified whatever means we had to take. I did feel bad about it, not that I felt that this was unethical . . . personally, I mean, in terms of my personal ethics, I didn't violate my personal ethics.

Q: What would you include in your personal ethics?

I think lying—I don't mean not telling white lies, we all do that, and everybody has budgets and plays with numbers [and here he talked about pressures on technical judgments and strategies for dealing with that] and being, well, I like to think of myself as being nonprejudiced. When I start generalizing that this person is like that person and because I don't like that person I'm not going to like this one. . . . This guy came up with a flaky bill, and I didn't even look at the bill because he's come up with flaky bills in the past. Whenever you prejudge something . . .

So truth and fairness and, as Stuart talked some more, a certain degree of openness with the public made up the baseline, but that left lots of room for strategic choices. While some rule utilitarians were more "strict" than this, he was not unusual.

Public Interest Planners

The single largest group in the sample, in terms of approach to ethics, was the group of twenty-six public interest planners. Unlike the rule utilitarians, the public interest planners took an approach to ethics that was much more like that taken by the pure deontologists. However, they added to this basic orientation a consequentialist idea of the public interest.

It is not difficult to see why this would have been a common approach. In our society, people commonly think of ethics in terms of right and wrong, rules and duties. Even the consequentialists did this. Pure consequentialist Paul Michaud talked almost in puzzlement about not thinking about right and wrong, and one of the rule utilitarians said, "When the end isn't that important to me, then I go through the ethical process," meaning that he followed deontological rules. Thus, deontologists were simply using the most commonly accepted idea of ethics. However, people in a policy profession really needed some principle that would provide a guideline for identifying good policy. For planners who did not accept a substantive deontological or a procedural definition of the public interest, this need was filled by the consequentialist idea of the public interest.

Most of these public interest planners were technical planners: 46 percent were traditional technicians and another 42 percent were divided almost evenly between passive hybrids and technician activists (see Table 7.2). When it came to thinking about whose idea of the public interest should predominate, 56 percent were technicians (see Table 7.4).

Their fundamental ethical approach was a fairly narrow, bureaucratically oriented, deontological one, not unlike the narrow deontologists. There was a strong tendency to identify professional ethics with control of corruption, conflicts of interest, and doing favors, not because they worked in communities that posed these problems—only a few did—but because that was just how they thought about ethics (see Table 7.3). Accountability was a fairly important issue for them since it was an aspect of the technical role, but in this they were not very different from the process planners or even the act utilitarians, who were especially concerned about keeping confidences. A bit like the rule utilitarians, their consequentialist idea of the public interest helped to prevent this commitment from becoming unquestioned or uncritical. They had an image of the planning process in which decision makers made the final decisions, which they would loyally accept, but their own role was to make the strongest technical case for what, in their professional judgment, would best serve the community.

They thought about the public interest in two related but slightly different ways. Half of them talked about a concern with a project or policy's broad, long-term impacts on the community. Here a planner talked about this as an institutional responsibility:

> The planning board's function—institutionally, our charge is the future generations of county residents. My dealing with the imple-

menting agencies and so on is [from] the long-term or the comprehensive perspective as opposed to the short-term and the expedient
thing.

Another third of the planners used a formal definition of the public
interest (Leys and Perry 1959). Laws, plans, and policies were adopted
after research and public discussion to express what the broad, long-term
interests of the community were. When asked how he would know that
something was in the public interest, a planner from west Texas first said:

> I'm not sure I can answer that. I think the plans themselves
> articulate policy and those policies articulate the public interest. Is
> it in the public interest to grow in a contiguous kind of fashion or is
> it in the public interest to let people scatter farther out? We've
> decided that it really isn't in the public interest to let people extend
> water and sewer lines anywhere they want and build in floodways.

Both of these definitions of the public interest were used by planners
other than those using a mixed deontological and consequentialist approach, but among the public interest planners, 42 percent used a broad,
long-term view and 35 percent used a formal one, compared with 22 and
13 percent, respectively, for the sample as a whole.

These public interest planners were not committed to particular
substantive goals, but they did have, in the broad, long-term idea of the
public interest, an independent criterion for judging the goodness of
policies. Thus, it was perhaps not surprising that they raised issues of
political pressure on technical judgments (13 percent of all issues) more
often than the narrow deontologists (5 percent), who did not use any idea
of the public interest. These were often situations where a planner's own
idea of the public interest conflicted with that of a superior.

Technician activist Richard Breitman and passive hybrid George
Walters both serve as examples, particularly of the role of the public
interest in identifying ethical issues like these. Breitman began with a
couple of obvious issues—bribery, which he had some experience with
in a previous job some years before, and not violating the law even if he
disagreed with it. The latter issue led naturally to the question of loyalty
and policy disagreements. He talked about how he expected his staff to
be loyal and how he, in turn, was loyal to the mayor.

However, Breitman was quick to point out several situations where
that loyalty had conflicted with what he thought was in the public interest.
He gave the example of an area zoned for commercial use that the mayor
wanted to rezone to industrial in an effort to attract additional industry.

Breitman thought that it was a poor idea: There were some retail stores in the area that would have been made nonconforming. In the end, he went along but said:

> I'm not admitting anything as far as being unethical is concerned . . . that might be close.

Walters, who had worked in his community for thirty years and fit into its political scene, raised a set of issues similar to those of Smith and Breitman: not taking small gifts, avoiding conflicts of interest, being fair, and being careful to keep some kinds of information confidential in a fairly small, close-knit community where he knew most of the developers.

He also raised several larger issues involving conflicts between loyalty and other principles. In one case, Walters faced a choice between loyalty and honesty. The chairman of the planning board had a direct but undeclared conflict of interest in a case coming up for decision. The fundamental question was whether to blow the whistle on the chairman, but for Walters this decision against loyalty was made easier because of his judgment about the public interest. As he described it:

> I felt that in that situation the community was the higher responsibility. The community would be shortchanged because the developer had a project that was not a good proposal. It was in the flight pattern of the airport, and I felt that locating in that area and placing a subdivision with families and children gave me lots of concerns of conscience, and I just couldn't let that pass.

These public interest planners were practical people, using analysis, existing policy, and technical judgment to make planning recommendations. Even so, there was still sometimes an intuitive quality that crept into the way they described the process of making decisions, an intuitive quality that seemed characteristically deontological. On procedural ethical issues, they listened to their consciences, and even when decisions involved a substantial analytical component, some still saw the process as at least partly intuitive. As one said, sometimes

> the conscious process—it is a negative, it keeps you from coming up with this answer, and you're sitting there, looking at numbers and reading laws and getting facts and all of this, and really, the answer is beyond your putting all that together. It is not possible— the more you muddle with it, the worse it may get—and somehow, when I'm able to get my whole being, my mind and my body and

my thought, into neutral, the answer comes to me. There used to be an expression about your conscience being a wee small voice and you have to listen to it, and the same is true in professional issues.

This was not a way that the more rationalistic teleological planners talked about making ethical decisions.

Aethical Planners

Finally, the four aethical planners seemed to embody the consequences of having no ethical standards at all. It is difficult to make any generalizations in such an uncharted area based on a group of four people. These planners did not seem to be actively evil. However, they did not accept with certainty even the idea that legal issues were ethical in nature. The questionnaire, for instance, included two questions involving legal issues. One asked about bribery and the other about conflicts of interest. Three of these planners checked only one of these as clearly posing an issue of ethics and one checked neither. This pattern was confirmed in their interviews, which indicated that they had very impoverished ideas of ethics.

A couple of examples of the cases they raised give a sense of why they seemed aethical. One youngish planner spent most of his interview describing how he had gotten involved in a private business that used data that he developed in his job with a public agency. He accepted the idea that other people would consider this a conflict of interest. In fact, he was worried about this aspect of it, but he also justified his behavior by explaining how frustrated he had become with the passivity of his agency and how this was a way of using the results of his work.

Another planner took on a project after his colleague had refused it on the grounds that it violated the procedural regulations of the program under which it was funded. The planner who finally did it was not motivated by a commitment to the project itself, and he was quite clear about his friend's objections and the fact that the project violated the rules. He simply did not seem to feel that this mattered.

These were the most striking examples they gave, which suggested a very narrow and rather uncertain definition of the realm of ethics. These planners also raised a number of other rather narrow issues in a more conventional way, but it seemed characteristic that their definitions of the realm of ethics were, at least in some cases, quite uncertain. They gave examples of experiences that they thought others would define as ethical in nature but about which they were not sure. Since these fell in the category of legal issues, which others overwhelmingly defined as clearly posing ethical problems, this suggested an unusually limited view of ethics.

These planners all worked in situations that either were corrupt or produced disappointment and cynicism. They were not the only ones who had become cynics, however, or who worked in corrupt political systems, raising the question of why only these four should find themselves apparently armed with no ethical standards at all. In actuality, these four were only the most extreme examples of a pattern that did affect other planners as well and that will be explored more in chapter 8 on factors that shaped planners' ethical values and then in chapters 10 and 11 on action.

Working in a corrupt environment seemed to have negative consequences for most of the planners who did it. The two here were simply the most obvious examples. If ethical principles were lost, a kind of cynicism resulted. One planner who had begun her career in a very corrupt, machine-dominated city said:

> The system was so closed . . . I didn't like it at all. It was very upsetting. There was a lot of grumbling about it all the time, but there was no choice if you wished to retain your job. I have a feeling that if I had stayed there, I would have just become very burnt out, very cynical.

Not all aethical planners worked in corrupt communities, though, and perhaps the two who did not were the more interesting because they suggest that overt corruption is not the only force that can undermine a commitment to ethics. Both of these planners were simply examples of the corrosive power of cynicism to undermine the idealism that may be a prerequisite for an ethical perspective.

The most troubling case was that of a planner whose only image of the role of the planner was a technical one but who, it seemed, should have been playing a more active role. He had brought to planning a strong interest in environmental issues and in seeing results from planning, but his training in the traditional technical role, and the general support of that role by his department, had convinced him that advocacy or the injection of personal values into his work was not professionally appropriate. He did work as an environmental planner for some time but finally left it in frustration for more technically oriented work. He did not define protecting the environment as an ethical issue, even on the questionnaire. When asked about his ethical values, he floundered. Several principles,

such as honesty, loyalty, and equity, were suggested as things that others
had talked about, but he replied:

> None of them strike me as very crucial. My approach to planning is
> that it is a job and I don't have the illusion or the delusion that I am
> necessarily constructing some sort of great social fabric or some-
> thing that is so important that I have to worry about the nature of
> the fabrication. I look upon my job as to anticipate needs within an
> organization and put in an honest day's work in solving them and to
> be reasonably creative about it and efficient. I really haven't thought
> about this kind of thing. Probably the trouble I'm having with all of
> this is that I don't think I've portrayed my ethical values very well.
> It comes out that I believe in a good honest day's work, and that's
> not really it.
> Q: Well, what is it?
> Well, I do believe in basic honesty and I'm fairly oriented toward
> principles—certain principles, they may not be . . . and they have
> to do with social issues of our times. In fact, I'm very opinionated
> about a lot of those.
> Q: Do you draw a line between your opinions and your job?
> Oh yeah, I do it all the time, and it is really not that hard to—or at
> least we think it's not. Maybe we're a lot more opinionated in our
> so-called objective assessments than we think we are, but it's not
> hard to look at things with a methodology that requires you to pick
> up all the facets and present them even if they work against the sort
> of decision that you would have liked to have seen if you could
> make it yourself.

This was an able planner who apparently had a strong interest in seeing
results, but his image of what his own role should be denigrated these
qualities and supported only the use of his technical skills. This left him
open to frustration and to a cynicism that did not allow him to identify
with the idea that planning was "constructing some sort of great social
fabric." It was not surprising that his idea of professional ethics sounded
thin and incoherent even to himself.

Conclusion

The planners in this sample raised a wide range of legal, procedural, and
substantive issues of ethics, but the weight they placed on each of these
kinds of issues varied from one person to another. Virtually everyone had

cases in their own experience in which they had dealt with deontological issues of legality and process, though this was less true of legal issues simply because most planners worked in communities where the politics were fairly clean. In addition, fully 84 percent used the idea of the public interest either generally (26 percent) or in their specific ethics cases (58 percent).

While these definitions of the realm of ethics were common to most planners, the way they thought about ethics varied considerably accord- ing to whether they took a basically deontological or a consequentialist view of ethics and what kind of role they played as planners. Technicians of all kinds took a deontological view (see Table 7.1), emphasizing the importance of legality, of duties of justice, and of accountability (Table 7.5). This role, of course, imposed accountability as a particular ethical value since the technicians' responsibility to the public was served indirectly through their service to elected officials. In addition, the nature of the role focused attention away from ends, which were largely consid- ered to be the province of those officials, and toward basic honesty and bureaucratic obligations. This was reflected in their view of ethics, which was also more legal and procedural.

Sixty-two percent of the active planners took a consequentialist view of ethics while most of the rest had a deontological concern with rights (see Table 7.1). Their ideas of rights or of the public interest provided the goals toward which they actively worked. These goals were central both to their view of ethics and to their professional identities. Almost a quarter of the ethics cases they raised involved these ends (see Table 7.5). They were exceeded in this only by the closet politicians, who were committed to rights but did not act.

Finally, the process planners were overwhelmingly deontologists (see Table 7.1). Their idea of the public interest as a process shows up in the high proportion of their cases that involved duties of justice or procedural issues, such as fairness and openness—the highest of any of the groups (see Table 7.5). Again, their moral commitment to these procedural values shaped the facilitating role they played in reality.

The simple distinction between consequentialist and deontological approaches to ethics highlights much of the basic difference among planners with different approaches to planning, but from the point of view of ethics itself, one of the most interesting things about these planners was perhaps the variety of approaches they took. These primarily in- volved a number of different combinations of deontological and conse- quentialist elements, though three involved quite different interpretations within a deontological framework. This would seem to suggest that, empirically at least, many of these people in a policy profession found it

TABLE 7.5

Relative Importance of Ethical Issues by Role

Role	Ethical Issues (percents)					Total	
	Legal	Duties of Justice	Accountability	Public Interest	Substantive	Number	Percent
Traditional Technicians	34	37	16	10	3	50	100
Passive Hybrids	35	38	18	88	1	53	100
Technician Activists	31	34	16	14	5	47	100
Active Planners	31	39	7	13	10	38	100
Process Planners	22	47	15	13	3	37	100
Closet Politicians	20	39	9	18	14	29	100

useful to have an ethical framework that could balance concerns with both means and ends. Because there was no single obvious way that this should be done, planners developed a variety of options.

The three deontological perspectives all drew primarily from Judeo-Christian traditions, but their specific forms were shaped by professional influences as well. The narrow deontologists followed most closely the Progressive idea of the neutral expert. The process and substantive deontologists both seem to have been using newer and rather different, post-1960s, politically active roles that were generated by, or at least required them to have, a broader view of ethics than one focusing largely on basic honesty and bureaucratic obligations. While the difference between older and newer ways of thinking about planning was especially clear in these three approaches to a deontological professional ethic, this change within the profession may well also have encouraged the more general diversity of ways of thinking about ethics. Over the thirty years of professional practice represented by the planners in this sample, people had come into planning for different reasons, with varying images of the role that planning should play in the world and with different ethical premises.

The public interest and rule utilitarian approaches that combined deontological and consequentialist ways of thinking also raised a somewhat different, more general issue. These two approaches to ethics represent two great traditions in normative moral philosophy. They tend to be thought of as incompatible, and among philosophers they have clashed for more than two hundred years without resolution. Each approach has its characteristic strengths but also its weaknesses. Utilitarianism focuses on the goodness of the consequences of action but neglects the claims of rights. It can be interpreted to mean that the end justifies means that override rights. Deontology emphasizes the rightness of actions in and of themselves but, except for its attention to certain ends, such as justice, it largely excludes ends from the realm of ethics. These strengths and weaknesses are not just found in philosophical debates. They were exactly the problems faced by at least some of the pure consequentialists and deontologists in this sample. These are the dilemmas we will look at in more detail in part 3.

Because these strengths and weaknesses are so complementary, ideas for combined approaches have proliferated both in philosophy and in policy fields. Rule utilitarianism is one such combination that has already been described and used here. Among people interested in public policy, the basic assumption has been that consequentialist approaches to ethics seem to easily fit the political arena, with its authoritative public decisions concerning the good of large numbers of people. Held (1984), for example, argues for "role morality" in which the ethical norms that would guide behavior in one area of life might be different from those in others. Public roles for those engaged in politics would largely be guided by consequentialist ethics, though the same individuals might rely on deontological rules in their roles as family members or friends.

Such an idea of different ethical approaches for different roles in life may perhaps help to explain the choices made by the planners in the study. Many did use a consequentialist idea of the public interest on policy issues even if they took a primarily deontological approach to dealing with individuals; indeed, it was difficult to operate as a planner without some idea of the public interest. Planners who were more politicized and more committed to seeing results were, in many cases, more likely to take a more thoroughly consequentialist approach to ethics. Even so, the older, Progressive line of development in the profession focused attention on the role of the planner as neutral bureaucrat. Here an active, consequentialist ethic would be inappropriate. One largely concerned with procedural values, such as honesty, truthfulness, and fairness, would be more suited to this very different role. And what about social justice in public policy? Given this diversity of ethical responsibilities, it is not surprising that the idea of balancing a concern with good consequences and a concern with rights has been applied by some theorists to the idea of policy analysis in general (Anderson 1979; Howe 1990; Moore 1981).

Indeed, this theoretical discussion in philosophy and policy/planning theory seems to have parallels in the actual behavior of practicing planners. Many did use mixed consequentialist and deontological approaches. Because there was still considerable tension between the two, there was a tendency for one or the other to predominate. Rule utilitarians, for example, seemed primarily to be utilitarians (that is, consequentialists) while public interest planners were primarily deontologists, but each group sensed in some way (since this hardly seemed to have been a conscious choice) that a "pure" approach was inadequate and that some principles from the complementary approach were necessary.

As part 3 on the actions they took will show more clearly, the planners we interviewed often seemed to recognize that planners should have both a concern for ends and a respect for ethically appropriate means. This meant maintaining a balance in ethics between their own independent idea of the public good and their deontological obligations to be responsive to officials and the public.

8

Influences on Ethical Values

Some planners chose roles deliberately; others probably evolved into them. This process of choice and of evolution through experience was the result of the interaction between planners' values and personalities and the nature of their political and social environments. In part, planners could shape their own roles and the jobs and agency settings they would work in, but the nature of their communities and their agencies shaped them, in turn, in ways they were hardly aware of.

Each role also involved a commitment to moral principles that would serve as guides to action. The kinds of principles that were used by consequentialists were substantive values, the public interest, or some idea of the balance between costs and benefits. Those who were deontologists used principles such as loyalty, openness, and truthfulness. A few with very narrow views of ethics talked about relying only on laws and specific systems of rules, such as departmental regulations or professional codes.

How did these planners come to have the ethical values and approaches they did and to choose the roles they played? The answers to such questions go far beyond this research, but the planners themselves did give some indication of what they thought had shaped their ethical values. In addition, it is also possible to explore whether personal characteristics or aspects of the planners' work environments seem to have been related to different ways of thinking about ethics and role.

When they were asked about what influences had shaped their values, planners mentioned such things as family upbringing, religious training, formal education, social movements, and professional experience. These same influences were also asked about on the questionnaire using a scale ranging from one (no influence) to five (a strong influence). While there were some strong common threads in what had influenced

181

them, planners with different approaches to ethics or different roles or from different parts of the country emphasized somewhat different shaping factors. In addition, even when people talked about the same factor—family, for instance—the exact nature or effect of the influence could vary considerably.[1]

In talking about the forces that had shaped their values, planners tended to make a distinction between three different groups of influences. The first were basic influences from childhood—family, religion, elementary and secondary school, and the ethical climate of the community they had grown up in. These institutions inculcated the duties of justice. The second were influences that came as they were choosing a career—the influence of college, graduate school, experience in the military, and social movements they had been involved in as young adults. These institutions primarily had an impact on values related to loyalty, responsiveness to officials and the public, and ideas of the public interest. The third influence was professional experience, which shaped the way their values played out in practice in the roles they had chosen.

Basic Values

When they were asked what had shaped the way they thought about ethics, many people thought of the influence of "upbringing" first. Overall, one of the strongest influences on ethical values was the values of planners' families. For 55 percent of the planners it was the first thing they thought of in the interview, and it ranked second among the items on the questionnaire (Table 8.1). They came from families of diverse ethnicity and origin, but their first answers to the question of what had influenced them sounded surprisingly similar. This planner was typical of many others:

> Anybody's a reflection of the values they grow up with. I tend to believe that I grew up with some notion of equity and fairness and try and reflect that in my day-to-day dealings, and some notion of what is reasonable behavior and consistency in terms of not telling somebody one thing in the office and somebody else something completely different.

Thus, "background" was the base of ethical values: 12 percent said flatly that their values had been set in childhood and had not really changed since then. When people mentioned specific values they had

TABLE 8.1

Importance of Influences by Approach to Ethics

	Total Sample (n = 72)[a]		Deontologists (n = 55)		Consequentialists (n = 17)	
	Mean[b]	Rank	Mean[b]	Rank	Mean[b]	Rank
Work experience	4.3	1	4.3	2	4.3	1
Family[c]	4.1	2	4.4	1	3.6	3/4
Professional education	3.7	3	3.7	3	3.7	2
Preprofessional education	3.3	4	3.4	5	3.6	3/4
Religion[c]	3.2	5	3.5	4	2.3	7
Social movements	3.0	6	3.0	6	3.4	5
Codes of ethics	2.6	7	2.6	7	2.5	6

Notes:

[a] Since these tabulations are based on data from the questionnaire, 6 planners who did not fill out the questionnaire are not included. In addition, the 9 vague planners are not included. Approximately 9 planners had missing values on these questions. This varies a bit from question to question. The *n*'s at the top of the columns are averages for all questions.

[b] Scale: 1 = no influence; 3 = some influence; 5 = strong influence.

[c] Difference of mean scores of deontologists and consequentialists significant at the 0.05 level.

learned as children, they tended to refer, as the planners did above, to duties of justice, such as truthfulness and fairness.

For most people who mentioned it, the influence of religion went hand in hand with that of family. When asked what had influenced her, one planner said:

> My family. My background. [We are] Sicilian—very strong on family ties. Catholic. I think religion has [an influence].

On the average among all the planners, religion was not a strong influence, ranking sixth of the eight items on the questionnaire, but it was a significantly greater influence for planners from the Bible Belt states of Texas and Tennessee than it was for others. It was also a much stronger influence for process planners, some of whom talked about religion not just as an influence in childhood but as something that was a guiding force for them as practicing planners (Table 8.2). Rebecca Giulini said:

> I went to a private school [that was influenced by] Jesuit thinking. The Jesuits have a very strong way—I think it's just an issue of fairness and treating people as people, treating them as humans, and knowing there is an intrinsic good in each person and going from there. Here I've joined a Christian life community that is all made up of professionals. I've got strong religious beliefs. That doesn't mean that I always do everything right, of course, but I do know what is right and wrong. It helps me to think carefully. It's easy to be caught up in the momentum of what you are doing.

Religion and family were also significantly more important influences for deontological than for consequentialist planners (see Table 8.1). The central values that guided most deontologists were ones that were learned in childhood. Principles such as the public interest or substantive values, however, which were especially important to consequentialists, were likely to come later.

It was perhaps in part this sequential process of learning values that produced so many mixed planners. Virtually everyone learned in childhood that it was important to be truthful, honest, and fair. Then as they matured and moved toward choosing a career, other, more substantive or consequentialist values might be added to their complement of values. Three planners who talked specifically about loyalty, for example, said they had learned it in the military.

The more specifically political value of responsibility to decision makers and the public was probably learned as a planning student or as a

TABLE 8.2

Importance of Influences by Roles

	Total Sample (n = 82)[b]	All Technicians (n = 41)	Roles (means[a]) Process Planners (n = 11)	Active Planners (n = 22)	Closet Politicians (n = 8)	Difference High/Low[c]
Work experience	4.3	4.3	4.2	4.4	4.1	ns
Family	4.1	4.2	4.6	3.9	3.7	.11
Professional education	3.7	3.9	3.7	3.5	3.4	ns
Preprofessional education	3.3	3.1	3.8	3.5	3.1	.05
Religion	3.2	3.2	4.5	2.5	3.1	.05
Social movements	3.0	2.7	3.2	3.2	3.8	.03
Codes of ethics	2.6	2.8	2.8	2.6	1.7	.04

Notes:

[a] Scale: 1 = no influence; 3 = some influence; 5 = strong influence.

[b] Since these tabulations are based on data from the questionnaire, 6 planners who did not fill out the questionnaire are not included. Approximately 8 planners had missing values on these questions. This varies slightly from question to question. The *n*'s at the top of the columns are averages for all questions.

[c] ns = not significant. The results of a t-test between the group with the highest and that with the lowest score on each item. Only those meeting the usual .05 level of significance are shown except in the case of "family," where the result almost meets the still reasonable test of significance at the .10 level. The results are affected by the small numbers of planners in each group; this is why all the technicians were combined.

185

junior-level planner, though few members of the sample were explicit about this. Only two pointed out how the idea of loyalty to decision makers had been a central lesson of their planning education, but this was a value held by most of the planners, and it may have been acquired during this period of life along with other values related to citizen participation and the nature of the political process.

Overall, the influence of planning school ranked third among the items on the questionnaire. While Tables 8.1 and 8.2 indicate that there were statistically no significant differences between planners taking different approaches to ethics or playing different roles, the interviews revealed that planning school was clearly more important for some planners. Those whose ethics were closely tied to substantive ideas of good land-use planning or urban design, for instance, were likely to emphasize the importance of what they had learned there:

> The first thing that most planners are exposed to is their education, and the "University of Timbuktu" turns out planners to do just what I'm doing—to do local planning. We're very design-oriented, very much drilled in the basics of [Edward] Bassett and [Alfred] Bettman and all of the fathers of city planning. We study their viewpoints and read a lot of their essays and things like that just to try to get a feel for what is the profession because it's such an ambiguous profession.

Another planner talked about the role that planning school had played in reinforcing his commitment to the public interest:

> I took planning school very seriously. It was at a time when you could. It was in the fifties. We always thought that that's where— we were the public interest. They don't teach kids that stuff anymore.

Commitments to substantive values or to other ideas of the public interest seem to have developed when people were older, though they might have roots in earlier influences. Several planners talked about having environmental values that were shaped by their parents but also by books they had read by Aldo Leopold, William O. Douglas, or Ian McHarg.[2] Similarly, many planners with a commitment to social justice traced it back in one way or another to early experience. One, when asked what had influenced her, said:

> I guess that my family had pretty strong values about social equity and personal responsibility and that came through to me when I was

a kid. Then we moved to the New York area and I went to high
school back in the 1950s on Long Island, which is about as ultimately uptight, narrow-minded suburban as you can find. I just
didn't like it at all. I didn't like the in-crowd in high school, thought
they were a bunch of narrow-minded, rah-rah bigots, and they were,
and so I sort of hung around with the intelligentsia in my high
school, and they were all considered Communists, of course, but
we saw ourselves as the out-group and we liked to raise issues about
social issues. So having that sort of out-group position in a very
conformist environment led me into thinking very seriously about
social equity.

Other planners had experiences as children or in high school that made
them aware of the issue of social justice. One was black; another had
grown up in Israel but had then moved to England as a teenager and had
been angered by the class divisions he found there. Several came from
radical, union-oriented families, others from families with strong religious
commitments to the civil rights movement. Many but not all of these
planners with heightened consciousness of the issue of social justice were
substantive deontologists and became active planners.

In a different vein, a planner with a commitment to a broad, long-
range view of the public interest talked about how he had become aware
of the existence of collective goods and the tragedy of the commons:

I was brought up in Minnesota and we had a place at a lake and we
used to go there all the time. We saw it go downhill, and the fishing
deteriorated and it got algae problems and everything. I did some
research on it and found out that the reason it was becoming that
way was because of a lot of the development around the lake. That's
kind of what got me interested in planning from the start.

These values were generally reinforced about the time they went to
planning school. As the descriptions of the active and process planners
and of the closet politicians showed, many, though not all, went to college
or planning school during the 1960s and were influenced by the antiwar,
black power, and environmental movements:

I came out of school in the sixties when all we were taught in college
was to challenge the system and to question everything and so forth,
so there's no question that . . . at least part of my educational
background influenced that. I was a typical, right-out-of-college
planner in 1967 who was going to turn the world upside down. I was

going to wipe out the special interests and power to the people. I was here in California [with] the antiwar, protect the environment [movements and] that whole thing. So I'm sure that influenced me.

This was the period that ended, during the Nixon administration, in Watergate, whose lessons for public service ethics were not lost on some of the planners. A woman who blew the whistle on her boss said:

It goes back to your question about influences. I think a lot of what influences me is having gone to college during the Vietnam War years, and I started college in 1967, and [the protests at] Columbia were in 1968. I was there in all the exciting years—it was very intense in terms of strikes. So I think that had a lot of influence in terms of seeing the dishonesty of what I thought was the war and feeling very strongly against the war and the draft and then Watergate—you know, the Deep Throat thing. Watergate was during the 1972 presidential election. I guess my feeling was that the people who talked to Woodward and Bernstein were *right* in talking to them.

Social movements seemed to play the same role among California planners as that played by religion in shaping values in Texas and Tennessee. The closet politicians ranked it as the second most important influence on their values (see Table 8.2). There was no significant difference between consequentialists and deontologists in the influence of social movements (see Table 8.1). The goals of the movements of the 1960s, at least—peace, social justice, and environmentalism—could be interpreted in either consequentialist or deontological terms, and the idea that they provided of working actively for broad social change was a powerful one for active planners regardless of their ethical approach. In line with this overall pattern, nine of those who talked in the interview about the importance of social movements were active planners, three were process planners, and three were closet politicians. Reinforcement for these values came from other sources, too. Three of these planners had been conscientious objectors and two had been in the Peace Corps.

Grace Sumner was this kind of planner. She had grown up in a politically active family in the Midwest and went to California for college and graduate school:

I have a mother who's very concerned about ethical issues. My mother calls herself a radical still; in fact, she's to the left of me, which is a great disappointment to her. We had a lot of political discussions around the table, so the ethical aspects of politics and doing good was a big issue. Then I went to school between 1965 and 1969, which was a real watershed, kind of a neat time to go to school, looking back at it. So there was the black revolution and then there was Vietnam. I lived in a dorm that was kind of the radical hotbed, if you like, and I participated in demonstrations and I took a couple of courses in institutional racism, so I had a very strong concern about ethical values, and I got into planning because I had some idea that I would be able to help the problems of the cities. When I went to Berkeley in 1969 to 1971, that was a pretty exciting time, too. I think Kent State was in 1970 and there was a quarter where I really didn't do any work. So I guess I went to school during a time . . . and I had that family background . . . and I think that's why I was originally interested in housing. That was just a long-term interest.

She was not among the most radical of the students of the 1960s—she would probably never have gone into a profession such as planning if she had been—but her political activism and then her service in the Peace Corps working on housing issues in Central America reaffirmed and focused her commitment to work for social justice at home as well.

Taken together, the planners' discussions of the forces that had shaped their ethical values suggested that some basic ones were learned early and remained fairly fixed. More substantive, professionally oriented values were apparently acquired later, though not necessarily through the medium of formal education.

Patterns of Moral Development

This sketch of the "moral development" of these planners reflects how they thought in retrospect, as adults, about the way their moral values had been shaped. It does not represent a psychological theory of moral development, such as the one proposed and tested by Kohlberg (1971, 1987). He argues that all children, regardless of nationality, culture, social class, or other social distinctions, go through a series of invariant stages of moral development. Each stage involves a characteristic way of thinking about moral dilemmas, and movement through the stages involves a process of maturation.

This is a much more elaborate theory than the sketch of moral development presented here, but the two may not be incompatible. It is interesting that in Kohlberg's research, fairness is a central aspect of younger stages of moral thinking. The idea of fairness as an exchange is a characteristic moral point of view of children at about age ten. This then shifts to a broader, Golden Rule image of fairness as a teenager. This kind of individually oriented morality gives way in later teenage years to an idea of morality concerned with a shared set of social or community rules. Respect for law and institutional loyalty are characteristic concerns. This stage, in turn, is followed by one that allows for the moral evaluation of laws and institutions themselves according to some standard, such as a consequentialist idea of the public interest or a deontological idea of the primacy of rights. These stages do seem to bear some relationship to the way the planners described their own sequences of moral development, though their descriptions sounded more like a gradual accretion of principles rather than a passage through a series of distinctly different modes of thought.[3]

All these experiences as children and as students, however, were only a prelude to these planners' professional careers. What happened to their ethical values once they began working as planners? Were they reinforced or changed and how?

Values, Behavior, and Experience

The planners' own discussions of the effect of experience convey a series of thumbnail sketches of the interactions between an individual's personality and the more or less unyielding nature of the outside political world. The adaptations they made varied according to their roles. In addition, the nature of the political and organizational structures in which they worked also affected their values and actions in ways in which they were usually not aware.

While some planners insisted that their values were set in childhood and had not changed through their professional lives, most did feel that their professional experience had shaped their approach to ethics or had at least clarified their values. This was the highest ranked shaping factor on the questionnaire and was rated a strong influence by 48 percent of the sample. As Tables 8.1 and 8.2 show, there was little difference in this rating among planners with different approaches to ethics or those playing different roles nor were there differences among those working in different parts of the country.

These planners' perceptions do seem to support the findings by Hendler (1991) that planners' views about ethics seem to change as they make the transition from school to practice. She found that Ontario planning students had somewhat different ethical views than practicing planners in the province, but as planning experience among the students increased, their values were more like those of practitioners.

If experience did little else, it could make clear to planners what their ethical values were and how these applied to their professional lives. For technicians, the most common lesson of experience was to reinforce their values. Often it was negative experiences that provided this reinforcement. One planner talked about having little respect for some of his coworkers because of their sloppy work:

> If anything, the contrast has heightened some of the values. Some influences in the opposite direction have just reinforced my consciousness of my values and the determination not to jeopardize those.

For some, experience had the effect of making them more cautious. They had been too quick to advise, too blunt, inconsistent, or they had seen others who were and had gotten into trouble. The concomitants to being cautious were to do careful analysis and to be straight. Several planners said that their departments helped by being straight, but two of the aethical planners who worked in corrupt political systems were also made cautious by experience.

Some active planners said that experience had made them more political and/or more concerned with being effective. One of the planners who was influenced by the social movements of the 1960s said:

> I learned very quickly that I wasn't going to turn the world upside down. I happened to be one who believed in working within the system for change. I felt I wanted to be in a place where I could change, and so that has certainly been a driving force in my career here because this has been my only planning job, and I came here as a planning technician, and I can guarantee you in 1967 I didn't think I would ever be the planning director. As I got more involved in the thing professionally, I felt the higher up I got in the organization, the more influence I had on the decisions that are made in the city, and so that became a goal of mine very quickly to get to that point. I want to leave my working career with some sense of looking back at what I've accomplished and be able to see that in some tangible kinds of ways. So that is really very much a driving force, and I hope, again, that I'm not trying to plan a city or direct the growth of the city or policy of the city to meet my own personal needs or desires but, again, to create some kind of better situation

for the public and try to balance my own personal preference on things toward the public interest.

However, most active planners had not been shaped by social movements or by political activism in college or graduate school. It was really only when they got out into planning jobs that they found that effectiveness was something they really cared about and which they had the skills to achieve. A planner who worked before he went back to school for his master's degree described the change in the way he thought about planning:

> When I was in planning school, I felt that the right way [to plan was to prepare plans] because I worked with the planning commission [and] they prepared plans. But when I graduated, I went back to work for the planning commission here for a couple of years, and I became involved more with a project planning line of work, [and] that's when I really began to think that the planning commission wasn't doing a fraction of what they could be doing in actively trying to work with [developers] and trying to get with them on the front end and work with them, and that really just sort of did change my attitude, my ethics a lot.

Another planner described how he had developed an effective approach over the years:

> I used to get very angry about things and I'd take direct issue and express myself very openly. I think through the years I've learned there are other ways of doing that more effectively rather than to be out-front.

These planners often said little about how this change related to ethics, but the import of their cases was that they had become more consequentialist. The planner who learned to be less out-front went around on the pros and cons of extreme consequentialism:

> Well, if it's a good end, you know . . . and it means enough . . . and it's not a violation of what you think is honest, decent . . . I think the ends do justify the means, but, you know, you have to be careful when you say that because you run into situations like what happens in Russia.

He said that he probably had been tempted to use means he thought were questionable for a good end but drew back from giving any specific examples.

If these active planners found themselves liberated, in some sense, by their experience, there were others with strong policy concerns whose careers proved to be frustrating because their ability to act fell so far short of what they had hoped to achieve. One who came back from World War II with a commitment to right social injustices found himself sidetracked in midcareer by political infighting and personal problems. In hindsight, he felt that both he and the profession more generally had simply helped to maintain the status quo. Planning had lost its value as an agent of change for him, except within severely prescribed limits.

There were many more planners whose idealism had not been so high and whose careers had run more smoothly who said that experience had mellowed them and given them patience, humor, or a willingness to compromise. It had made them more accepting of the political side of planning and of the ethical gray areas in which right and wrong were not easy to distinguish. A technician, trained as an engineer, who had come to accept the role of politics in planning as he had risen to become the director of his department, talked about how the change in his own views had corresponded to the rise of citizen participation in his city:

> I think in a sense that as you get closer and closer to the decision-making process you see some of the reasons and some of the so-called logic behind certain decision-making issues: that not everything is black and white. While I may feel strongly about it, the person on the other side of the fence has got some real good reasons why it should be that way. As an engineer, one and one make two all the time, there's no other way of coming out. Things have changed. You've got the variable of the peoples' concern, and that changes everything. We used to have a plan commissioner who was a CPA and who then became an attorney, and he told me one of the hardest things he had to deal with when he was going to law school was the fact that not everything was black and white: "Now I go to law school, everything is gray, nothing is black and white." That's the interesting part about planning, I find, is that you've got the people aspect of the thing, and trying to help them, and what we think is right for them, still recognizing that they've got a feeling for their neighborhood.
>
> Q: For yourself, how was that transition from a view of things black and white to a lot gray?
>
> I think it was gradual and it really came out in the last ten years or so, when we got more public participation.

The technician activists were especially likely to see themselves as having mellowed as they reached positions of power. Richard Breitman joked:

I've been accused of mellowing in my old age [laughter]. I think I have mellowed a little bit, and maybe more nearly matured is a better word. Maybe I go about doing what I think needs to be done in a little less dramatic way or in a little less pronounced way. I'm not as emphatic, as vociferous, or whatever you want to call it, as I might have been when I was twenty years younger. You get co-opted a lot more when you have the ultimate responsibility. Sometimes I wish I was just a freelance planner, that I could say exactly what I think when I think it. I'm not going to say that we don't, but we do it in a different way than I might have if I were just on my own.

These planners clearly thought that experience had been important in shaping their approach to ethics. What they described, however, was concerned less with the way experience had shaped their values and more with how it had shaped their behavior. They described the playing out of the role choices they had made. Some planners' roles had changed. The drive of the technician activists made them more active but also more mellow as they reached their career peaks. Some other active planners also seem to have learned on the job that they could be active, just as closet politicians may have learned that they could not. Whether they changed over their careers or did not, their roles had significant implications for their ethical values.

Values and Structure: Community and Agency Values

What the planners usually did not see about their own experience was the way the political and organizational systems in which they worked had subtly shaped their values and therefore their actions. They simply lacked the distance or comparative framework that would have made these influences clear. Both community and agency values were important. The most obvious, though not the most common or even the most important, factor was whether the planner worked in a corrupt setting. On the other side, agency or community norms could also encourage planners to try to achieve certain kinds of substantive goals, such as environmental protection.

Corruption

Really corrupt political systems, of which there were seven in the sample, did not necessarily create corrupt planners, but they often produced cynical ones. Corruption seemed to generate two rather distinct responses. One was to fight it. Several planners blew the whistle on corrupt activities. One consciously refused to stoop to the kind of tactics he was fighting. Another fought fire with fire, using tactics that she herself called "not wonderful."

The other response to corruption was a kind of passive acceptance and survival. If ethical principles were lost, a kind of cynicism resulted in which activities that appeared to have ethical meaning were taken only because of instrumental practicality or fear of consequences. Alternatively, planners who retained their ethical standards only seemed to be more frustrated and alienated.

Three of the four aethical planners worked in political systems that either had been corrupt in the past or were at least somewhat corrupt at the time of the interview. Whether planners resisted or became passive may well have been a function of individual circumstance and personality, but in all these cases, it was very difficult to do planning at all, much less effective planning, when decision makers and sometimes other planners had little concern for basic standards of fairness and honesty. This undermined the obligation to be responsible to elected officials, leaving these planners to rely primarily on their own judgments of the public interest. Those who were active were the ones who had dirty hands. Such actions seemed to be a natural outgrowth of the environment in which they worked.

The Culture of Planning

These corrupt communities were extreme cases and not very common ones, at least in this sample. Much more pervasive were differences across regions of the country in terms of expectations about not only the role to be played by planning but also the kind of activities that were appropriate for individual planners. A comparison between northern California and the two southern states of Texas and Tennessee can show how this influence operated, but other places also seemed to have a distinct "climate" of their own. New York City, for example, was especially difficult to work in because of its extreme bureaucratization and corruption.

Northern California and the two southern states stood at opposite ends of the spectrum among the states in the sample. Citizens and politicians in northern California were somewhat skeptical about the benefits of uncontrolled development and, as a result, were interested in and supportive of planning. The politics seemed to be generally open and participatory. It was clean as well: 74 percent of the nineteen planners portrayed their communities as having very clean politics. Texas and Tennessee, though, were both strongly prodevelopment, the latter fighting to get economic growth, the former on the verge of a tremendous economic boom. Texas was the only state in the country where large cities had little planning and no zoning, though this was not uniform throughout the state. Tennessee was hardly more accepting of planning despite a long tradition of state planning assistance to localities. Both states seemed to have many political systems dominated by old-boy networks, though Tennessee seemed to be more corrupt than Texas: nine of the ten Tennessee planners who gave any indication about corruption portrayed their communities as very or fairly corrupt.

These differences affected perceptions of appropriate planning behavior. A small example can begin to give a sense of the difference. It concerns the question of whether planners considered it appropriate to accept lunches from developers. The lunch was, in effect, a small gift, like flowers or a bottle of liquor at Christmas. It provided an opportunity for influence and, by extension, could be seen as a small bribe. Opinions differed among the planners as to whether they were vulnerable to such influence. One said:

> If I'm going to compromise my principles, it should be worth more than lunch [laughter]!

However, another argued that:

> I think a lot of planners are corruptible—I don't mean for payoffs— but corruptible in the sense that if you wine and dine them enough, you know, they'll change their opinion.

Several planners who worked in land-use regulation and had to deal with the same developers over and over did indicate that it was difficult to maintain neutrality and distance, and, indeed, they were raising on a small, personal scale an example of the classic problem of regulators being co-opted by the industries that they regulate. Lunches provided a situation in which formality was broken down and the distinction between planners' public and private roles could be blurred. Moreover, even if none of these consequences resulted, the appearance of influence could be a problem:

> I think the appearance is much more important than the reality. I mean, I can't believe that if somebody bought you lunch or bought me lunch, it would change my mind on their development project,

but I think the appearance is critically important. It has happened at the county level to several individuals where they've been labeled such and such . . . and have been forced to leave because of it whether or not there was any basis in truth or not.

The thing that was interesting about lunches with developers was how acceptance of it varied from state to state. Altogether, seventeen people gave their opinion on it. In Texas and Tennessee, the states with the most prodevelopment values and the least acceptance of planning, five planners accepted lunches and two did not. In California, it hardly came up, and both planners who talked about it said that such lunches were unacceptable.

This would remain only an intriguing and trivial example except that it was indicative, in a larger sense, both of the nature of the politics of these states and of expectations about planning. It was not altogether surprising to find a Tennessee planner complaining about his agency's policy of prohibiting consulting by planners or one who owned a construction business or Texas planners who were working as developers or real estate agents in their own cities. These activities were officially discouraged but widely accepted in the community at large and apparently among planners. A planner who had a strong commitment to neighborhood revitalization talked about how he and some friends had begun to think about getting involved in development:

We began to talk about our frustration with nothing really happening. [There was a] group [that] was trying to be a neighborhood development corporation and do some developmental kinds of things in the neighborhood—not for profit—and we began to realize that nothing was going to happen, no development was going to take place unless there was an incentive for it—that incentive being profit, particularly here. So we started talking about getting together and buying some property and renovating it just to show that it could be done and also to make a profit from it, because when you're in this kind of position, you recognize the possibilities for doing that kind of thing—it's very tempting to go out and do that—and I did have a concern about whether or not that would be inappropriate activity for me to be involved in, so . . .
Q: What happened?
It just fell apart primarily because of my concern about that and because another person moved away. Numerous things happened. I don't think we ever would have done it because it would have posed serious ethical problems in my mind, although I'm sure that other

people—that certainly is a matter of departmental precedent. One person in the department owned, I think, a whole block in a subdivision that was later developed, and I'm sure that other people in the department do own land for speculation, so that is a problem.

In northern California the situation was different. Planners initially often had trouble thinking of ethical issues because the obvious things, such as bribery and conflicts of interest, were so far from their everyday experience. Only 5 percent of the cases they raised involved legal issues they had dealt with firsthand. Some said that such issues as political pressure on technical judgments were clearly ethical issues "but not here." As one explained:

> Corruption here is knocking over a parking meter, you know, and taking the change out of it. I mean, we don't have the New Jersey syndrome here . . . people indicted, running for office. California has its faults, but it is relatively free of the corrupting problem, and that's what I mean when honesty is not the big thing in mind because, you know, it goes without saying that we're all going to be personally honest. We're not going to take favors for a decision around here.

For a planner to have owned or developed property would have been considered obviously unethical. The only example of this that was given had occurred ten years before, and the planner involved had been excoriated in the press.

What this pattern indicated was not simply that planners in Texas and Tennessee were more likely to get involved in actions that would be defined as unethical in northern California; it suggested that in Texas and Tennessee, planners had somewhat different values and saw their roles differently from planners in California.

Where planning was less accepted, as in Texas and Tennessee, planners had to tread more carefully and were less likely to play active roles, except occasionally in large-city agencies. The passive hybrid and technician activist roles seemed to be especially suited to the sometimes corrupt, old-boy style of politics. By the same token, the planners were somewhat less likely to lean on developers in negotiations in order to gain concessions in return for permission to undertake a project.

They also had more ties to their states—they were more likely to have grown up there, to have gone to school there, and to have worked there for their whole careers.[4] Perhaps also as a way of establishing their local legitimacy, they were more likely to talk about their local ties as important:

> I think maybe that's one of the things that I have an advantage on over someone who might come in here from another place. I feel like I know the way most of the people around here think and where they're coming from and why they think that way. My dad and I, we really get into some good arguments about building . . . he has this land ethic that most people in west Texas have and I think you have to understand that in order to deal in this kind of an environment. I know where most of the people come from and maybe that gives me a little bit of an edge, and, too, I talk like the other people [laughter].

Planners from Texas and Tennessee had lower scores on the scale measuring attitudes about favoring low-income and minority groups. They were politically more conservative and had higher scores on a scale measuring attitudes favoring development.[5] They were less likely to have a clear idea of the public interest, and fewer of them thought of the public interest as a balance between their own ideas of the public interest and those of decision makers and members of the public. Essentially, decisions were more likely to be made on particularistic grounds rather than through an open process of debate over what would most benefit the community.

Planners in California were more likely to be active or process planners. Support for planning and the participatory open politics of many communities gave planners scope for a more active role, though traditional technicians did also exist in this environment. The idea of the public interest was used by all but one planner, and three-quarters saw it as a balance between their views and those of other participants in the process.

They were less likely to have come originally from California, and no one talked about the importance of being local. While many did share the values of people in their communities, this was the only state where several planners talked about the problem of being co-opted into local values.

Co-optation was a concern because, as the statewide average on the scale measuring attitudes about low-income/minority issues indicated, some of these planners had strong moral commitments to social equity that they were actively trying to promote. In this they were aided by the state government itself, which was trying to influence affluent communities to provide more affordable housing. Only one of the five planners who talked about this issue was content to simply let his city council's opposition kill action on the issue. The other four worked actively, though in somewhat different ways, to get their communities to accept such housing. Several talked about the ethical issue involved in balancing their own values against those of citizens and officials.

If housing was an issue on which planners had to push, the environment was one on which the values of many California communities were very supportive. It was several California planners at both the state and the local level who saw no trade-off between equity and environmental concerns. While planners in Texas and Tennessee had environmental values just as strong as those in California, in a prodevelopment environment, the protection of even critical environmental resources, such as aquifers, posed an uphill battle.[6] The planner who was a real estate agent spoke proudly about how he would not sell houses built on the local aquifer, though development there was proceeding apace. While California hardly eschewed development, a much larger and more active constituency existed for dealing with environmental issues in the planning process. This meant that environmentally oriented planners in California had more room and leverage to act on those values in negotiations with developers.

All of these factors contributed to the development of distinct local "cultures of planning" with their own values and ethical norms. The cultures were not uniform. Dallas and Austin, for example, were more cosmopolitan than the smaller cities of west Texas, just as the Bay Area was more cosmopolitan than the cities of the Central Valley, but despite the internal differences, the culture of each region established limits on the nature of planning activity. Understanding the values of a community could be an advantage, especially if planning was not fully accepted, but the other side of understanding was the co-optation that some of the California planners were concerned about.

These different local cultures were also associated with rather different ethical issues and different ways of dealing with them. Any effort to change "the ethics" of planners would have to contend with the opportunities and constraints established by this larger structural setting.

Agency Climate

On a smaller scale, as well, planners seemed to be influenced by the ethical climate of their agencies. There were tensions in relationships between supervisors and subordinates that were viewed as ethical in nature. They revolved around discretion, responsibility, loyalty, and support. Particularly in larger, more bureaucratic departments, planners at lower levels had relatively little autonomy to act on issues they saw as ethical. These subordinates saw it as the role of superiors to act on such issues. This was especially a problem for planners like the closet politicians, who wanted to see positive action on politically difficult policy issues, such as affordable housing or more equitable transit fares. As one of these planners said about an important issue he thought had been handled badly:

> I had a role to play in making those recommendations [but] working in a city this size, what finally is decided and what you've done is miles apart.

Lack of action by superiors was equally a problem for planners who wanted support in resisting pressures to change technical recommendations. One planner whose director had stood by him under a lot of pressure said:

> I was a very young planner. She was very political, a political appointee, but dedicated as a planner, and she kept asking me if I was sure I was giving her the right advice, and I had to tell her what I thought was right. In the end, she followed my advice. She gave me a lot of consideration—more than my position really would have deserved normally.

Those whose superiors had been the ones to apply the pressure were usually hesitant to be critical out of a sense of loyalty, but they raised the issues as ethical ones because of their sense that this pressure was wrong even if it did come from an elected or appointed official.

Lack of such support or, indeed, corruption by superiors could result in problems of controlling subordinates. The worst-case scenario from the point of view of a director was the junior-level planner who, frustrated with the lack of support from higher up, became a bureaucratic guerrilla. Because of the study by Needleman and Needleman (1974), this conjures up images of neighborhood planners working, sometimes covertly, for disadvantaged communities. A director who had some experience with active and independent neighborhood planners said:

> There has been a conflict that has developed occasionally when a district planner would sort of take on the coloration of a community organization to the degree that he finds himself fighting the city council, the mayor's office, the planning department, and all that. I

told [one planner in particular] that "You have to realize which side your bread is buttered on. You are working for the city administration and that in all your official roles you have to be reflective of what's going on in city hall, in the planning department, and elsewhere." Now, I said, "that doesn't mean that you as an individual can't have certain beliefs. You can say what you think, but you have to be careful how you say it. You cannot say it in your role as a member of city government."

Bureaucratic guerrillas were not by any means limited to neighborhood planners. As part 3 on action will show, all that was needed to push the planner over into covert defiance was a consequentialist approach to ethics, an active orientation, and a sufficient level of frustration. These led to end runs of various sorts and even to conflicts of interest.

Curiously, no director talked about having a stronger obligation to act on substantive ethical issues because they had more control or autonomy or because it was important to members of their staff. Their greater responsibility and visibility may have meant that this was, in fact, the case, but they did not see it as an ethical obligation.

There were some directors who did see it as their duty to keep their agencies honest. For several in corrupt communities, this involved taking the heat and protecting their staff. Some, in communities where the pressures were not so extreme, tried to create a more general agency climate. Several talked about their efforts to establish a reputation for their agency as being open, honest, and "straight." While this was primarily for the consumption of the public and of decision makers, it had to be based on the behavior of people within the agency. One said:

I want to build as much credibility into this program as possible. I want people to know that when they're dealing with this department, they're getting a straight answer, they're getting all of the information that's available to help them with the decision. They are not getting half-truths, they are not getting information withheld, they know that we're going to do our best to provide them with everything that everybody wanted to know about that subject—and we're still going to take a position on it if we're asked.

Particular cases of wrongdoing might serve as object lessons to employees of what not to do. Several times in certain cities, we heard the same case from several different people in the same agency.

This strategy of deliberately creating a departmental ethos did seem to have some effect in supporting ethical behavior. However, as broader control was exerted, the results could be a little unpredictable. In one agency that had a statewide reputation as a professional, effective, and honest agency, all the employees we talked to, from the director on down, adopted the dominant image of the straight technician. For some people, such as a zoning administrator, this fit their values and worked well, but this was also the agency of the aethical planner whose commitment to getting results and ultimately to planning itself was undermined by this ethos. Accepting the dominant ideology meant denying the activism and value commitment that had attracted him into planning. He engaged in some small acts of defiance but primarily felt overcontrolled and alienated. He apparently had a reputation in the department for being more outspoken than was useful:

> It's perhaps my sense of paranoia more than there really is a problem—where the lid has been so tight on communication, it gets to the point where people ask you for your opinion and you are extremely reticent to say anything.

As this example suggests, an agency's climate could go beyond providing support for actions or values. It could be a real shaping force for the planners within it. Whether the climate was deliberately created, as this agency's was, or was simply the result of happenstance, it could serve to encourage or discourage ethical behavior.

Thus, experience was important to ethics in the sense that planners adapted to the culture or expectations of the organizational and political systems they worked in. This adaptation affected both values themselves and the expression of those values in action. If communities were corrupt, planners' values could be corrupted or they might simply become cynical about the capacity to act effectively. In a similar way, the culture of planning in California allowed for the development and expression of proequity and proenvironmental values more than was possible in the prodevelopment climate in Texas and Tennessee.

Because they were only slightly aware of the shaping force of their environments, planners tended to take these influences or expectations as given. If they found themselves at odds with these structural values, they could exit by finding another job, but some did voice disagreement by blowing the whistle on illegal actions, promoting policies that required a change in local values, or trying to create a particular ethical climate in their agency.

Like the influence of family, religion, or schooling, the shaping force of professional experience and environment was long term, gradual, and pervasive. It shaped planners' principles or values, what they identified as ethical issues, the roles they played, and the ways they dealt with the ethical issues they faced. It is these actions that will be explored in part 3.

PART 3

Actions

9

A Framework for Evaluation

Now the pieces of this puzzle begin to come together. It is all very well to know what planners identified as ethical issues and how they thought about them, but the bottom line in ethics is what they did about these issues. In the end, ethics involved being able to sustain a sequence of actions. Initially, an issue had to be defined as posing an ethical dilemma. Once the issue had been identified, the planner had to analyze the issue in such a way as to come up with a justifiable course of action. Finally, he or she had to actually act on the issue. Problems could arise at any stage. Characteristically, different kinds of planners encountered problems at different points in this sequence—technicians with seeing issues, consequentialists with justification, and closet politicians with action, for example. On the whole, however, most planners negotiated the whole sequence, though, as usual, in rather different ways.

Part 1 of our discussion examined how the planners defined the realm of planning ethics. Part 2 explored factors, such as roles and approaches, that shaped their definitions. This part will examine what they did and how they justified it. As with the issues, what they did can simply be described. In a book about ethics, this begs the question of whether what they did was right or wrong, good or bad. One aspect of the planners' descriptions of their actions was their own evaluation of them, but must the rest of us accept only people's own judgments as the final word about what is ethical? If a thief says that theft is not wrong, must we accept that judgment? Of course not. It is quite possible to have an explicit, reasoned standard against which ethical behavior can be judged. In the case of these planners, the profession itself has a *Code of Ethics and Professional Conduct* (American Institute of Certified Planners [AICP] 1981) that provides a good starting place for a framework for evaluating the planners' behavior. It seems obvious to ask how closely the values embodied in this code corresponded to what the planners in the sample were actually doing. The purpose is not to point the finger at individual "wrongdoers" but, rather, explicitly to identify areas of possible difficulty that planners in different situations and with different images of their roles might find themselves facing.

Most of this chapter is devoted to developing a framework for evaluating the planners' actions, using the code and my additional idea of a hierarchy of values. It is based on the premises that planners have their own particular professional ideas about the public interest but that these must be balanced against the need to be accountable to elected officials and to the ordinary moral values of the broader public. Chapter 10 will focus on the way that different kinds of ethical issues and conflicts were handled while chapter 11 will look at the characteristic patterns of behavior among planners playing different roles and taking different approaches to ethical issues. Chapter 12 will explore some of the factors besides role and approach to ethics that shaped their actions. Finally, chapter 13 will look at the question of how ethical action can be encouraged.

On the whole, the planners in the sample did generally accept the principles laid out in the code and my idea of a hierarchy of values. They did not always act on their beliefs for a variety of reasons, which will be explored in these chapters. The greatest disparity between the provisions of the code and the planners' values and actions existed in substantive definitions of the public interest. The code places more emphasis than these planners did on the principles of preserving the natural environment, striving for good urban design, and working for social justice. Politically, these were not easy principles for planners to act on, and they were notable not because planners acted unethically in relation to them but because the issues so rarely came up or had to be acted on at all. On these issues, at least, I would suggest that they may have been too responsive to the values of their elected officials and of dominant groups in their communities.

The Nature of Moral Standards

In a world in which we are aware of many cultural and religious traditions, and apparently conflicting moral judgments even within our own moral tradition, many people are cautious about accepting the idea that it is possible to have general standards against which the behavior of a large group of people, such as the members of a profession, can be judged. Indeed, the different deontological and consequentialist approaches to ethics taken by the planners in the sample suggest the difficulties of developing a unified standard. However, it is possible to consider and to lay out explicitly the elements necessary for a set of moral guidelines. Frankena (1973, p. 108), for instance, says that normative discourse in general

> is a language in which we may express our sentiments—approvals, disapprovals, evaluations, recommendations, advice, instruction, prescriptions—and put them out into the public arena for rational scrutiny and discussion, claiming that they will hold up under such scrutiny and discussion and that all our audience will concur with us if they will also choose the same common point of view.

Frankena suggests that the justification of moral decisions should be impartial and should be based on a test that accepts as guidelines in particular cases only those principles that we are willing to accept as universal ones. These are requirements for generalization and consistency.

Baier (1965) is another of the many philosophers who have elaborated on the importance and nature of universalizable principles. He argues that the moral point of view is not self-interested. It involves using principles that prevent making exceptions, that is, treating people in similar circumstances differently. Principles are meant to apply to everybody equally.

These basic and general criteria of consistency, universalization, and disinterestedness suggest that it is possible to have moral guidelines that are widely accepted. They would not resolve all difficult ethical conflicts but could be used as the basis for "rational scrutiny and discussion" of such choices.

Criteria for Professional Ethics

In professional ethics, this same issue about the universality of moral values has generated a debate that concerns the question of whether a professional group could justifiably hold ethical principles that diverged from those of the broader public. This would mean that such professional principles would not be generalizable beyond the profession. Thus, for example, lying might be considered wrong in the broad society but it could be argued that doctors can justifiably lie to their dying patients about their illnesses.

Since the 1960s, sociologists have been analyzing sources of power among professionals. The key issue has been the considerable institutional autonomy granted to some professionals by society that has increasingly been seen as encroaching on the autonomy of clients or the legitimate concerns of the larger public (Freidson 1973; Haug and Sussman 1969; Larson 1977; May 1976). An older, functionalist image of the dedicated professional providing expert service to clients and the public has often given way to the image of elitist professionals protecting their social and economic power at the expense of clients and the public (Kultgen 1988).

Growing out of this sociological critique, the central debate in professional ethics has been over the "separatist thesis." This thesis argues that professional ethics are independent of "ordinary" ethics, that is, of the ethics of the people professionals serve. As Goldman (1980) explains it:

> The most fundamental question for professional ethics is whether those in professional roles require special norms and principles to guide their well-intentioned conduct. . . . We may define a professional role as *strongly differentiated* if it requires unique principles, or if it requires its norms to be weighted more heavily than they would be against other principles in other contexts.

There has been considerable debate back and forth among philosophers over the merits of differentiated professional ethics. The argument has turned primarily on whether violations of the rights of clients or the public can be justified by the professional purposes such violations serve. Overall, the balance of opinion among philosophers seems to lie with the argument that professional ethics should coincide with, or at least be functionally related to, ordinary ethics (Bayles 1981; Freedman 1978; Gewirth 1986; Goldman 1980; Kultgen 1988; Martin 1981).

In public professions in the United States, a similar question has an even longer history, largely because of public distrust of governmental power in general and of bureaucratic power in particular. Meyerson and Banfield's (1955) and Altshuler's (1965) empirical studies of planning in the 1950s and 1960s argued that planners held ideas of the public interest that were quite different from those held by elected officials in their cities. In both cases, they thought that the planners' ideas about the public interest were not justified, largely because they saw the public interest simply as a value judgment, an expression of opinion, not as the result of reasoned, moral argument. If it were simply an expression of opinion, only an elected official could make a legitimate determination of the public interest. Planners did not have this legitimacy, and their "differentiated" values were a cause for concern.

As chapter 4 indicated, the planners in this sample, at least, also had their own ideas of the public interest, and these could quite easily diverge from the values held by decision makers and members of the public, so differentiated values could present a possible problem that would need to be addressed in a justifiable set of ethical guidelines.

A Normative Framework for Planning Ethics

The criteria for a defensible ethical framework for planning is that it be made up of principles that are disinterested, universalizable, consistent, and not different from those held by the people served by the profession. The starting place for the normative framework that will be used to evaluate the actions of the planner in this sample is the AICP's *Code of Ethics and Professional Conduct* (1981; Figure 9.1). The nature of such a code is to lay out principles that apply universally, at least in the professional context, and that would encourage consistency. How closely these principles correspond to ordinary ethical values will have to be examined.

The AICP code is structured around the idea of obligations to various groups served by planners. The primary obligation is seen as the planner's responsibility to the public and to serving the public interest, which is defined in both procedural and substantive terms. In addition, secondary obligations are owed to clients and employers, to colleagues, to the profession, and, finally, to the planner himself or herself.

The code is used only as a starting place because I will argue, in addition, that the principles in it can usefully be thought of as forming a hierarchy in which some are more binding than others. Thus, laws and duties of justice are the most binding principles; accountability and service to the public interest take second place; and principles concerned with responsibilities to the profession constitute a third level of obligations.

The rationale for this hierarchy is both theoretical and empirical. The correspondence between the hierarchy and what planners were already doing would not, by itself, justify its use, but if independent arguments can provide justification, the correspondence would seem to be a practical advantage.

FIGURE 9.1

AICP Code of Ethics and Professional Conduct
(Adopted September 1981)

This Code is a guide to the ethical conduct required of members of the American Institute of Certified Planners. The Code also aims at informing the public of the principles to which professional planners are committed. Systematic discussion of the application of these principles, among planners and with the public, is itself essential behavior to bring the Code into daily use.

The Code's standards of behavior provide a basis for adjudicating any charge that a member has acted unethically. However, the Code also provides more than the minimum threshold of enforceable acceptability. It sets aspirational standards that require conscious striving to attain.

The principles of the Code derive both from the general values of society and from the planning profession's special responsibility to serve the public interest. As the basic values of society are often in competition with each other, so also do the principles of this Code sometimes compete. For example, the need to provide full public information may compete with the need to respect confidences. Plans and programs often result from a balancing among divergent interests. An ethical judgment often also requires a conscientious balancing, based on the facts and context of a particular situation and on the precepts of the entire Code. Formal procedures for filing of complaints, investigation and resolution of alleged violations and the issuance of advisory rulings are part of the Code.

The Planner's Responsibility to the Public

A. A planner's primary obligation is to serve the public interest. While the definition of the public interest is formulated through continuous debate, a planner owes allegiance to a conscientiously attained concept of the public interest, which requires these special obligations:

1) A planner must have special concern for the long range consequences of present actions.

2) A planner must pay special attention to the interrelatedness of decisions.

3) A planner must strive to provide full, clear and accurate information on planning issues to citizens and governmental decision-makers.

4) A planner must strive to give citizens the opportunity to have a meaningful impact on the development of plans and programs. Participation should be broad enough to include people who lack formal organization or influence.

5) A planner must strive to expand choice and opportunity for all persons, recognizing a special responsibility to plan for the needs of disadvantaged groups and persons, and must urge the alteration of policies, institutions and decisions which oppose such needs.

6) A planner must strive to protect the integrity of the natural environment.

7) A planner must strive for excellence of environmental design and endeavor to conserve the heritage of the built environment.

The Planner's Responsibility to Clients and Employers

B. A planner owes diligent, creative, independent and competent performance of work in pursuit of the client's or employer's interest. Such performance should be consistent with the planner's faithful service to the public interest.

1) A planner must exercise independent professional judgment on behalf of clients and employers.

2) A planner must accept the decisions of a client or employer concerning the objectives and nature of the professional services to be performed unless the course of action to be pursued involves conduct which is illegal or inconsistent with the planner's primary obligation to the public interest.

3) A planner must not, without the consent of the client or employer, and only after full disclosure, accept or continue to perform work if there is an actual, apparent, or reasonably foreseeable conflict between the interests of the client or employer and the personal or financial interest of the planner or of another past or present client or employer of the planner.

4) A planner must not solicit prospective clients or employment through use of false or misleading claims, harassment or duress.

5) A planner must not sell or offer to sell services by stating or implying an ability to influence decisions by improper means.

6) A planner must not use the power of any office to seek or obtain a special advantage that is not in the public interest nor any special advantage that is not a matter of public knowledge.

7) A planner must not accept or continue to perform work beyond the planner's professional competence or accept work which cannot be performed with the promptness required by the prospective client or employer, or which is required by the circumstances of the assignment.

8) A planner must not reveal information gained in a professional relationship which the client or employer has requested be held inviolate. Exceptions to this requirement of non-disclosure may be made only when (a) required by process of law, or (b) required to prevent a clear violation of law, or (c) required to prevent a substantial injury to the public. Disclosure pursuant to (b) and (c) must not be made until after the planner has verified the facts and issues involved and, when practicable, has exhausted efforts to obtain reconsideration of the matter and has sought separate opinions on the issue from other qualified professionals employed by the client or employer.

The Planner's Responsibility to the Profession and to Colleagues

C. A planner should contribute to the development of the profession by improving knowledge and techniques, making work relevant to solutions of community problems, and increasing public understanding of planning activities. A planner should treat fairly the professional views of qualified colleagues and members of other professions.

1) A planner must protect and enhance the integrity of the profession and must be responsible in criticism of the profession.

2) A planner must accurately represent the qualifications, views and findings of colleagues.

3) A planner, who has responsibility for reviewing the work of other professionals, must fulfill this responsibility in a fair, considerate, professional, and equitable manner.

4) A planner must share the results of experience and research which contribute to the body of planning knowledge.

5) A planner must examine the applicability of planning theories, methods and standards to the facts and analysis of each particular situation and must not accept the applicability of a customary solution without first establishing its appropriateness to the situation.

213

FIGURE 9.1 (continued)

6) A planner must contribute time and information to the professional development of students, interns, beginning professionals and other colleagues.

7) A planner must strive to increase the opportunities for women and members of recognized minorities to become professional planners.

The Planner's Self-Responsibility

D. A planner should strive for high standards of professional integrity, proficiency and knowledge.

1) A planner must not commit a deliberately wrongful act which reflects adversely on the planner's professional fitness.

2) A planner must respect the rights of others and, in particular, must not improperly discriminate against persons.

3) A planner must strive to continue professional education.

4) A planner must accurately represent professional qualifications, education and affiliations.

5) A planner must systematically and critically analyze ethical issues in the practice of planning.

6) A planner must strive to contribute time and effort to groups lacking in adequate planning resources and to voluntary professional activities.

Source: Reprinted with permission of the American Institute of Certified Planners. The American Institute of Certified Planners (AICP) and the American Planning Association (APA) revised this 1981 version of the AICP Code and adopted a restatement of Ethical Principles in Planning, including the AICP Code of Ethics and Professional Conduct, in 1992. For the current version of the AICP and APA documents, and for any subsequent amendments or additional advisory rulings, write to AICP, 1776 Massachusetts Avenue, Washington, D.C. 20036.

Justifying a Hierarchy of Principles

One of the most obvious problems the planners had in dealing with the ethical issues they raised was knowing what to do when their own ethical principles conflicted with each other. Formal codes of ethics like the AICP's can easily be faulted as providing little guidance in this area. They list many a priori principles that are presented as equal in weight. The AICP code, in this case, at least specifies that obligations to the public take precedence over those to employers, to colleagues, and to the profession. Even so, a more elaborated hierarchy of values that was normatively justified would be useful.

I proposed and provided a justification for such a hierarchy in chapter

2. It is consonant with the principles in the code and also seems to correspond moderately well to the planners' own ideas of ethics. The planners themselves were generally not explicit about using a hierarchy, though a few were. One who had just been talking about honesty and loyalty argued that ethical judgments were:

> an unconscious action, and I don't know that consciously you can sort that out easily.
> Q: But if you were ever in a situation where honesty and loyalty conflicted?
> Oh, honesty's first, for sure.
> Q: How do you know?
> I'm just built that way. I have a built-in mechanism to be honest. I need to be honest.

Implicitly, many of the others had similar ideas. Table 9.1 lists items from the AICP code that were included in the questionnaire. The rankings in the left-hand column indicate how clearly the planners accepted each issue as posing an issue of ethics. They placed adherence to the law at the top (ranks 1 and 2), followed by the duties of justice to be truthful (ranks 3, 5, and 6) and fair (rank 9). The one item on accountability (rank 4) ranked with duties of justice, which hardly seems surprising. Serving the public interest ranked lower (ranging from 8 to 23). Even the consequentialist planners in the sample, who might have been expected to emphasize the public interest more, seemed to accept this hierarchy. There were no statistically significant differences between deontological and consequentialist planners on the rankings in Table 9.1. Thus, the planner's own hierarchy and my proposed framework for evaluation differ only on the issue of loyalty/accountability, which I have argued is more problematic than it appeared to these planners.

The normative justification for this hierarchy rests largely on the argument made in chapter 2 that some of these obligations were more impartial or universalizable and so more binding than others. Legal obligations were the most binding of all, simply by virtue of their status as laws. The law is impartial and universally applicable to all people in similar circumstances. Among the moral obligations, duties of justice were the most binding, owed to all individuals. They were what Kant (1964) called "perfect duties," which did not allow for exceptions.

The weakness of the principle of loyalty is that it is not impartial or universalizable (Baron 1984). It involves an obligation whose only justification is that a special relationship exists, for example, within a family or an agency. For public civil servants, the duty to be accountable to the

TABLE 9.1

AICP (American Institute of Certified Planners) Code and Planners' Definitions of Ethics[a]

Rank by Planners	Item in the AICP Code	Mean for Planners[b]
Responsibility to the Public		
8	Not serve the public interest	1.49
11	Not concerned about long-range consequences of present action	2.00
18	Not concerned about interrelatedness of decisions	2.67
6	Not provide accurate information on planning issues	1.40
14	Not give citizens opportunity for real impact on plans	2.16
7	Knowingly reduce choice for disadvantaged	1.41
19	Unintentionally reduce choice for disadvantaged	2.72
12	Knowingly harm natural environment	2.05
23	Unintentionally harm natural environment	3.31
Responsibility to Clients and Employers		
10	Fail to exercise independent professional judgment	1.60
1	Sell services by implying influence by improper means	1.02
2	Use office for personal gain not in public interest	1.07
13	Work beyond professional competence	2.16
4	Reveal confidential information of employer	1.38
Responsibility to Profession and Colleagues		
5	Inaccurate representation of views of colleagues	1.38
9	Not fair in review of others' work	1.67
17	Not share results of experience/contribute to knowledge in field	2.60
15	Apply standard solution to planning problem	2.48
22	Not help professional development of students and beginning planners	2.98
16	Not increase opportunity for women and minorities as professionals	2.58
Self-Responsibility		
20	Not improve own professional education	2.76
3	Inaccurate representation of own professional qualifications	1.09
21	Never volunteer to help groups lacking resources	2.89

Notes:

[a] These statements are all worded negatively because of a quirk in the nature of ethics. While any ethical action can be thought of in positive terms, we often tend to think of ethics in terms of infractions. Thus, lying would be identified by most people as an issue of ethics, but we are less likely to think of this as an obligation to tell the truth. The import of some of these items—knowingly harming the environment, for example—is made almost meaningless by positive wording.

[b] Scale: 1 = clearly an ethical issue to 4 = clearly not an ethical issue.

public through elected officials is on more solid ground. It is impartially and universally owed to all. Thus, the issue of when the demands of accountability ended and those of loyalty took over was important for the legitimacy of the action but was also often difficult to determine.

Finally, the principle of serving the public interest, in all of its many deontological and consequentialist forms, was less like a perfect duty and more like a duty of benevolence simply because it was more discretionary. It could not be owed to each individual as a matter of right, as duties of justice were, but was owed to all the public.

This image of a hierarchy of values would suggest that the planners would always be obligated to obey the law, to be truthful and fair, and to do no harm. They would also be obligated to be accountable to decision makers, but they would have to be careful to analyze when issues really turned on the question of accountability and when they turned instead primarily on claims for personal loyalty. Finally, planners would be under a general obligation to serve the public interest, but exactly what form this would take would be more subject to their own definitions.

The AICP code, of course, does not use this hierarchy, though just as the planners in the sample did, it recognizes its logic implicitly. Legality, for example, clearly ranks higher than accountability. Among the provisions related to responsibilities to employers are those concerned with legal issues, such as conflicts of interest and improper use of influence or office (B.2 to B.6 in Figure 9.1). The provisions related to accountability (B.2) and to keeping confidences (B.8) are also in this section. When these two sets of responsibilities conflict, the code is quite clear that legal obligations take priority over accountability. Section B.2 states that "A planner must accept the decisions of a[n] . . . employer concerning . . . objectives . . . unless the course of action . . . involves conduct which is illegal"; Section B.8 enjoins keeping confidences except when disclosure would be "(a) required by process of law, or (b) required to prevent a clear violation of law."

Duties of justice are not clearly recognized in the code as a separate kind of principle at all nor, at times, as being broadly applicable to planning. Fairness is only referred to in relation to evaluating the work of colleagues (C.3), though the planners in the sample clearly saw it as a principle with application to their relations with the public as well. Not doing harm and respecting the rights of others (D.1 and D.2, respectively) wind up under self-responsibility, which somewhat blurs their strongly reciprocal quality.

Even so, the presence of three items on truth suggests the importance of duties of justice as well as the central role of truth in planning. One involves providing accurate information to the public and to decision makers (A.3), seen as an aspect of the planner's primary obligation to serve the public. Others relate to truthful representation of the views and qualifications of colleagues (C.2) and of one's own qualifications (D.4).

On the whole, in fact, this particular hierarchy does not seem to conflict in spirit with the AICP code. The code's own explicit wording places laws above loyalty. In the same spirit, it seems very unlikely that the AICP would condone sacrificing either the law or the truth to serving, for example, a broad, long-range view of the public interest.

Planners' Values Versus Ordinary Moral Values

Does the AICP code and the idea of a hierarchy of ethical values represent a set of strongly differentiated professional values that would separate planners off from the public they are supposed to serve? On the whole, the answer is "no," though the possibility of differentiated values could arise in relation to definitions of the public interest.

Many of the planners did not see their professional values as in any respect different from their values as ordinary people. One, when asked about the ethical values that guided him, said:

> I think that the major values that guide the work of a planner are the same values that guide any member of our society—go back to Christian or Judaic ethics—planners aren't much different.

This reaction was most characteristic of planners with a deontological view of ethics who were stressing the duties of justice such as truth and fairness. In their professional lives, these values were simply applied, as they are in the AICP code, to the characteristic problems raised by the context of planning. A few consequentialist planners did say that they thought their professional values diverged from their own private moral values. Tom Stuart made a distinction between his consequentialist ethics and his personal ethics in chapter 7. In the former, good ends encouraged him to use means that he felt would not be acceptable in the latter. Another consequentialist planner made much the same point but somewhat less directly:

> I guess what I would say is the more politically active a planner becomes, the more ethical compromise he's going to have to stand, but the trade-off is getting things done. You get into the political arena where budgets are made and laws are passed and decisions . . . then that's action. You're going to be a party to the wheeling

and dealing or the compromising or the concessions or the influence peddling or whatever the hell you got, and I found it very exciting to kind of be a part of all that.

Some other planners said that they thought that their own ideas about the public interest diverged from those held by the public. This raised the problems of elitism and differentiated values that concerned Meyerson and Banfield (1955), Altshuler (1965), and Vasu (1979). It could sometimes lead planners into covert pursuit of their goals. Accepting the idea that good ends could justify questionable means could lead to radically autonomous action.

The code provides little solution to these problems. It enjoins accountability (see Figure 9.1): (B.2) "A planner must accept the decisions of a[n] . . . employer concerning . . . objectives." However, it adds the caveat that this should be done only if "the course of action to be pursued is [not] inconsistent with the planner's primary obligation to the public interest."

If, as the idea of a hierarchy suggests, accountability to decision makers and serving the public interest are seen as equal obligations, the code also provides little guidance for this very common and central planning dilemma. Accountability to decision makers provides the critical link to the broader values of the community. It has always been intended to prevent the radical autonomy among public professionals that some private professionals have acquired. It is enforced through the bureaucratic structures in which public servants work. Unlike doctors and lawyers, who traditionally have worked either in private practices or in bureaucracies that they controlled, public planners have always worked in bureaucracies where they answered to elected officials or their appointees. Even so, however, should accountability always override planners' judgments about the "interests" of the communities they serve?

Here the planners' own ideas about this common dilemma, and the dictates of philosophy, both suggest procedural guidelines that provide a solution. The answer is open discussion of differing concepts of the public interest, with each side justifying its position through rational, generalizable argument.

Philosophical support comes from three rather different sources, one concerned about the public interest, the second concerned about lying, and the third concerned about loyalty. All three are consonant with the ideas presented earlier about moral justification as a process of rational discussion. They also coincide with the planners' own sense that the public interest should result from a process of balancing the ideas of planners, decision makers, and members of the public.

Positivist philosophers and the social scientists such as Altshuler (1965), who were influenced by them, thought that it was impossible to have rational justification of normative judgments. Decisions about values or goals or the public interest had to be made either by those with the greatest political power or by those with institutional legitimacy, but they could not be subject to rational decision or debate since value judgments were essentially only emotional statements.

Philosophers critical of positivism have maintained that normative judgments, including those about the public interest, can be justified rationally (Baier 1965; Bourke 1968; Hancock 1974; Toulmin 1950; Warnock 1978). Looking at how people actually think and talk about value judgments, they say that we treat ethical judgments as objectively true or false and subject to rational verification. In discussing them, we give "good reasons" for why we think an action is good or bad, right or wrong.

Working from this "good reasons" school of philosophy, several writers have argued that the public interest is a normative judgment, arrived at by a process in which various interests assert and justify claims that their recommended courses of action would serve the interests of the public (Flathman 1966; Held 1970; Sagoff 1988). This gives rise to the assertion that some policy that serves the public interest would only have legitimacy and weight in the policy-making process if it were based on the kind of impartial, universalizable justification discussed at the beginning of this chapter. The argument that a particular course of action would serve the public as opposed to some other, narrower interest would only make sense if it were framed in impartial terms and would apply equally to all members of whatever group would be affected (Flathman 1966).

Held (1970) adds the further requirement that the normative claims must be weighed by political decision makers who have legitimate authority to make rules and decide on claims. Flathman (1966) and Sagoff (1988) both argue in somewhat different ways that it is this authoritative decision making that makes the public interest a moral concept, giving decisions legitimacy even for people who see them as conflicting with their own individual self-interest.

In addition, fundamental in the arguments made by Held, Flathman, and Sagoff is the idea that the dialogue should be open, in the sense that any claim must be convincing not only to those who are already believers but also to those who are not: both to those who would benefit and to those who would be harmed. This theme is elaborated on in Bok's (1978) discussion of the ethics of lying. She considers the question of how a prima facie unethical act such as a lie might sometimes be justified. Her answer is what she calls "the test of publicity," which draws on the ideas of justification and generalization that are so central to public ethics (Bok 1978, pp. 92–93):

> I would like to combine this concept of *publicity* with the view of justification in ethics as being *directed to reasonable persons,* in order to formulate a workable test for looking at concrete moral choice. It will be a test to weigh the various excuses advanced for disputed choices. . . . Such a test counters . . . self-deception. . . . It challenges privately held assumptions and hasty calculations. It requires clear and understandable formulation of the arguments used. . . . It requires us to seek concrete and open performance of an exercise crucial to ethics: the Golden Rule. . . . We must share the perspective of those affected by our choices, and ask how we would react if the lies we are contemplating were told to us.

Such a test could not be satisfied by reference to the dictates of conscience, to imagining what others would say, or even necessarily by discussion with staff or coworkers. While these might all be helpful, they could all be biased toward a predetermined but wrong conclusion. Bok (1978) argues that only real public debate and justification would meet the test for issues of public policy. The requirement for such a process would also have the salutary effect of making people examine more carefully whether there were alternative courses of action available that might not raise ethical problems.

Bok's test of publicity would apply to the violation of any ethical duty. It seems most obvious in the case of duties of justice, where reciprocity is the key and the harm to another, in terms of violated rights, would generally fail the test. However, acting covertly in violation of the principle of accountability, for example, should certainly be subject to public justification as well.

If some philosophers have been concerned about rescuing the public interest as a valid moral principle, and more generally about the need for open justification of actions, a few others have been concerned about the limits of loyalty when it conflicts with the public interest. Baron (1984) looked at situations faced by engineers whose professional judgments about an appropriate course of action conflicted with loyalty to their companies and superiors. She also developed a test based on an open decision-making process. Loyalty should only take precedence if there has been a full discussion within the organization of the pros and cons of the proposed action. If in such a process the judgment of the engineer or planner is overruled, then "going along" may be appropriate.

While the planners in this study were clearly not thinking about the public interest in such abstract terms, their idea of the public interest as a balance was very similar. With few exceptions, they granted to elected officials the final authority to make decisions, but many saw their own role as more or less actively engaging in a discourse over what would best serve the public. In such a process, planners' values could be quite different from those of other participants, but they would have to submit their values to a process of scrutiny. One explained the way he saw such a process:

> The issue of what you do when you're at odds with the vast majority of your constituents—we have done that. There are certain plans and there are certain programs that we have worked on that have been not well accepted at all, both by the public and by the politicians. . . . Ethically, if you think you know what's right and nobody else agrees with you, you're probably wrong. However, you might not be. So you still give it your best shot. If you can't convince *anybody,* either you're wrong or your argument is so weak that you may as well forget about it. . . . If you can make a case and if you can convince anybody, then you're probably on some kind of right track. . . . If you can get yourself in the situation where you can maintain some kind of dialogue—that you say, "Okay, you say I'm wrong. Tell me why I'm wrong. I say I'm right. I'm going to tell you why I'm right." If you can get any kind of dialogue, you can usually find some midpoint . . . and, you know, maybe somebody has to give a little more than the other, depending on how strong their argument is or their information is or whatever. As long as you do that—and I think that's the ethical way to do it—then I think you're okay, and if you have to compromise from what you feel is less than the ideal, I don't think that's unethical.

Thus, taken together, the AICP code and my hierarchy of values can provide a justifiable set of nonself-interested, universalizable principles for guiding the behavior of planners. The use of the hierarchy also could increase consistency by giving them guidance in the many situations where several ethical principles could conflict.

The values embodied in the code and the hierarchy would serve to keep planners' values from diverging from those of ordinary people. Laws, made by representatives of the people, would take precedence over duties of justice, which themselves provide protection from violations of basic moral rights. Below them, accountability and service to the public interest would balance each other. Conflicts between any of these values would be resolved through a process of normative justification of competing claims, ideally through Bok's (1978) test of open publicity.

This image of balancing competing claims through rational argument serves as a reminder that the code, the hierarchy, and its associated procedural test are all normative guidelines. How closely these guidelines could be adhered to in actual daily planning practice was shaped by factors such as the roles the planners played, how they thought about ethics, the amount of risk that was involved in taking an action, and the practicality of acting. These influences will be explored in chapters 11 and 12. First, though, it is necessary in chapter 10 to look at the actions the planners actually took and how these corresponded to the evaluative framework laid out here.

10

Acting on Difficult Choices

The planners had to act on a wide range of issues. In many cases, it was easy to know what to do and easy to do it. These were bread-and-butter ethical choices, not glamorous but important to the effective functioning of any real ethical system. Other cases posed issues that were difficult to sort out or that involved conflict and risk to act on.

This chapter will examine the actions the planners took on the ethical cases that were described in chapters 2 and 3. In particular, it examines the general strategies available to the planners to deal with the issues they faced. It also applies the guidelines of the AICP code and the hierarchy of values to the eighty-two most difficult choices the planners had to make and compares this evaluation to their own evaluations of their actions. As before, this examination of the issues paves the way for looking in more depth at the decisions made by planners in different roles or with different approaches to ethics.

Perhaps not surprisingly, the planners themselves tended to evaluate their own behavior in a more favorable light than my "external" evaluation did. In general, they did accept the primacy of laws and duties of justice. They also accepted the principle of accountability, but loyalty created many ethical dilemmas, and demands for loyalty as opposed to accountability were not always easily disentangled. Generally, loyalty carried more weight for them than it did in my guidelines, and the issue of justice carried less.

Of the 480 cases of ethical issues that the planners identified, 260 involved situations in which they had to make decisions. In 244 of these cases, they talked about what they actually did. The rest were either still in process or, because of the flow of the interview, simply did not get explored in detail.

The classification of what a planner did about a case was based on a description of what he or she did and why. It included their own assessment of whether the action was ethical or not, as well as my assessment using the principles developed in chapter 9. For actions that the planners said were ethical, the strategies they used for acting ethically can be explored. In many cases, particularly where choices were difficult or where they thought they had acted unethically, they gave justifications for their decisions. These can provide additional information about why they chose as they did.

The planners themselves said that in 12 percent of the cases they acted unethically. The evaluation using the AICP code and my hierarchy suggests that they acted unethically in 16 percent. The line between ethical and unethical action was sometimes hard to define. Good reasons could sometimes be given for actions that seemed on their face to be wrong and some actions taken for good reasons proved to be flawed in other ways.

Difficulty of Issues

If the idea of the ethics of public servants produces any images beyond those of corrupt bureaucrats taking bribes or engaging in "honest graft," it is likely to produce the opposite image of true public servants, risking their jobs by blowing the whistle on corruption or waste or fighting for the powerless underdog. As one might expect, however, none of these images is very accurate, though each does have some connection to the reality of planning.

Of course, not all ethical choices are the same to deal with. Among the cases raised by the planners there were small ones and large ones, just as there were difficult ethical acts and easy ones. Either small or large decisions could lead to unethical behavior.

The cases can be examined from the point of view of how difficult each was to act on and what the planners did about them. Each was classified as "easy," "moderate," or "difficult."[1] About one-third of the issues fell into each of these three categories, and I will focus on the two extremes.

Easy Issues

Planners facing easy issues were less likely to be explicit about this aspect than ones who had to deal with difficult ones. One planner, for example, virtually defined an ethical issue by whether it was difficult or not.

Speaking about trying to raise the regional perspective on some local issue, she said:

> Those aren't ethical issues. They're diddly. I guess I didn't feel it was much of an ethical issue because I wasn't in much political danger. What creates ethical conflicts, I guess, is when I feel I'm constrained in doing something that I believe in because of political concerns.

In lots of cases, doing what was ethical was not difficult. This is important to recognize as central to the effectiveness of ethics. Difficult ethical dilemmas involving pressures and risks are much more glamorous for popular reporters and academics alike, but if being ethical mostly involved such choices and actions, it would be much more difficult to rely on ethics in everyday life. The best safeguard for ethics in the public service is not heroic individuals, though they certainly should be valued. Instead, it is political and organizational settings that encourage and reward routinely ethical behavior. The fact that many of these planners really had to think hard to come up with ethical issues with which they had been involved was often not due to lack of ethical awareness or imagination on their part but appeared to be a reflection of environments in which ethical dilemmas did not often arise. As one said in response to the question of whether she had a deliberate strategy for avoiding problems:

> No [laughter]. I think at least the position now that I have—there are certainly a lot of checks and balances on what you do. It's not that we're dealing as much with developers . . . in some of the things that we do here, but I really think that the department and the commissioner have a good reputation—you have to judge things on their technical merit.

Many of the easiest issues to deal with were small ones. Almost 40 percent related to legality. Avoiding conflicts of interest and not allowing developers to influence their judgments through small gifts or lunches were issues that many planners simply took in stride. Other examples resulted from their affirming obligations to adhere to standards or principles that they accepted as ethical. In 22 percent of the easy cases, planners talked about the need to be careful about being fair or open or objective or, occasionally, loyal or even legal. Personal or bureaucratic pressures sometimes drew them away from these basic standards.

Difficult Issues

Difficult issues often were difficult both to make and to act on. Of the 37 percent of these issues that involved the public interest and the 13 percent that involved equity, many raised conflicts with other ethical principles, such as loyalty or openness. This often made it difficult to decide the right thing to do, but the difficulty of acting was not primarily a function of the difficulty of deciding. These were issues that created conflicts not only in the planner's mind but also in the real world. Some were the stuff of popular portrayals of ethical public servants blowing the whistle on illegal actions within their agencies or throwing up a job and going to the press after heavy political pressure from a political boss. Actions such as these could place some planners at the eye of a storm of controversy and hostility, but even less dramatic or less public actions involved pressures that were difficult to withstand.

Twenty percent of the cases involved planners who were put under substantial pressure by developers or decision makers to tailor their analyses to a given political outcome. Thirteen percent involved favoritism or significant violations of the law. Some planners withstood the pressure under these circumstances. One director whose mayor and council were pressing her to be a little less "strong" in her comments on a project said:

> I've said "I understand what you're getting at . . . but it's still the responsibility of my department and my staff, including myself, to respond the way they feel is best for this project." I'm not willing to do that because if we do that on this one project, we should then assume that role on all the other projects. I think the issue is one of applying pressure.

Another more junior planner told how he had been drafting a sign ordinance and was told to exempt certain kinds of signs belonging to influential local businesses. He did.

Many of the difficult issues, including most of the public interest ones, involved conflicts within the bureaucracy that at least potentially pitted planners against agency or political superiors, such as city managers or mayors. Four involved personnel or budgeting issues in which directors felt caught between loyalty to their staffs and demands from above to cut staff or make personnel decisions that they opposed.

Actions

The planners' responses to these easy and difficult issues could be either ethical or unethical—by their own definitions or in light of the criteria developed in chapter 9. Ethical responses included resisting unethical behavior by avoidance or by various degrees of resistance (Table 10.1). Faced with an issue, especially if it involved a choice between two principles, planners in a third of the cases just said only that they acted ethically, often giving some reason why the action was ethical. In 12 percent of the cases, as we have seen, the planners themselves said they had acted unethically.

When the planners described themselves as acting ethically, the strategies they used seemed to vary with the difficulty of the ethical issue they were confronting. Easy issues were generally dealt with by preventive avoidance (9 percent), by moderate resistance (52 percent), or by just doing what the planner judged to be ethical (25 percent) (see Table 10.1). Difficult issues were likely to produce moderate resistance (23 percent) or active resistance (20 percent). Issues posing a moderate challenge involved using all the possible strategies.

Preventive Avoidance

Avoidance meant trying to make sure that an ethical issue would not come up. Keeping social distance from influential people to reduce pressures for favors, not owning property in the community, trying to

TABLE 10.1

Strategies for Action

| Strategy | Difficulty of Ethical Issues (percents) | | | |
	Easy	Moderate	Difficult	Total
Preventive avoidance	9	4	1	5
Moderate resistance	52	43	23	39
Active resistance	6	10	20	12
Ethical choice	25	30	45	33
Unethical action	7	14	11	12
Total	100	100	100	100

Note:

n = 222 ethical issues. Some cases are missing because they could not be classified according to difficulty.

ensure fairness through bureaucratic procedures or objective analysis, not talking to friends who were developers about certain kinds of issues— these were all preventive strategies.

One planner who reviewed large development proposals talked about the way strong political pressure was exerted in the review process. In this environment, undue pressure and corruption were two sides of the same coin. In order to protect himself, he indicated that:

> It is desirable to put everything in writing rather than to conduct anything orally, so that everything will remain on record. Also another thing, I find, is that it is important that the files should be maintained properly and all the information and correspondence should be available to the public so that if anybody has any doubt or any questions concerning the project, they should be able to see it. It's a public document.

This may have seemed an excessively bureaucratic response, but one of the purposes of such bureaucratic procedures, as several others pointed out as well, was to try to ensure fairness and openness.

There were also planners in the sample who raised issues hypothetically, explaining that it was not an issue for them because of their agency's rules or management style or the image they had created as an honest agency or the values of the decision makers or the community. One director in Texas discussed how the rules of his department prevented problems:

> For example, I won't let a planner design a subdivision if it's within our jurisdiction. I won't let any of the staff represent an applicant on a zoning case or anything that will appear on an agenda of any of the boards or commissions or the council. Now if they want to design a subdivision in the next county, I don't have a problem with that. People ask me to do that. As long as it's not in our jurisdiction, it's not a problem. . . . Every department head has to file a financial disclosure statement and we are subject to the city's ethics ordinance. So everything is very open.

At least one member of his staff who was also interviewed referred to these rules as well. Such mechanisms were more structural examples of avoidance.

Resistance

Moderate resistance was the most common strategy by far, used in 39 percent of all the cases. It was a largely reactive strategy, used against various kinds of pressure to behave unethically. It was the planners' equivalent of the injunction to teenagers to "just say no"—to bribes or gifts, to violations of the law, to lunches with developers, to offers of consulting work, or to anything that would pose a conflict of interest.

Resisting the temptation to violate positive principles was one form of moderate resistance and probably the easiest to do since it involved one's own actions. The temptation to be unfair to developers who were a pain, to get back at someone who had created problems for the department, or to close certain groups or individuals out of a decision-making process were all issues that the planners talked about. One planner talked about the temptation to violate the small details of the law, and her rationale for not doing it was both typical and telling:

> The laws in California are so complicated, it's very tempting to just kind of shoo over them and probably no one will sue you, and I occasionally make some error in notifying, and I have to decide if I want to do anything about it. But I really try to keep the council and the board and the commission very honest and not let them get away with stuff, and if we've screwed up and haven't notified someone, we admit our error and continue the issue. If it's something serious and if they want to do something, we say, "You can't do it. You've got to wait two weeks."
> Q: Do you do that for ethical or for strategic reasons or both?
> Both. I think maybe the ethical even stronger because . . . well, it's hard to separate them. Once you start screwing around with it, you . . . kind of all is lost and there aren't any rules for people.

More difficult was resisting pressures from other people—from decision makers to change findings or recommendations, from influential developers or citizens to see issues their way. In some contexts, these pressures were easy to withstand, but this was by no means always the case. One planner worked in a state agency in a position where he often had to deal with issues on which the governor or state legislators had already made decisions on political grounds. They then wanted analysis justifying the decisions:

> Professionally, in my own mind, when the political pressure is so great that I know the decision has been made, I still do profession-

ally anything I would have done anyway in terms of analysis, presenting all the pertinent facts to the decision makers. If they want to ignore it at that point, that's *their* decision. Hopefully, the case I've made will convince someone.

He then gave an example where such an analysis had identified a significant problem with a program of state land acquisition, resulting in some changes:

But, again, this is a political decision, but the principle was upheld and the community did get some money. In my mind, if we had just approved it because the governor said so, this would have been unethical, but the end result, if you really want to be honest about it, was not the best. In terms of operating within the political realm and doing as much as we could, I think it was probably not bad.

More difficult issues often went hand in hand with more active resistance. In 12 percent of the cases, planners faced ethical challenges that they felt had to be dealt with more forcefully than through quiet resistance. These planners took issues of corruption to agency leaders or to the district attorney, fired staff members for unethical behavior, blew the whistle on officials who engaged in illegal acts, or actively fought against policies that they thought would harm the public interest.

In a more positive vein, a few of these "active resistors" felt it was their duty actively to raise the issue of affordable housing or to help empower the poor. The fact that they were counted as, in effect, resisting the dominant values of their communities shows the difficulty of dealing with the issue of social justice.

Acting on Choices

Finally, there were the cases where people said only that they had acted ethically or unethically. A substantial number of these decisions were fairly easy to make and act on. A quarter (25 percent; see Table 10.1) of the ethical actions were of this sort. These usually involved situations where someone might argue that the planner had done something improper but where they felt confident they had not. One planner gave the example of an irate landowner who accused him of making an illegal deal when a change in the location of a road meant that the owner's property was no longer needed. However, the planner knew that the road had been changed for planning reasons and not in order to benefit another landowner.

Forty-five percent of all of the difficult issues involved this kind of ethical choice (see Table 10.1), including conflicts between competing ethical principles, such as different definitions of the public interest or between accountability and the public interest. Either choice might be thought of as ethical and planners just had to choose.

Among issues where the planners said they had acted unethically, two-thirds were easy or moderately easy. People were naturally more likely to talk about unethical actions that did not reflect too badly on themselves; in reality, they may not have been engaging in highly unethical behavior. Easy unethical issues included cases of political etiquette or the ones where people were saying, in effect, "I'm human. I aspire to follow certain principles but I don't always succeed."

Some choices did reflect less well on those who made them. Some planners reported cheating on their time sheets. This was a reflection of their negative attitudes about the large bureaucracies in which they worked. These instances were one example of a somewhat wider range of behaviors that were supported by the idea that "everyone does it." These included not providing truthful evaluations of employees, passing difficult decisions off onto someone else, and even selective enforcement of some laws.

Many of these decisions, though, both ethical and unethical, involved difficult choices between competing principles. Since the planners' judgments about these choices differ somewhat from mine, it will be useful to discuss these choices together and to examine how their reasons compare to my hierarchy of laws, duties of justice, accountability, and the public interest.

Acting on Competing Principles

The planners made choices between competing principles in eighty-two cases (Table 10.2). In relation to the categorization of cases as easy or difficult, fifty-eight of these cases were difficult ones. As one might expect, they included almost three-quarters of all the difficult cases. The remainder of the difficult cases were primarily situations where the action that needed to be taken was fairly obvious but it was the action itself that was difficult to take for some reason. These will be dealt with more in chapter 11 as well. In addition, Table 10.1 includes twenty moderate and four easy cases involving conflicts.

A look at Table 10.2 suggests several things. One is that there were

TABLE 10.2
Ethical Conflicts

	Law	Duties of Justice					Accountability		Public Interest		Total
	Law	Truth	Fairness	Promises	Openness	Not Doing Harm	Loyalty	Keeping Confidences	Justice	Consequentialist	
Law	0										
Duties of Justice											
Truth	0	0									
Fairness	3	0	0								
Promises	0	0	0	0							
Openness	0	0	0	0	0						
Not doing harm	0	0	0	0	0	0					
Accountability											
Loyalty	10	7	2	1	3	0	2				
Confidences	0	0	1	0	0	0	1	0			
Public Interest											
Justice	2	0	0	0	2	0	4	0	2		
Consequentialist	5	0	3	0	3	1	25	1	2	8	
Total[a]	20	7	9	1	8	1	55	3	12	48	82[b]

Notes:

[a] The total is arrived at by adding all items in both the row and column with the same heading.

[b] This is half the number of total conflicts since each case involved two conflicting principles. Adding as in (a) counts every case twice. For example, the case of the woman who blew the whistle on her boss involved legality and loyalty. It is counted among the ten legal issues in the first column and with all the issues involving loyalty—adding across that row—10, 7, 2, 1, and 3—and then down the loyalty column in the middle of the page—2, 1, 4, and 25—to total 55.

233

no conflicts among duties of justice. The single largest group of conflicts (twenty-five) was between consequentialist ideas of the public interest and loyalty. Loyalty also conflicted frequently with the various duties of justice (thirteen times) and with the law (ten times). Another group of twelve conflicts occurred between different ideas of the public interest.

In many of these cases, the explicit idea of a hierarchy of values could provide some guidance and consistency when principles conflicted, but this was not always the case. For example, in Table 10.2, the twelve conflicts that lay along the diagonal all presented cases involving conflicts between two versions of the same principle—two different ideas of the public interest or conflicting loyalties to different groups, for instance. By and large, the question of which action would be the right or the best one turned primarily on empirical evidence and careful analysis. Compromises might be possible and appropriate, but, in the end, these equal choices simply serve as a reminder that these were difficult decisions.

Loyalty and Accountability

In a public profession, the purpose of loyalty to officials is to ensure accountability to the public, but these two elements of accountability exist in tension and can conflict. For these planners, loyalty was the largest generator of conflicts, producing fifty-five or a third of all the conflicts in Table 10.2. Its questionable status in philosophy seemed to be reflected in the sense that many planners had that there were other obligations or ideas of the good that could legitimately compete with it. Traditional Progressive administrative theory, however, places a high priority on the accountability of non-elected officials. So how was a planner to know whether loyalty should be or should not be a binding obligation? This depended both on the nature of the competing principle and on the process by which the decision was made. The AICP code and my hierarchy of values suggest that laws and duties of justice should take primacy over accountability and that accountability should take precedence over a planner's own idea of the public interest if the decision was made in an open process.

There were twenty-three cases that presented conflicts between loyalty and the law or loyalty and duties of justice: truth, fairness, keeping a promise, openness, and not doing harm. An additional twenty-five cases presented conflicts between loyalty and consequentialist ideas of the public interest. The balance involved conflicts with justice or with competing ideas of loyalty itself.

Loyalty Versus the Law

In the specific cases involving loyalty and the law, the planners were generally clear that loyalty, or accountability, could not justify a violation of law. This judgment corresponded with Section B.2 of the AICP code (see Figure 9.1). Ten cases involved conflicts between laws and loyalty (see Table 10.2). In six, the planners chose the law; in two, they chose loyalty but said that what they had done was wrong. The final two, one vague planner and one aethical planner, did not say that what they had done was wrong. This suggests a clear recognition among planners with an ethical viewpoint that laws took precedence over the demands of their superiors.

For those who chose the law, these were often very difficult and sometimes dramatic choices, but the planners involved all felt that their decisions were right. The planners knew they were on solid ground even if they had to blow the whistle on elected officials, as these did. A planner whose plan commission sued the city council for violating the zoning ordinance had come into his position after the conflict was well under way. He could perhaps have left the issue primarily to his commission, which had raised it in the first place, but instead he became an active participant, saying:

> I didn't feel that I had any choice. The worst thing that I could have . . . the most neutral thing that I could have done was just to do nothing—let it play itself out. I was involved as a professional. I mean, this is a position, I guess, where the professional aspect of the thing was central because I saw the position of the commission as being right. The decision [that is, the violation] wasn't in support of the planning principles and was the opposite of everything that we were supposed to be doing, and that was the "right" way to go.

Loyalty and Duties of Justice

Conflicts between loyalty and moral duties of justice produced less consensus among the planners. Some felt they were on solid ground in resisting what they saw as unwarranted demands for loyalty. The same planner whose commission sued the city council was also engaged in a dispute with his council over changes in the personnel system. There was no issue of legality involved, but he did think the case posed issues of fairness to the employees and of pressure to "toe the line":

I suspect part of what I'm trying to do now is show that I do disagree with the system, with the style and the politics of this place. I don't know whether it's being interpreted that way or interpreted as stubbornness, as lack of a team player, a trouble-maker, and that kind of stuff. Whereas I see it as I'm just trying to do it fairly, the ethical way, and that kind of stuff—that is, consistent with trying to do away with the kinds of abuses that we have seen in the past, of favoritism.

In a sense, he had little to lose given the nature of his council and his already poor relations with them. The same might be said of the planner who kept his promise to a neighborhood group not to divulge their housing demands to city officials.

In the thirteen cases that involved conflicts between loyalty and duties of justice, such as truth, fairness, and openness, planners chose loyalty in seven. Five of the seven planners who raised cases of pressure to lie were in this group who chose to act loyally. One lied to a reporter; the others changed studies or projections or came up with predetermined findings. None was willing to say that these actions were unethical, though they did raise them as problematic. One was a planner whose environmental impact statement (EIS) supported the location of an indus-trial facility in an industrially zoned area. However, influential nearby residents pressured the agency's board to have the EIS modified to show negative environmental impacts. The director then pressured the planner, a loyal technician, who changed the EIS. Afterward, he was not willing to go any further than to say that the change "deviated from professional planning principles," but he clearly had difficulty accepting its legitimacy:

> The final EIS essentially says the use was inappropriate because of the impacts da-da da-da da-da. And to me, that's the closest thing I've seen as something that sort of tore at me from a professional ethical standpoint because if I was called into court, I in good conscience could not testify and support that final environmental impact statement. However, knowing the way we prepare affidavits in the agency, if that was the case, I would probably not be asked to testify. It's a fine line because the people who worked on it had a certain value system. Part of that's personal, part of it's profes-sional. . . . You could interpret it that the board had a different opinion of community and public welfare values than the staff did. I try to console myself and say that was the case.

This planner and the others were all technicians.

The AICP code's requirement to provide full, clear, and accurate information and the principle of the primacy of duties of justice would define these cases of "waffling" on the truth as unethical. In a profession whose primary function is to analyze policy issues and provide advice, the obligation to be truthful might be considered especially central. Since the underlying purpose of loyalty to officials was accountability to the public, how well was this served by putting the stamp of technical legitimacy on inaccurate analysis that would be used as public justification for a policy? Both of these arguments suggest that the choices these planners made were wrong and that this duty of justice, at least, should supersede loyalty for planners.

While they tried to justify their behavior on the grounds of loyalty, the real problem these planners faced was lack of leverage in their bureaucratic jobs. Some were more willing to resist pressures to fudge analysis if the data they were dealing with were "hard" statistics rather than softer, more judgmental analysis, such as a population projection. This distinction, in effect, gave them a little extra leverage—an argument that decision makers sometimes accepted as legitimate—but otherwise, they had few options for countering these pressures from superiors.

Leverage, Accountability, and Covert Action

These decisions involving loyalty and truth and loyalty and other duties of justice were not easy and could involve risk. The one other option the planners sometimes had was to act covertly. One planner who saw his technical analyses misused did sometimes go outside the normal channels to correct matters, but he went carefully:

> With the planning commission, say, there may be times when I realize that information about a certain project is not well represented by the city manager's office. It's not unusual to have what you consider to be very important information just not get to the public officials. Sometimes they would call on the phone and say, "What's up?" With, say, a particular commissioner or somebody that I knew was very trustworthy and who I thought was smart enough to protect their sources, there are times when I have occasionally brought up things that I'm sure the management would not have wanted me to bring up. . . . It would be purely verbal communication. . . . I'm sure there was some substantial risk involved. In other words, I'm not necessarily someone to go out on a big limb, certainly not if it would get back to me.

Covert action did violate the principle of accountability, though. Quiet action, which minimized publicity, was not the same as covert action. George Walters, who quietly alerted a plan commissioner and through him the mayor to the conflict of interest of the commission chair, was acting quietly but was still "going through channels." The planner who blew the whistle on illegal activity by her boss by giving a negative evaluation of him to her board was also not acting covertly. She followed the procedures specified in the AICP code for blowing the whistle. She did it quietly, but the board was the official decision-making body for the agency. She had to "live with" them later and had to deal with the consequences, both positive and negative, as it turned out, for the action she took. She said:

> I've gotten feedback from people. In fact, when the new executive came in, who was on the board at the time and who I knew, just to talk to, [he said] he was very wary of me and my role in this and that "I had to prove myself." I thought it was overblown, actually, but people had talked to him, so in that sense that made me very aware. And we don't intend to leave this area—it's a very small town.

These planners were on more solid ethical ground than the planner quoted above who was making a covert end run around his boss or another planner who went to a local newspaper to reveal a corrupt zoning deal by a councilperson. While these latter individuals acted for good purposes and this kind of covert action has acquired a romantic aura, these cases did raise the real problem that the planners, who were obviously not elected officials, could not be held accountable for their actions by their superiors. They wanted to have their cake and eat it too—to act for good ends but not be responsible for their actions.

Again, the issue seems in part to be one of options and leverage. Several planners in the sample who had tried to report cases of corruption found an unwillingness among their superiors or other appropriate officials to look into their charges. Was going to a newspaper instead an action that was more accountable to the larger public or less so? If data were manipulated or even accidentally distorted in a public presentation, did it improve or short-circuit accountability for a planner to communicate with an elected official not in the regular chain of command? Technicians were certainly more likely to choose loyalty in these situations; activists were more likely to act covertly to achieve a goal that they could still argue involved accountability in a larger sense.

While these are arguments over the actual meaning of accountability, there is an additional consequentialist argument that weighs against covert action. Acting covertly did seem to come from, but also perhaps could contribute to, a sense of cynicism about the need for accountability. The planner who covertly blew the whistle on corruption was equally willing to act in a similar, covert manner in a substantial policy disagreement with his council. The planner who made an end run for "truth" was one of the aethical ones. If these very few cases are anything to go on, one covert action might encourage additional covert action; that could be the fundamental consequence of a lack of accountability.

Loyalty, Accountability, and the Public Interest

In cases where loyalty conflicted with duties of justice, the latter should and generally would take precedence over the former. However, in situations where loyalty conflicted with a consequentialist idea of the public interest, the obvious choice was less clear. Here again, accountability was a central issue. Planners might argue for their own ideas of the public interest, but they did not have the authority to make the final decisions. This was where the test of an open process of discussion could help planners decide whether or not to go along as loyal team players. It would suggest that they should resist pressures from others to "go along" if discussion has been inadequate. The underlying premise is that proposed actions that would have bad public consequences would be less likely to survive such a process of open discussion.

Conflicts between loyalty and a planner's own consequentialist idea of the public interest arose in twenty-five cases. The planners in nine of these had a chance to engage in an open process of developing the agency's or the city's position and did not feel that they were pushed into being loyal. Several said that they could live with losing on some issues as long as they were not "muzzled." One planner, when asked how he handled such conflicts with his manager, said:

> Very carefully [laughter]! Well, I've always tried to say what I think, and I feel comfortable now in being fairly open and honest with my comments. It's a very sensitive area.

Another who loyally gave way when his city manager was put under pressure by a developer indicated that his relations with the manager were sufficiently open to allow for argument on other occasions:

> We just had to stand up and be soldiers and do it, and generally we rationalized on just that basis. In fact, we've used it to advantage

subsequently since then to curb the manager from doing that kind
of thing: "This is the kind of problem you get when you do that.
Why don't you let us play it straight?"

These planners recognized that they were expected by their agencies to
give up some of their autonomous judgment and act as team players.

"Going along" was sometimes seen as a cop-out, however, and this
was more likely to be the case if the planner felt he was being railroaded
by not having a chance to express his views. Five cases of this sort were
given, and two of these were the only ones involving the public interest
where the planners themselves said that what they had done was unethical. One of these planners who disagreed with several policies he had
been involved in developing said:

> I've never found a way to successfully subscribe or to enunciate my
> disagreement with that. There are no mechanisms that I feel com-
> fortable or confident of using, saying, "I think this is a wrong
> process." I think that's basically one of the conflicts that I've dealt
> with, and I think it's symptomatic of working for a powerful agency
> which has close relationship with a mayor who has a particular
> point of view. What do you do when you see a policy that you think
> is not what it really is? This is not an agency where it's easy to
> dissent, where there are regular . . . At least in the last five or six
> years during this administration, there's no sort of a mechanism in
> the agency now—we don't even have nonconfrontational
> discussions.

If planners had little respect for their decision makers, their acquiescence
left them with the gnawing feeling that they had been weak and wrong.

There were also situations where planners resisted the demands of
loyalty when it conflicted with their ideas of the public interest. As with
conflict between loyalty and duties of justice, there were several ways
they could do this. They could resist openly or covertly within the system
or, in extreme cases, they could resign in protest. Open resistance
corresponds to what Hirschman (1970) described as "voice," resignation
is a means of "exit," while covert resistance again seems to be a case of
wanting to have your cake and eat it too through a kind of quasi-exit.

Resistance and Resignation in Protest

When planners were put under pressure to take positions they thought
were indefensible, they had only a few choices. They could say no, they
could resign in protest over the policy, or they could undercut it covertly.

Some did "just say no" directly or occasionally by getting someone with more leverage to make their case for them. Implicitly, this was a threat that they would "go public" with their disagreement, though no one gave a case where they actually had. Five cases of this kind of resistance were given. A health planner considered having a showdown with her board but, in the end, drew back:

> All right. We're talking about an excess of beds and all we have is a number for a region—it in no way tells you how to get from that region down to hospitals . . . there are myriad ways that you can get down to the hospital level. The decisions were how do you make the breaks. If you did it as pure, pure planning, you could come up with all kinds of things—well, this number in this area. Instead, the discussions went around about excluding certain hospitals from consideration. They're either too big or they're too powerful—powerful being a big part of it—the two are interrelated, and in this town the hospital politics are unbelievable. . . . Well, in this particular instance, I in fact pulled out the canons and looked at them again and there was one on the public interest because—and it's hard at this point to reconstruct—it had to do with who we were excluding and why, and I think it was at a point where there was no basis for the exclusion. It was purely on power. I was ready to sort of go the route and say "I won't do this and here are my ethics" or the principles in the canons. We were able to work it further and sort of pull back—this is within the staff—pull back from a confrontation that allowed me to say that what we were doing was okay.

Covert disloyalty over policy disagreements was about as common as covert resistance to illegality. Four planners made end runs around officials or leaked information to people who supported policy positions that they agreed with but that their departments did not support. A planner who worked in a highly politicized and corrupt environment leaked information to supporters of a project on which her agency was officially neutral. She made no attempt to say that what she did was "nice," but she did say it was justified:

> There's another sensitivity here. There's a sensitivity that certain of the developer's attorneys are very well placed governmentally. They are friends of [my agency], and it would not be nice to do that to them, to stab them. But I don't care. I think these guys are worms! So I think the agency's interests in this are very narrow and kind of dirty and so going behind this, I think, is totally ethical. . . .

I do think that basically sneaking around behind and offering people information is not a wonderful quality. I think that there is an ends justifies the means situation, but I don't think the means are wonderful by any means.

The problem with this approach to resistance was simply the same as covert action to challenge illegal behavior, though with even less justification. The planner could not be held accountable for this decision to support a policy different from that of her agency. This was not exactly a case of dirty hands in the sense of violating rights or doing harm, but, at least implicitly, it was an assertion of radical autonomy from decision makers.

Theoretically, at least, planners, particularly those in senior positions such as directors, also had the option to resign in protest over decisions with which they strongly disagreed. One planner had done it, not over a policy disagreement but over pressure to illegally approve a project. Another had threatened his council that he would. Several others talked about circumstances where they thought it would be necessary—if they were asked to violate the law or if their own ideas of the public interest were consistently at variance with those of their officials. One technician, for example, said:

> There is what I call the "best" decision that can be made and the "right" decision, and I sit down and I have to make that distinction in my own mind each time. The right decision is the one where I think it ought to go. The right decision doesn't always come out of the process because I'm aware that it is a process, a political process, and that there are a whole number of variables involved in the process. There are the issues of local community participation in terms of neighborhood association participation, there are the prevailing political attitudes of the majority of the planning commission or the city council. Those will change year to year, and so I have to step back and view the decision that comes out as to how much variance there is between what I perceive to be the best decision and the right decision and I have to balance those out all the time. To go back to the question you raised earlier, at what point would I leave the community or would my values influence my leaving it—probably when I think there weren't enough right decisions being made over some period of time.

There was a somewhat unreal quality about these efforts to specify ultimate limits. One wondered whether, if the ultimate situation ever arose, resigning in protest would really be the choice. When faced with situations they saw as unethical, planners were more likely to resign quietly and go elsewhere. This was done by six people. This action, of course, saved them personally from being pressured into unethical behavior, but it probably would not affect the problem that caused them to resign. In this sense, it was not an example of active resistance.

The planners who resigned quietly as well as the others who talked vaguely of resignation may have been reflecting more general attitudes about organizational "disloyalty," which seems to be disapproved of not only in public organizations but in private ones as well (Baron 1984; James 1983). A survey of ninety whistle-blowers found that many were harassed by superiors and, less often, by peers at work (Farnsworth 1987). Those in the private sector all lost their jobs; half of those in government were no longer in the same agency. While many believed that their actions were right and had affirmed their sense of honesty and self-esteem, the price in financial and emotional terms was prohibitively high. One planner in our sample who was involved in uncovering unauthorized use of public resources by elected officials had to have police protection. We saw earlier the distrust faced by the woman who went to her board about illegal actions by her boss. Both of these cases involved "heavier" issues of legality and not simply policy disagreements over the public interest.

Resignation in protest over policy issues seems to be regarded in largely the same light. Weisband and Franck's (1975) study of appointed officials in the federal government found that of 398 officials who resigned of their own free will between 1900 and 1970, only thirty-four (8.7 percent) left in protest. The reason seemed to be that resignation in public protest over a policy effectively ended their careers. Only 3 percent ever held a similar or higher level job in the federal government again. Internal pressure against resignation was very strong, and such resignations left people open to systematic ad hominem attacks organized by loyalists to the administration and unrelated to the issue that prompted their protest. This vilification was quite different from the pattern in Britain, where such principled resignations were considered to be quite appropriate.

Because the cost of resigning in protest was so high in the United States, Weisband and Franck (1975) showed that officials who disagreed either resigned quietly or often stayed on, arguing that they could be more effective exercising "voice" from inside an administration than by exiting. Several planners who bowed to decisions they did not agree with said that in fleshing out the way the decision would be carried out in practice they tried to mitigate the harm that they thought would be done. A planner whose city wanted to build a marina on a lake said:

If there is going to be bad impacts on the lake because of the marina, from a professional standpoint that's bad to do that and maybe we shouldn't have the marina, but from the city standpoint, you try and play down those impacts and mitigate them wherever you can.

Some of the discussions of conditions that would have to exist to justify resignation simply sounded like excuses because planners felt, quite justifiably, that the price of such public disagreement was too high.

The lack of an effective "exit" option encouraged the development of covert activities, such as end runs and leaks. This may have had the effect of allowing debate on the issue to take place in the public arena but it reduced the accountability and increased the autonomy of the bureaucrats who did it.

Duties of Justice and the Consequentialist Idea of the Public Interest

If loyalty posed difficult conflicts with planners' ideas of the public interest, ideas of the public interest were also capable of generating conflicts with laws or duties of justice. Here again, the principle of the primacy of laws and duties of justice should hold, but the problem was whether a good end could, indeed, ever justify infringing on such a duty. In a similar way, accountability and the openness of the process of argument seemed to be key factors in the legitimacy of the decision. These conflicts produced a variety of actions, ranging from some clearly involving dirty hands to others in which achieving the end of serving the public interest did not require the sacrifice of rights.

Dirty Hands

There were five cases where planners' commitments to the public interest carried them into clear violations of laws or strict duties of justice. Of these planners, only two really had dirty hands, and their hands were not very dirty. They were not Robert Moses destroying neighborhoods and reputations to build parks or highways (Caro 1974). One was a transportation planner, a self-confessed "bike freak" who was so committed to his issue that he used office resources to lobby on his own despite orders not to. The other was the environmental planner who was trying to get conservative rural communities to plan. He designed a subdivision for a local official, wired a grant competition to give money to communities that needed to plan, and disregarded some violations of state contractual obligations for strategic reasons.

Both these planners accepted the idea that what they did was unethical in the sense that it violated laws or was obviously unfair. Indeed, the wired competition gave the environmental planner considerable unease because he could put himself in the other person's shoes:

> It is a bias in what we are doing. First in this specific case, where I was involved, we were trying to channel money into an area that had serious environmental threats posed to it, and also to give money to jurisdictions that haven't been involved with the program . . . [to] get them in the swing of things and become more informed, more active planners. That was the intent, and the intent was not to have a fair solicitation of proposals—so it was highly unethical in that sense. It was wired, so to speak, which used to very much trouble me in the private sector when I knew that that was going on. It was one of my highest complaints of unethical activity, and here I am on the other side.

Both of these planners felt that the end really did justify the means in these cases.

These actions were not as covert as the covert violations of loyalty, but they were done quietly because the planners both knew that their behavior would not stand up to open scrutiny. Even if one accepted the argument that the harm done was not very great, acceptance of their approach provided no guideline for preventing greater harm. Greater harm was likely to grow out of greater cynicism than either of these planners had and would probably be more covert and so less controllable.

Clean Hands

In other cases where duties of justice appeared to conflict with planners' ideas of the public interest, the conflicts proved to be more apparent than real and the planners said they had served the public interest without recourse to dirty hands. All of these cases involved processes of negotiation or exchange in which the planner dealt fairly openly and directly with those who would be affected by the decision. The possibility of doing harm was real—this was why the planners raised the issues—but in most cases they felt harm had been avoided.

One planner saw this as an issue of fairness. She was negotiating for renovations in a housing project. The issue was whether the owner could really afford all the necessary improvements. Because the negotiation was not fully open, she was unsure of his financial capacity and, sensitive to the principle of fairness, the planner accepted some compromises, but she did not give up the renovations she thought were essential for the public good.

Several other cases involved conflicts between the planners' ideas of the public interest and openness to the public. The AICP code includes such openness as one of the elements of serving the public interest, thus making it a strong obligation. The planners' own evaluations of their actions in these cases indicated that they accepted the idea that the public had a right to have access to the planning process but that planners were not bound to accept as final the public's views on issues. This, of course, was the same approach that many of them took to defining the public interest. A transportation planner was the point man for a plan for the expansion of a subway system. The proposal for a new station was opposed by a group of nearby residents. He was convinced that the station served the interests of the larger community and of future residents and justified his disregard of the opposition on these grounds, but still the conflict bothered him.

The pattern that these decisions suggest was that in conflicts between duties of justice and the public interest, duties of justice, such as being fair and ensuring access to an open planning process, were accepted as binding even by the planners who violated them. Dirty hands were a problem but not a very large one. Moreover, in some respects, the "conflict" between ends and means was sometimes illusory. The obligation to be fair or open did not preclude a planner from achieving what she thought was in the public interest. Compromises were sometimes possible that avoided violations of rights, and an open process did not mean that planners felt they had to accept citizens' definitions of the public interest as binding.

Justice

Finally, where in the hierarchy of ethical obligations and values did social justice fit? The AICP code has as one element of the public interest the obligation to "strive to expand choice and opportunity for all persons, recognizing a special responsibility to plan for the needs of disadvantaged groups." Should justice be thought of as a strict duty of justice? The way the planners acted on it suggested that most dealt with it as simply another concept of the public interest, at most coequal with the consequentialist idea. For many, it seemed to be thought of as a general "duty of benevolence."

In two conflicts with legality, not surprisingly, legality won out. Neither was a case of principled civil disobedience. One was the case of the neighborhood planner who had discussed with some friends the idea of trying to do some private demonstration projects in a run-down neighborhood to show how revitalization might be done, but nothing came of the idea in part because it raised problems of conflicts of interest with their jobs as public planners.

In four cases that the planners described as involving conflicts between justice and accountability, they chose accountability. In all four cases, planners described problems of affordable housing or slum conditions in their communities and talked about how decision makers were unwilling to come to grips with them. These issues were risky and difficult to raise. None of the planners had actively worked to get the issue on the public agenda. They justified their behavior on the grounds of accountability but they still felt that they should have done more. One said that what he had done was unethical, and the clear indication given by the others was that they had taken the easy way out.

One talked about how he had gone into planning to serve the public interest. However, given his own caution and the parochial views of his officials, he found himself unable to accomplish very much. On the issue of affordable housing, he identified the unresolved conflict:

> I support affordable housing in the region, but realistically I have to plug it into Shelby. What the city council wants is what becomes important to me, which creates these conflicts. I just work for the council and the plan commission, providing information. It's their job to make the big decisions. The council has agreed to do a lot in their housing element, but they don't have anything now and lots of private groups believe they won't do much.

This sense of "copping out" stood in direct contrast to the way that people who did take on the issue of equity in housing talked about their choices. They did not raise the issue of loyalty but instead were concerned about being able to maintain their own commitment to equity and yet not close out the legitimate concerns of people who were not committed. They were trying to generate an open process in which discussion played a central role and which, characteristically, would result in some kind of compromise.

All of these planners at least were directly raising the issue of social justice as an obligation of some kind. However, the tip of a much more difficult problem was raised by the planner from Yonkers, who did not see equity as an issue in his community's use of urban renewal to promote revitalization. This case was evident only because Yonkers later became such a highly publicized controversy when a U.S. District Court found that Yonkers's renewal and public housing programs had been intentionally used to increase segregation in both housing and schools and that such action was illegal (Feld 1989).

There almost certainly were other instances where justice conflicted with consequentialist ideas of the public interest. Every zoning ordinance that restricts affordable or multifamily housing is based on an implicit idea of the public good that does not consider justice, but only three of the twenty-one planners who worked in the suburban areas likely to have such zoning raised this as an issue. A closet politician who worked in a state agency discussed this particular problem and identified the pressures that kept planners from raising it:

> Housing is a moral issue really. If you talk about ethics in planning . . . one of my pet beefs has been that planning, which is essentially a progressive concept, has been used for regressive . . . to buttress regressive social attitudes, you know, you wall off people from each other. You have your nice single-family land here and you put the mobile home people and you put the renters in the less desirable areas, and it's all sanctioned as part of the progressive land-use regulation idea. Every planner [is] confronted with questions of when to . . . subjugate their own personal concerns with what their boss or whoever pays their check is asking them to do. Obviously, if you're a suburban planner, you know what you're doing: you don't become a suburban planner to help poor people. That's kind of the nature of the game when you go into that job.

The equity issues raised by the planners usually did not involve legally guaranteed rights. Many of the planners may well have reflected general social attitudes in thinking of justice as having at most only the status of a duty of benevolence, an obligation that should be acted on but is not owed to everyone. Even one of the equity-oriented planners identified the practical difficulty, saying, "If [I] had an ethical imperative [to pursue social justice], I'd be working more hours. Why am I sitting around on Saturdays?" One might have a duty always to tell the truth or always to be fair, but the duty to right politically and socially ingrained injustices seemed overwhelming. Many other planners could see this as a moral obligation but not one that was binding on them in their particular work. One who did question the basic land-use policy of his town said:

It's not like it's discrimination—I mean . . . you can see that sometimes if a black person would come up with a request for something and he would be turned down and people would joke about it—"Hey, we got that guy, didn't we"—that would cause indignation, I think, to a reasonable person. In this case, it takes time to kind of see. [At] first, I wasn't at all sure that it was a cognizant action on their part, but after a while, I began to see request after request—good quality requests—for this type of housing being turned down. You bring this up as a matter for discussion; you know, on the next request, you say, "There is a demand, so much of our population is within this age group and within this income category," and you point out to them that there's nothing in the market in town right now that would provide housing for these people at a cost they can afford, but they choose to just totally discount [it]: "Too bad. They can go elsewhere or they will get here eventually. If they really want to live here, they just need to wait until they make more money." Now we have not had a lot of confrontations over that issue. We don't come in and say, "We want more apartments." In fact, the reverse is true since the community isn't supportive of that. So to a certain extent, if you are a true believer in the idea of democracy, you know—what the majority says, this is what you want—that gets a lot of the guilt feeling out of it, but at the same time it is very difficult to see and accept.

The active planners who used social justice as their central concept of the public interest gave it the status of a duty of justice, but other planners did not. Modifying this way of thinking would not be just a matter of clarifying the status of justice as an important ethical principle. Planners did not raise the issue more frequently in part because it was politically extremely controversial in the communities in which they worked. The planner who said that housing was a moral issue also talked about mobilization of bias in relation to equity issues. It was in the interest of dominant groups to keep this issue off the public agenda, and most planners were unwilling to challenge this bias for good reasons:

If a clear-cut decision can be made, black or white, then a planner should have a moral obligation to choose the white, but in the day-to-day world, most things—a great deal of policies—are not decided frontally. It's a process of past traditions: There are certain presuppositions that are simply not questioned. In going back to housing, the basic presupposition is that part of the American dream is to own your own home, and it's a legitimate government function to support homeownership through mortgage deductions et cetera. That's really a nondecision at this point; it's not questioned. It's not really questioned, so then it becomes a tough issue for an individual planner to raise this thing to the level of consciousness that there is a decision here. Keep in mind that we spend five times as much on middle-class homeowners as we spend for poor people on housing. . . . A nondecision is where the parameters are already set within which you operate.

Conclusion

These planners faced both difficult and easy issues in acting on ethics. Difficult ones, particularly those involving choices between competing ethical principles, are more interesting and provide an opportunity for exploring and evaluating what choices planners made in practice and under stress. However, if life were made up completely of difficult ethical decisions, ethics would be much less useful as a guide to behavior. Much of the real fabric of ethics for these planners was made up of the many small, easy choices that they made: to act on principles they held or to resist pressures to do what they knew was wrong. Creating environments that would support and encourage people in this kind of routine behavior would probably have an impact over a wide range of ethical issues, perhaps even including those involving dirty hands, which arose more out of cynicism than out of evil intent.

The planners' choices in the eighty-two cases of mostly difficult choices did suggest that they accepted the idea of the primacy of laws and duties of justice. If they did not always act on these principles, they were usually clear about why they did not and whether they had dirty hands. The demands of organizational and personal loyalty posed especially difficult choices. In cases where they were pressured to do inaccurate analysis or where they felt that a judgment about the public interest had been rammed through without giving them sufficient voice, they often felt bad even if they did go along. Sometimes they just said that what they had done was unethical. Sometimes they made an argument for the appropriateness of the choice despite their misgivings. A few chose covert resistance, but that posed ethical problems of its own.

The major disparity between their own evaluations of their behavior and mine was on issues involving justice. The AICP code places much greater emphasis on social equity than these planners did. This was the one notable example where the aspirations of the code were not matched by the behavior or at least the values of the planners. This hardly seems surprising since the moral obligation to serve justice is often given more lip service than actual adherence. Planners reflected the values of their communities in giving it low priority. This seems to me to pose a much more fundamental ethical issue than some of the actions the planners clearly recognized as wrong.

Even so, there were some planners who were concerned with social justice just as there were ones whose first thought was for accountability and others who worked actively to achieve the consequentialist public good. Chapter 11 will examine, at least in part, how the various groups in the sample did take on rather different issues and act in rather different ways.

11

Action, Justification, and Effectiveness

Planners' actions on ethical issues were closely tied to the way they acted as planners in general. The different roles that planners played were associated not only with different ways of thinking about ethics but also with different ways of acting. Active, consequentialist planners were more driven by goals and more willing to take on conflicts, for example, than were deontological technicians whose style was more reactive.

Of the three elements needed for effective ethical action—seeing issues, analyzing and justifying action, and acting—the first and some of the second have already been described. This chapter will evaluate how able the planners were to justify their decisions and to act on them. It explores how their actions were shaped by their approaches to ethical reasoning and to defining planners' roles. Empirically, the planners in the sample were quite varied in the kinds of actions their definitions of ethics imposed, in how they chose to act on ethical issues, and in how able they were to justify their actions.

Reasoning and Acting

Knowing whether they were able to act was fairly straightforward from their descriptions of what they did. If they should have acted in a certain way, either by their own definition of ethical duties or by mine, and they did not—not just on one isolated issue but on several—then they were considered to be unable to act. The question of whether they were able to justify their actions was more difficult to answer. What does it mean to be able to justify an ethical judgment? The standard given by a philosopher such as Frankena (1973) is strict. He suggests that justification of ethical judgments should involve being rational: that is, impartial, conceptually clear, and informed on the facts of the case. It also involves taking the moral point of view. Here he draws on Baier (1965), who argues that the moral point of view involves not being egoistic, doing things on principle, and being willing to universalize one's principles, that is, accepting the idea that an action that is right for one person in a particular situation would be right for all people in similar circumstances.

The planners in this sample varied a good deal in how well they lived up to this standard. It was also difficult to "operationalize" how rational their process of justification was, but a couple of indicators give some idea.

Almost no one talked explicitly about the idea that principles should be universalizable except, perhaps, for the four people who used the Golden Rule, which captures the essence of universalization. Many planners, though, when asked, were able to articulate the general principles they held. If they could articulate them as general, then this seemed to suggest that they thought of them as generalizable to all situations. The principle of telling the truth, for example, is a general injunction not to lie in all or most situations. There certainly were planners in the sample who were not able to come up with any general ethical principles. This did not indicate that they had no principles—most did and were able to use them to identify and decide on ethical issues—but in the abstract, some people had difficulty identifying them as general principles.

The conceptual clarity of their reasoning on their ethics cases could also be assessed. Some people made inconsistent arguments or were quite vague or confused in their framing of issues, indicating a lack of clarity in their ethical thinking. One planner, for instance, described in some detail how his department had a policy to prevent conflicts of interest and then went on to describe a conflict that he had and that he said posed no problem. Two others had developed fairly elaborate frameworks before the interview for talking about ethics. One could fit his own experiences into his framework, thereby giving them some clarity, but the other could not, so that the actual issues he talked about were rather vaguely defined.

Two other possible indicators of the adequacy of moral reasoning showed little variation among the planners but should be mentioned. Almost everyone took an impartial or nonegotistical approach to talking about ethics. The very few who did not were quite notable; this almost in itself defined them as aethical. Virtually everyone also recognized the need for facts as a basis for ethical decisions.

Even by their own definitions of ethical behavior, at least a quarter of the planners in the sample had problems with either justification or action. Among the vague and aethical planners and the narrow deontologists, more than half and even up to three-quarters of the planners were not able to articulate the principles that guided them, and similar proportions of these groups used muddled reasoning in discussing the ethical issues they raised (Table 11.1). Figure 11.1 indicates the relationship between justification and action. The vague planners were really able to do neither. Narrow deontologists were handicapped by their very restricted view of ethics. The aethical and some active, consequentialist planners (act utilitarians) ran the risk of being willing to act in ways that they could not fully justify. The closet politicians had the opposite problem, being able to justify why it was important to act without being able to do so. Beyond these twenty-four planners, most in the sample were both able to act and to justify their actions to themselves.

Ethics, Effectiveness, and Role

The planners' actions on ethical issues were shaped both by their approach to ethics and by their roles. Their approach to ethics defined what they saw as ethical issues and how they thought about dealing with those issues. Their roles were shaped, in part, by their ethical commitments but, in turn, also shaped what kinds of issues were likely to arise and how the planners acted on those issues.

The combination of a planner's role and ethical approach suggested what kinds of obligations were especially important. The various kinds of technicians, who were mostly deontologists, did not act the same way on ethical issues as did process planners or active consequentialists. Not only did their goals differ, but so did their attitudes about the means that would be appropriate for a planner to use.

Planners playing different roles and taking different approaches to ethics also had quite different ideas about what effectiveness in planning meant. For active consequentialists, effectiveness meant having an impact on achieving goals. For deontological technicians, it meant providing good advice. For process planners, it meant facilitating an open planning process. What was the relationship between being ethical and being effective? Was being ethical associated with being ineffective? Some planners wondered if there was a trade-off between them, but there were planners in the sample with quite varied approaches who were highly ethical and apparently effective and who seemed to disprove the idea that such a trade-off was inevitable.

The relationship between the ability to act and the ability to justify that action provides a framework for a look at the relationship between ethics and effectiveness. Here ethics is represented by the ability to

TABLE 11.1

Ability to Justify Ethical Decisions by Approach to Ethics

	Vague	Aethical	Narrow Deontologists	Process Planners	Substantive Deontologists	Public Interest	Rule Utilitarians	Act Utilitarians	Total
Principles Justifying Ethical Decisions									
None	2	3	2	1	2	1	0	3	14
Some	4	0	4	4	0	4	0	0	16
General principles	3	1	5	7	12	21	8	9	66
Percent with general principles	33	25	45	58	86	81	100	75	69
Clarity of Reasoning Regarding Ethical Action[a]									
Unclear	4	3	5	2	0	3	0	1	18
Some problems	4	0	1	1	2	1	0	1	10
Clear	1	1	4	9	12	22	8	10	67
Percent with clear reasoning	11	25	40	75	86	85	100	83	70

Notes:

n = 96.

[a] One (1) planner reasoned clearly but within a framework that was so unusual that he was not included here.

255

FIGURE 11.1

Ability to Act Ethically: Roles and Approaches

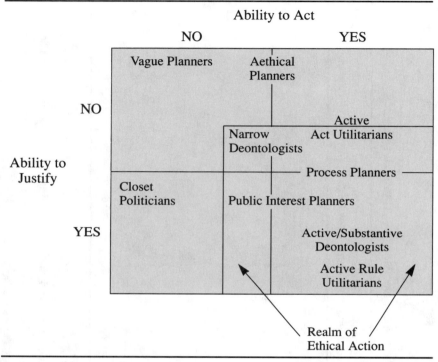

justify actions while effectiveness is represented by the ability to act. This framework can be used to identify the most obvious problems in the search for strategies of effective ethical action. Then we can focus in more detail on the strengths and weaknesses of different strategies and the forces that led planners to choose one or another.

This chapter will focus on groups of planners who combined particular roles with particular approaches to ethics (Table 11.2). The examination of groups that had difficulty acting on ethics will look at the vague and aethical planners first, regardless of their roles. The other two groups with particular problems were the closet politicians, regardless of their approach to ethics, and a few of the most active consequentialists (act utilitarians). In Figure 11.1, these various groups who either could not act or could not adequately justify their actions form a partial "frame" above and to the left of the majority of planners who were able both to act and to justify their actions.

TABLE 11.2

Planners' Role by Approach to Ethics

Roles	Approach to Ethics (percents)							
	Vague	Aethical	Narrow Deontologists	Process Planners	Substantive Deontologists	Public Interest	Rule Utilitarians	Act Utilitarians
Traditional Technicians	67	25	46	17	0	46	0	0
Passive Hybrids	11	50	27	0	14	19	12	0
Technician Activists	0	0	18	0	7	23	0	8
Active Planners	22	25	0	25	29	0	88	75
Process Planners	0	0	9	58	7	4	0	8
Closet Politicians	0	0	0	0	43	8	0	8
Total	100	100	100	100	100	100	100	100
Number	9	4	11	12	14	26	8	12

The seventy-two planners at the bottom right of Figure 11.1, in contrast, all met what might be thought of as the minimum requirements for ethical action. Their paths to ethical action were varied, however, because the way they defined both their roles and their ethics imposed different means for achieving ethical and effective action. Within this "bottom right" subset, we will look at two groups of active planners—the fourteen active consequentialists (plus one technician activist), and the four substantive deontologists who were also active planners. Then the actions of the thirty-three technicians who were narrow deontologists or public interest planners will be explored. They include the bulk (two-thirds) of all technicians (another 20 percent were vague or aethical planners). The chapter will close with an examination of the sixteen planners defined either by role or by approach to ethics as process planners.

Action and Justification: The Extremes

Ethical action required both the ability to act and the ability to analyze whether an action was ethically justifiable. Neither alone was sufficient, and all the twenty-four planners discussed in the next several sections had problems with either one or the other.

The Vague Planners

The nine planners who were vague in their approach to ethics were both unable to make a coherent justification for ethical action and unwilling to act (see Figure 11.1). Most were traditional technicians or passive hybrids. All had some kind of problem with justification. They often talked around issues without defining what the central ethical question or principle was. These planners were often unable to identify principles that they used as guides for ethical action.

If there was a common thread that tied these vague planners together, it may have been caution. Even the most politicized one was a cautious survivor, and a primary "obligation" for most appeared to be risk avoidance. This may have included avoidance of too clear an idea of ethics which might have raised uncomfortable issues. Indeed, one said of himself that he was a bureaucrat who "almost never makes a definite statement."

Since they shied away from conflict, they were less likely than others to have had any personal experience with ethical issues. Two raised no ethical issues on which they had had to act and three others had only one or two. Because of this, only two gave examples of situations where I thought they had acted unethically (Table 11.3). When they did have to act, their caution was a handicap for taking appropriate action. One said that he had been unethical in waffling on two issues where he should have defended the public interest more strongly. When they did act, resistance to political and other pressures was their primary strategy. They did not use active resistance or proactive efforts to accomplish positive goals.

Such a description makes them sound like straw men, set up as a model of ineffectiveness, but these were, in reality, just ordinary planners. They were rather mild-mannered and sometimes seemed anxious or uncomfortable with their responsibilities. Some had dealt with ethical issues even if they could not generalize about how they had done it. One had refused to pay a bribe required for a promotion, one of the most

TABLE 11.3

Planners Who Acted Unethically by Typology Combining Role and Approach to Ethics

	Unethical Planners[a] (percent)		
Role and Approach to Ethics	*Author's Definition*	*Planner's Definition*	*Total Number*
Vague	22	11	9
Aethical	75	75	4
Closet Politicians	44	44	9
Active Consequentialists			
Act Utilitarian	50	30	10
Rule Utilitarian	25	12	8
Active Substantive			
Deontologists[b]	0	0	4
Technicians			
Narrow Deontologists	60	20	10
Public Interest	22	22	23
Process Planners	0	0	16
All Planners	30	18	93

Notes:

[a] Planners characterized as engaged in unethical action, as defined by the author and by the planners themselves.

[b] Three (3) people who were not active planners were classified as substantive deontologists. They are not included here or in the discussion.

personal ethical challenges in the whole study. But in the end, their ability to act effectively on ethical issues in a deliberate and rational manner seemed to be weak.

The Aethical Planners

The vague planners shared some similarities with the aethical ones who were also unable to make reasoned and valid justifications for their actions. The difference was that the vague planners were simply vague; the aethical ones had a cynicism that prevented them from grappling sincerely and seriously with ethical choices. Three of the four aethical planners had done things that both they and I thought were unethical (see Table 11.3). Two of the four planners did not take a nonegoistic view of ethical issues. They thought not of what was right but of what would be personally safest or easiest. They could articulate principles like other planners, but these did not seem to be real guidelines for their own actions. Their reasons for acting on issues posing obvious ethical problems included avoiding hassles or risks or simply satisfying personal whims or desires. One, when asked why he had leaked information to a defendant in a suit, simply said, "It was fun." At least overtly, they rejected ethics as naive or troublesome. One could not help wondering if this was some kind of pose that they assumed for the interview, but the fact of assuming such a pose would itself be an indicator of their attitude toward ethics.

The other two aethical planners, while also cynical, were more confused about the roles they should play as planners. They lacked principles because they seemed to have little moral direction. Both seemed to have a drive to play an active role, but lacking any image of what an ethical active role might be like, they became cynical about the technical role they did play. Occasionally, they broke out into unprincipled revolt, acting covertly to do things they thought needed to be done.

As this suggests, active planners who had incoherent or cynical ideas about ethics were potentially loose cannons whose willingness to act could get ahead of their ability to justify those actions. In reality, this was not a major problem, at least in this sample, but it was not a hypothetical one either.

Two of the vague planners and one aethical one were active planners. Neither of the vague planners was motivated to act by strong personal values, so neither was really tempted to undertake risky, possibly unethical actions in order to achieve some important goal.

The aethical activist was strongly motivated by frustration, by ambition, and, in some part, by an idea of the public interest. By planning standards at least, he was an extreme example of a planner acting with the radical autonomy that affected a number of other consequentialist planners to a lesser degree.

Active Consequentialists with Dirty Hands

Two examples of radical autonomy will be given here to illustrate two rather different aspects of the problem. One, shown by the case of the aethical planner, was simply that consequentialist arguments could be used to at least try to justify very questionable actions. The other example relates less to the specific nature of the arguments made and more to an attitude that underlay them, an attitude that allowed other people to be treated as means for achieving ends.

The aethical planner was a young man with a rather narrow and unformed view of ethics. He was anxious to see results from his work in computer mapping and was frustrated by what he saw as the ineffectiveness of his agency. As a result, he got involved on the side with a private company, a direct competitor to his agency, which he thought could help to accomplish what he wanted to see done. The experience was heady, transforming him from a middle-level traditional technician into a covert activist. The initial justification for his action might have been adequate if the action he had taken had been less extreme:

> I wanted to do this for a personal challenge because it was sort of obvious that I couldn't do this in the context [of my agency]—I couldn't get any support. So I thought, "Well, okay, there's a real important need for this information, and it should be made available to the public," so [I went to] a business . . . to make the information available.

As it was, he recognized that his action was a violation of the principle of accountability to his agency and involved a conflict of interest—selling for profit information he had developed as a civil servant. Once he was involved, the need for rationalization was even stronger, and he began to see additional justification for his action because, he argued, it had more or less inadvertently produced some good consequences for his agency as well. In the end, he felt torn between his own direct sense of excitement and accomplishment and the more abstract sense that what he was doing was wrong. His ultimate justification showed a growing cynicism that allowed him to downplay ethical principles that restricted action:

> I think planners are a real naive bunch, and I think particularly in this town, where it is so dominated by the private sector and wheeling and dealing and stuff like that and big money and major development things—those things are not always real ethical. But that doesn't mean that they are wrong either—I mean, not entirely. It's like a man sees what needs to be done and you go about doing that, and you may or may not choose the right way, but I'm not as naive as I used to be to think that all good is accomplished by following the rules. It just doesn't happen. . . . The political process itself is not entirely ethical, and the fact that it's not ethical doesn't mean that it's bad, but it doesn't mean that you do everything according to Ann Landers or whoever wrote the book of etiquette. It's not always as open and honest.

His confusion between ethics and etiquette was not accidental since it reduced the claims of ethical duty to the status of table manners. He was well on his way to becoming a radically independent act utilitarian, guided only by his own ideas of the good.

The other example of radical autonomy was given by a planner who worked in a powerful agency in a corrupt political system. She had only disdain for the corrupt bureaucrats and officials she dealt with but shared the ambition and drive for effectiveness of others in her agency. When she found a project she thought was a good one, she worked hard to see it come to fruition regardless of principles such as loyalty or openness. A specific example she gave was the case of a mixed-use commercial and residential project on which her agency was officially neutral, but she believed it to be particularly good and in danger of being sidetracked by the city's internecine warfare between agencies and powerful interests. As a result, she set to work covertly to see that the proponents got helpful information, not only about the project itself but also about relationships and deals among opponents. In this case, her commitment to a clearly defined idea of the public interest might have justified her lack of accountability to her agency. She talked in some detail about the excellent study that had convinced her in the first place of the merits of the project and about the weak reasons for her agency's neutrality and about what she really suspected was going on:

> What I suspect is that the developer really wants to get a rezoning and sell the property off piece by piece—has no intention of developing the particular complex that he has proposed.

However, her willingness to act covertly made her a completely independent agent, free from responsibility to any representative of the public.

What was even more disturbing was that, more generally, in her drive for effectiveness, other people simply became means to her ends. She seemed to have only scorn for others who disagreed with her judgment about the public interest. In relation to protecting herself from exposure of her leaks on the mixed-use project, she said:

> The woman next door is a very good friend of some of the developer's lawyers and other people, and we are very friendly, and I've been very, very careful in what I've said to her to put a smokescreen up, to, you know, give myself some insurance, some protection.

More generally, she talked about her secretary as if she was a useful, if flawed, tool:

> I think sometimes that to be fair you have to be dishonest. I have a secretary who is shitty. I have one of the top ten world's worst secretaries. She is a very sensitive person, and good in other ways; she's confidential . . . she will lie for me. I value that very highly, she's very loyal; and even though she does not do good work, I give her good reviews.

The radical autonomy of these planners verged on becoming a problem of "dirty hands," involving violations of law or of duties of justice. A conflict of interest, even one intended to achieve a good end, is still unethical and in some cases illegal. A person who treats others as a means to her ends deprives them of autonomy and treats them, in effect, as objects, not as people. By adopting this kind of instrumental consequentialism, this planner was contributing to the very corruption and distrust that she saw herself as fighting.

These planners who were most vulnerable to the problem of radical autonomy faced a problem of the ethical justification not only of their means but of their ends as well. They recognized that their means failed the test of being ethical, but they justified their actions as serving good ends. However, the ends they acted to achieve had not been arrived at by any open process of decision making. They substituted their own ideas of the public interest for some idea arrived at through a public process. If their actions to achieve these ends were covert, as these both were, their usurpation of the role commonly played by elected officials and members of the public was complete. If their values happened to be shared by members of the public, this was entirely fortuitous. They themselves did not care.

These two cases, while particularly clear and extreme, were not the only ones raising these problems. In a number of other cases, planners were trying to achieve good ends—providing better planning in communities where planning was not well established or improving the transportation system, for example. Their means were wrong, though not necessarily earthshakingly so. They involved using office resources for private activities, doing a favor for an influential person, or "wiring" the results of a grant competition in advance.

The problem was not just the means, though. It was a cynicism about the honesty of the larger system in which they worked that reduced their faith in an open process. This cynicism, joined to strong policy commitments and sometimes to the sense of excitement and accomplishment that came from the action itself, could convince otherwise well-intentioned planners that wrong actions were right.

Justification Without Action: The Closet Politicians

The third group that failed the test of being able both to act and to justify their actions was the closet politicians. They faced the opposite problem from the autonomous planners. They were able to justify why action should be taken on issues they defined as ethical but they themselves were unable to act. Some people would have said that they were highly ethical but ineffective. They themselves, however, saw this ineffectiveness as fundamentally unethical.

Closet politicians had a broad view of the realm of ethics that made them unusually aware of ethical dilemmas. Two-thirds (six people) were substantive deontologists while the others were public interest planners (two people) or act utilitarians (one person). They not only saw the public interest as an ethical issue but were particularly concerned about social equity, which they saw as a duty of justice, not to be sacrificed for other principles. Largely because of this broad view, they were more likely than any other group to raise difficult issues and issues that presented choices between conflicting principles: loyalty and equity, loyalty and fairness or truth, or between different ideas of the public interest. They were also the only ones to talk about sins of omission—issues they should have raised but did not—rather than just sins of commission. If "being ethical" was a matter of seeing more difficult ethical issues and of having a strict view of duty, these planners probably did have a higher ethical standard than most others.

The closet politicians, though, were not very effective at acting. Unlike the vague planners, the issues that they were concerned with could not be dealt with by resistance alone. If they were to be effective, they had to act affirmatively, fighting for justice or environmental preservation, for example. But they shied away from the substantial conflict that this would have involved. As a result, when they did act, it was quietly—writing a memo or signing a petition. One said:

> I have given information to people who I know are at odds with the planning commission but I have not done it in a way where they could then use that information to come back to the planning commission. There is a network—there are many, many networks, and one of the networks is people who share certain values that I do in terms of housing in particular and planning for minorities and so forth. And I . . . I wouldn't say I have leaked . . . you know, I've given data and information on request where I knew that if the request had gone through the head of the agency, it would be lost. So it's more . . . it's basic facts and information to people which is available to everybody, not a special kind of thing, but make sure that they have it.

This action not only raised the problem of covert action but was in itself inadequate given the large goal he wished to achieve.

At least one planner who was not actually a closet politician but who shared some of their characteristics suggested that a focus on ethics might substitute for a concern with effectiveness:

> When I meet people who are much concerned with ethical considerations, I come away with the sense that they are preoccupied with that to the exclusion of other things. Why I am ethical is because I like myself. I have a very good opinion of myself. Being ethical, I don't do any bad things and I can think of myself that way. . . . For me, being concerned with ethics sort of fills a void, in the sense that [I feel] that I'm being involved in the public interest. . . . I just think that a concern with ethics may go hand in hand with a position of relatively less effectiveness . . . and I guess maybe I think that many people who are planners tend to be a little more retiring and cautious and have an appreciation and also an inclination to fill the void, not being as effective as a person who is in a more aggressive role. When I say it's not all that good, it's much easier to go along being ineffective if you have a lofty ethical behavior to take its place.

In fact, except for the aethical planners, the closet politicians were the group most likely to see their own actions as unethical (see Table 11.3). Even when they could justify choices on the grounds of loyalty to agencies or superiors, they saw their actions as waffling or worse. Since the choices they raised involved conflict between loyalty, equity, and duties of justice, such as truth and fairness, their judgments, as Table 11.3 also shows, were correct by my standards as well. They set themselves up for failure. One planner described efforts he had been involved in to recommend an organizational structure for addressing the many problems of a large slum area. Ultimately, the department and the mayor chose an organizational framework that he saw as ''a sellout—there was going to be a lot of activity and no action because there was a lack of commitment on the part of the administration to doing something about the area.'' At the time, he did nothing:

> In my deep subconscious, it's very unethical not to have spoken out. For many reasons, I would find that this is extremely unethical behavior, and I think that there are times in my professional career when I would have resigned over some of these issues, and I'm not resigning.

Sometimes they could make no justification at all but just had to accept the feeling that in action they were morally weak.

If the judgment of moral weakness seems unduly harsh, it was largely the way these planners saw themselves. They cared about large ethical issues but were unable to act on them in ways that they thought were appropriate. Their inability to act was not an isolated incident but was a chronic problem in their lives. This is why their interviews were overlaid with such a feeling of guilt and dissatisfaction.

Effective Action: Matching Means and Ends

Other than the vague and aethical planners and the closet politicians, most of the sample appear to have generally been able to act and were also able to justify their actions (see Table 11.1). They met the minimum requirements for ethical action, but they did not all act in the same ways.

By combining the two typologies of roles and approaches to ethics, four rather different approaches to moral reasoning and action emerge. Active planners could take either a deontological or a consequentialist approach to ethics, but they shared a sense of commitment and independence. Active consequentialists had a tendency toward extreme independence while the small group of active deontologists was notably meticulous about both process and ends. Technicians, with a less ambitious role, took a narrower, deontological approach to ethics focusing on legality and accountability. Their characteristic problem was a tendency to be co-opted by the decision makers they worked for. Process planners had an awareness of the perspectives of others that seemed to make them ethically quite scrupulous. They focused on trying to ensure that the planning process was open and fair and that all interests were represented.

Active Consequentialists

Active consequentialists were strongly goal-oriented, sometimes guided by very specific purposes, such as assuring personal mobility or improving urban design, sometimes by a more general idea of the public interest. Like their deontological counterparts, the substantive deontologists, they had a broad view of ethics. Thus, they were more likely than any other group except the substantive deontologists to raise difficult ethical issues and issues that involved choices between ethical principles, such as loyalty and the public interest. Their consequentialist ethics left them somewhat at risk of having dirty hands or of acting autonomously, but generally they stopped short of such behavior.

Unlike the closet politicians, they were not hesitant about taking on conflicts if the issues were important. They used the strategy of active resistance against pressures to do things they thought were unethical, and they were willing to rock the boat by reporting graft or blowing the whistle on illegal activities. A planner who covertly blew the whistle on an illegal deal over a rezoning described what it was like:

> I cooperated with the media. I met with editorial people at the newspaper and directed them in, in my opinion, an appropriate direction. Now I know that the word among those people involved within the city administration was that anybody talking to the media was not loyal to the administration, and, in fact, they were looking for those people or that person. Eventually, the media turned its attention to the council not dealing with the issue as rapidly [and] definitively, and then some council people who would have otherwise been friendly were beginning to say, "Boy, the media's really beating up on me now. Maybe we ought to know who's providing all this information to the media." And suddenly what is incredible is how the perspective of who's guilty suddenly changed. The people who did the wrong weren't the guilty any more but it was the guy who was generating the heat. The media became guilty, leaks became guilty.

Active consequentialists were often fairly autonomous actors in the political process. They were less likely than any other group to be automatically loyal to their agencies or superiors. Their scores on a scale measuring loyalty to their agencies were lower than those of any group except the closet politicians and were significantly lower than those for technicians who were narrow deontologists or public interest planners.[1] One active planner spoke for many others in describing the leeway he saw in his relationship to the administration he worked in. He was specifically talking about the issue of resignation in protest:

> When you work for a public official, there are matters of discretion, and loyalty isn't quite the word. You have to accept the general point of view of that administration, but that doesn't mean you agree all the time. You have to decide if the issue is so great, or if your problem with it is so great, or would you have a greater effect on the circumstances if you quit. I'm not trying to say I'm confronted with that every day. You're always going to be in a debate of some kind.

Nine of forty-three cases involving a choice between loyalty and some other principle were raised by active consequentialists. In six of those nine cases, the planners chose the other principle, such as the public interest or keeping a promise over loyalty. Several of these choices involved significant conflicts.

Because they were active, these planners used a wide variety of means for trying to get policies adopted or implemented. Doing studies and providing information and advice were at the heart of this for most, but they also lobbied decision makers and staff people and dealt with the press. They worked with community groups and sometimes helped to organize or activate them. They negotiated with developers over the nature of projects and worked with other government agencies to get action on projects. As a result, the ethics of tactics played a larger role in their interviews than in those of any other group.

Several raised specific cases that posed conflicts between ethical principles and political effectiveness. Others raised the broader issue of whether their drive for effectiveness led them into unethical behavior. This was, of course, the issue of dirty hands and the exact opposite of the ethical-but-ineffective problem of the closet politicians. One planner argued that being passive was in itself unethical for a planner:

> I think you're hired for a reason and it isn't to sit there and agree with everything your boss says or sit there and do nothing because you're afraid that if you do anything it's going to be wrong.

Even so, as he raised the image of the "ethical purist" who would say "I know what's right," his immediate reaction to the conjunction of ethics and effectiveness was:

> The purist would be ethical and ineffective and the most effective would probably be the most unethical.

For any particular planner, whether there was, in fact, a trade-off between ethics and effectiveness depended on what sort of tactics they were actually willing to use. As one might expect, the act utilitarians were among the most likely to have acted unethically (see Table 11.3). Only the narrow deontologists had more problems. Their common consequentialist rationale was that the ends justified the means. Both the unethical actions and the consequentialist rationale were less common among rule utilitarians.

Some tactics were more questionable than others. When the planners were asked about tactics that might be thought of as unethical, in most cases they said they would not use them, but acceptance varied a great deal (Table 11.4).[2] As before, though, utilitarians were more likely than other groups to say they were acceptable. In this case, the rule utilitarians were more likely to say that they would use some of the tactics, such as expendables and withholding information.

In all these cases, the planners were likely to say that such tactics were acceptable only under certain conditions. Building expendable provisions into a plan that could then later be bargained away, for example, was considered to be acceptable by many planners. The key criterion was that the tactic be used only in situations that were "fair," meaning that both sides were aware that they were being used:

> [It's] part of the standard budgetary game, really, because you know you're going to get cut, so you go with a little more, hoping that there will be some minimum that you'll stay at it. I wouldn't see anything unethical about that because everyone knows the rules of the game . . . [but] I think you should play it as straightly as you can with the public in general [who don't necessarily know the rules].

Some other tactics were accepted or used only by the most politicized of planners, and then only quietly. Leaking of information or end runs around superiors would both be violations of the principle of accountability. Withholding information from opponents, for example, would certainly violate the idea of an open political process. Again, for

TABLE 11.4

Tactics by Role and Approach to Ethics

	Number of Planners Who Would Use Tactic[a]				
Tactic	Using Expendables[b]	Lies	End Runs	Leaks	Withholding Information
Principle	Truth	Truth	Loyalty	Loyalty	Openness
Role and Approach to Ethics					
Aethical	0	1	0	3	0
Closet Politician	2	0	0	1	0
Active Consequentialist					
Act Utilitarian	1	0	2	2	1
Rule Utilitarian	5	0	0	1	4
Active Substantive					
Deontologist	0	0	0	0	0
Technician					
Narrow Deontologist	0	0	0	1	0
Public Interest	2	0	0	1	2
Process Planner	2	0	0	0	0
Percent Would Use	12	1	2	10	7
Percent Would Not Use	2	61	5	18	18

Notes:

[a] These numbers indicate how many planners either gave an example of the use of one of these tactics or said explicitly that they would or would not use it. Each of the columns is independent of the others since a planner might use more than one of the tactics.

[b] Using expendables means putting provisions in a plan, a budget, or some other policy proposal that are intended to be bargained away later, if necessary, to protect key provisions.

these tactics, some planners said that their use would depend on the context. As one rule utilitarian said:

> The question is whether you are dealing with people who will play fair with you. To some extent, you have to judge your opposition, if it's opposition, and what these people are; also judging what the situation is.

If the opposition leaked or withheld or manipulated information, then it might be appropriate for the planner to do so as well.

This kind of argument was exactly what left these cynical consequentialists open to having dirty hands. The contextual condition for expendables was that the game be fair and the actual use of the tactic in the bargaining situation be open. For the other tactics, however, the contextual condition was simply whether the planner was distrustful of or cynical about the people he was dealing with. The use of the tactic was largely covert. Any public justification, even of an implicit kind, was thus avoided and the planner's own judgment about the appropriateness of the action was under no scrutiny.

The tactic that was clearly considered the most unethical by consequentialists and deontologists alike was lying, particularly in developing and giving policy advice. Only one aethical planner said he would lie:

> I don't find enough problems with honesty/dishonesty sorts of issues to say that I worry that much about them. I consider myself to be a very honest person, but I consider my actions to be flexible enough so that if I get into a situation where I have to be deceptive, I can be deceptive. I don't have an outright ban against those sorts of deceptions because I have certainly participated in deceptions working for the city.

Even the woman who leaked information to support a project and who put up a smokescreen with her colleague to protect herself believed that technical analysis should be correct and thorough. Talking about the study that had convinced her about the benefits of the project, she stressed its quality:

> We were chosen as an agency that is very respectable in doing market studies . . . and we're seen also as a neutral party who didn't care to get involved in the question one way or another, and initially we were. Initially I was as well. I didn't care one way or another which way it came out, and I managed to keep the study objective because there were plenty of people who were trying to influence me one way and another. I said, "No, I'm not going to listen to you guys, I'm just going to have my consultants do the work and we're going to do a good, solid study that we know is respectable and we're not going to have any of you people perverting it." So I kept the mayor's people at bay, I kept the state people at bay, I kept all these other jerks off my back, and my consultant, XYZ, Inc., did a marvelous job and a lot of people said it was a very, very good job. . . . So it was a wonderful public service.

Seven active consequentialists said that they would present a case to emphasize their preferred alternative, especially once a conclusion had been reached based on initial objective analysis. Not presenting the other side at all or making up or distorting data would be unethical, though. Two planning directors fired planners who did it.

Act utilitarian Paul Michaud, with his drive to achieve good projects and his earlier cynicism about the political process, was willing to use some of the more questionable tactics if the issue was important enough. Using expendables was a taken-for-granted fact of negotiating with developers. As he explained it, the department's position was worked out in internal discussions:

> This was done with the full consent of other people in the organization, that we are presenting these controls and we have a fallback situation. Unless we take a tougher position at the beginning, they will ask for more, and we like to end up with a compromise. . . . The developer files his application with the commission and he proposes a level of development, maybe, for example, rezoning which will allow him three thousand units. We know that we can go up to twenty-five hundred maximum, not three thousand, but for bargaining purposes, we start with a lower figure, maybe less than two thousand, and later the application will be reviewed and later we will tell him how much we will allow. We may cut back. In connection with the Sitwell Building, the district permitted building with a floor area ratio of like 11.6 and the developer wanted to reach that level. We started with a much lower figure and then slowly reached an intermediate point where the settlement was made. We knew that we have to start with a lower base in order to bargain with him on other things, such as public access, for other facilities, and in exchange we may allow him to increase the FAR—but it was always within the permissible maximum. There's nothing unethical about it, but it's a game.

Michaud insisted that the project analysis by his staff that underlay this bargaining be as accurate as possible. The city and its officials should know as clearly as possible what the benefits would be and what problems might result from a development, but in negotiations, there was no reason to put all the city's data or cards on the table.

Once he was convinced that a particular project would benefit the city, Michaud did not stop with analysis. Normally, he primarily focused on trying to convince those above him who were in a position to decide. Sometimes he would go outside the governmental structure to apply a little extra pressure for a good cause. For example, Michaud talked about efforts to get land for a park:

It was 175 acres owned by this guy and next to it was a thirty-acre parcel that he owned as part of the 175 and I wanted him to donate it to expand the six- to eight-acre park in one of the low-income areas in New Bristol. So it was just a great piece of land and actually not very good for development, which is often the case. So I wanted him to donate it as a condition of the zoning. I was selling the zoning—no question about it—and so I had my commission going from here to Sunday about whether they were going to do it. Now my commission had said no, and what was I going to do? So I called the president of Citizens for a Better New Bristol and told him what my problem was and we agreed that he would write me a letter that I would draft for him because I knew the situation, asking the questions that would give me . . . that I would have to give the answers that I wanted to give. So we did that. I drafted the letter and he sent me the letter with a copy to the *New Bristol News* and that took care of that and we got the thirty acres.

Michaud also said that he didn't do this as a rule:

I think we begin getting to a point where our role becomes too much of an advocate planner, working from the outside in versus working from the inside out, and I, in my own mind, do tend to draw the line there somewhat.
Q: Now do you draw that line for strategic reasons or because of some principle that it might involve?
I think there's a certain amount of principle involved. I work for the city government first, and they are my bosses, so to speak, the mayor and the city council, and so I think, from a professional point of view or behavioral view, I view them sort of as my first loyalty, so to speak, and so that does impact it. To be candid about it, there's some risks involved, politically, even if I didn't have a strong feeling that . . . I think that also probably tempers my view toward [it].

On one notable occasion, which Michaud described with a bit of bravado, he had taken on the risk and violated this loyalty. His department, under considerable political pressure from powerful interests in the city, had backed a major project that he was sure was misguided. He finally had become so frustrated with his inability to have any impact from within that he quietly had given information against it to a couple of friends—one in the office of a city councilman and the other in another city agency that was opposed to the project. The information was primarily about the substance of the project, but Michaud also said rather indirectly:

> Sometimes people have made headway, and other people don't know where they are coming from. . . . The truth can be . . . you enlighten people about the interests that they have, and sometimes those interests can be personal interests.

When he was asked whether he thought any of this was wrong, Michaud said that he thought the pressure politics and the bad consequences of the project justified what he had done:

> I felt this was a real risk-taking sort of a thing, but I felt so strongly, again, on an ethical base, in my mind that the future of the city . . . was so critical at that time that I had to do some extraordinary activity, so I did.

He was not caught, and due to a variety of political events, of which his information was only a small part, the project ultimately died.

Michaud's case illustrates well how the commitment of an act utilitarian planner to such deontological principles as loyalty was balanced against a consequentialist idea of the public interest. In addition, ambition, a little cynicism, and a willingness to take risks if the goal was important enough could all combine to lead him to autonomous action or to dirtying his hands. Michaud did have some recognition of this:

> I would like to think I wouldn't hurt anybody, but since I really have a vision that I think I know what's right, which may be overinflated, I think I probably overlook that a bit because if I think I know what the right is, I may excuse myself for not being as careful about what other people may think is right.

As this rueful statement suggests, the drive to be effective in achieving "the good" was a strong one.

So, clearly, there could sometimes be a trade-off between being effective and being ethical. However, there was no evidence from this sample that such a trade-off was inevitable. Even active consequentialists kept their political strategies within fairly strict bounds and accepted the constraints of the democratic process (see Table 11.4).

What these planners did was to develop ethical strategies suitable to their communities that allowed them to achieve goals they thought were important. A state-level planner who was a rule utilitarian explicitly raised the issue of a trade-off between ethics and effectiveness. He talked about how, after eight years, he had been able to develop a strategy for having some impact and remaining ethical as well:

> You smack your head against the wall so many times that you realize the wall is not going to move, or maybe you find out that the wall is moving a little at a time. . . . Once you start seeing this, you see that the system does work—it doesn't work perfectly but it works—and then mentally I went through a process of saying, "I've done some things that have come to fruition and other things that have died on the vine." You start putting together in your mind a scenario for how you can operate within the system. I hate to say that I'm now part of the system, but I guess I am in the sense that I fully understand how the system works, and I realize what I can and what I can't do, and, more importantly, I realize how I can also help to change that system. Once you reach that point—it's kind of a threshold which varies from person to person—when that threshold's met, that's when I think . . . ethically, I sort of put [it] together. I guess it's a rationalization for how I can operate as a professional within this political decision-making process, still maintain what I hope are high ethics as far as I'm concerned, and still be able to live with the end result, which maybe isn't the most ethical decision or the most professionally sound decision at the end, but still realizing that if I wasn't there, it would have been *worse*, and that's, I think, a key point.

Some consequentialists played a broker role between various interests to try to work out compromises on development proposals that served the public interest—balancing, for example, pressures for development with the need to preserve the environment. Several gave examples of projects in which they had helped to develop nonzero-sum solutions that could meet the desires and financial needs of a variety of parties.

Tom Stuart, the rule utilitarian, thought of the ideal planning process as one in which groups with differing views on a policy or project would engage in an open process of discussion and negotiation that would produce a reasonable solution. He was somewhat tempted by the utilitarian idea of the end justifying the means, but he was not as comfortable with it as Michaud. He thought that the purely political lobbying tactics he had used on the recreation areas program bills, while not violating his personal ethics, were unprofessional from a planning standpoint. Talking about another project he had been involved in, Stuart said:

> [They should have] come in and said, "You know, we just have a difference of opinion here. We feel that it should be done this way, and you don't agree so let's discuss it." Then we would have sat down—and not just me and Rob and them but other people who were involved: the governor's office, people who were brought in as members of this citizens' group, and other people who were interested in this project—and we could have worked for a solution to it. Maybe their approach would have been made the better by a group.

He recognized, though, that on this project, as on others, political reality did not operate this way. Especially as he became committed to a particular policy, Stuart ended up being manipulative or less than fully open himself:

> For example, on this ag land project . . . you know you're going to have a certain group of people who are going to be opposed to anything you do, and we've got this legislator in particular who's taking this on as a cause and he doesn't understand the project. He's just one of these who doesn't want to be involved in something like this, period, and he doesn't see things like we do at all. When he comes up here, we're pleasant to him; there's no need to be antagonistic to him. We give him information he needs, but, you know, I'm not going to go out of my way to give this guy ammunition that he can use to cause all the problems that the guy's got the potential to cause.

While this lack of openness bothered him, Stuart ended up saying:

> You know, I do believe strongly that planners have to take sides, they have to make decisions, and they have to support what they feel is correct. They also have to realize that there have to be compromises.

Consequentialists like Stuart generally were optimists about the possibility of a participatory process and about the ability to get workable compromises among conflicting groups that would produce good planning results, but they were realists as well about how such a process worked in practice. They balanced their own, often strong ideas about the public interest against those of others, sometimes being a facilitator to encourage compromise but at other times playing a more direct advocacy role.

Active Substantive Deontologists

If there was a single group for whom ethics seemed to be a central motive force for action, it was the active planners who were substantive deontologists. Only these planners and the process planners described no cases in which they had acted unethically (see Table 11.3). This was a small group, only four planners who made up 29 percent of the substantive deontologists and 15 percent of the active planners. Remember that 43 percent of the substantive deontologists were closet politicians who have already been discussed; the rest were spread across other roles.

The active substantive planners were attracted to planning because they saw in it an opportunity to work for social equity and sometimes for environmental preservation as well. All were working for the disadvantaged—for more and better housing, for a more active voice by tenants in housing policy, for economic and physical revitalization of disadvantaged neighborhoods.

Other active planners raised different kinds of moral issues. One gave an example of how she was trying to get reluctant officials to act on a project she thought posed a basic safety hazard. Her discussion of this case was an especially clear example of moral reasoning as well as of action:

> There's one issue that I'm really having problems about—kind of moral problems. We have a project under construction near the freeway that has three sinkholes that have opened under the places that were going to be built on. So the first thing we did, we told the guys to stop work and not to build the houses and have the soils engineer come in with a report. He came in with a report that recommended that certain things be done, but it's a really wishy-washy report. I mean, it says, "This was an unusual situation and you don't plan for that, and we don't expect it to happen again. . . . " So it doesn't give me much support, but I can't get support from our engineer—who is really supposedly the technical person—to just shut them down. He says that it is a reasonable report. So I feel up a creek.
> Q: Why do you see that as a moral problem?
> Because I feel like people . . . somebody might get killed there and

that I would have had a role in letting that thing . . . If I have any
chance to keep it . . . either make them do some things to change
that and not have that happen or I would feel personally responsible.
Q: But what can you do in that case?
Well, I did a couple of things. I said that I thought there was a whole
legal issue here, so I shipped the thing off to our attorney. Our
engineer didn't even want to do an independent review of it because
he felt that the soils engineer that had done the initial work was
from a competent firm. They are a competent firm, but one never
knows what pressure they're getting from the developer, how much
money they had, or . . . you know. There are uncertainties there. I
was frankly surprised that they were willing to put themselves out
that much. Anyway, I got our attorney to agree that we should do
an independent review, so that's one thing, so we are going to go
ahead and have that done. Another thing is that the county open
space district was supposed to take title to the open space where
one of the holes occurred, and there's been a recent court case that
says that if you own the property where they occur, even if they
occur naturally, you may be liable for the damage. So I told the
county open space district about that and they're going to hire their
own geologist to go out and look, and so we may have two independent geologists looking at it. I also talked to the council and the
commission a lot and told them about the real problems I had with
it, and they're all pretty nervous, but . . . So I really hope to get
something a little more definitive from one of these geologists, either
that it probably really is okay or that they really should do more or
they should move the units or something.

By calling this a moral rather than simply an ethical issue she meant that
it was really serious—an issue of life and death. She could clearly
articulate the general principle involved, searched for more information
to help her decide whether there really was a problem, and explored
alternative ways of dealing with it. In such a case, she was willing to
argue with experts, involve her citizen's board, and push any group that
might be activated to get more independent information to try to resolve
the issue.

Active substantive planners were strongly goal-oriented. They were
not just reacting to ethical challenges that happened to come their way.
They felt that they had an affirmative responsibility to do what they could
in their communities to right social wrongs. Two were neighborhood
planners and held jobs in which they were responsible for advocating the
interests of low-income residents. The others hardly spent all their time

on issues of social justice and the environment but they did create legitimacy for raising these issues. One who had been fairly successful in getting her suburban community to consider affordable housing talked about how she had built the groundwork to be able to raise the issue:

> I probably can do more now than I felt I could when I first started. They were very suspicious of their planner after what had happened with the last one . . . and I hadn't established any kind of a track record. Now that I've established enough of a track record, they know I don't generally go out in left field in the way I approach an issue, and they're willing to listen.

They were not "holier than thou" or Pollyannas but they were committed and optimistic about what could be accomplished through the democratic process. They were also energetic and apparently effective.

They saw no conflict between being ethical and being effective. Like the active consequentialists, they did not hesitate to get involved in conflicts and were just as likely to actively resist pressures to behave in ways they thought were unethical. As deontologists, though, they were concerned about the rightness of actions themselves; for them, a good end could not justify a wrong act. So they were very scrupulous about means. They did not use questionable tactics, such as doing end runs around their elected officials or withholding information from participants in the planning process (see Table 11.4).

Grace Sumner was this kind of a planner—willing to take on conflicts in order to get things done, especially on affordable housing—but as a deontologist, she acted within quite strict procedural limits that she took more or less for granted. She talked about the political difficulty of dealing with the issue of affordable housing and how she had become more pragmatic about it. Talking about student interns, Sumner said:

> I see that with the students here. The kids come in: "Things *should* be this way. This is right." Well yes, that's true, but being right isn't always enough. I have said that to planners a lot of times and I guess that is a matter of ethics. Sometimes they're not going to win for political reasons and they should know enough that they're not destroyed. Sometimes it will be necessary for them maybe to do some hand-holding . . . that they don't really want to do, like a neighborhood group is opposing a project and I'll say, "Well, you should really go out there and talk with them."

In terms of her own strategy for dealing with this divisive issue, Sumner said:

So how do you handle that as a planner? Well, by making sure that the projects are good ones that you're going to support, by making sure that the applicants know that they have a lot of homework to do and it's important for them to be out there in the community talking to people about what's going on, and by helping to get the projects designed in such a way that there are perceived benefits to the community to support, by making sure that the valid concerns of the community are being met. So there's the element of conflict there, but I think there's an element of conflict in just about everything you do. I mean, you can't just go for social justice or environmental protection or any one single value that is probably a very good one, but you can't just go for that one thing.

Some issues she knew she wouldn't win, but if the issue was important enough, Sumner didn't mind taking on a direct conflict:

On some things, even where I know I'll lose, I make a technical staff report, if you like, and then I let them do it. We talk about doing a "Custer's last stand" on projects, . . . and it's kind of a joke, on projects where we know we're going to go down but we want to stick to our guns.

While she didn't want to fritter away her credibility on opposing lots of issues this way, Sumner also was not much tempted by the idea of going behind the scenes to try to change the probable outcome. When asked if she would manipulate data, she said she would not though she would highlight the benefits of the position she supported. Openness was a major ethical value for her, so that she rejected the idea of leaking or withholding information for purely strategic reasons. These tactics would be neither ethical nor effective for what she was trying to do.

Technicians: Narrow Deontologists and Public Interest Planners

The various kinds of technicians saw their role in completely different terms from the active planners. The kind of effectiveness that active consequentialists talked about as possibly conflicting with being ethical was not what the technicians thought of as effectiveness, nor was acting for social justice. Effectiveness for them was providing objective advice to decision makers. If they were persuasive and lucky enough to have decision makers who cared about making good planning decisions, the information would be well used. If this was not the case, they had at least done their best. Ethical action to them meant resisting pressures to do things that were illegal and loyally serving their decision makers by giving advice and accepting the decisions that were made.

While most did judge policy against some idea of the public interest, they were much less goal-oriented than active planners, granting much more freely to elected officials the right and the obligation to make the final determination of the public interest. They were predominantly deontologists—30 percent were narrow deontologists who did not use the public interest at all. The balance were public interest planners, but even the technician activists were more committed to the goals of their administrations than they were to their own personal images of what planning should accomplish.

These technicians' well-defined and more limited role meant that they were less likely to find themselves in situations where they felt they had to make choices between two ethical principles. This did not mean that they faced no dilemmas at all, but their decisions were, in many instances, much more straightforward than was the case for other planners. Thus, they were the most likely of any group to raise issues that they described as being easy to deal with, and they did seem to have a more black-and-white view of ethics.

However, their rather narrow, simplified image of ethics left them vulnerable to their own particular ethical problems. These were not the problems of too much independence and dirty hands faced by the active planners. Rather, they revolved around the opposite problem of too little independence. Loyalty and accountability played a central role for technicians. Their scores on the scale measuring loyalty to their agencies were significantly higher than all other groups. One expressed the unconditional nature of his loyalty:

> If I work for the individual, I've got to support him. If it's wrong, he's going to pay the price. So I guess, ethically speaking, I'm on his side, even though it's the [technically] wrong thing to do. It's not going to change my opinion of what's right in the case or not.

Behind this individual and organizational loyalty, many planners articulated the principle of accountability that was central to public planners:

> [It's] the primacy of the local elected official . . . the fact that he or she makes the final decision and their responsibility on that.

Of the forty-three cases that involved choices between loyalty and other ethical principles, the largest group, 37 percent, were raised by the narrow deontological and public interest technicians, somewhat outstripping their 34 percent representation in the sample. These technicians chose loyalty in 62 percent of these cases, a very different outcome from the choices made by active consequentialists who rejected loyalty in two-thirds of the cases they raised.

Those who did not use the idea of the public interest were especially vulnerable. A clear idea of the public interest could provide an image of what was professionally required and could balance the pressures of loyalty. Taken together, narrow deontologists and public interest planners who were technicians made about the same proportion of the unjustifiable decisions to be loyal as their representation in the sample. These were decisions that conflicted with laws or duties of justice or where they were pushed into going along even if issues had not been adequately discussed. However, narrow deontologists made half of these unjustifiable decisions though they were only 30 percent of this group.

More generally, aside from the aethical and vague planners, the narrow deontologists had the most difficulty justifying their ethical choices (see Table 11.1). Two were preoccupied, in their interviews at least, with personal problems that seemed to preclude their being able to take a broad view of ethics, but the others simply had such narrow views of the realm of ethics that they had difficulty seeing the ethical problems they themselves raised. With no clear idea of the public interest, they could hardly articulate the choice they sometimes had to make when they disagreed on the content of policy. The planner from Yonkers was also a narrow deontologist, and between having no idea of either the consequentialist public interest or of social equity, he was entirely unable to see the issue that his planning presented. Perhaps not surprisingly, 60 percent of these narrow deontologists acted unethically by my criteria but only 20 percent saw their own actions in this light (see Table 11.3).

Edward Smith, Jr., largely defined ethics as legality and loyalty. He thought of himself as a practical person doing things for practical reasons rather than for ideological or ethical ones. In an environment where he felt that there were pressures both on himself and on the officials he worked with to be unethical, Smith talked about how important it was both ethically and practically to be objective and consistent:

> It's very difficult to become a little bit flexible; it's very difficult to contain flexibility. You suffer the consequences so quickly on that that it causes you to think twice before you do it. Because if you're not consistent they will burn you—that will happen very quickly. You make one decision that's inconsistent with what you've done before, everybody in the community—every developer—knows

about it. It spreads like wildfire. The same engineers or surveyors that handled [the case] for Mr. A have Mr. B, Mr. C, and Mr. D all lined up to come in.

Laws and policies were the framework, the backbone, for this consistency, and Smith tried to be sure that he stuck to them.

Favoritism was something he worried about and tried hard to avoid. In his dealings with the downtown business community, he would give advice but would go no further. In the case of a particular project that they wanted city assistance on, Smith thought that the action being proposed might be an illegal use of government power to benefit a special interest group. He took his hesitation to the city attorney, who explored the state case law in the area and was able to reassure him that the action would be legal, though Smith himself was never entirely convinced.

Beyond trying to stick to the law, he defined what was appropriate primarily by reference to what his manager, planning board, and council chose. In one case, a local developer wanted to rezone a parcel of land for town houses and a shopping center. The proposal was poorly developed and relied heavily on the developer's assurance that, as a local person, he would act responsibly. The professional analysis Smith did indicated that an insufficient case had been made for changing the zoning, so he recommended that the project be rejected. The developer was influential, though. The community was conservative, and the members of the city council were worried about appearing to impede private development. At a briefing on the project, the council told Smith to change the recommendation to favor the rezoning: they did not want to approve it without some apparent technical support. Afterward, being forced to change his recommendation continued to rankle, but Smith said that both his behavior and the council's had been ethical:

And the reason I think that is that if I were to put myself in the position of a city councilman—assuming politics aside and the interaction that takes place on that front—those people are elected to represent the public and supposedly to reach some kinds of decisions that will benefit the majority of the citizenry. . . . It's their prerogative. If you've got any faith at all, which I do, in a democratic process, you've got to hold true that that's the best system going, and so I think, within that context, you've got to have that kind of flexibility to deviate from "a professional planning principle," if you will, if it's counterbalanced in that public official's mind with something more important than what maybe the professional planning principle may dictate.

While this issue implicitly raised the question of his own view of the public interest, Smith did not articulate the public interest as a real countervailing obligation that could legitimately compete with the claims of loyalty to elected officials. He did not articulate it as an issue of truth versus loyalty either. He felt that, somehow, something was wrong, but he could not see what it was.

Thus, in the end, though Smith was personally careful not to favor certain groups, such as the downtown businessmen, if his policymakers wanted to do it, he had no alternative to going along. His image of his role did not include pushing for a different vision of what the city should be doing or encouraging the participation of normally unrepresented groups.

In many respects, the public interest technicians who used a consequentialist view of the public interest did not think or behave very differently from the narrow deontologists. Legality and loyalty were still the dominant principles they used, but their greater faith in their own definitions of the public interest could give them grounds for resisting the pressure that Smith unhappily accepted. This did seem to matter. They acted unethically in only 22 percent of the cases they discussed, and their evaluation of their actions and mine coincided exactly (see Table 11.3).

Like Edward Smith, Jr., many of the issues that George Walters raised simply involved resistance to or avoidance of small illegalities, but he did raise several other issues that showed where his priorities lay. One was the case of the plan commissioner who was employed by the developer with a proposal for a subdivision in the flight path of the airport. In this instance, Walters chose legality over loyalty, taking the issue to another plan commissioner, who took it to the mayor, who, in turn, fired the commissioner with the conflict. He was reinforced in his decision by the judgment that the subdivision would not be in the long-run interest of the community.

However, on an issue where there was no problem of legality but just a disagreement over the public interest, Walters said:

> We're given an opportunity to prepare a full and complete written report and to make a full and complete recommendation to the planning commission and the legislative bodies, and what falls out falls out from there.

While his clearer idea of the public interest could help to make these reports more convincing to decision makers, he was subject to the same kind of indirect co-optation that Smith was.

The limits of this approach can be seen in a case where he chose loyalty over openness. The case involved an industrial development across some railroad tracks from a residential area. The manager and certain members of the council were strongly for the development while the neighbors were opposed. Walters developed a performance zoning approach to dealing with the site that he hoped would satisfy both sides. However, the manager was not interested, and when the neighborhood group came to talk to him, Walters felt he was obligated to say nothing about the performance zoning even though it would have been of considerable interest and use to them. Here he had a mechanism for encouraging negotiation and compromise but he felt that it was not the place of the planner to play a more active, mediating role.

Since many of the issues raised by the narrow deontological and public interest technicians involved pressures to do clearly unethical things—to do favors, accept bribes, change technical findings—they were more likely than any other group to use the strategy of resistance. In most cases, the pressures to be resisted were not dramatic and the resistance was not difficult, but it was typical of their narrow view of ethics that a large proportion of the cases in which they engaged in active resistance involved pressures to do or to condone something that was clearly illegal. Technicians may, on the average, have been less comfortable about getting involved in conflicts than active planners, but when basic legality was at stake, there were many who were willing to stand up and be counted. They accounted for five of the nine cases of justifiably resisting pressures to act illegally. Some of these cases were quite dramatic. The case of the planner who helped his commission to sue the city council for violating the zoning ordinance has been discussed already, as has the planner who, under pressure from a political boss, quit his job and went to the press. Still another planner also exposed illegal use by local officials of public resources in a private development scheme. The conflict generated by this exposure was so great that he came close to being fired and had to have police protection for a time.

These were black-and-white situations. They required moral courage to act on, but they did not require a very broad or subtle idea of ethics to see what should be done. The mirror image of this pattern could be seen when technicians did things they themselves thought were unethical. These were commonly actions that either were or verged on the illegal, where they had been unable to "just say no" to a developer or to a friend. Unlike the consequentialists, who usually justified unethical actions by saying that they had been done for a good purpose, these deontologists had little counterjustification to give. They did sometimes say that their action had caused no harm or that they had somehow tried to make amends, but these arguments were not justifications. They were simply efforts to mitigate what they saw as their own guilt.

However, once the narrow deontological and public interest technicians moved away from issues that were illegal or clearly unethical into the area of issues concerned with process and the public interest, accountability became the dominant principle. They might chafe against it—almost all their difficult issues did involve conflicts between loyalty and some other ethical principle—but they accepted it unless they were asked to do something illegal. Thus, in terms of action, at least, their moral world was a fairly simple one of resisting illegal behavior and otherwise of serving decision makers loyally.

Because of this more limited view of their obligations, they did not see a possible trade-off between being ethical and being effective as an issue. Unlike the closet politicians and the substantive deontologists, they did not see it as their duty do try to achieve ambitious goals, such as reducing social injustice. Their less active approach to planning grew substantially, though not entirely, from an affirmative commitment to a limited role. By the same token, the practice of using bad means for good ends was one that also had little relevance or that they rejected. Indeed, relatively few technicians talked explicitly about the ethics of political tactics, and many of those who were specifically asked rejected out of hand such tactics as slanting a technical case, leaking or withholding information, or doing an end run around a superior (see Table 11.4). Technician activists, who were generally public interest planners, were the one group who were sometimes willing to use expendables or withhold information strategically, but for most deontological technicians, these actions would have no place in the professional life of a planner whose central obligations were to give objective technical advice and to be loyal to superiors.

As this comparison suggests, however, technician activists had a somewhat stronger concern with being proactive and effective in political terms. They were more willing to be active in somewhat the same sense that active planners were, but they shared with other public interest technicians a fairly narrow view of ethics that emphasized legality and loyalty. For them, though, loyalty went beyond a generalized institutional attitude. They were embedded in particular political systems whose policies they had actively been involved in shaping. On the scale of agency loyalty, their scores were the highest of any group.

Like active planners, they were more likely to use active boat-rocking resistance against pressures to behave unethically. They were not afraid to disagree with superiors, to fire staff who did unethical things, or even, in one case, to resign in protest. One experienced regional planner gave an example that illustrated his willingness to lobby actively if it was necessary in order to get action:

> I have to look at the project, as to what is its impact on the community, what is the long-range impact of the project. I just went through a situation where we have one city which is kind of a retirement community but they are violently opposed to any kind of subsidized housing. They have never approved a project, and this last time I went up and talked to their city council about it and I had some senior citizens who live there demonstrate a need for it, and it's well planned and in an area that would bother no one, and that is the first time that council has ever adopted both projects, and HUD's now approved one of them. I just went up and talked with the people at the senior center, who said, "We need this." I said, "Come to the council meeting and tell the council." I went to the nutrition center and talked to seniors there. I knew there was a need, I don't care what the mayor might have said, and when he heard it from people he knew—"I'm on a fixed income while you're a very wealthy rancher"—he heard it and don't you think that senior citizens don't vote in a block. I met with the planning director, the city manager, the council—talked with them and they unanimously approved and wrote me a letter of endorsement. That is the first time in their lives they've done it.

Their technician roots did seem to prevent them from going far enough to have problems of dirty hands, but they had an independence that was not characteristic of most technicians, and they thought strategically. As one said:

> Strategy is awfully important. If you don't get anything done . . . from a planner's standpoint, there are certain things that, you know, that should be done and you try to work them together.

Even so, they were generally too embedded in and loyal to the power structures of which they were a part to undertake radically independent action.

Richard Breitman had been around a long time and had earned his responsible position and curmudgeonish independence both by his ability and honesty as a planner and by his ability to survive in the bureaucracy. He had worked first for a regional agency planning for his city and then had moved over to the city's planning department at a time when a reform administration was challenging the political machine. Breitman's career was tied to the new administration and its commitment to planning.

Given this background, he had the autonomy to give honest advice and to disagree with the mayor and with other agency heads, but as one of the policymakers, his obligation to be loyal was clear, and, as a practical matter, his commitment to policies he had actively been involved in making set the limits to his independence. Breitman may have felt that he gave in to the mayor in the case of industrial zoning somewhat against his better judgment, but the issue itself was not a fundamental one. On the whole, he said there was a great deal of consensus on what needed to be done in the city, and on major issues, his involvement was generally large enough to preclude disagreement.

For technician activists, and, indeed, for technicians in general, loyalty was their particular weakness. It was a problem in two ways. One was that it was the organizationally easy choice, the one that did not rock the boat. Cautious planners could argue that they had made an ethical choice even if they had rejected a more binding duty of justice. They were on even stronger ground if they chose accountability over an equal but more uncomfortable principle, such as the public interest.

The other problem was that they were more likely to be co-opted by the values of their communities and of the elites that were most active and influential in their politics. Smith and Walters were indirectly co-opted through their acceptance of the principle of accountability and their fairly passive roles. Breitman was more directly and actively involved in his own co-optation; indeed, he saw it himself. There was, perhaps, no inherent reason why this should be a problem. Many planners said they lived in and shared the values of their communities and thought this was a good thing, but local planning is a somewhat parochial endeavor, and communities as well as neighborhood or other special interest groups have every incentive to adopt policies that allow them to benefit at the expense of larger or less well organized groups or units. Most planners who used some idea of the public interest said that they were concerned about the larger picture and the longer run, but the technician role, with its strong pressures for accountability and its lack of a well-defined alternative vision, gave many of these planners little leverage for acting effectively on this perspective in difficult cases.

Some certainly recognized the dilemma. Several technicians talked about their disagreements with the policies set by their officials on housing, environmental, or design issues. One said that, in general:

> If a planner finds himself ethically at odds with the governing body
> or the city manager, even if it's on little things, but it's time after

> time after time, then you need to sit back and analyze what you're doing there. . . . I think that a planner's ethics would require him to resign the position, and I think that's one of the things that I feel strongly about.

He had earlier talked about a disagreement with this council over the community's policy of excluding all apartments, thereby keeping out lower income people. About that specific issue, he said:

> You know, the planner has a job and I'm working for the city manager, and if I feel that things are not being done, I can quit and maybe approach it from a different direction if I feel strongly enough about it. But at this point I don't. I think it's a shortcoming but I don't think it's a fatal flaw.

A few did leave jobs in which disagreements became a chronic problem, but others like this planner were content to leave this as an unresolved issue. As we have already seen, principled resignation may have been more difficult to act on in reality than it was in imagination.

This planner's example illustrates a further problem with loyalty and co-optation. Governing groups in many communities, certainly in this one, did not represent the entire range of interests. The politics of planning was often dominated by propertied interests, such as developers and middle-class homeowners. Other areas of planning, such as health planning, had a similar bias, if one that differed in the specific nature of the groups involved. In such a political system, co-optation specifically meant that technicians had little support for raising issues of social justice or of any other issue unpopular with the dominant groups. As a young planner, Breitman had been associated with a reform administration that identified itself with helping the disadvantaged. Years later, as planning director, he retained the image of himself as committed to social justice, but he did not have quite the independence he had had as a younger man. In his city, there was some disagreement over exactly who had benefited most from the city government's active revitalization efforts. When asked about this, Breitman said a bit defensively:

> Of course we did an analysis of the expenditure and funds in the last decade, and actually 30 percent of the funds that have been spent have gone to the central city and 70 percent to the other communities—in capital program expenditures. So how can one say that the downtown area has been built up at the expense of the other parts of the city?

He might well have been correct, but his position itself made a critical perspective difficult.

Process Planners

The final group that was distinctive in the way it acted was the process planners or mediators. To say that they stood between the active planners and the technicians makes them sound as if they were just a residual, transitional group between the other two. They could be seen this way in some sense since there were some technicians and active planners who had a strong mediating streak as well. Here I have included all the sixteen planners who were identified as process planners on either role or approach to ethics. About 60 percent were process planners in both typologies, but the rest were spread over a variety of other roles and approaches to ethics.

In terms of the way they acted on ethical issues, the process planners had a substantially different approach than either active planners or technicians. All but one were deontologists, and, like the substantive deontologists, they were notable for raising no cases on which they acted unethically (see Table 11.3).

What made the process planners distinctively ethical was their apparent ability to empathize with others in the planning process. This meant that they were particularly sensitive to not trading off the rights of a minority in return for benefits for the whole community. As a result, they tried to work out problems through an open process of negotiation. In some cases, this seemed in part to be the result of their own somewhat tenuous positions—in regional agencies without a strong power base, for example, or in communities divided by factional conflict—but this was not universal; some simply seemed to be balancers or negotiators by nature. Even if the role seemed to fit their situations, they also seemed to have an ideological commitment to a process orientation. Not surprisingly, they had higher scores than both technicians and active consequentialists on a scale measuring attitudes in favor of citizen participation.[3]

The core group were the people who not only played this kind of role but who also had a purely deontological idea of the public interest as a process. Several others held a deontological idea of the public interest as social justice. They were not dogmatic about this value but seemed to be open to the values of others as well. They were balancers or compromisers, searching for a middle ground that could satisfy all parties to a controversy. In their eight cases of conflicts between the public interest and other principles, process planners chose compromise solutions in five.

One planner who worked in a community divided between prodevelopment and antidevelopment factions spent most of her interview describing in a detached and humorous way how she walked a tightrope between the two. Initially targeted by the antidevelopment group to be fired because of her prodevelopment views, she had survived by being objective and open:

Right now we've got another prodevelopment group. This past May a new group went in, which was another 100 percent change. Yeah, they were thrown out 100 percent in May of this year, so I'm working under my third council, my third city manager.

Q: The manager always changes?

Well, I didn't tell you that [general hilarity] the manager that came in with this antidevelopment group—that's his one claim to fame here—he would not fire people for political reasons. But he was just at a loss to do anything else, it was just chaotic, and he got another job . . . so now we have manager number three . . . and so things are sort of stabilizing. I've got friends on both sides, I mean, I think more on the more prodevelopment [side], but actually I feel, and I don't think I'm just being naive, that I got along pretty well with the antidevelopment plan commission, and they kind of knew where I was coming from and I kind of knew where they were coming from. I don't feel that I'm pro development or pro nondevelopment—I try to be pro planning and look for ways to balance competing objectives. . . . I hope I'm not just being a Pollyanna, that I'm seeing more consensus maybe developing. Another thing that's going to help in that respect is that everybody is interested in improving our downtown. So once you get an issue that brings people together rather than pulls them apart, like the highway did or like residential neighborhoods do, I think that can help. . . . So I see it as looking for that middle ground in a community like this—mediation, balancing competing objectives, trying to make the best out of sometimes a difficult situation for which there is no immediate solution. . . . I guess I'm more comfortable working in a mediator role and I think that, although it takes time, in the long run sometimes the chances of success are better than when you play a more conflict kind of role. I'm not saying that I don't think there is a time and place for that too, but probably it would take another planner to do it.

For her, substantive values had to take a secondary place to trying to work with these two opposed but apparently stable factions. She had enough patience, detachment, humor, and credibility to do it.

Ethically, these planners were independent, and most did not shy away from conflict if it was necessary. More than half raised issues that involved substantial conflicts between ethical principles. They had faced their share of pressures to change technical analyses or to condone illegal actions. The planner who finally went to her board with information on the wrongdoings of her boss was a process planner.

They were also apparently not overawed by the idea of loyalty, though their scores on the agency loyalty scale were between those of technicians and of active consequentialists. Three were technicians, and they were more accepting of the idea of automatic accountability. For the others, in the six cases that they raised involving a choice between loyalty and some other principle, five went against loyalty. One planner, for example, withstood pressure from several elected officials to approve a project for a powerful developer even though the review process had excluded groups that would have been harmed by it.

They were also notable for raising more subtle issues that indicated a sensitivity to the values or concerns of others or to their vulnerability and humanity. These issues ranged from examples that were almost trivially small to ones that posed serious dilemmas. One individual was struggling with what to do about a lawsuit in which both he and the city were attacked:

> Most people, when they are hit, the first thing they want to do is get the person who is doing it, but if you draw back your fist to hit somebody and you happen to hit the guy standing in back of you who just happened to be there . . . I feel that "getting" a person, making me feel good, will in the long run damage . . . quite a number of people that really should not be damaged because they had nothing to do with it.

It may well have been this ability to put themselves in other people's shoes that made them unlikely to get involved in the problem of dirty hands. They did not have either the driving commitment to particular ends or the cynicism about other participants that would have allowed them to treat people as means rather than as whole people with feelings and rights.

As planners who were often involved in negotiations, several did talk about using expendables (see Table 11.4), but they put a high priority on trying to keep the decision-making process open. As a result, tactics that would bias information itself or its availability to different groups were either not considered at all or were thought to be unacceptable.

If they were not vulnerable to dirty hands, they were also less vulnerable than technicians to co-optation. Acceptance of the general idea of the public interest as a process certainly opened the possibility of co-optation by powerful and active groups, but these planners seemed to be somewhat armed against this. Their style was not to be obvious leaders in raising difficult issues, such as social equity, and in that sense, their aims were modest. like the technicians, but they were not afraid to take on such issues if they did come up, and several had considerable interest in equity, in particular. Primarily, however, they were firm believers in an open process, involving all groups who might be affected by a decision. This was a commitment that tended to make them champions of the underdog rather than of the powerful. Thus, for instance, a couple of regional planners whose agencies did not really have a very strong local political base were quick to identify issues in which disadvantaged groups were closed out of the political process by powerful ones. Institutionally, their role was to try to represent the regional public interest, but about all they could do was to use their own limited powers to try to open the political process up somewhat.

Rebecca Giulini's community had many well-organized, active groups. It was not deeply divided over development in general, but particular issues could be hard-fought. She felt she had an obligation to both developers and to citizen groups to see that the process was fair and open. In the case of the neighborhood that wanted development, Giulini tried to make sure that the developer did not take advantage of the neighborhood group and that they were both party to negotiations on the issue.

In another case, however, her own ideas of the public interest were stronger and conflicted with the values of people in the community. The issue involved a proposal to construct high-density, affordable housing in a largely developed area. The residents argued that the traffic impact of a large development would be devastating for their neighborhood. Giulini felt that the community badly needed the housing:

> We've got a real need for housing and I personally have a very, very high place . . . I put housing in a very, very high priority, especially housing that can be somewhat more affordable than traditional market-rate housing in this environment. That means low-income, moderate-to-middle income. The trouble we're having on that one is that the site is located in the middle of one of the worst transportation access messes we have. . . . How strongly do I push as a

planning director for that project because I think housing is a good thing versus the overall community perspective, which would say that putting a lot of housing in an area which is already heavily impacted by traffic may not be the best thing to do?

Her solution was to talk extensively with the planning staff and the city manager and to do a particularly thorough analysis of the whole project and its traffic impacts. Giulini argued that this provided more information to everyone involved in the process, and she was able to suggest ways in which the traffic impacts might be mitigated and a compromise developed:

> We are not trying to hide the negative information. If an effort was made to suppress information, or an effort was made not to try to obtain as good a mitigation package as possible, that I would regard as unethical behavior. Now here that would be more difficult to do than in most communities because the level of involvement here and the types of people that are involved in the process are pretty good quality—there's some very bright people. . . . What we will end up doing is trying to create a situation where the project is accompanied by enough mitigation issues that major problems in that area will at least not be worsened and try to minimize the negative impacts.

From an ethical standpoint, the most notable aspect of this relatively small group of process planners was how ethical they did seem to be. It was characteristic, if maybe not definitive, that none of them talked about having done anything unethical, though several agreed with the planner who said, "I assume I have—I wouldn't be human otherwise." In the eight situations where they had faced choices between duties of justice and other ethical principles, they always chose the duty of justice. These were not easy cases. Several involved loyalty in conflict with the public interest or legality. Two involved advocacy for affordable housing in exclusive suburban areas.

Despite these two equity cases, these planners generally were not trying to achieve ambitious goals. Their primary commitment was to an open planning process. They accepted the primacy of elected officials, but they were independent actors, with clear ideas of ethics that they were willing to work to achieve, sometimes in difficult circumstances.

Conclusion

I argued in chapter 9 that planners should use a set of three principles that would embody a balance between binding deontological obligations in relation to means and a commitment to ends. Not surprisingly, then, the application of this framework to the planners' actions does support the idea that a balanced approach to ethics is the most satisfactory.

In order to be ethical, the planners (1) had to be able to see that an ethical issue existed; (2) had to be able to analyze the issue so that they could make a decision that would be justifiable on ethical grounds; and (3) had to be able to act on it. There were planners who had trouble with each of these. A very narrow view of ethics made it difficult to see any issues beyond legality and loyalty. Aethical and vague planners were unable to make rational, impartial justifications for their decisions. Closet politicians were unable to act on their ethical principles. It was the rule utilitarians, the active substantive planners, and the public interest planners who were able to see a range of ethical issues, act on them, and articulate why they had acted.

Using the AICP code and my principles of adherence to the law and to duties of justice, accountability, and the public interest, these same three groups were judged to be the most ethical. They were joined by the process planners as well. These groups were all guided by an idea of the purposes that planning should serve. They used both deontological and teleological ideas of the public interest. They were also guided by a commitment to achieve those purposes through a legitimate, open process that included planners, decision makers, and the public in a process of give-and-take. Many were optimists about the public interest.

Among the more active of these planners, the least ambitious were the process planners, who focused primarily on the process itself; substantive planners and rule utilitarians actively pursued their ideas of the public interest with few violations of procedural rights. These were not planners for whom effectiveness involved a trade-off with ethics.

As technicians, the public interest planners had a more limited view of the planner's role, one that placed more emphasis on accountability to decision makers, but they were able to balance this commitment to loyalty with a fairly clear idea of the public interest, which protected them somewhat from co-optation.

The framework of these three principles also serves to identify several kinds of behavior that could be seen as ethically problematical. Aethical planners lacked the idealism that was necessary to a real commitment to ethical means or ends. Act utilitarians ran the risk of having their commitment to ends and to acting on them outrun their ability to justify that action. They sometimes felt that good ends justified means that even they saw as questionable. They did violate duties of justice, though not often, and when they acted covertly, they acted with radical independence, breaking the tie of responsibility to decision makers and the public. Half of the act utilitarians had acted unethically (see Table 11.3).

Narrow deontologists ran the risk of too little independence. The commitment to legality and to loyalty did not constitute a sufficient code of ethics for a planner. A concern with legality was a fundamental beginning point for ethics, but it was too narrow. It prevented some planners from seeing ethical dilemmas concerned with other principles of justice or the public interest. Loyalty, while an important and legitimate principle for public planners, could not be accepted uncritically. Both the nature of the demand and the process by which decisions were made affected whether the decision to be loyal was ethical or not. Taken together, an exclusive concern with legality and loyalty contributed to the ease with which planners could be co-opted by the political systems they worked in. Among the narrow deontologists, who were the mirror image of the act utilitarians, about half had also acted unethically (see Table 11.3).

These problems came either from a lack of basic ethical commitment or from a lack of balance among ethical principles. There seems to be no inherent reason why balance in itself should be desirable, but since the two great Western ethical traditions have different but at least somewhat complementary perspectives, the use of elements from both would seem, in a policy profession at least, to produce a more workable approach to ethics.

The AICP code and my hierarchy of principles provide a standard of evaluation that is somewhat independent of the ideas used by these planners, though both clearly come out of the same professional context. Perhaps it is not surprising, then, that there was some real agreement among the planners in the sample that these were principles that should be adhered to. This would perhaps augur well for their acceptance in the profession.

Even for the most strict principles—adherence to the law and to duties of justice—acceptance was high, though living up to the principles sometimes proved to be more difficult. The planners upheld duties of justice in 60 percent of the cases involving them. Most of the rest who did not accepted that what they had done was unethical or at least problematic.

Even the most aggressive consequentialists in the sample accepted these principles, though they did sometimes violate them. They did not want to lie or do harm to other individuals in order to achieve their own ideas of the public interest. The woman who leaked information on the mixed-use project she favored made this clear. She valued and relied on some of the very principles, such as loyalty, that she herself violated.

She made a clear distinction between right and wrong actions. She did engage in the wrong ones, but she also recognized and used the right ones:

> I think that basically sneaking around behind and offering people information is not a wonderful quality. I think that, you know, there is an ends justifies the means situation, but I don't think the means are wonderful by any means. . . . The good qualities are honesty, the good qualities are working hard and being efficient and being correct, doing a good job and knowing that you are correct, and checking to see if you are correct. Thoroughness.

By especially highlighting the importance of "correct" analysis, she implicitly marked off the one area where, for her, trust was critical. It was an area that should not be touched by dirty hands.

Cynicism and a lack of trust made some planners violate duties of justice. Removing the sources of that cynicism would remove much of the motivation to act with dirty hands or with radical autonomy.

The principle of accountability was widely accepted as well, though interpreted in different ways. Issues involving loyalty were by far the most common, and sorting through the demands of personal loyalty versus democratic accountability was not easy. Technicians gave loyalty a broader interpretation than others did, but, ultimately, only 11 percent of the planners rejected the legitimacy of officials as final decision makers.

Finally, the idea of the public interest as an ethical principle was accepted by the 84 percent of the sample who used it. Active, consequentialist planners were more likely to do unethical things in service to the public interest, but they did see these actions as questionable. Indeed, there was a general sense in the sample that the public interest should take second place, at least to the law and to duties of justice. The idea of the public interest as a process, though articulated by only half the sample, does help to sort out the legitimate claims of accountability. If the process of decision making is open, then a planner's own idea of the public interest should take second place to that of superior officials.

Substantively, however, the elements in the AICP code's definition of the public interest were accepted only to a limited degree by the planners. Only the idea of the broad, long-term public interest was widely shared, though it was particularly characteristic of the public interest planners.

This analysis of the relationship between approaches to ethics and actions clarifies further what was evident in chapter 10, the disparity between the aspirations in the code on environmental preservation, good environmental design, and especially on social justice and the actual performance of the planners. Environmental preservation and good environmental design were definitions of the public interest that were central to only a few planners. Social justice was very important to most of the substantive planners and was somewhat important to the process planners as well, but to most others in the sample, none of these goals apparently had much direct relationship to their everyday practice.

Some of this disparity was probably due to the values that the planners held as individuals. Overall, on the scale measuring attitudes about protecting the environment, the planners scored 4.1 on a scale on which 6.0 was strongly supportive. This was one of the highest means for substantive values and suggests considerable support. Was it, then, a matter of the political systems they worked in that might discourage action on these issues? Chapter 12 will explore some forces, including the nature of their political systems, that seemed to shape their actions.

12

Shaping Action on Ethics

Why did the planners act as they did? The explanation must deal with factors that influenced them at several different levels. In one sense, they acted as they did because of the values they held, values we examined in chapter 8. Their actions on certain cases, though, were also shaped by more immediate influences. The political systems of the community or the planner's agency could influence specific actions. The risk or practicality of particular actions and the inclination of the planner all played a role as well, as did social support and just the way events played out. In addition, on a larger scale, structural factors could shape the kind of issues that planners dealt with as well as community interest in and support for them.

In many cases, the planners had explanations for why they acted as they did. Taking a distinction from Kant, motivations were usually either moral or prudential, as I discuss below, but there were also influences on their behavior of which they were not aware. The structural factors, such as the values of their communities and agencies, were often below the threshold of consciousness of a particular individual.

Acting from Duty and Prudence

Generally, teleologists have not been greatly concerned about ethical motivation. A good act is good whether it is produced for good or bad reasons. Thus, the elements of pride, ambition, and excitement that seemed in part to motivate some consequentialist planners would have no bearing on the ethical nature of their actions if they were judged from a purely teleological point of view.

Motivation has been a concern for deontologists perhaps because their focus on the rightness of actions themselves seems much more difficult to separate from the motivations for action. Kant (1964), who placed great emphasis on the capacity of man to act from reason, made a distinction between acting from goodwill versus acting from prudence or inclination. Prudence involved acting in seif-interest. Inclination involved doing as one wished. However, for Kant, the only actions that were moral in nature were those taken from goodwill, duty, or from a rational willing to do right.

Sketched in this way, this test of motivation has a severe quality, but it is easy to act morally as long as such actions correspond to the dictates of prudence or desire. Indeed, we have seen already how important easy actions were to everyday ethics. It is when these motivations conflict that the ability to act morally is tested. At that point, the ability to see clearly where duty lies and then to deliberately act on it becomes critical. This does require the kind of resolve and perhaps the severity that Kant's idea of duty suggests.

Aethical planners seemed to be aethical not simply because of their actions. Much of what they described was perfectly "ethical." Being aethical reflected, in part, acting primarily from prudence or inclination rather than from a sense of duty. This was action that did not involve any real commitment to determining what was right, and, since it was based largely on what was easy, it was an approach to ethics that was unlikely to withstand any very difficult challenge. Thus, one planner whose politically connected subordinate did favors on zoning cases looked the other way, saying only that no one was being hurt.

One of these planners compared himself to someone else who he knew was also in the sample:

> To me, it's sort of ethical—whether you choose to do something that is a conflict of interest. When you first called, I thought, "Oh no! Of all the people—she's got a good one here," and then when I found out you were talking to James Sheldon, I thought, "Oh no! Exact contrast," because he is Mr. Precision and straight, and I thought, "Well, she's going to get it when she comes here."

By "straight" he apparently meant that his colleague acted from duty. It was a term used by others as well in much the same way. It was a quality held by perhaps 20 percent of the sample overall and about 30 percent of the deontologists, for whom it was most relevant.[1] It implied that these people could act, perhaps in the face of risk, and that the action was moral in its motivation, that is, based on duty. While this minority of "straight" planners seemed to have a particular kind of certainty about ethics, the majority of the planners who came between them and the few aethical planners could also act from moral motivations. When people talked about listening to their consciences as a guide, this was what they meant, but it was also natural and inevitable, if not very Kantian, that most people considered prudence and practicality as well.

Influences on Behavior: Bureaucracy and Politics

None of the planners in this sample were evil. Some, such as the aethical planners, were cynical about the usefulness of acting on ethical grounds. They felt it was "naive" to expect well-intentioned action to be effective in a political world, but this was not a common attitude. So why did people act in ways that they themselves often thought were unethical?

The first obvious explanation is that they may have felt they had little choice given their limited bureaucratic and political autonomy. This is the image of Baum's (1983) Maryland planners who had difficulty seeing results from their work and who were confused by the complexity of the planning process over which they felt they had no control. His lower-level planners were especially likely to be cynical about having any influence.

The nature of bureaucratic and political systems did seem to play a role in the actions of the planners in this sample. The cases involving loyalty raised situations in which the planners were likely to feel constrained by their bureaucratic and political environment. Formal measures of such factors in this study were minimal and rather crude, but they do give some sense of the difference between the planners who acted ethically and those who acted unethically according to the AICP code and my hierarchy.

Occupying a higher position in an agency seems to have given the ethical planners greater leverage to resist pressures (Table 12.1). Among those who were faced with issues of loyalty, 72 percent of the directors compared with only 22 percent of those who held middle- or lower-level positions in the bureaucracy acted ethically. In cases involving conflicts between loyalty and their own ideas of the public interest, directors were in a better position to press their views until they were satisfied that they had been heard. On the other side, on the six issues in which a planner acted covertly, four of the planners worked in middle- or lower-level positions. Some did feel frustrated and limited by the bureaucracy, and this was their response.

On the issue of the location of a large industrial facility, Paul Michaud was busy plotting means and setting his staff to work on analyses to

TABLE 12.1

Influence of Political and Bureaucratic Factors on Actions

| | Action Taken (percents) | | Total |
	Ethical	Unethical[a]	Cases
Position in Agency:			
Director or			
Assistant Director	72	28	29
Division Head	54	46	11
Middle/Low	22	78	9
State:			
Maryland	73	27	11
California	69	31	13
Tennessee	55	45	9
Texas	44	56	9
New York	43	57	7

Notes:

n = 49 cases involving loyalty.

[a] Ethical and unethical actions are defined in relation to the AICP code and my hierarchy of principles.

change the mayor's ideas about the site. On this issue, he did not have to worry about being heard, but the middle-level project manager who had become committed to the mixed-use project was sure that interagency bureaucratic politics would prevent her from convincing her superiors of its merits. She said in justification of her covert efforts in support of the project:

> [My agency's] perspective on the ethics here is that we're neutral, we take no position on this because we don't want to be positioned in it. If we take a position, we're stabbing a sister agency, which is not nice, and I don't care about that, really. I mean, I think it's a very stupid issue.

The larger political climate did also seem to make a difference. In California and Maryland, which were more accepting of planning and in which even local civil service was quite professionalized, planners were somewhat more likely to make ethical choices than in Texas and Tennessee, where planning played a more marginal role (see Table 12.1). Chapter 8 portrayed the differences in general values, in the nature of political systems, and in expectations about planning and planners between California relative to Texas and Tennessee. The provisions of the AICP code were closer to the values prevalent in California. Holding planners in Texas and Tennessee, with their strongly prodevelopment values, to at least some of the provisions in the code would have involved more risk for them. In New York, the problem was primarily in New York City, where the size and corruption of the bureaucracy made acting difficult.

A California planning director who worked in a community that was less supportive of planning than many others still portrayed his relations with his decision makers as open and straightforward:

> There have always been council members who come in and attempt to sell you their point of view. I think that most reasonable people can listen to them and sympathize with them but still indicate that it may not be the appropriate direction for the city to move. I don't know if I call it politicking, but you certainly have to be aware of the interests of those people who are going to vote on it and couch it in a language that is acceptable to them.

His image of his political system contrasted strongly with the bureaucratic image presented by a middle-level planner in New York City:

> There's basically no willingness to say honestly, "This is a good idea, this is a bad idea," no matter what the waste of resources. Just smile and go ahead and do whatever thing they want. . . . When that's an external thing with other agencies or to the public and you're not in a position to make a decision, that's one thing. Somebody else has made policy for you, but if it's [at] an internal, in-house level of consideration before decisions are made or before they are brought to the outside, then I think that when honest advice is not given that there is certainly questionable judgment going on.

A more detailed comparative study of the politics of planning in a variety of communities would be required to look at the way local political and bureaucratic structures either constrained or provided opportunities for ethical action. Some of the planners in the sample described themselves as lacking the resources to resist pressures to be loyal, but it was difficult to sort out how much this was due to the nature of the community's politics and how much to the planner's approach to that politics. A planner from New York, for example, argued that the nature of its political and bureaucratic system had the effect of reducing planners either to ineffective passivity or to covert revolt; certainly both kinds of reaction were evident in the cases related to loyalty.

Influences on Behavior: Prudence

This variability in planners' responses to ethical issues raised in their political systems depended in part on their attitudes about prudence. Prudence is the skillful and rational choice of means for achieving one's own well-being. The two prudential considerations most frequently raised by the planners were the risk and the practicality of possible ethical actions. While it was possible for these considerations to play too large a role in people's decisions, outweighing ethical principles that should have been acted on, risk and practicality were generally useful guides allowing planners to gauge the kind of response they might encounter. If the dictates of morality and of prudence coincided, then acting ethically would be substantially easier.

Risk

Many ethical decisions involved little or no risk at all. That was why some were easy to make and act on. Even so, of the seventy-four planners who talked explicitly about the factors they considered when they made an ethical decision, 60 percent talked in one way or another about risk.

Risk and conflict went hand in hand, though they were not quite the same. The primary risk that planners talked about was the fear of loss of their jobs; any action that would have put their jobs in jeopardy would clearly have been fraught with conflict as well. It was possible that planners who had a higher tolerance for conflict were somewhat less likely to see their jobs on the line when they made decisions, but even so, such planners did sometimes get involved in situations that put their jobs at risk. People who blew the whistle on illegal activities were the obvious case in point. While one resigned and went to the press, several others stayed in their jobs and had to face attempts to fire them or face criticism and distrust by other people. A planner who was involved in revealing illegal activities by his manager and an elected official described the result:

> There was a slight reign of terror afterward. The police department had to stake out my house when I was away. There was an orchestrated campaign to show that the planning commission was slowing down the development review process too much, but the real objective was to get rid of me. We countered it by asking for an engineering task force to look at our review procedures.

Planners accepted risk as a practical constraint on their behavior:

> You know where you're getting your pay from and you know that
> you don't want to antagonize too many people who have certain
> clout or a question could arise about your own continued tenure
> with the agency. Now, this isn't something that you have on your
> mind all the time . . . I mean, thinking about the ethical dilemmas of
> what you're doing. You just kind of develop a sense of what will fly
> and what won't. You make a decision that says, "I'm not going to
> rock any boats because I've got to eat."

Some could also see that there were times when it was important to take
a risk as well.

Consequentialist planners tended to see this as a situation where the
end was sufficiently important to overcome the risk involved in the
means:

> I might take a certain amount of risk, like Southwest Freeway . . . I
> have a number of problems with it, but there are several solutions
> for it and not a clear wrong solution. With the Rosebud bypass and
> with certain other things I've gotten involved in, I could see that
> there is clearly a wrong solution which is the one that, in fact, is
> being pressed and a number of right solutions that weren't being
> pressed. I think the answer to your question is, "Is the proposed
> solution clearly and overtly wrong?" Maybe how wrong it is is a
> question of how much I will get myself involved.

In general, active consequentialists did seem to have a higher tolerance
for risk than most of the technicians, except for the technician activists.
The project planner who provided covert support for the mixed-used
development said with a little bravado:

> If I were caught with my hand in the jar, what would happen? Would
> I get slapped or would I get fired? I tend to think that I would be
> slapped and ostracized but not fired.

A few planners became so caught up in the challenge of acting on the goal
that they seemed almost to forget about the risk. Deontologists, though,
saw the choice more as a matter of how binding a duty was. They were
not so likely to discount the risk.

Some planners talked explicitly about why they could afford to have
a higher tolerance for risk that allowed them to act in ways they knew

others could not afford to do. Four planners ended up in situations where
they knew they were already on a "hit list" to be fired, so that they did
not run much additional risk by acting. One planner who worked behind
the scenes to stave off changes in a plan that he had been involved in
developing said:

> In terms of fear, yeah, that was there, but then, on the other hand,
> I figured if these people prevail, I'd be out anyway, my policies
> would probably be out, and I had nothing to lose from that perspec-
> tive, really, from a losing-my-job type of perspective.

The other group that had a higher tolerance for risk was women, who
saw their financial risk as lower. The planner who blew the whistle on her
boss compared herself to a colleague who left the agency rather than act:

> I do have a lot of faith in what the agency does, and I wanted to see
> it through. . . . I tend to be a stayer; I tend to be inertial. I didn't
> want to leave at the time, for personal reasons, and he [the col-
> league] just made an effort to leave. I guess I also had a sense that—
> because my husband was working, that if it ever came to it and I
> had to quit on the spot or I was fired on the spot—it would not get
> me in financial trouble, whereas this other person was the sole
> support of his kids. So I was able to tolerate more.

Not all women had this luxury, of course. One talked about being the
sole support of her children, but it was notable that no men with working
wives raised this point. A few men who were single and one with a
military pension did make similar comments.

When planners did not feel that they had this higher tolerance for
risk, they calculated as best they could how much risk they would run
and balanced it against the strength of their ethical obligation. One
planner who worked in a community with "down and dirty politics" and
a closely divided council counted votes even on keeping his own job:

> That whole three years, you count your votes for what you should
> bring up and what you should not do, and if you know you're going
> to lose, then don't even bring it up. . . . Well, it depends on the
> significance of the issue and whether or not you need to keep
> plugging away at something. . . . Right now, with the existing
> charter, I'm appointed by the mayor and the council and I need a
> vote of four to one if the mayor disagrees with firing and three to
> two if he does agree—which, by the way, for the first two years I

was here was what kept me on the job because it was a three to two vote and the mayor was on my side. So that's what kept a lot of us going.

Practicality

Practicality played a somewhat similar balancing role, often one that supported ethical action. The most commonly mentioned practical consideration, raised by ten planners, was long-run effectiveness. Generally, they said that they would not lie or be disloyal or do favors, not only because it was not ethical but because it was not practical either. Relationships with decision makers, developers, or community groups had to be relations based on trust. The cost of losing such trust would substantially outweigh any short-term political advantage that an unethical action might bring. If it were lost, it would be very difficult to regain:

> I've always considered ethics honesty. . . . I believe for the people's sake and for your own sake, you better let them know everything.
> Q: Is that partly not just a matter of ethics but also a matter of strategy?
> I think strategy. I think it could possibly be damaging not only to that project but to any future projects that you may come up with. You may have a project that you sell and at a future project that is really valuable, that you really need to sell, if they find out that you have lied back here, you're not going to sell that other one whether the first project worked well or not.

Other considerations of practicality also involved tactics. Several planners simply pointed out that certain tactics were not practically useful in the context in which they worked. A planner was told by his city council to restructure the personnel system. He did not think the new system proposed by the council's consultant was an improvement, but he was being put under considerable pressure to toe the line anyway. He had thought of trying to blow the whistle by going to the press, but it just did not seem practical. It would only have given the council an excuse to get rid of him, and it would probably have had little impact in a city where press reports of internal city hall squabbling were routine. Another planner talked about his own personal style and how that limited the kind of tactics he could effectively use, even on an issue on which he was very strongly committed.

Often, but not always, practical considerations supported ethical action. Not surprisingly, people did not like to give examples where practicality had triumphed over principle. Often, practicality seemed to be a secondary justification made by people to show that they were not impractical ethical dreamers but hard-nosed realists. Ethics might sometimes be risky, but it could be useful as well.

Influences on Behavior: The Process of Acting

When the planners talked about what encouraged them to act, they often talked about how the process of decision and action had played out. As with prudential considerations, the process did not shape their values but it did affect how they acted. They particularly talked about two things. One was how they got caught up in the process. The other was the support they had gotten from other people. Support was by far the more important of the two. Even though planners were motivated by their own individual values and sometimes acted alone, making ethical decisions was generally a social process.

Getting Caught Up in the Process

The effect of getting caught up in the process was similar to the feeling of excitement that some consequentialist planners had when they were involved in risky actions, though it could also affect deontological planners as well. It only happened when people were engaged in major conflicts, so it was not very common. Covert actions could heighten the excitement partly because of the risk and partly because, in some sense, contact with the prosaic outside world was cut off. The planner who took his mapping skills and data to an outside consultant told an extraordinary tale of how he had been drawn in more and more deeply until he found his persona as a consultant competing directly with his agency persona. The competition climaxed at a computer mapping conference:

> The climax was the computer mapping conference in November—the university is sponsoring this workshop that will bring together all the people. Okay, so here's my partner and here's me—we planned this big production—this is our visibility image, the emergence of this division trying to market itself. Well, believe me, I did not sleep for about the whole month before because I stayed up here late at night working. . . . Well, we set up a display—our reports and everything like that—but we were trying to market

ourselves as a mapping service or resource within the community, but then on weekends me and my partner were working double time trying to get the consultant's products in a good condition. In the meantime, it became obvious to the staff people here that this competitor . . . the competitor surfaced, and it became obvious to the boss and my programmer that "Ah ha! There's someone else that has it too."

Q: And your friend is the front man.

Right, and I'm the silent partner. So I'm just gritting my teeth, and for a while there was some suspect that I might be involved, but that passed, but the bottom line was that at the workshop, he has his reports [and] we have ours. [Then the public agency] programmer [who he had been unable to get to do the work he wanted before] gets a copy of his stuff and she begins scrutinizing it to see what he has that she doesn't have, and she, in a flash of motivation, comes to me and goes, "We need to do this, this, and this," and she has the legends circled in red, and says, "We need to do all of this. I want to do this." So as a result of my conflicting interests, our own reports got better because we came back in with a revised edition that had some additional information that we didn't have in the beginning, so our agency reports got better as a direct result of that conference.

Support from other people heightened commitment and solidarity and also had the effect of reducing connections to the everyday world. The planner who blew the whistle on her boss and who talked about the influence of Watergate's Deep Throat said:

It's hard. It gets very romantic, and it's hard to pull back from the romanticism to what you're doing.

The planner whose commission sued the city council said of that time:

Of course, the other thing probably too was getting caught up in events. . . . I didn't have to advocate to the state representative in the state capital [but in fact I did have] to advocate to him that I think it is a state interest because we're talking about the department of state planning, [which] is [supposed] to promote good planning practices across the state, [and] here is an obvious example of good planning practices not being followed.

Another planner, who got involved in defending a development proposal from what he saw as unfair opposition in a referendum after it had been approved by elected officials, thought that he had been carried away in the heat of the moment:

> I think, as I look back at that, and it was a very, very intense situation, I developed a vested interest in that vote [though], in retrospect, I kept the brakes on reasonably well, and by that I mean that it would have been very, very easy for staff to become active, combatant, in the election process. It was a situation where that objectivity, that openness to the process, started to slide away and could have slid a hell of a lot farther and faster.

Social Support

Social support could even draw these three straight, deontological planners into getting caught up in events. While these were extreme cases, 61 percent of the planners talked about involving other people in the process of deciding or acting. In fact, this involvement was critical in encouraging planners to act, especially if the action was a difficult one. Of course, as with most of these influences, support could encourage either ethical or unethical action.

Other people were involved in ethical decisions in a variety of ways. They could supply information on which a choice could be based, they could suggest options, or they could provide clarification or other perspectives. They could provide reinforcement or allies for action, and they might be equally involved in making and acting on a decision. On these professional issues, the planners generally talked to other professionals, either in their agency or outside, though some talked with family members or friends especially if they were knowledgeable about the field. No one went to clergy or to anyone who might be thought of as an expert on ethics nor did anyone go to a professional organization unless they were charging someone else with unethical conduct.

Information or analysis was often necessary in order to make ethical choices. It was critical to any consequentialist decision concerning the public interest or good policy. The information was necessary both to weigh consequences and then to make a case. Thus, it was not surprising that two-thirds of the consequentialist planners specifically talked about this kind of process, along with 20 percent of the deontologists.

In many planning agencies, the collection and analysis of such data were likely to involve a number of people who thereby served as some check on its accuracy and on the reasonableness of the arguments being made from it. Some planners said explicitly that they were more thorough about this marshaling of information if a decision was a difficult one. Rebecca Giulini, who was urging affordable housing on a reluctant community, was one of these:

> I felt what I saw as an ethical issue was my desire to get more housing, and . . . at that point there was a danger, I think, that staff could become so enamored of getting more housing that we wouldn't ask the tough questions. . . . It caused us to go into greater depth than we probably would have before. . . . Those types of concerns caused us to go back and double-check and make sure we did ask the tough questions.

Sometimes getting information involved drawing in outside people who were experts. This was often at least partly a strategy of recruiting allies as well. The planner who had the problem of what to do about sinkholes in a subdivision was looking not only for better information but also for an authoritative source who could provide weight to her argument if the problem seemed to require more forceful action. Other planners went to lawyers for similar support on legally complex issues. The planner who was convinced, somewhat against his better judgment, to withhold information from the press said he had been influenced by the fact that it was the department's legal counsel who had told him to do it.

Gathering information was also closely related to getting advice, generating and considering options, and trying out ideas on other people. Considering alternatives was not discussed as much as one might expect from a sample of planners: only 16 percent of the planners talked about it. It was especially important if an action that appeared to be necessary would involve doing harm or violating some other ethical principle. The planner who had to consider what to do about a suit against himself and his city thought at first that the only course of action open was to make all the information public, thereby harming some innocent people who had been caught up in the case. Further discussion, though, made him reconsider:

> I really wanted to let them [the plaintiffs] have it, and after talking with the counsel, even he had this inclination at the beginning, "Let's just shut it up right now." But after a long discussion—several discussions . . . and I've had several talks with the council in executive sessions and I guess through the talks . . .
> Q: So what did change your mind?
> I honestly don't know . . . whether it was me or the attorney or the

council or all of us combined. I do know that we just said, "Let's back off. Let's stop a minute."

As well as helping to search for alternative courses of action, these discussions allowed the planners to lay out ideas about possible actions and to get other perspectives. This role of providing feedback was the one most commonly discussed. Planners often went to experienced people or ones whose judgment they particularly trusted. A younger planner said:

> On a day-to-day basis, when questions come up regarding the correct way to posture myself within the community vis-à-vis developers or the board of standards and appeals or the city planning commission, in cases where I can't fully trust my intuition or hard knowledge or what's contained in the executive orders and those clear cases of violations of the city law, I guess I turn to more experienced colleagues for guidance and advice. I've found . . . a lot of people who work in a likewise intuitive fashion and also engage in a good amount of soul-searching and discussion with their peers as to how . . .
> Q: Is there discussion of things that you would define as ethical issues among your contemporaries?
> Generally not explicitly discussed as ethical issues but rather in the context of particular problems as they develop. I think there is an awareness of the ethical underpinnings or implications of our actions. Nominally, we're supposed to be taking guidance from various executive orders and laws which pertain to behavior of public servants, but on a day-to-day basis they don't really offer that much.

Directors used their staffs to give them feedback on whether they were going in directions that seemed reasonable. One said:

> What I usually do is check my thinking—I'm not a loner. There are planners who are loners. I have a management team that I have a lot of respect for. They offer me a constant check of whether I'm doing the right thing or not. There are about eight people involved in that process. We meet every Monday at lunch and we talk about the management questions or the larger questions, and I think that is an important check for a person like myself that has to work with a larger agency.

Of course, how good the feedback was depended in part on how open the climate of the department was. Several planners gave examples of situations in which their concerns about some issue had been brushed aside; there were the cases too where pressure to make a wrong judgment had been applied by the department director rather than by some outside politician.

From getting feedback to getting reinforcement was only a small step, though it was also the step from an open consideration of options to a decision that had already been made. Reinforcement was critical for action that involved substantial risk, whether it was ethical or unethical. The planner who took his computer maps to an outside firm talked about the support he had gotten from the friend in the firm whom he had worked with:

> I did consult with him a lot—like, "How far can we go before I really jeopardize my position there?"

The woman in the corrupt agency who covertly gave out information supporting a project she favored talked about her husband's support:

> [He] works in city government, not in city planning, and he finds it so terribly frustrating that he considers 50 percent of his job fomenting the citizenry . . . I mean, you know, he spends plenty of his time on bunches of issues, doing exactly what I'm doing but to a much, much greater degree. I mean, I'll make a couple of phone calls a day but he spends 50 percent . . .

This seemed to be a case of like finding like.

On the other side, a planning director who struggled to operate honestly in a very political and corrupt city said that he got some support from other agency heads who were trying to do the same. This was difficult, since they were all under pressure "straight out of Nixon" to be loyal to the council.

Planners who were concerned about trying to raise politically difficult issues, such as social justice, also needed long-term support from other like-minded people in order to combat co-optation and burnout. A neighborhood planner, for example, said that involvements in groups outside his job and constant contact with his constituency kept his commitment up.

Planners who wanted to take on a single ethical issue also needed reinforcement if the consequences could be unpleasant. Several planners talked about issues that they had thought at the time posed ethical problems but on which they had not acted. The critical factor had been the lack of concern by colleagues about the issues or their unwillingness to get involved:

> I was working on the analysis of the new sports stadium a couple years ago—three years ago—and we did an analysis for the chairman of the planning commission and came up with a dollar value and the chairman publicly said that "It's going to cost this much. We've had a thorough review." Well, shortly thereafter, the state agency, which has greater powers and some financing capability, did a study contracted with one of the largest engineering firms, and I was speaking to the analyst at the engineering firm and learned that they were making some funny debt service assumptions—stretching it out—and [that] changed the cost a lot, so that the project, when it was announced by the state, cost $50 million more. The way I handled it was that I discussed that as a story with lots of people, and I was waiting for somebody to pick up on it, you know: "Hey, don't you think this is really odd? We did a study and then nine months later the state comes out with a study and there's a $50 million overrun." And nobody thought that much of it except they might raise an eyebrow as if to say, "Tough that it happened, but what do we know."

In the end, he did nothing.

Reinforcement, in turn, was closely tied to recruiting allies. In a number of cases, the planner was willing to act alone as long as others were supportive, but allies, particularly if they had influence, were obviously an advantage. In his study of planners in conflict, Hoch (1988) found both statistically and qualitatively that organizing allies was a significant factor in producing outcomes that were more favorable to the planners involved.

Just being one of several people helped. A planner who tried, unsuccessfully, to blow the whistle on what he thought had been a kickback scheme was clearly emboldened by being one of several complainants:

> Two or three of us were very seriously involved in documenting and collecting evidence of what had gone on. Not directly, but through a fellow planner, [we] contacted the district attorney and asked if there was anything that could be prosecuted, and we were told that there was no legal evidence. So the people that were behind the whole thing were never affected.

None of these people had any more influence than he did, but planners were sometimes able to recruit powerful allies to their cause. The planner who helped his plan commission sue the city council for violating the zoning ordinance not only had the commission's support—in fact, it was more of a case of them having his help—but he was also able to get assistance from the state planning agency, which ultimately supported the commission in their suit. George Walters was able to deal with several ethical issues through the intervention of an influential plan commissioner. Several others, such as Michaud, were able to use connections with city councilmen to raise issues that would have been difficult for them to deal with openly and directly. Of course, planners who were trying to achieve substantive goals, such as affordable housing, were, in a more open way, trying to do exactly the same thing—gain support from community groups or decision makers on an issue that was risky to raise.

Almost everyone who raised difficult or risky issues talked about having or recruiting support, except for one group—the closet politicians. While it is a bit tenuous to attribute significance to what people did not talk about in these interviews, it was notable that only one of the closet politicians talked about having any contact with other people in regard to ethical issues. Given that they were raising difficult equity and environmental issues, only with substantial support could they have gotten any serious consideration of them, but this was simply symptomatic of why they could not act. They tended to portray themselves as loners—Don Quixote tilting at windmills.

Hoch (1988) argued from his survey data that planners' images of professional autonomy and power prompted them to try to cope with conflicts as individuals rather than by getting help from others. Similarly, they attributed successful outcomes primarily to their own "technical competence and professional integrity" (Hoch 1988, p. 30) rather than to help from others, though failures were often attributed to lack of support and alliances.

Our interviews, however, suggest a somewhat different picture, perhaps because people's descriptions of what they did in particular cases made it possible to see patterns that they did not necessarily see themselves. There certainly was a tendency to talk about these ethical issues as cases of individual action, but when the planners were asked how they had decided and what action they had taken, the people who had been involved in risky, conflictual, or otherwise difficult decisions talked about other people who had helped them decide or act. Aside from the principles that told them that they should act, which might correspond to Hoch's technical competence and integrity, this support was probably the most critical factor in encouraging action. Active planners, in particular, needed it since they were eager to take on difficult issues. Even if technicians generally did not go out looking for issues to take on, they came by their share of difficult cases too and needed the support just as much.

Influences on Behavior: Structural Constraints

All of these factors of bureaucratic and political setting, prudence, inclination, and social support affected the planners' ability to act on issues that came up and about which they were aware. They influenced the behavior of individual planners on individual issues, but at a broader level, the kinds of issues the planners faced were shaped by structural factors that were inherent in all planning in the United States. These structural factors meant that the planners were more often faced, for example, with ethical issues in relation to fairness to individual developers than they were with justice toward low-income people.

As planning has tried since the Progressive period to create an institutionalized, bureaucratic role for itself in American government, it has had to deal with the structures of power in the political and economic systems. The political importance of economic development in general and land development in particular has shaped a public profession whose job it is both to encourage and to regulate development.

Planning grew up primarily as a local activity in a decentralized political system and a market economy. Local communities in such an economy are vulnerable to the movement of jobs and economic activity in general. Because local communities depend for their general economic and fiscal health on export-oriented economic activity within their boundaries, development, that is, attracting and keeping such businesses, has been central to local politics. Business interests and affluent and mobile middle-class residents have generally played a privileged though not necessarily a completely dominant role in this politics (Kantor 1988; Peterson 1981).

Redistribution of resources to working or lower class groups places any except a wealthy, growing community at an economic disadvantage relative to its neighbors. Using taxes from the affluent to help the less advantaged encourages the former to migrate to jurisdictions with either lower taxes or with services that benefit them more directly. Similarly, protection of the natural environment or a concern with aesthetic development, while often popular with the affluent middle class, can impose costs on a wide range of economic actors who are quick to point out that they may thereby be forced to move.

Among the various municipal functions, planning has probably been shaped significantly by these political and economic constraints. It is concerned with regulating the nature and location of public and private land uses, and all locational decisions have implications for the fiscal and economic base of a community. Planning is also a mechanism for providing public subsidies to various kinds of development that are deemed worthy by policymakers. The reasons may be equitable or environmental, but most often they appear to be economic.

If economic competition between communities means that issues of environmental preservation, aesthetics, and social justice are less likely to draw attention than issues of economic development, this bias is strengthened by patterns of citizen participation in local politics. Empirical research on participation in politics indicates that less educated, lower income people are less involved in various kinds of political activities (Verba and Nie 1972). On issues involving collective goods, such as aesthetics and environmental quality, Olson's (1965) theoretical analysis that many people will not participate because they can be free riders on the active few has been shown to be empirically valid (Walsh and Warland 1983)—though this is an area of active academic debate, given the obvious existence of environmental and other groups concerned with collective goods (Goodwin and Mitchell 1982; Mitchell 1979; Tillock and Morrison 1979).

The shaping of planning issues and practice by these structural forces is not some unusual characteristic of planning as a profession. It simply reflects the nature of local politics and economics. It highlights why some planners talked about the mobilization of bias, which could keep certain kinds of issues, such as social equity, off the agenda of local decision makers, and why substantive and process planners found themselves concerned about groups that were largely shut out of the political process. Many of the planners, though, never raised either substantive or procedural equity or environmental issues, even if these issues might have had some relevance in their communities.

The effect of this structural bias was not completely uniform. As we have seen, it was stronger in Texas and Tennessee than in California or Maryland. In central cities with large minority populations and a history of redistributive programs, the issue of social justice was bound to be somewhat more salient than it was in suburban areas. In California, at the time of the interviews, the state government was raising the issue of affordable housing, providing an opening for some planners concerned about equity, but, in general, planners raising these issues would be going across the political grain, and given the resources they could command, most were reluctant to do so.

In these cases, responsiveness to elected officials and to the politically organized public systematically sustained the bias inherent in the distribution of local power. Planners could argue that their moral obligations were met by this responsiveness and that as nonelected bureaucrats they had no legitimacy for dictating to a local community policies related to race, income, environmental preservation, or urban design.

This is a difficult dilemma for the profession. High-sounding words in a code of ethics were not enough to change planners' behavior on these issues. However, changed incentives might help. Chapter 13 will explore ideas for encouraging attention to these issues.

Conclusion

Planners acted because their ethical values told them to, because they judged that their actions would be prudent, and because they were supported in various ways by others. Ultimately, action was shaped by values. Without the motivation provided by some principle, action was unlikely. Conversely, someone who was initially motivated to act on some ethical value might choose, for prudential or strategic reasons, not to.

Acting also required a certain minimum level of idealism and faith that ethical action was possible, expected, and not hopelessly naive. A few planners who worked in corrupt or particularly frustrating circumstances became cynical. They lost this idealism and, with it, the will to act on ethical grounds. However, most planners believed that acting ethically was a duty. Whether they could bring themselves to do so, though, depended as well on how important the issue was to them, their estimation of the risks involved, their stomach for conflict, the support they received from others, and sometimes just on the vagaries of the way the process played out.

On the whole, active planners were more motivated to act by their own value commitments to particular ideas of the public interest. They were also less deterred by prudential considerations, both because of their own personalities and probably because of the kind of communities they worked in. These forces combined to define them as active planners in the first place. Technicians often seemed to be more cautious, both personally and probably in some cases because their environments were less supportive of active planning. The value of responsibility to officials provided an ethical underpinning for this more cautious role. If they were to go beyond a commitment to legality and loyalty, they needed not only a broader set of ethical values but more support as well.

All planners needed support in order to act ethically. Acting on duty was not always easy, and to assume that part of that duty was to bear all of the risk and burden alone would be, unfortunately, puritanical. Other people could provide support. So could institutional structures in communities and in the profession. How ethical action might be encouraged institutionally is the subject of chapter 13.

13

Encouraging Ethical Action

The motivation for ethical action was not simple. Acts were influenced by a variety of factors within individuals and in their social environments. Principles, prudence, and even inclination were balanced one against another while social support and the excitement of the moment encouraged or impelled the planners toward action. Principles, which themselves had diverse origins, some in childhood, some in early adulthood, were then used and reinforced through experience. The planners in this study brought a variety of principles with them into planning that interacted with values that have been characteristic of the profession often since its early days.

The ethical issues raised in this study of public planners were largely concerned with public duties. At the most basic level, many planners raised issues concerning honesty and corruption, though these were real problems in only a few communities. All the planners were concerned as well with procedural obligations to members of the public and to appointed and elected decision makers. They discussed cases that were related to fairness, providing truthful analysis, opening or restricting access to the planning process, and being accountable to elected and appointed officials. Most, but not all, also raised issues that were concerned with the public interest. They defined this in a number of rather different ways, although all versions could be reduced to the idea of the broad, long-run good of the community. Some simply used this most basic consequentialist definition of the public interest. Others were committed to particular substantive principles—social justice or preservation of the environment—that they thought were especially critical to that long-term good. About half also saw the public interest as arising out of a process of discussion among planners, members of the public, and elected officials. For some, this was their dominant image of the public interest.

Ethical issues arose both from simple challenges to ethical values and from conflicts between competing ethical values. Some issues were easy to deal with. These were the bread-and-butter, day-to-day issues that represented the normal functioning of a viable ethical system. Others, especially conflicts among ethical values, posed difficult issues that required both the ability to decide how to act and the ability and will to actually take action. The most difficult issues were those related to conflicts between loyalty to superiors and other ethical obligations, ranging from the law to truthfulness to the public interest. Here the problem was to determine where the legitimate claims of public accountability gave way to the illegitimate claims of personal loyalty.

The planners in the sample dealt with these ethical issues in ways that varied depending both on their own approach to ethics and on the role that they thought planning should play in the political system. In particular cases, their actions were also shaped by a variety of other factors, including prudence, support received from others, and/or simply the sweep of events.

Technicians generally held a view of planning as simply providing objective technical advice to elected officials. The line between planning and politics was clear, and decision makers were the ones who determined the public interest for their communities. Exactly how this was interpreted varied somewhat. Traditional technicians and passive hybrids were more "strict" than technician activists, who had stronger ideas of what they wanted to see done and were more willing to work to get it. All, though, ultimately deferred loyally to their elected officials.

Ethically, the most limited of all the technicians were the narrow deontologists, whose idea of ethics extended only to legal and procedural duties. Their Achilles' heel was loyalty since they had no clear concept of the public interest to help them sort out legitimate from illegitimate demands for loyalty by their superiors. Edward Smith, Jr., the traditional technician from Texas, had little clear image of how he wanted his growing city to develop. He relied on existing plans and laws as the backbone for recommendations to his officials, but if they wanted to adopt proposals that, though legal, were technically weak or favored their buddies, Smith felt he had no legitimate grounds for disagreement.

The narrow deontologists were a small group, however, and most technicians did have some notion of the public interest that they could use to balance the demands of loyalty. Richard Breitman, the technician activist, was more colorful and emphatically opinionated than George Walters, his passive hybrid counterpart. Their styles reflected somewhat different mind-sets as well as adaptations to rather different kinds of political systems. Breitman had always been more concerned with seeing results, and his influential role as an insider in a fairly closed, large-city administration gave him leverage to achieve them. Walters wanted less, and his influence came from many years of providing information and building trust in a low-key way among officials, the press, and community groups.

Both of these planners held a consequentialist idea of the broad, long-run public interest of their communities. They were willing to argue with their decision makers over whether particular policies would or would not serve that interest. Breitman was more comfortable mobilizing support from other agencies or citizen groups, but once the mayor or the council had decided, both men expected to be good "soldiers." Loyalty was central to their role. Indeed, for all of Breitman's more obvious appearance of independence, his insider role bound him perhaps even more firmly to his administration, whose policies he had been instrumental in shaping.

If loyalty was the bugaboo of the technicians, radical autonomy in the form of dirty hands or covert actions could be a problem for more active planners. This was a less pervasive problem than loyalty was for technicians, and it primarily affected consequentialist activists.

Consequentialist planners, especially cynical ones, were the most likely to think both that there might be a trade-off between being ethical and being effective and that a good end could justify the use of questionable or alienating means. Paul Michaud was an act utilitarian. He was ambitious, strongly committed to what he defined as "good planning," and a bit of a cynic. While he normally marshaled data and arguments to support projects he favored, he was quite willing to bargain strategically, to instigate pressure on decision makers, and even to act covertly to sabotage a project he thought was misguided. All indications were that he was an effective planner. Michaud was living proof that there could be a trade-off between being ethical, at least in a deontological sense, and being effective.

Rule utilitarian Tom Stuart, who had much the same kind of drive and apparent effectiveness, suggested that this trade-off was not inevitable, even for consequentialist planners. He just drew a line and said that there were "personal" ethical rules, such as being truthful, fair, and open, that he tried not to violate. Some aspects of his active role as a lobbyist, such as playing on the natural dislike between legislative houses or not volunteering information, gave him pause. Stuart thought, ideally, that planners should convince others about policies on their merits, but he recognized that in his state government, things did not always work that way. So he lobbied hard, trying just as hard not to be pushed over the line of what he thought was wrong.

His consequentialist ethics, however, left him somewhat vulnerable to being flexible. It was really the substantive deontologists like Grace Sumner who defined what it meant to be a "straight" active planner. She, too, was strongly motivated, especially by her commitment to affordable housing for suburban Denton. She did not shy away from conflict, thought strategically, and seemed to be effective, but for Sumner, means such as lies, withholding information, or end runs violated the very commitment to justice and to autonomy in a larger sense that she was trying to achieve, so she did not use them. In the open politics of her community, she also did not have to.

Indeed, if there were two groups in the sample who indicated that it was possible for planning to be both active and ethical, it was the substantive deontologists and the process planners. They came closer than any others to being "communicatively competent," though none had probably ever heard of Jurgen Habermas (Forester 1980).

The process role is one that seems to have emerged fairly clearly in recent years. It shares ethical commitments—to fairness and openness— with the substantive deontologists but may be especially appropriate in situations where planning is not as politically accepted or the process is not as open as it was in Grace Sumner's Denton. Rebecca Giulini shared much with Sumner, but her priorities were different. She subordinated her personal concern with social equity to her overriding commitment to see that the planning process in her community was open to weak as well as to strong groups.

Most of the active and process planners were optimists about the role of planners, citizens, and decision makers in the planning process. For a few, experience had not dulled their activism but had made them cynical. They were the most vulnerable to problems of dirty hands and covert action. There were also some ethical casualties to the idea of an active role for planning. These were the closet politicians. Sam French showed very clearly that it was not enough to hold strong ethical values. It was also necessary to be able to act on them. His inability to act left him with a corroding sense of moral weakness.

As this summary suggests, ethics is not a simple matter. It requires being able to see ethical issues, to decide in some systematic way what action would be right or good, and then to act on that decision. Many but not all of these planners had resources of their own that enabled them to act ethically. Many had clear ethical principles that enabled them to see issues and to decide how to act. Some were tolerant of conflict or risk. Honest and open bureaucratic and political settings gave them additional leverage. Support could also be garnered from colleagues or other allies.

This book is intended to provide support of a somewhat different kind. In looking at the kinds of ethical dilemmas planners faced, I have tried to develop guidelines for decision that might contribute to a stronger sense of a professional ethic for planning.

The framework used here for evaluating the actions of these planners draws both on the AICP code of ethics and on my own ideas for a mixed but primarily deontological planning ethic. Both of these guidelines corresponded fairly closely to the planners' own understanding of ethics, except in relation to the substantive meaning of the public interest. The code's strong emphasis on protecting the natural environment, on striving for good urban design, and, especially, on achieving social justice was not reflected in the practice of most of the planners in the sample and, in some cases, not in their personal values either.

My own values are more similar to those in the code of ethics than to those of at least some of the planners. Ethics are essential to an authentic relationship between people. Planners must treat others, whether in a professional or a personal context, with respect, as ends not as means. Actions that would violate duties of justice, such as truthfulness or fairness, should be resisted and should not be justified by appeal to serving the public interest. Professionally, it is important for planners to be responsive and accountable to the elected officials they serve. It is unfortunate that principled resignation has so little role in American politics. The lack of an ethically justifiable expression of protest inevitably lends support to much less justifiable covert action.

However, planners do not have to give up all judgment and autonomy in the name of accountability. A clear idea of the public interest, both as a substantive concept and as an approach to the process of decision making, can give planners independence from excessive demands for loyalty. The AICP code identifies three collective "goods"—social justice, environmental preservation, and aesthetic design—as central to its definition of the public interest. It must be left to others to develop detailed reasons why these particular principles should be central ethical commitments in planning (Beatley 1991; Howe forthcoming). All three have been motivating values in the profession since the Progressive era. In part, it is the commitment of planners to the substantive values of social equity, aesthetics, and preservation of the environment that distinguishes them from other public professionals, such as public administrators and policy analysts (Alterman and MacRae 1983; Nigro and Richardson 1990).

Given the diverse influences on planners' ethical values and the similarities and differences between these values and those laid out in the code, what possibilities exist for encouraging ethical action among planners? Two issues need to be addressed here. One is how to encourage planners like the ones in this sample in the actions that they already defined as ethical. The other is whether it is possible to close the gap between the aspirations of the code and planners' actual practice. The two tasks are rather different, though some of the tools for accomplishing them both might be the same.

Doing Better at What We Do Now

The idea of encouraging ethical action may suggest that if people are left to their own devices, they would not act ethically but must somehow be encouraged by some outside force. This was not the case for these planners. A few seemed to be adrift, in need of ethical support and guidance, but many had principles to guide them and sufficient will to act. What problems there were came from two primary sources.

One was the external environment. In some communities, even minimum levels of legal behavior were not supported because of corruption. A related but more subtle problem resulted from the clash between community values and professional values that suggested that communities should play an active role in dealing, for example, with equity or environmental problems.

The other problem arose from the range of roles and ethical approaches taken by the planners. The framework used here identifies as problematic the two ends of the spectrum of ethical approaches. Technicians of all varieties tended to overemphasize loyalty. Active planners, driven by ends, could become casual about the propriety of the means they used.

Given these specific problems, what could be done to encourage planners to act more ethically within the institutions available to a profession such as planning? Many of the forces that shaped behavior were beyond the influence of professional institutions. The culture of planning in particular communities, the early socialization of children, even the long-term influence of experience are largely beyond reach. The two most powerful tools available to the profession are its ability to socialize at least some of the people coming into the field and its ability to provide even limited kinds of support once they are out in practice.

The External Environment: The Culture of Planning

The structural conditions that shaped the ethical behavior of these planners were malleable to only a limited extent. No community was without ethical issues since the bureaucratic nature of public planning and the

competing "goods" that planners were trying to achieve guaranteed the
existence of ethical choices. There were communities in the sample in
which basic issues of corruption did not exist, though. For many planners
working in communities where corruption was an issue, this achievement
in itself would have been a great improvement, leaving them free to get
on with the always complex business of trying to make planning effective
rather than just minimally honest.

The general ethical climate of a community had to be taken more or
less as a given by any particular planner at any given time, but it was not
fixed for all time. Maryland was a state in which the corrupt old patterns
of Spiro Agnew's day lived on only in some areas. In terms of the
acceptance and professionalization of planning, Maryland was more like
California than it was like Tennessee.

It would be difficult for individual planners or for a professional
organization to have much impact on the culture itself. They could,
however, be active in discouraging corrupt behavior and in encouraging
planners who chose to resist corruption. The provisions of the AICP code
are clear on conflicts of interest and misuse of the power of office.
Prosecution under a professional code is not easy, especially in a profession without strong powers of self-regulation, and several examples were
raised by members of the sample where efforts to discipline particular
planners under the code had failed. Cases of corruption would be the
most clear and straightforward. Indeed, such behavior would be prohibited by local law as well. The central difficulty, and not an easy one to
deal with, would be breaking with the local culture that allows corruption
to exist. Here legal and investigatory support from the American Planning
Association, whether through its state chapters or through the national
organization, could provide support for someone bringing a case.[1]

Perhaps more important, both in the case of corruption and in the
broader case of conflicts between professional and community values,
would be to provide support and assistance to planners who were trying
to "do right." If ethics and a commitment to the public interest are to
represent anything more than meaningless platitudes, planners would
need support for raising issues that might generate conflict. This might be
done in a variety of ways, through training, support within an agency, or
professional support from outside. In Hoch's (1987) report to the APA on
Planning Threatened: A Final Report on Planners and Political Conflict,
he showed that planners themselves, both those who had been involved
in conflicts and those who had not, ranked improved training in handling
conflicts highest, followed by networking, legal support, research support, and support from colleagues (Hoch 1988; Hoch and Cibulskis 1987).

Hendler (forthcoming), in a study of conflicts experienced by members of one Canadian planning office, had similar findings. Except for training, which shapes the individual's approach to and competence in handling conflict, all of these kinds of support would be expected to change or improve the planner's power resources for dealing with his or her political environment. One planner in Hendler's study "said that the professional organization should act more like a union in this regard" (Hendler forthcoming).

Support from colleagues and institutional support from one's own agency could provide help in resisting corruption or co-optation. Planning directors who tried to establish an ethical climate in their agencies were trying to encourage ethical behavior, not only by setting rules and expectations but also by taking the heat for their employees. The examples in this study were primarily concerned with maintaining standards of basic honesty, but the equity-oriented planning effort in Cleveland was strengthened not only by Krumholz's encouragement of his staff but also by his willingness to shield them when necessary (Krumholz and Forester 1990). Support by the planning commission was also consistent and helpful. One agency director in this sample appears to have operated in a somewhat similar manner.

Beyond agency support, Hoch (1987) proposed the creation of a "Planners' Contact" discussion and referral service. The purpose would be to use the APA to put planners engaged in conflicts in touch with others who had an interest in or expertise with such conflicts. The other person could provide social support but also ideas about how the conflict might be analyzed or dealt with. Such advice or feedback might improve the outcome from the planner's point of view.

Finally, external legal and research support might operate in similar ways to improve the technical resources available to planners in conflicts. Knowing one's own legal rights is useful, and the backing of a lawyer makes other players more cautious. Hoch (1987) suggests that each APA member be allowed to contact the organization's legal staff up to one time each year.

Outside research support might provide a more general source of leverage, especially when combined with legal assistance. This might be especially useful on substantive issues related to social equity or the environment. Especially in court suits such as those against Yonkers or Mount Laurel, which challenge local programs or ordinances on the grounds of racial discrimination, APA might give expert testimony and might be able to provide technical assistance to communities that showed some willingness to change discriminatory ordinances or to deal with significant environmental problems.

The possibility of such support would probably be only a slight inducement for planners to raise conflictual issues. The planners in this study suggested that organized local support or pressure or money from higher levels of government were sometimes helpful in reducing the costs of action for planners already disposed to act, both because of their substantive values and because of their active approach.

Individual Roles and Conflict

The idea of helping planners to do better what they are already doing precludes efforts to produce major changes in their procedural or substantive approaches to planning, but within the context of what planners already did, Hoch's (1988) survey indicated that planners themselves, especially those who had not been involved in threatening conflicts, wanted more education in how to deal with conflict.

Exactly what this might involve is less clear. In recent years, there has been a growing interest in systematically teaching methods for dispute resolution (Dotson et al. 1989; Rabinovitz 1989; Susskind and Ozawa 1984). The planners in this study were involved in negotiations and even, on occasion, in mediation situations, but their knowledge of how to handle these was largely intuitive. For process planners, especially, greater understanding about different kinds of disputes and a more analytic and strategic approach to dealing with them might not only help to further define their role but might also give them greater legitimacy in it. Many active planners might also find such skills useful.

Typically, the negotiation/mediation literature focuses on situations in which the planner serves to help other contending parties to work out solutions to disputes (Forester 1987). The conflicts described by Hoch (1988) and the ethical dilemmas faced by planners in this study were more commonly ones in which they were one of the contending parties, often a relatively weak one. Here the principles and techniques for dispute resolution could still apply but at a deeper, more personal level, which perhaps complicates their application. Diagnostic tests are available that can be used by individuals to analyze and understand their own approach to conflict (Dotson et al. 1989). Some planners may be conflict avoiders; others typically see conflicts in zero-sum, I win/you lose terms. Still others are by nature compromisers or people who look for and help others to find win-win solutions. Of course, understanding does not automatically translate into action. Understanding will not magically transform a conflict avoider into a problem solver, but insight can be a starting place for change. Training in negotiation and mediation skills, which provides a framework for systematic analysis of conflict situations and suggests appropriate strategies, can provide support for such change. This kind of training might be provided in planning schools or it might be available through the national APA, regional or chapter conferences, or short courses.

Encouraging a New Ethic

Over the years, planners have worried about whether planning really is a profession and what kinds of institutions and behavior would make it one. On the whole, it seems to be a fairly well-established if small and not highly visible one. Even so, it is diffuse because planners work in a wide variety of public and private jobs spread over a range of substantive fields. Planners themselves often seem to have a desire for a stronger professional identity—a sense of commonality more specific than the rational planning approach. The planners in Hendler's (forthcoming) Canadian agency, for instance, wanted the profession to present itself and its role more clearly and positively to the public, to create a more defined and accepted professional identity that would support their individual actions.

The AICP code lays out a framework for a professional ethic for planners. It has the advantage of having a basis in the values that planners already hold both as individuals and as a profession. It draws on principles such as accountability and the public interest, which have guided public professionals since the Progressive period. While these principles fell out of favor during the 1960s, the post-Watergate revival of interest in ethics seems to have brought them back to respectability.

Even so, while these principles have historical roots in the field, and in the present values of some planners, they are not clearly accepted by practitioners and teachers as the basic tenets for public planners. Some are accepted in theory but not acted on in reality.

I believe that these values are important to the field. Because they are politically controversial and neglect of them is sometimes supported by institutional structures in political systems, we cannot make every planner care about them or adhere to them. They have to be discretionary "duties of benevolence" rather than binding "duties of justice." However, we can encourage members of the profession to care about them, to see how structural bias weakens their "voice," and to see how a planner might act effectively to raise them. One lesson to be learned from the planners in this study is that these principles could be acted on, if not by all planners everywhere at least by some in particular circumstances. The challenge is to increase the number of people willing and able to act and the number of opportunities for action.

Several mechanisms would be available to the profession to encourage their actual use. One would simply be to place more emphasis on the existing code. The other would be more systematic socialization to these values in planning school.

The Role of Codes of Ethics in Regulating Behavior

For a variety of reasons, codes of ethics in planning do not appear to have much influence over the values or behavior of planners. As a shaping force on ethics, they ranked the lowest of any of the influences measured on the questionnaire given to the planners in this sample and were rated as a strong influence by only 8 percent of the sample. This does not necessarily mean that they could not, or did not, serve a useful function, but it was not primarily as a force shaping ethics. The planners who did use a code of ethics used it as a public support for decisions that they arrived at using their own internalized principles. One planner, already quoted, said about a conflict she had with her policy board:

> In this particular instance . . . I in fact pulled out the canons and looked at them again, and there was one on the public interest. . . . I was ready to sort of go the route and say, "I won't do this, and here are my ethics"—the principles in the canons.

Since the adoption of the AICP code in 1981 and of a more general APA code in 1987, both organizations have devoted attention to familiarizing planners with their content and to encouraging systematic thought about ethics (American Institute of Certified Planners 1983; Barrett 1984, 1989; Martin 1989). Workshops have also been held at national and chapter meetings that give people a chance to talk about real and hypothetical cases and to explore the nature of ethical action.

However, the AICP code also has to compete for attention, in a sense, with those of states, municipalities, or agencies. More people in the sample mentioned state or local ethics laws or departmental regulations as guides that regulated their behavior than mentioned a professional code. This poses in a specific way the more general problem faced by all professions whose members work in bureaucratic agencies. This is that the agencies exert much more real day-to-day control over behavior than the profession can. Public planners, as civil servants, do owe loyalty or accountability to elected officials. Their professional effectiveness, advancement, and, in the end, their jobs depend on the approval of those officials and not in any way on the organized planning profession. They do not have the institutionalized autonomy that society has granted to such traditional professions as law and medicine (Howe 1980b).

This is not necessarily a disadvantage for society. The autonomy of professionals such as doctors has proved to be a mixed blessing for everyone else. For the past twenty years, the consuming public and governments have been engaged in a running battle to withdraw some of the autonomy they have granted. Indeed, the major issue in the academic study of professional ethics has been the issue of whether professions could justifiably hold ethical principles that conflicted with or contravened ordinary ethical values (Bayles 1981; Freedman 1978; Gewirth 1986; Goldman 1980; Kultgen 1988; Martin 1981). This question has produced considerable disagreement, but a majority of scholars who have thought about it suggest that they should not.

Public professionals, including planners, have never been in a position to argue for this kind of autonomy. Public servants are seen as exactly that. They serve elected officials and, by extension, the public. This is the quid pro quo for their power to regulate property and behavior by law.

As professionals, though, many planners are not content simply to serve as the tools of elected decision makers. They bring to their jobs ideas of what appropriate patterns of development should be. These are embodied in their own ideas of the public interest. In effect, planners assert some claims of autonomy within the bureaucratic structure. Their own ethical values support this idea of limited autonomy—asserting, for example, that it is possible to have a conflict between loyalty to officials and their own ideas of the public interest.

Ultimately, in a small way, the AICP code of ethics, which governs professional as opposed to lay planners, contributes weight on the side of autonomy. It gives a planner, like the one quoted above, some external support. If the suggestions made earlier were also followed, professional organizations could also back the code with some institutionalized support as well.

State and local ethics laws and regulations are primarily concerned with corruption and conflicts of interest while the professional code deals much more with general positive principles, such as a concern for the public interest or social equity. Because of this difference, the professional code could provide a kind of external balance force that public laws do not, albeit one with a much weaker authority. This role of the code in increasing a sense of professional solidarity was discussed by the woman who did use it as such a balance. She had been active in her APA

chapter and that had increased her awareness of and perhaps her commitment to using the code:

> Somehow I do have a sense of my professional self, and maybe part
> of that is through being active in the planning association. I think
> that's helped because I started when I was a student, . . . and at
> that time I had a sense of planners . . . looking for a profession, so
> maybe I wanted to define it. My husband's an attorney, and that is
> so well-defined as to what you are . . . when he got admitted to the
> bar, having to learn those canons . . . that made me aware of looking
> for planning canons, too.

Education as a Force for Change

While codes of ethics may tend to operate as support for ethical positions
rather than as a shaping force, professional education would be a way in
which the ethical values of new planners could be shaped. Many basic
ethical values seem to be set in childhood, and planning schools can only
assume that people come with them, but the application of those principles to planning practice is something that planning school can clarify.
Values about the public interest and responsibility to officials might be
more shaped, particularly for students who had not given these issues
much thought. Planning school can also make explicit the role choices
that are available to planners and the ethical assumptions embedded in
each. Finally, it can help students to explore different approaches to
thinking about ethical issues.

Professional education, by its nature, indoctrinates students to the
techniques and values of the field, though students may well choose a
profession in part because of the perceived fit between their own values
and those of people in the field. Since values go hand in hand with
substance and technique, it is important to recognize that issues of ethics
and principle can and do arise not just in introductory courses or those
dealing with theory or specifically with ethics but in all courses. This is
why at least some degree of consensus on central ethical values is
important. Such consensus may well exist in planning, though more
explicit recognition of it might be useful. If the AICP code and perhaps
the idea of a hierarchy, like the one suggested here, were seen as a central
guiding force for the profession, what would the implications be for the
way planning is taught?

The specific application in planning of duties of justice can be
explored in a variety of ways. Since there is quite a lot of agreement on

procedural principles, this is probably done in most planning programs already, but it could be dealt with more explicitly. The importance of truthfulness and accuracy in data collection and analysis, for example, is probably implicit in most methods courses, but some discussion of the kind of ethical pressures and temptations that planners can face could make students think about how they might deal with them and what behavior would be justifiable (Wachs 1982). Similarly, fairness is a value that might be discussed explicitly in courses on zoning and other regulatory techniques to which it has particular relevance.

A variety of kinds of courses might help to clarify role choices. In addition to the obvious introductory and theory courses, other courses dealing with the politics of planning, with strategic thinking, with mediation and negotiation skills, and even with methods of analysis would deal with roles in one way or another. Planning school can be critical in helping students to make deliberate choices about the kind of roles they will play and about their relationships to appointed and elected officials and to others in the planning process. This provides an opportunity for dealing with the very real and difficult issue of the difference between democratic accountability and personal loyalty.

The choice of a role need not involve a lifelong commitment, though for many of the planners in the sample it did seem to be a fairly stable choice that implied certain moral commitments as well. Some people may be comfortable taking a purely contingent approach in which they may shift roles from one issue to another, providing technical information on one or serving as a mediator on another or a lobbyist on a third. Others may change roles as their careers change—as they move up in the bureaucracy or move from one kind of work to another. A young planner at the bottom of a bureaucracy may largely be expected to play a technical role but may adopt a more active one as he or she moves up or into project planning, for instance. Still others may find that a particular role fits their own personal approach to planning and that they should seek out jobs where they can then play that role. The purpose about being explicit about role choices is to try to help young planners to have a realistic idea about the kind of role they could actually play. This could help them to retain the sense of idealism that is so important to ethical action.

Acceptance of the principles of accountability and of the public interest would reduce, at least in the realm of public sector planning, some of the variation in roles and approaches to ethics found among the planners in this sample. The narrow deontological approach in which loyalty was the primary underlying principle or an extreme act utilitarian approach focusing only on the public interest would be seen as too restricted. These values, while obviously very important, would have to be balanced by other, complementary ones.

Within these limits, choices in style and in values would still cover a substantial range. We are long past the time when the traditional model of the technician can be or probably is presented as the only legitimate one. There is also no sense in discarding that model just because postpositivist philosophy argues that it is impossible to be value free. It is a role that is well suited to some people, to some kinds of planning, such as regulation, to some kinds of states and political systems (Rabinovitz 1969), and, often, to lower levels of the bureaucracy.

While deNeufville (1986) argued that the nature of more politicized roles has not been developed systematically enough to make them viable alternatives, this really seems no longer to be true. This research is just the latest in a series of empirical studies that give form to more politicized roles (Baum 1983; Benveniste 1989; Forester 1987; Howe and Kaufman 1979; Needleman and Needleman 1974; Rabinovitz 1969). These roles are now supported by more normative guides as well (Kaufman 1978, 1986; Rabinovitz 1989; Susskind and Ozawa 1984). This study supports the idea, originally developed by Rabinovitz, that a process or broker role is quite distinct from an active or mobilizer one. The logic that underlies the former is concerned with the legitimacy of the planning process while the latter, in a broadening of Davidoff's (1965) original formulation, is primarily concerned with the achievement of substantive goals. Just as with the technician role, Rabinovitz's research indicates that each of these roles may be particularly appropriate to certain kinds of political systems. They also fit particular kinds of people and may well be better suited either to jobs higher in the bureaucracy or in which the planner has considerable freedom of action.

The central educational issue here is simply that students should see the choice of a role in the same way that they see the choice of a substantive area, such as environmental planning or economic development. Clearly, such a choice is partly shaped by experience once planners leave school; it is a case of learning by doing. But schools can give students some preparation by giving them an opportunity to understand the nature of the political and organizational systems in which planners work and the political nature of planning issues. Students can also think about their attitudes toward risk and conflict and be trained in process skills, such as negotiation and mediation, as well as analytical ones.

Clarification of role choices fits easily with efforts to help students think about ways of approaching ethical issues. A variety of pedagogical approaches could be used. One is to encourage familiarity with the norms that the profession formally accepts in its codes of ethics. Another is to help people to clarify the approach to ethics that they bring with them from family, religion, schooling, and whatever other kinds of experience they have had. The third is to provide people with methods for thinking through ethical issues when they do arise.

Even if the AICP code were more widely known and used, the major influences shaping ethical decisions and action would still be the values of individual planners themselves, many of whom seem to bring to the profession well-developed ethical values and approaches to thinking about ethical issues. These were often values and approaches of which they were only partially aware. Sharpening of their awareness of these existing patterns, and additional training in using them, might improve the quality of ethical decisions and action. Understanding whether they take a deontological or a consequentialist approach to ethical issues has broad implications for the kind of role planners are likely to play. Game playing (*Where Do You Draw the Line? An Ethics Game*, 1977) and discussion of hypothetical scenarios can help students to analyze what kind of approach to ethics they tend to use. If the findings of this study are any indication, mixed approaches may be common, but each person may still take a predominantly deontological or teleological approach. Awareness of one's ethical approach can sensitize students to the possible problems they may encounter.

While clarifying the approach that they bring to professional ethics is one important element in ethical training, it is not the only one. Learning to think through ethical issues systematically is what moral justification is all about. The process of thinking through ethical issues requires some kind of criteria for making choices in specific situations. The overarching deontological question of "is it right" and the consequentialist question of "is it good" provide a starting place but only a beginning. In evaluating the procedural issues faced by the planners in the sample, I have used the criterion that laws and duties of justice have more weight than other principles. This was justified using the idea of universalization embodied in Kant's (1964) categorical imperative. For teleological choices, the utilitarian test has been "the greatest good for the greatest number," which finds its modern, policy-oriented form in cost-benefit analysis.

The use of criteria such as these can be learned by ordinary planners. There is nothing exceedingly arcane about them. Bok (1978) has proposed two additional, particularly concrete tests for ethical judgments, tests that would be compatible with the others just given. One is that if some necessary action would appear to involve an ethical problem, it is necessary to explore whether there are alternatives that would not. This was not something that many planners in this sample talked explicitly about doing.

Thinking about alternatives may be especially important to consequentialist planners because their commitment to ends may give them tunnel vision, and their weaker concern with the rightness of means leaves them more open to the idea that doing good may inevitably cause harm to some—"you can't make omelets without breaking eggs." Just as cost-benefit analysis, the descendant of utilitarianism, suggests that a planner should look at the efficiency of a variety of alternatives, so it is necessary to think about their ethical implications as well. What may appear to be the most efficient solution to a problem may impose costs on some group that might be avoided by a different strategy. The point here is simply that looking at alternatives and considering their consequences are as important for ethics as they are for efficiency.

Consequentialist planners must also recognize the temptation of covert action and of dirty hands and guard against casual acceptance of them. Bok's (1978) other criterion for justification is the test of publicity, already discussed in chapter 9. This really is the teeth in the idea of considering alternatives, especially for consequentialists. It would consider violation of an ethical principle such as truthfulness or fairness to be justified only if the argument for it would be strong enough to convince even those who would be harmed.

The more open the discussion of ethical choices, the more this test is satisfied. Covert decisions and actions would be the most suspect. By involving others in their decisions, the planners in the sample did meet this requirement to some degree, though the search for support and reinforcement probably reduced their willingness to seek out a full range of opinions.

This test of publicity is a concrete, procedural version of the Golden Rule, which emphasizes reciprocity between people and "putting yourself in the other person's shoes." Kant's (1964) categorical imperative that "I ought never to act except in such a way *that I can also will that my maxim should become a universal law*" is a stronger version of the same idea. It focuses attention not simply on behavior that has bad consequences but on behavior that is logically self-contradictory. If lying were accepted as a universal law, the very idea of truth would cease to have any meaning, and lies would lose their meaning as well. Thus, the categorical imperative demonstrates how much ethical action is a collective good, a matter of mutual trust, dependent on acceptance by all without free riders. Its alternative form, that people should be treated as ends, not as means, emphasizes the underlying premise of the worth and autonomy of each individual that should not be violated by a free rider on their trust.

These tests—of seeking alternatives, of publicity, and of universalization—are practical, fairly easily learned, and not easily forgotten. They take people beyond intuition or conscience to some kind of structured analysis. They are strict because they are intended to force people not simply to accept what inclination tells them to do but to show what it is that duty commands. Acting on that duty may not be a simple matter; it may not always be possible, but a clear view of duty is more likely than a fuzzy or self-serving one to lead to ethical action.

Finally, planners can be encouraged in school to have a clear idea of the public interest, thought of as both a process of decision making and in substantive terms. Many students come to planning school in part because they have ideas of the public interest they want to serve. Historically, planning has been a field in which value commitments have played an important role. In the Progressive period, planning espoused the very different values of the City Beautiful and the housing reform movements. Since then, these aesthetic and equity goals have been joined by others concerned with good land use, environmental protection, and sound economic development. The AICP code emphasizes equity, an environmental ethic, and a concern with good urban design as the central substantive elements of the public interest. Whether we do it implicitly and quietly or explicitly and actively, the institutional role of planning is to represent these collective values in the policy process.

The idea of the public interest would probably have to pervade all aspects of a planning program, but rather than simply being an implicit "background" assumption, it should be examined explicitly in a variety of ways. In addition to treatment in specialized substantive courses, it might make sense to encourage planners to have at least some familiarity with each of these areas as part of their knowledge of the core of planning. It would be especially important to provide some systematic treatment of the politics of each of these issues and how they have historically been dealt with by planners. Land-use planning may be one of the best-developed areas of planning, for example, but it is also important to understand how its underlying causal models and developing techniques have supported patterns of racial and class segregation in cities or of enviromentally wasteful land-use patterns. Examination of these kinds of issues can provide a framework for exploring, in addition, the kinds of roles that planners can play to represent these interests more effectively.

Inevitably, such discussion would raise the issue of the interplay between planners' own ideas of the public interest and those of other participants in a process of asserting claims. A more consistent commitment to substantive ideas of the public interest might, on the whole, serve to make planners more active in style. However, it would be important to recognize that this is not workable for all people or for planners in all positions or communities. The process used to determine the public interest and the role of the planner in it could vary considerably.

Overall, education and professional support may well have less influence on ethical values than other factors, such as childhood upbringing or the constraints inherent in a local culture of planning, but these are the levers that are available to an organized profession for trying to deliberately support and shape ethical action.

Appendixes

Appendix A

Methodology

Ideally, qualitative research is used initially to explore an area such as ethics that is not well researched or understood. Then quantitative research can be used to test hypotheses that have been generated by previous work. In this study, this ideal sequence was reversed. This book is a qualitative study based on personal interviews with ninety-six planners. It grew out of an earlier national survey on the ethics of 614 public planners (Howe 1980a; Howe and Kaufman 1979, 1981). While the first study provided a variety of interesting insights into the ethics and roles of planners, it seemed to raise more questions than it answered. A survey made up of closed-ended questions forces responses into the categories defined in advance by the researchers. It does not allow for the emergence of significantly different patterns.

Once my colleague, Jerry Kaufman, and I had become convinced by the survey that the issue of ethics was an interesting one, it seemed necessary, in effect, to go back to the beginning and go out to talk to planners in an open-ended way about how they thought about and dealt with ethical issues in their work. As a result, this study is based on in-person interviews with ninety-six planners in five states—Maryland, New York, northern California, Tennessee, and Texas. The planners were all members of the national professional organization, the American Institute of Certified Planners (AICP) and all worked in public planning agencies.

The inductive, qualitative research design used here draws substantially on Glaser and Strauss's (1967) ideas of grounded theory, though, in the end, the approach differed in significant ways as well. They argue that theoretical insights arise inductively out of the interaction between emergent hypotheses and field data. Strauss (1987, p. 5) characterizes it as a "style of doing qualitative analysis" in which the coding or interpretation of an initial set of data generates an emerging theory, which then guides additional data collection designed to allow for making systematic comparisons. While the sample used here was not drawn according to Strauss's idea of "theoretical sampling," the methods for coding and analyzing the interviews were similar to those used in grounded theory.

The Sample

As a statistical sample of public planners, this sample represents a series of compromises. On the one hand, we wanted to have a sample that was large and random enough for some simple statistical analysis. We also wanted it to be national in scope. On the other hand, it had to be small enough for three people with a very limited budget to get to all of the respondents in a single summer. We decided that one hundred was the largest number of planners we could get to in the allotted time. To make the travel more efficient, we decided to go to only five states. Thus, the sample was a cluster sample drawn in a two-stage process.

The sampling strategy involved using the American Institute of Certified Planners (AICP) list of planners by state. We deleted all planners who could be identified as not working in public agencies. This produced 2,849 planners. To choose five states, this number was divided by five and every 569th planner in the roster was chosen, beginning with the 156th, who was chosen randomly as the starting place. California, because of its large size and number of planners, was divided in half while some contiguous smaller states were grouped together to create units with at least forty public agency planners in each one. The units selected were northern California, Texas, Tennessee, Maryland/Delaware, and New York.

Then within each of these units, thirty-eight planners were selected using a similar systematic sampling strategy, though, in order to produce equal numbers for each unit, the sampling fraction varied for each one. The aim was to have a final sample of twenty planners in each state. The larger number was arrived at by using the nonresponse rate from the 1978 questionnaire. Then we sent letters to the selected planners to ask for their participation, to determine whether they were in fact eligible, and to ask them if they were interested in participating. If they were, they were asked to fill out and send back the consent form. Once those were returned, we called to set up appointments until twenty interviews had been scheduled in each state. We did make a real effort to get to single planners in outlying places, even using a private airplane in large states. Only two people were eliminated from the sample because they were simply too far away to get to. The overall response was much higher than we expected so that ultimately 20 percent of the sample was willing to participate but was simply not needed.

While the actual number of interviews completed was ninety-nine (one person was ill on the day of the interview), the number in the analysis is only ninety-six. One interview from each state except California was lost. All the interviews were expected to be tape-recorded, but sometimes they were not. Where a respondent declined to be taped (one case) or the recorder was not turned on (three cases), detailed notes were taken at the time, which allowed these four interviews to be included. However, one tape from Tennessee was physically lost at a later time and one from Maryland was entirely spoiled by air-conditioning noise. Unrelated to the tapes, one person in New York was eliminated as not being a planner in a public agency. The planner who was not interviewed because he was ill was from Texas.

Despite the initial intent, the sample is not a random one for a variety of reasons. (Even if the sample had been truly random, the sampling error in a sample of only one hundred cases would be as high as 14 percent, hardly resulting in precise estimates.) One reason why the sample is not random is that the planners from each state are not represented in proportion to their numbers in the national membership of AICP. When we originally designed the study, we thought that planners from the five states might be rather different, so we wanted to be sure that there was a good representation from smaller as well as larger states. At that time, we intended to weight the sample to correct for the disproportionate weight given to the smaller states, but once I had begun the analysis and was thinking about ninety-six real individuals, some of whom would, in effect, be "cloned" in the weighting scheme, this just seemed to be a confusing additional bit of manipulation. Moreover, it was already clear that the sample was far from random for other reasons.

One reason for this is that the states did turn out to be quite different, one from another. Each had its own distinctive "culture of planning." I would hesitate to generalize nationally from these five states on the assumption that other states are probably equally unique.

In addition, from the start, we knew that the membership of AICP did not include all professional planners. We found once we began interviewing that it is strongly biased toward senior-level planners. Often the director of an agency "subscribes" for the whole agency. In addition, junior-level planners may find membership too expensive. In any case, 44 percent of the sample was agency directors and only 4 percent occupied the lower levels of agency hierarchies. Thus, ethical issues that might be characteristic of junior-level planners are very poorly represented here.

Taking all of these factors together, it is important to say clearly that generalizations from this sample to all public planners nationwide are not justified.

The Interviews

The interviews were completed in the summer of 1982. They were done in person, usually at the planner's office, by one of three interviewers. All but four were taped. For the four that were not, detailed notes were taken after the interview. The interviews generally lasted from an hour to an hour and a half.

The respondent was guaranteed anonymity, and some planners talked about controversial or questionable actions only because of that guarantee. Thus, when cases are reported in the text, names of people and places and sometimes even the subject matter have been changed. The characters, such as Edward Smith, Jr., and Grace Sumner, who are described in the text, are composites of several members of the sample.

The interviews were guided by a general set of questions or "protocol" (see Appendix B). In any interview, most of the questions in the protocol would be asked in more or less the order shown. However, considerable discussion occurred around each question so that the protocol represents only the skeleton of the interview.

As the protocol shows, the focus of the interview was primarily on what might be thought of as the "dependent variables" listed in Table A.1—the way the planner defined ethics, the ethical dilemmas he or she had faced on the job, and how they had been dealt with. The various "independent variables," such as the role they played, their ideas about the public interest, or the organizational factors influencing their behavior, were explicitly explored only at the beginning and the end of the interview or if they came up explicitly during the interview. However, the interviewers had all been involved in the project since the earlier survey stage and were familiar with the issues and questions that had come out of the earlier work. The detailed discussion of each of the cases raised by the respondent was expected to bring out the factors that had influenced him or her. By and large, this did work.

After each interview was completed, the planner was also given a revised version of the original survey questionnaire (see Appendix B), which they were asked to fill out and mail back. The return rate for these questionnaires was 93 percent. The questionnaire was intended to allow both for examination of the adequacy of the original survey as a way of exploring the ethics of planners and, perhaps, for comparison between

TABLE A.1

Variables in the Study

Independent Variables	*Dependent Variables*
Personal Background	Approach to Ethics
Age	Scope/Breadth
Education	Deontological/Consequentialist
Sex	Strictness of Judgments
Family	Substance of Ethics
Religion	Issues Raised
Political Values	Principles Used
Substantive Values	Actions
Characteristics of Work Environment	Nature of Issues
State	Choice
Community	Difficulty
Growth	Choice of Strategy
Size	Action Taken
Central City/Suburb	Outcome
Degree of Corruption	Justification
Agency	
Size	
Level in Agency	
Attitude about Agency	
Professional Influences	
Nature of Work	
Ideal Role	
Actual Role	
Concern with Effectiveness	
Proactivity	
Interest in Implementation	
Attitudes Toward Citizen Participation	
Attitude about Value Neutrality	
Ideas about Public Interest	
Own Idea	
Role of Public	
Role of Decision Makers	

the interview sample and the original survey group. As the analysis of the personal interviews developed, comparison with the original sample became a marginal concern.

The Analysis

Once the interviews were completed, the tapes were transcribed and coded. An average transcript was about twenty single-spaced pages, so coding was necessary simply to concentrate the raw data and to arrange it in such a way that comparisons between planners could easily be made. To accomplish these purposes, the coding was done on note cards with relevant quotations attached. These could then be filed and used by subject. However, the coding also meant much more. The categories developed for it represented the independent and dependent variables that formed the framework for the analysis (see Table A.1). It was important to the analysis to be open to the "emergent properties" of the data, that is, to what the planners were saying about their own experiences. That meant not becoming too strongly committed too early to particular interpretations. Even after the analysis was quite advanced, interpretations remained open to change. The initial set of about thirty coding categories was developed from the first twenty to twenty-five transcripts, but new ones were added later in the process of doing the transcripts or during the analysis.

Some variables were coded quantitatively, though this coding was all nominal or ordinal in nature. These quantitative data were added to the computer file of the data from the respondents' mail questionnaires. The quantitative data were generally used to check more qualitative ideas that might be unduly influenced by particularly interesting or vivid cases that might prove not to be typical of the larger group.

The process of analysis in this kind of qualitative, exploratory study might be likened to assembling a jigsaw puzzle whose picture you could initially only guess at. You might guess, for example, that it was a map and that the two primary features were land and water. Using the colors and markings on the pieces as guides, you could gradually assemble many pieces into the two separate parts of the picture. Then it would be possible to work out the relationship between the two sections until the picture was complete.

This analysis proceeded in a similar way by focusing on two central concepts—role and approach to ethics. Each central concept was represented by a typology for classifying the members of the sample. The typologies were constructed by examining a number of related variables.

Once the two typologies had been developed, the relationship between them was explored. In addition, both could also be used as independent variables to explore how the planners defined and acted upon ethical issues and as dependent variables in an examination of how the planners came to play certain roles or to hold particular ethical values.

I have tried in the analysis to account for the real diversity of the planners. This results in typologies with lots of categories and sometimes produces discussions of the attitudes or actions of small groups of people. Take the variable role, for example. In the earlier survey research, we came up with a logically neat set of three roles: technician, politician, and hybrid (Howe 1980a; Howe and Kaufman 1979). Here, however, the ninety-six planners are divided into six different roles, some including as few as ten people. People are diverse, though, and rather than dealing with numbers in the hundreds in tables generated by a computer, I have worked with the clear images of ninety-six sometimes dull, sometimes thoughtful, sometimes funny planners. In the search for patterns and generalities, I have tried not to lose track of these individuals. Keeping their images clear also reminded me not to generalize too much from them.

Validity, Reliability, and Replicability

Issues of validity, reliability, and replicability are especially difficult to deal with in qualitative research. Data from open-ended interviews are quite variable. Coding involves considerable judgment, and the process of getting from the raw data to some interpretation of it is not as clear or easily replicated as it is in a quantitative study.

Miles and Huberman (1984) identify as a characteristic problem of qualitative research the validity of the measures used. They recommend that whenever possible several independent sources of information about a single variable be used as a check of validity. This is referred to as "triangulation." In this study, independent measures, such as an interview and a separate documentary source, do not exist, but in the case of some variables, there were both qualitative measures from the interview and quantitative measures from the questionnaire. Each source could, in effect, be used to make some judgments about the validity of data from the other.

The face validity of the codes and quantitative measures from the interviews probably are better than those from the survey instrument simply because the coding schemes were developed from listening to the interviews themselves and not thought up before the data were collected.

We always intended to use the interviews to examine the validity of the measures developed for the survey, but in the end, the survey measures also helped to clarify the validity of some of the interview coding as well.

I would argue overall that the variables developed were fairly valid—that is, they did measure what they were supposed to measure. For example, analysis of planners' responses on the substantive scales on the questionnaire indicated that these scales mirrored their values as expressed in the interview but were not good predictors of their actions.

The reliability of the various individual measures was probably quite variable. The measure of the planners' concern for implementation, for example, was fairly simple: either they did not mention it at all; they mentioned it once and did not return to it later in the interview; they discussed it at some length; or it was central to the interview. Such a measure might produce fairly similar results for independent observers. The other two measures of role—actual role and whether they were proactive—were much more judgmental, though criteria were developed for each so that I could remain consistent over the six summers it took me to transcribe and code all the interviews.

If different researchers might code members of the sample differently on a central variable, such as their actual role, how replicable could a study like this be? More broadly, would a different researcher see the same variables and patterns in this set of interviews?

The first issue is one of accuracy and might be solved with clear criteria for coding. The second is more a matter of the values that the researcher brings to the analysis. I have a strong interest in planners' roles and am essentially a deontologist on ethics. These values have shaped the analysis here. My colleague, Jerry Kaufman, has less interest in role and is a consequentialist, though probably a mixed one. His detailed analysis of the interviews might well have been substantially different from mine, though in an early and independent beginning at an analysis he started with a typology not unlike some combination of the two ultimately developed here (Kaufman 1987). This kind of differing interpretation of data is a natural and interesting aspect of qualitative analysis and does not necessarily pose a problem as long as an effort is made to deal with other possible problems, such as validity and consistency.

Appendix B

Questionnaires

B.1. Interview Protocol—Planners' Ethics

1. I'd like to start by getting some background on what you do in your job.
   a. If you had to describe your job to another planner, what would you say about it?
      What kind of projects do you work on?
      Who do you commonly work with?
   b. What do you like most and least about your work, briefly?

2. Now I'd like to ask you about any situations you've been involved in as a public agency planner that posed ethical problems for you.
   a. Could you briefly describe them (limit to 3)?
   b. Why do you think each posed an ethical problem for you? (If respondent mentions no more than 1 situation, go to 4a.)

3. Are there other things beyond these experiences you've mentioned that you think pose ethical problems for public planners?
   a. (for each) Is it always a problem or just sometimes? Why?

4. Now going back to the situation about _____:
   a. What did you do? (Ask only if not already answered.)
   b. Why did you do what you did? (Probe for reasons.)
   c. Did you think what you did was ethical or unethical and why?
   d. How did you reach the conclusion what you did was ethical or unethical?
      (Ask only for first situation.) Do you think the way you reached this conclusion is the way you generally make ethical judgments in your work?

   e. (If a switcher) Why did you do something you thought was unethical? Did you feel guilty?

   f. (If not a switcher) Have you ever done anything in your work that you thought was unethical? If so, did you feel guilty?

     (If respondent says no to f, then ask) It sounds like you end up in situations where you don't do unethical things. Do you have a strategy for avoiding such things?

4a. (If respondent mentions no more than one personal experience in 2, then ask): Are there any situations you know of in your work where another planner faced something you would have defined as an ethical problem? Why?

What did he/she do?

Did you think it was ethical or unethical? Why?

Would you have done the same thing? Why or why not?

5. Now that you've talked about a few examples, what would you say are the major ethical values that guide you in your work as a planner?

   a. (If respondent already discussed a conflict between ethical values, then restate it and ask) Is the way you handled this conflict, the way you think you'd generally resolve such conflicts?

   b. (If respondent hasn't mentioned any conflicts in specific cases, then ask) What would you do if a couple of your ethical values conflicted?

     (If no answer) Have you ever been in a situation where they did?

6. What would you say has had the most effect on shaping your views about what is ethical or unethical for public planners to do? (e.g. family, religion, books, experience, professional codes of ethics?)

7. How would you say your professional experience or the people you work with in your job have affected your views about what is ethical?

8. One final question—since we've talked for quite a while, are there any other thoughts you have now about: ethical problems for planners *or* how you might deal with conflicts among your principal ethical values?

B.2. Study of Planners' Ethics

This questionnaire consists of four parts, and should take you about 50 minutes to fill out. As you can see we have put your name on it so we can analyze it together with your personal interview. However, your answers will be treated as entirely confidential in any report of the findings. We hope you will be as frank as possible; and any additional comments you may want to add to your answers would be useful to us as well.

I. Boundaries of Ethics

To begin with, we are interested in what you consider to be issues that fall within and outside the realm of planning ethics. Below are a number of statements, each involving an action by a planner. For each statement please circle the appropriate letter (a, b, c or d) which indicates whether you think the behavior

a—clearly involves an ethical issue for planners
b—probably involves an ethical issue for planners
c—probably does not involve an ethical issue for planners
d—clearly does not involve an ethical issue for planners

In addition, would you please place a check mark in the last column for each statement if you think your choice would depend on the situation.

Note: We are not concerned here with whether you agree or not with the actions listed below. We only want to know whether you consider the behavior to fall within or outside the realm of planning ethics.

	Clearly an ethical issue	*Probably an ethical issue*	*Probably not an ethical issue*	*Clearly not an ethical issue*	*Depends on situation*
1. A planner does not provide accurate information on planning issues to citizens or government decision-makers.	a	b	c	d	
2. A planner does not contribute some of his or her time and information to the professional development of students, interns, and beginning professionals.	a	b	c	d	

	Clearly an ethical issue	Probably an ethical issue	Probably not an ethical issue	Clearly not an ethical issue	Depends on situation
3. A planner doesn't improve his or her own professional education while working as a professional planner.	a	b	c	d	
4. A planner lobbies actively outside his/her agency to get a policy adopted.	a	b	c	d	
5. A planner through his/her actions knowingly harms the natural environment.	a	b	c	d	
6. A planner applies a standard solution to a planning problem without first establishing its appropriateness to the situation.	a	b	c	d	
7. A planner reveals information gained in a professional relationship which the employer has requested be held inviolate.	a	b	c	d	
8. A planner inaccurately represents the views or findings of colleagues.	a	b	c	d	
9. A planner tries to sell his or her services by stating or implying an ability to influence decisions by improper means.	a	b	c	d	
10. A planner's actions unintentionally lead to reducing choice and opportunity for disadvantaged groups and persons.	a	b	c	d	

	Clearly an ethical issue	Probably an ethical issue	Probably not an ethical issue	Clearly not an ethical issue	Depends on situation
11. A planner fails to exercise independent judgment on behalf of the clients he or she serves.	a	b	c	d	
12. A planner never volunteers his or her services to groups which lack adequate resources.	a	b	c	d	
13. A planner does not serve the public interest.	a	b	c	d	
14. A planner does not share the results of his/her experience and research, which would contribute to the body of planning knowledge, with other members of the profession.	a	b	c	d	
15. A planner provides accurate but not complete information to citizens or decision-makers.	a	b	c	d	
16. A planner uses coercive pressure on a decision-maker to get a planning proposal adopted.	a	b	c	d	
17. A planner fails to give citizens an opportunity to have a meaningful impact on the development of plans and programs.	a	b	c	d	
18. A planner does not work to increase the opportunities for women and minorities to become professional planners.	a	b	c	d	

	Clearly an ethical issue	Probably an ethical issue	Probably not an ethical issue	Clearly not an ethical issue	Depends on situation
19. A planner inaccurately represents his/her professional qualifications, education, or affiliations.	a	b	c	d	
20. A planner is not fair and considerate in reviewing the work of other professionals.	a	b	c	d	
21. A planner's actions unintentionally lead to harming the natural environment.	a	b	c	d	
22. A planner reveals information which the employer requests be kept confidential, because the planner feels the revelation of this information is required to prevent substantial injury to the public.	a	b	c	d	
23. A planner performs work beyond his/her professional competence.	a	b	c	d	
24. A planner uses the power of his/her office to obtain a special personal advantage which is not in the public interest.	a	b	c	d	
25. A planner through his/her actions knowingly reduces choice and opportunity for disadvantaged groups and persons.	a	b	c	d	
26. A planner does not pay special attention to the interrelatedness of decisions in his/her work.	a	b	c	d	

	Clearly an ethical issue	Probably an ethical issue	Probably not an ethical issue	Clearly not an ethical issue	Depends on situation
27. A planner is not concerned about the long-range consequences of present actions in his/her work.	a	b	c	d	
28. A planner "waffles" (changes position) on a technical judgment because of political pressure.	a	b	c	d	

II. Ethics Scenarios

On the following pages there are a number of short scenarios involving ethical issues for planners. Each scenario is followed by two questions about whether you think the behavior described is ethical, and whether you would do the same yourself. Please answer both questions by circling the number on the scale from 1 to 5 that corresponds to the answer you would choose.

We realize that reality is more complex than these short scenarios can portray. Please answer as honestly as you can, given the information presented.

1. A representative of an environmental group comes into a city planning office and asks a staff planner for a copy of the recommendations of a plan for the reduction of pollution in the city's streams which is in the process of being prepared. The planner gives the representative the draft recommendations. The agency has no specific policy about releasing such information before a plan is completed.

   a. Is the planner's action:

1	2	3	4	5
clearly ethical	probably ethical	not sure	probably unethical	clearly unethical

   b. If you were faced with such a situation, would you:

1	2	3	4	5
do it	probably do it	not sure	probably not do it	not do it

2. A regional transportation plan is being prepared. The city planning agency is strongly in favor of a 25¢ fare to make the system as accessible as possible to poorer people. The regional planners are opposed to this because they think a higher fare is necessary to break even. Technical meetings between city planning and regional planning representatives are being held in order to determine the economic feasibility of the two options. The chief planner for the city planning agency believes the regional planners' estimates are always conservative about the number of riders, so that they can argue that the system would not pay for itself at the lower fare. In order to justify the lower fare, she always purposely develops estimates that indicate that the system would attract more riders, thus yielding higher revenues.

   a. Is the action of the planner from the city planning agency:

1	2	3	4	5
clearly ethical	probably ethical	not sure	probably unethical	clearly unethical

   b. If you were faced with such a situation, would you:

1	2	3	4	5
do it	probably do it	not sure	probably not do it	not do it

3. A public planning agency has recently completed the first draft of a plan to establish several "park and ride" facilities in outlying areas of the city. The head of the agency has been meeting with a variety of neighborhood groups to gain their support for this plan. Less than half of the groups consulted have agreed to support it. She then meets with representatives of a city-wide civic group whose approval is particularly critical but who are especially sensitive to the opinion of neighborhood groups. The planner urges the civic group to publicly endorse the plan, indicating without being specific, that many of the neighborhood groups consulted so far have supported the plan.

   a. Is the planner's action:

1	2	3	4	5
clearly ethical	probably ethical	not sure	probably unethical	clearly unethical

   b. If you were faced with such a situation, would you:

1	2	3	4	5
do it	probably do it	not sure	probably not do it	not do it

4. A planner who works for a city planning agency is assigned by her agency to work with the residents of an inner city, low-income neighborhood. She finds out that another unit in the agency is doing a study for the same neighborhood which will recommend clearing 20 acres of land to be used to provide housing for students at a nearby college. Without being authorized to do so, the planner decides to give the information and draft findings of this study to the head of the community group in the area.

   a. Is the planner's action:

1	2	3	4	5
clearly ethical	probably ethical	not sure	probably unethical	clearly unethical

   b. If you were faced with such a situation, would you:

1	2	3	4	5
do it	probably do it	not sure	probably not do it	not do it

5. A comprehensive plan has just been completed for the X metropolitan area, calling for each community to prepare its own growth management plan. It must now be adopted by the planning commission, made up in part of local elected officials. The regional planning director has made it clear in meetings with local elected officials and planners that if they do not support the plan he will selectively use the agency's A-95 review authority to recommend denial of projects—not limited just to the growth issue—that such localities seek from the federal government.

   a. Is the regional planning director's action:

1	2	3	4	5
clearly ethical	probably ethical	not sure	probably unethical	clearly unethical

   b. If you were faced with such a situation, would you:

1	2	3	4	5
do it	probably do it	not sure	probably not do it	not do it

6. A regional planner is preparing a fair share housing plan for the communities in a several county region. Knowing that the idea of every community taking its fair share of low and moderate income housing will be tough to get accepted by the COG-type regional commission, he puts into the plan several strong recommendations which will generate very strong opposition, but which he feels are expendables that might be traded off for support from some of the commissioners for the central aspects of the fair share plan.

a. Is the regional planner's action:

1	2	3	4	5
clearly ethical	probably ethical	not sure	probably unethical	clearly unethical

b. If you were faced with such a situation, would you:

1	2	3	4	5
do it	probably do it	not sure	probably not do it	not do it

7. A planner who works for a high-income suburban community recognizes that the community's land development regulations are exclusionary, with large lot zoning, expensive subdivision improvement requirements and few bedrooms allowed in the only zoned multiple family district. This makes it quite difficult for poor people and all but a few minority group members to live there, even though job opportunities for poor people exist in the area. She decides, as part of her regular job activities, to organize support from local people she knows are in favor of opening up the community so that they will put pressure on the suburban government's officials to change the community's zoning policy.

a. Is the planner's action:

1	2	3	4	5
clearly ethical	probably ethical	not sure	probably unethical	clearly unethical

b. If you were faced with such a situation, would you:

1	2	3	4	5
do it	probably do it	not sure	probably not do it	not do it

8. A staff planner for a regional planning agency is fairly certain that the agency's director purposely left out certain findings from a draft of a wetlands preservation study that were objectively documented and presented by the staff planner, because the agency director felt it presented a point of view that the regional planning commission does not support. The staff planner feels these findings should not be kept from the public and, without authorization, gives them to an environmental group which is strongly in favor of a wetlands preservation program.

a. Is the regional planning agency staff planner's action:

1	2	3	4	5
clearly ethical	probably ethical	not sure	probably unethical	clearly unethical

b. If you were faced with such a situation, would you:

1	2	3	4	5
do it	probably do it	not sure	probably not do it	not do it

9. A planner is preparing a study on the need for increased mass transit in the community. The planner's own policy preference is for increased mass transit. A citizens group did a reasonably thorough study several years ago where it found that a majority of the community's residents opposed an expanded mass transit system. The planner decides not to use this particular information in writing up the recommendations of the study.

a. Is the planner's action:

1	2	3	4	5
clearly ethical	probably ethical	not sure	probably unethical	clearly unethical

b. If you were faced with such a situation, would you:

1	2	3	4	5
do it	probably do it	not sure	probably not do it	not do it

10. A representative of a white homeowner's group comes into a city planning office and asks a staff planner for a copy of the recommendations being developed for a scattered city public housing plan which

the agency is preparing. The planner gives the representative the draft recommendations. The agency has no specific policy about releasing such information before a plan is completed.

a. Is the planner's action:

1	2	3	4	5
clearly ethical	probably ethical	not sure	probably unethical	clearly unethical

b. If you were faced with such a situation, would you:

1	2	3	4	5
do it	probably do it	not sure	probably not do it	not do it

11. An oil company decided to build a refinery on several thousand acres of tree-covered waterfront property which it owned. The land was zoned rural, and the oil company requested a change in zoning to a heavy industrial classification. The county planning staff opposed the rezoning and said that the area should be recognized as a valuable natural resource and preserved for recreational and residential uses. The staff was overruled by the county planning commission and subsequently by the county commissioners who approved the rezoning. A group of residents who lived near the refinery site took the case to court. One county planning staff member provided assistance on her own time—information and advice—to the citizens' group in preparing their case.

a. Is the county planner's action:

1	2	3	4	5
clearly ethical	probably ethical	not sure	probably unethical	clearly unethical

b. If you were faced with such a situation, would you:

1	2	3	4	5
do it	probably do it	not sure	probably not do it	not do it

III. Attitudes

On the following pages you will find a series of statements about planning, planners and issues related to planning. They are strongly worded to try to elicit differences of opinion between people. This gives them a black-

and-white quality which may not always feel comfortable to you. But as with the scenarios, we want you to indicate the answer which comes closest to your real opinion. The set of items may also seem contradictory or inconsistent. We are in no way trying to trip you up; there are no right or wrong answers.

Each question has six possible answers:

strongly disagree	disagree	slightly disagree	slightly agree	agree	strongly agree
1	2	3	4	5	6

Beside each question there is a box. Write the number which corresponds to your opinion in that box. Please write legibly to avoid coding errors. The scale appears at the top of each page of the questionnaire so that you can easily keep it in mind. Please answer every question.

1. Preserving clean air and water should be high priority issues even if this means that economic development in the community may be slowed. ☐

2. Planning is primarily a political activity. ☐

3. Developers are only concerned to make money for themselves. ☐

4. Planners have a responsibility to advocate the development of mass transit systems because they are more efficient and less polluting than automobile travel. ☐

5. Planners have a special responsibility to try to ensure that resources are redistributed to the have-nots of the community, particularly the poor and minority groups. ☐

6. Planners should keep their notions about public policy in check, resisting public revelation of strong attitudes which might raise doubts about their objectivity. ☐

7. Citizen groups should not have veto power over plans. ☐

8. Planners should not place a great deal of emphasis on mass transit as a solution to urban problems. ☐

9. Planners should accept and work within the rules of their departments, even if they do not always agree with them. ☐

strongly disagree	disagree	slightly disagree	slightly agree	agree	strongly agree
1	2	3	4	5	6

10. Planners should recognize that developers, in responding to market forces, are only giving people what they want. ☐

11. Where few or no already established groups exist in support of a particular planning effort, the planner should help form such groups and actively make use of them. ☐

12. If the planner's recommended alternative is not chosen by the decision-makers, s/he should not try to change that decision. ☐

13. People have a right to control what kind of people live in their communities with them. ☐

14. Technical expertise is sometimes most useful for providing a screen for building political support for a plan. ☐

15. Planners know better what the needs of the community are than do residents—that is what they are trained to do. ☐

16. A planner may have to work covertly to gain support for planning policies. ☐

17. If people want to drive cars, they should be able to even if it costs the taxpayers money for highways, parking lots and other automobile-oriented facilities. ☐

18. Plans should stand or fall for their acceptance on their technical quality and internal logic. ☐

19. Developers have an unjustified bad image. ☐

20. Planners have become too much concerned about protecting the environment. ☐

21. Residents of existing neighborhoods are justified in organizing to maintain the integrity of their communities in the face of economic or racial change. ☐

22. It is not a good idea for a planner to bring pressure to bear on people if s/he wants them to do something. ☐

23. A planner's effectiveness is based primarily on his/her reputation for objective, accurate and in-depth analysis. ☐

strongly disagree	disagree	slightly disagree	slightly agree	agree	strongly agree
1	2	3	4	5	6

24. The pollution in cities from the use of automobiles should be reduced, even if it requires such measures as parking bans or heavy auto use taxes. ☐

25. Equal opportunity should not mean giving some groups special treatment or preference over others. ☐

26. Planning should be placed in the governmental structure so that it can easily get involved in political disputes that relate to its areas of competence. ☐

27. Overemphasis on accommodating to the automobile seriously impairs the quality of urban life. ☐

28. Developers have a legitimate complaint against many communities for imposing unnecessary and cost-increasing requirements on their developments. ☐

29. While citizens should be kept aware of developments during the planning process, they shouldn't get deeply involved in the technical work. ☐

30. Planners should primarily be trained to develop technically correct solutions to planning problems. ☐

31. There is a strong need for planning to be long-range (10–20 years). ☐

32. Planning has become too concerned with the demands and concerns of low income and minority group members. ☐

33. If planners meet opposition to their plan from non-governmental interest groups, they should try to neutralize or counteract it by mobilizing support in favor of the plan from other interest groups. ☐

34. If a plan is accepted by decision-makers it is a success, even if it is an inadequate piece of analysis technically. ☐

35. Concern for protecting the environment is important, but planners should temper that concern by recognizing that other legitimate objectives which come in conflict with environmental protection may be even more important. ☐

strongly disagree	disagree	slightly disagree	slightly agree	agree	strongly agree
1	2	3	4	5	6

36. In a democratic system opposition to a policy held by one's own agency should be just as normal and appropriate as support for it. ☐

37. The essence of planning is rationality. ☐

38. Mass transit systems should not be developed or expanded if they can't pay for themselves. ☐

39. There should be tighter controls on private development to protect the public interest. ☐

40. No one can better define the needs of a community than its residents. ☐

41. Planners should lobby actively to defeat proposals that they think are harmful, even if it means challenging powerful interests. ☐

42. The planner's job is to understand the point of view of the administration s/he serves, and assist it in achieving its objectives. ☐

43. Planning must go beyond merely allowing citizens to be heard, to having them participate in making judgments on technical aspects of planning. ☐

44. Planners should allow their values to influence the choice of policy in drawing up plans. ☐

45. The price being paid by the taxpayers to clean up the environment is too high. ☐

46. Planners should undertake an impact analysis for any major proposal that comes before them to see what its effects are on low income and minority groups. ☐

47. Planners should try to influence decisions primarily by disseminating and facilitating the use of technical planning information. ☐

48. People should be encouraged to use mass transit instead of automobiles. ☐

strongly disagree	disagree	slightly disagree	slightly agree	agree	strongly agree
1	2	3	4	5	6

49. Planners should be open participants in the planning process, staking their values in competition with others, and openly striving to achieve their ends. □

50. Private developers have little or no concern for the good of the community as a whole. □

51. The quality and depth of analyses done by planners has little to do with their effectiveness. □

52. The right of property owners to benefit from increases in the value of their property can legitimately be limited so that land can be preserved in its natural or agricultural state. □

53. Planners should involve citizens in every phase of the planning process. □

IV. Background Data

Finally, we would like to ask you some background questions to help us interpret our results. Where the possible answer to the question is preceded by brackets [ ], please check one or more boxes, as specified. Where the possible answer is followed by an underlined space, please supply the information requested.

EDUCATION
1. Check each degree that you have received, and indicate what field it was in.

   DEGREE   FIELD

   [ ] BA/BS _____

   [ ] MA/MS _____

   [ ] Ph.D. _____

   [ ] Other (specify degree) _____

2. If you have a planning degree(s), what university did you receive it from, and in what year?

	University	Location	Year
BA/BS	_____	_____	____
MA/MS	_____	_____	____
Ph.D.	_____	_____	____

Took courses, but received no degree at _____

　　　Year(s): _____

EMPLOYMENT

3. How many years have you worked as a planner? _____ years.

4. Of those, how many have been spent as a planner for public agencies? _____ years.

5. What size is the jurisdiction of the agency you serve? (in 1980)?

[ ] over 1 million
[ ] 500,000 to 1 million
[ ] 100,000 to 500,000
[ ] 50,000 to 100,000
[ ] 10,000 to 50,000
[ ] under 10,000

6. In terms of population growth, is the jurisdiction your agency serves:

[ ] declining
[ ] stable
[ ] growing

7. Indicate the substantive area you primarily work in. You may choose up to three areas, and rank them according to the time spent on each, with "1" denoting the most time, and "3", the least.

_____ Economic/fiscal analysis   _____ Land use
_____ Environment   _____ Neighborhood planning
_____ General planning   _____ Social services
_____ Health   _____ Transportation
_____ Housing   _____ Urban design
                                    _____ Other, specify _____

8. Listed below are a number of kinds of groups that you might have contact with in your job. Choose up to 4 which you have worked with most frequently over the past year, and rank them, with "1" indicating the largest amount of contact, and "4", the least. For any group that

you very rarely or never have any contact with, please put a "0" in the space.

Rank

_____ Citizen groups
_____ People in other public agencies
_____ Groups regulated by your agency (e.g. developers, industries, health service providers)
_____ Community influentials
_____ Decision-makers (e.g. elected officials, planning boards, a city manager)
_____ other people in your own agency
_____ other, specify _____

9. Of the following items, choose the five that are of most importance to you in your job, and rank them with "1" indicating the highest priority, and "5" the lowest.

Rank

_____ The quality of your work.
_____ Autonomy in performing your job.
_____ Respect or recognition from the community or groups in it.
_____ The security of the job.
_____ Respect of other professionals you work with.
_____ The inherent interest of the work.
_____ Respect of elected or other high level officials.
_____ Service to the community.
_____ The ability to influence policy decisions.

PERSONAL BACKGROUND

10. Age: _____

11. In the interview we talked about factors which had influenced your views about professional ethics. A number of possible influences are listed below. Would you please rate each one on the scale provided, (circle the appropriate number) and then rank them in the order of their importance for you.

Rank		No influence		Some influence		Strong influence
		1	2	3	4	5
_____ Family		1	2	3	4	5
_____ Religion		1	2	3	4	5

Rank	No influence		Some influence		Strong influence
	1	2	3	4	5
_____ Pre-professional education	1	2	3	4	5
_____ Professional education	1	2	3	4	5
_____ Work experience	1	2	3	4	5
_____ Professional colleagues	1	2	3	4	5
_____ Social movements (e.g. env'tal movement, civil rights movement, etc.)	1	2	3	4	5
_____ Professional codes of ethics	1	2	3	4	5
_____ Other, specify:	1	2	3	4	5

12. What was your father's occupation (e.g. small businessman, lawyer, auto mechanic)?

13. In general, how would you characterize your political views? (Circle the number which is most appropriate.)

radical		liberal		moderate		conservative
1	2	3	4	5	6	7

Notes

Notes

1. A 1989 survey of members of the American Planning Association found that 19 percent of respondents (Hecimovich 1989) were private consultants whose ethical issues might be more like those of other consulting professionals.

2. This code technically covers only members of the American Institute of Certified Planners (AICP), who gain membership by meeting a requirement for professional experience and by taking a written examination of professional proficiency. Not all practicing planners choose to be AICP members. However, this code is designed to cover the behavior of the kind of professional planners who made up the sample in this study. The American Planning Association's "Statement of Ethical Principles for Planning" (1987) is more general, covering lay plan commissioners as well as practicing planners, and so is less appropriate as a standard.

Part 1: Issues

CHAPTER 2: THE NATURE OF ETHICAL ISSUES

1. The planners came up with 480 cases, about five per person. A variety of factors may have affected the kind of issues or cases they raised. There certainly was room for shaping their presentation of self, and there were a few who I thought might have done this. There was a general tendency to focus on recent and/or major ethical dilemmas and not to think about the day-to-day situations where they made the "right" decisions without thinking. Some people had difficulty coming up with any cases, either because their idea of ethics was so undeveloped or because experience had presented them with few real dilemmas. When this was the case, ideas about ethics were explored by focusing on cases they knew or through hypothetical, general issues. There was plenty of room in the interview for the planners to discuss and to differentiate between values that were ethical and those that were important to them but were outside the realm of ethics. Since many had not thought carefully about this distinction, it was explored with many but not all of the respondents.

2. I originally developed thirty categories in the process of coding the interviews. Some with only one or two cases were theoretically interesting, and they are included here, but some were dropped.

3. The questionnaire included a section with twenty-eight short descriptions of actions taken by a planner (see Appendix B). Respondents were asked whether each statement "clearly involves an ethical issue for planners," "probably involves an ethical issue," "probably does not," or "clearly does not" involve an ethical issue. They could also answer that they thought it "depends on the situation." Many but not all of the items were taken from the American Institute of Certified Planners' *Code of Ethics and Professional Conduct* (1981).

4. Burke's (1986) idea of the ethics of public professionals differs somewhat

from the argument being made here that separates duties of justice from account-ability. The difference arises less from intentions, which are similar, than from differences in perspective. Burke's analysis is theoretical, though it draws for illustrations on case studies done by others of particular issues. In the interviews done for this study, however, the separate importance of duties of justice was so clear that to subsume them in various ways under the heading of responsibility, as Burke does, would, for example, mask possible conflicts between responsibility and duties of justice.

CHAPTER 3: PROCEDURAL ISSUES

1. A systematic effort was made to classify the nature of the political environment in each community, at least as its planner saw it. The four categories used were: (1) very corrupt, enough so that it impinged on the planner's practice; (2) somewhat corrupt; (3) basically clean; and (4) very clean and open. It must be remembered that this is based on what the planner said about the community and not on independent research. However, that perception in itself was an interesting variable. In addition, only seventy-nine people (82 percent of the sample) talked enough about this for any estimate to be made.

CHAPTER 4: THE PUBLIC INTEREST

1. The citizen participation scale was made up of six attitude items from the questionnaire. Two dealt with whether citizens or planners know better what the needs of a community are. The rest were concerned with how much role citizens should have in the planning process. Should they be just kept aware, be involved in making technical judgments, be involved in all phases, or have a veto over plans? Respondents were asked whether they agreed or disagreed with these items, using a six-point scale (see Appendix B).

Part 2: Planners

CHAPTER 5: PLANNERS: AN INTRODUCTION

1. Many quotations will be used to characterize the groups in the two typologies. The characters, while they are composites rather than specific individuals in the sample, also are given these kind of "lines" to "speak." In all cases, the quotations are drawn only from the people in the particular group being discussed.

2. These roles were originally used by Bolan (1969). The other roles in both Bolan's and Mayo's (1982) typology are: community knowledgeable, initiator, technical expert, and expert on process.

3. This idea of role grew out of the research in the first phase of this study (Howe 1980a; Howe and Kaufman 1979). Role was measured using two Likert-type scales, measuring attitudes to specific statements with a scale from "strongly agree" to "strongly disagree." One measured the respondents' attitudes about the importance of rationality, objective analysis, and long-range thinking. This was the technical dimension. The other scale measured attitudes about the use of

political tactics to develop support for plans or to oppose potentially harmful proposals. This was thought of as the political dimension. Some planners approved of one activity and disapproved of the other. Those who favored (or scored high on) the political dimension were called "politicians." Those who favored the technical aspects of planning were called "technicians." Planners who thought that technical analysis was important but that planners should be politically active as well were called "hybrids." There was a final possibility, low scores on both scales (called here low/low), but very few planners scored this way.

CHAPTER 6: PLANNERS' ROLES

1. Remember that these characters are composites of the real people who were classified as playing each role (see Figure 5.1). Their cases and the quotations for them are all real, from planners playing that role.

2. Value commitment was measured using a four-item Likert-type attitude scale. Two of the items made the point that planners should be openly committed to values and should allow such values to affect their work. Another item stated that for planners to be objective, they need to keep their ideas about policy in check. The last stated that opposition to agency policy should be acceptable. Respondents were asked whether they agreed or disagreed with these items using a six-point scale.

3. In 1965, when positivism in planning was just beginning to wane in the face of national events but pluralist theories of politics were still in the ascendant, Paul Davidoff wrote a powerful article arguing that planners should play a politically active, value-committed role as advocate planners for low-income groups that had historically been closed out of or actually harmed by planning (Davidoff 1965). This idea of the active advocate for the disadvantaged took root in planning practice. After the urban riots of the 1960s, many older central cities instituted formal neighborhood planning programs (Needleman and Needleman 1974), which did and still do provide opportunities for this kind of equity-oriented planning. Other niches for Davidoff-type planners include housing authorities, neighborhood community development corporations, and nonprofit housing advocacy organizations.

4. His sample (Baum 1983) was different from the sample here in two respects that might account for some of the difference in the number of planners who seemed to suffer from dissonance. One is the larger proportion of junior-level, public planners in his sample—34 percent compared with only 27 percent in this one. The other is the more bureaucratic nature of Maryland planning agencies. Local government there takes place primarily at the county level, and many of the county agencies were very large, with as many as fifty professional staff members.

5. There were two kinds of dissonance—between ideal and actual role and between interest in implementation and action. Evidence of such dissonance in the interviews was generally obvious. Some planners talked about how their actions as planners did not live up to their image of what a planner should do,

either because they were not politicized enough or were too politicized. Others talked about a disparity between what they wanted to accomplish and the results they actually achieved. Some discussed both problems.

CHAPTER 8: INFLUENCES ON ETHICAL VALUES

1. These questions in the interview and on the questionnaire were not an effort to plumb the psychological depths or early influences in these planners' lives, and, in fact, they did not. Most people gave rather brief matter-of-fact answers.

2. Aldo Leopold's *A Sand County Almanac, and Sketches Here and There* (1968 [1949]) has the distinction of being one of the clearest, most direct, and personal expositions of the need for an environmental ethic. The natural environment should be seen as a community of which man was not the master but simply another member. Like Leopold, liberal Supreme Court Justice William O. Douglas had begun life loving nature but viewing it through a utilitarian perspective. In 1951, he was converted to a perspective similar to Leopold's idea of the land ethic in which man is seen as simply a part of nature. He wrote actively about nature (Douglas 1952, 1960, 1965, 1972) and campaigned for the preservation of wild areas (Fox 1981). Ian McHarg also shares the image of man as part of nature, and as a planner and landscape architect, he has had a more direct influence on planning. In *Design with Nature* (1969), he developed a methodology for planning that would be sensitive to the natural environment.

3. I do not accept all of the implications that Kohlberg (1977) draws, such as the idea that empirically some cultures are more morally evolved than others and that any given culture also evolves morally over time. He argues that in the United States, most adults probably never go through the last two stages. That is, they stop at the stage that stresses the maintenance of existing social rules and institutions. This makes one wonder whether the last two are really "higher" states like the others or just different adult approaches to ethics. The idea that they are "higher" really depends on a justification that they are morally "better," but this is a task not for empirical research but for rational moral argument. In "From Is to Ought: How to Commit the Naturalistic Fallacy and Get Away with It in the Study of Moral Development" (1971), Kohlberg does make an explicit reasoned argument for the idea that each successive stage can be thought of as morally better than the one before it, ending with the highest state (not described above), which uses the idea of justice and consistent universal moral principles, such as Kant's (1964) principle of humanity, as the basis for autonomous moral choice.

4. Because this kind of question was not anticipated when the interviews were done, information on where they came from and on their job histories was spotty. The most systematic information was where they had gotten their planning degree, if they had one, which was asked on the questionnaire.

5. The scales on substantive values were made up of value statements, about half for and half against any particular issue. The planners responded on a six-point scale ranging from "strongly agree" to "strongly disagree." In the tabula-

tion of the scale, the "against" items were reverse coded so that the final scale measures attitudes in favor of the value being measured.

The scale on attitudes toward low-income/minority groups was made up of six attitude items. Two emphasized the responsibility of the planner to analyze impacts of projects on disadvantaged groups and to see that the resources were redistributed to them. Two stated that neighborhoods or communities should be able to control who lived there. One said that planning is too concerned with low-income/minority issues, and the final one said that equal opportunity should not mean giving special treatment.

The development scale was made up of five attitude items. Two suggested that developers give people what they want and have an unjustified bad image. Two suggested that they only want to make money and have little or no concern for the good of the community. The final one said that there should be tighter controls on development.

On neither scale was the difference between Texas/Tennessee and California significant at the usual 0.05 level. On the low-income/minority scale, the scores were: California 3.85, Texas/Tennessee 3.42, significant = .06; on the prodevelopment scale, they were California 3.35, Texas/Tennessee 3.64, significant = .17.

Political views were measured by a seven-point scale labeled from "radical" to "conservative."

6. Attitudes about the environment were measured with a six-item scale. Two items were concerned with protecting the environment even if development were slowed or the measures necessary were hard. One said that limits on property rights were acceptable to preserve agricultural land. Two others said that planners were too concerned with the environment and that the cost of cleanup was too high. The final one said that the environment was important but that other objectives may be more so.

Part 3: Actions

CHAPTER 10: ACTING ON DIFFICULT CHOICES

1. Planners talked about such things as pressure, risk, or resistance, which allowed the difficulty of action to be gauged. They also talked about their own willingness or reluctance to raise issues or to act.

CHAPTER 11: ACTION, JUSTIFICATION, AND EFFECTIVENESS

1. The agency orientation scale was made up of five Likert-type attitude items coded on a six-point scale from "strongly disagree" to "strongly agree." Three of the items were concerned with the legitimacy of disagreement with rules or policies set by decision makers. One stated that the role of the planner is to understand the point of view of his or her administration and to assist in achieving its objectives. The last stated that a plan adopted by decision makers is a success even if it involved poor technical analysis.

2. The information on what tactics the planners would use is not comprehen-

sive. Tactics sometimes came up in cases and were discussed in that context. If the planner talked about tactics in a more general way, they were asked about whether they had used or would use certain tactics, such as manipulating data, leaking or withholding information, including expendables in plans that could later be bargained away, or doing end runs around superiors. In most cases, only one or a few of these tactics were actually discussed. One of the interviewers was also more likely to ask about it than the other two. In all, twenty-eight planners did not talk about tactics and were not asked.

3. This difference was not statistically significant, due in part to the fairly small numbers of cases in each group of planners. However, a t-test using role produced statistically significant differences between that smaller group of process planners and both the technicians and active planners.

CHAPTER 12: SHAPING ACTION ON ETHICS

1. "Straightness" was difficult to define empirically and therefore to measure precisely. It was not identical simply to acting ethically—it implied something about the motivation for action, a strictness that made the person act ethically from a sense of duty. The tally of straight planners is simply a tabulation of the people who I designated as "straight" based on an overall evaluation of their interview, using Kant's (1964) idea of duty as a criterion.

CHAPTER 13: ENCOURAGING ETHICAL ACTION

1. The relationship between the American Planning Association (APA) and the American Institute of Certified Planners (AICP) may need some clarification here. APA was formed out of the union of the American Institute of Planners, which represented professional planners, and the American Society of Planning Officials, which represented a broader group of professionals, plan commissioners, and other interested people. The American Institute of Planners became AICP, a unit within APA. It has its own code of ethics, which applies to professional planners, while APA has a somewhat more general code covering plan commissioners as well. The structure of state chapters is part of APA, not of AICP. At present, none of these parts of APA have as a policy or a mission to provide assistance to planners who work in corrupt communities. If APA undertook to provide such support, it would most likely be provided by state chapters, though AICP or the national APA might also play a supportive role.

Bibliography

Bibliography

Acton, H. B. 1946. Moral ends and means. In *Philosophical studies: essays in memory of L. Susan Stebbing*. London: Aristotelian Society. Reprinted 1970 as Does the end justify the means? In Singer, M., ed. 1970. *Morals and values*. New York: Charles Scribner.

Alinsky, S. 1946. *Reveille for radicals*. New York: Vintage Books.

Alterman, R. and MacRae, D., Jr. 1983. Planning and policy analysis: converging or diverging trends? *Journal of the American Planning Association* 49:2, 200–215.

Altshuler, A. 1965. *The city planning process*. Ithaca: Cornell University Press.

American Institute of Certified Planners (AICP). 1981. *Code of ethics and professional conduct*. Washington, DC: AICP.

———. 1983. *Ethical awareness in planning*. Washington, DC: AICP.

American Planning Association. 1987. Statement of ethical principles for planning. *Planning* 53:7, 35–38.

Anderson, C. W. 1979. The place of principles in policy analysis. *American Political Science Review* 73:3, 711–723.

Baier, K. 1965. *The moral point of view: a rational basis of ethics*. New York: Random House.

Baron, M. 1984. *The moral status of loyalty*. Dubuque, IA: Kendall/Hunt.

Barrett, C. 1984. Ethics in planning: you be the judge. *Planning* 50:11, 22–25.

———. 1989. Four perspectives on ethics. *Journal of the American Planning Association* 55:4, 474–483.

Barry, B. M. 1964. The public interest. *Proceedings of the Aristotelian Society*. London: Harrison and Sons.

Baum, H. 1983. *Planners and public expectations*. Cambridge, MA: Schenckman Publishing.

Bayles, M. 1981. *Professional ethics*. Belmont, CA: Wadsworth Publishing.

Beatley, T. 1991. A set of ethical principles to guide land use policy. *Land Use Policy* 8:1, 3–8.

Beauregard, R. 1978. Planning in an advanced capitalist state. In Burchell, R. and Sternlieb, G., eds. *Planning theory in the 1980s: a search for future directions*. New Brunswick, NJ: Center for Urban Policy Research, Rutgers University.

Beckman, N. 1964. The planner as a bureaucrat. *Journal of the American Institute of Planners* 30:4, 323–327.

Bellah, R., Madsen, R., Sullivan, W., Swindler, A., and Tipton, S. 1985. *Habits of the heart: individualism and commitment in American life*. Berkeley: University of California Press.

Benditt, T. 1973. The public interest. *Philosophy and Public Affairs* 2:3, 291–311.

Bentham, J. 1948 [1789]. *An introduction to the principles of morals and legislation*. Oxford: Blackwell.

Benveniste, G. 1989. *Mastering the politics of planning*. San Francisco: Jossey-Bass.

379

Bok, S. 1978. *Lying: moral choice in public and private life*. New York: Pantheon Books.
————. 1983. *Secrets: on the ethics of concealment and revelation*. New York: Vintage Books.
Bolan, R. 1969. Community decision behavior: the culture of planning. *Journal of the American Institute of Planners* 35:5, 301–310.
Bourke, V. 1968. *History of ethics*. New York: Doubleday.
Burke, J. 1986. *Bureaucratic responsibility*. Baltimore: Johns Hopkins University Press.
Caro, R. 1974. *The power broker: Robert Moses and the fall of New York*. New York: Alfred Knopf.
Davidoff, P. 1965. Advocacy and pluralism in planning. *Journal of the American Institute of Planners* 31:4, 331–339.
deNeufville, J. I. 1986. Usable planning theory: an agenda for research and education. In Checkoway, B., ed. *Strategic perspectives on planning practice*. Lexington, MA: Lexington Books.
Dotson, B., Godschalk, D., and Kaufman, J. 1989. *The planner as dispute resolver: concepts and teaching materials*. Washington, DC: National Institute for Dispute Resolution.
Douglas, W. 1952. *Beyond the high Himalayas*. Garden City, NY: Doubleday.
————. 1960. *My wilderness: the Pacific West*. Garden City, NY: Doubleday.
————. 1965. *A wilderness bill of rights*. Boston: Little, Brown.
————. 1972. *The three-hundred-year war: a chronicle of ecological disaster*. New York: Random House.
Dworkin, R. 1977. *Taking rights seriously*. Cambridge, MA: Harvard University Press.
Fainstein, N. and Fainstein, S. 1982. New debates in urban planning: the impact of Marxist theory within the United States. In Paris, C., ed. *Critical readings in planning theory*. Oxford: Pergamon Press.
Farnsworth, C. 1987. Survey of whistleblowers finds retaliation but few regrets. *New York Times*, February 22.
Feld, M. M. 1989. The Yonkers case and its implications for the teaching and practice of planning. *Journal of Planning Education and Research* 8:3, 169–176.
Finer, H. 1941. Administrative responsibility in democratic government. *Public Administration Review* 1:4, 335–350.
Flathman, R. 1966. *The public interest: an essay concerning the normative discourse of politics*. New York: John Wiley and Sons.
Forester, J. 1980. Critical theory and planning practice. *Journal of the American Planning Association* 46:3, 275–286.
————. 1987. Planning in the face of conflict: negotiation and mediation strategies in local land use regulation. *Journal of the American Planning Association* 53:3, 303–314.
Fox, S. 1981. *John Muir and his legacy*. Boston: Little, Brown.
Frankena, W. 1973. *Ethics*. 2d ed. Englewood Cliffs, NJ: Prentice Hall.

Freedman, B. 1978. A meta-ethics for professional morality. *Ethics* 89:1, 1–19.

Freidson, E. 1973. *Profession of medicine: a study of the sociology of applied knowledge*. New York: Dodd, Mead.

Gerth, H. H. and Mills, C. W. 1946. *From Max Weber: essays in sociology*. New York: Oxford University Press.

Gewirth, A. 1986. Professional ethics: the separatist thesis. *Ethics* 96:1, 282–300.

Glaser, B. and Strauss, A. 1967. *The discovery of grounded theory: strategies for qualitative research*. Chicago: Aldine Publishing.

Goldman, A. 1980. *The moral foundations of professional ethics*. Totowa, NJ: Rowman and Littlefield.

Goodwin, K. and Mitchell, R. 1982. Rational models, collective goods and nonelectoral political behavior. *Western Political Quarterly* 35:2, 161–181.

Habermas, J. 1975. *Legitimation crisis*. Translated by Thomas McCarthy. Boston: Beacon Press.

————. 1979. *Communication and the evolution of society*. Translated by Thomas McCarthy. Boston: Beacon Press.

Hancock, R. 1974. *Twentieth century ethics*. New York: Columbia University Press.

Haug, M. and Sussman, M. 1969. Professional autonomy and the revolt of the client. *Social Problems* 17, 153–161.

Hecimovich, J. 1989. *Planners' salaries and employment trends, 1989*. Chicago: American Planning Association, PAS Report, no. 423.

Held, V. 1970. *The public interest and individual interests*. New York: Basic Books.

————. 1984. *Rights and goods*. New York: Free Press.

Hendler, S. 1991. Ethics in planning: the views of students and practitioners. *Journal of Planning Education and Research* 10:2, 99–105.

————. Forthcoming. Planners talking about professional conflicts. *Journal of Architectural and Planning Research*.

Hill, S. B. 1975. Self-determination and autonomy. In Wasserstrom, R., ed. *Today's moral problems*. New York: Macmillan.

Hirschman, A. 1970. *Exit, voice and loyalty*. Cambridge, MA: Harvard University Press.

Hoch, C. 1987. *Planning threatened: a final report on planners and political conflict*. Chicago: American Planning Association.

————. 1988. Conflict at large: a national survey of planners and political conflict. *Journal of Planning Education and Research* 8:1, 25–34.

Hoch, C. and Cibulskis, A. 1987. Planning threatened: a preliminary report of planners and political conflict. *Journal of Planning Education and Research* 6:2, 99–107.

Howe, E. 1980a. Role choices of urban planners. *Journal of the American Planning Association* 46:4, 398–409.

————. 1980b. Public professions and the private model of professionalism. *Social Work* 25:3, 179–191.

————. 1990. Normative ethics in planning. *Journal of Planning Literature* 5:2, 123–150.

———. 1992. Professional roles and the public interest in planning. *Journal of Planning Literature* 6:3, 230–248.

———. Forthcoming. Introduction: ethical theory in practice. In Hendler, S., ed. *Planning ethics: a reader in planning theory, practice and education.* New Brunswick, NJ: Center for Urban Policy Research, Rutgers University.

Howe, E. and Kaufman, J. 1979. The ethics of contemporary American planners. *Journal of the American Planning Association* 45:3, 243–255.

———. 1981. The values of contemporary American planners. *Journal of the American Planning Association* 47:3, 266–278.

Innes, J. E. 1990. *Knowledge and public policy: the search for meaningful indicators.* 2d ed. New Brunswick, NJ: Transaction Publishers.

James, G. 1983. Whistleblowing: its nature and justification. In Robinson, W., Pritchard, M., and Ellin, J., eds. *Profits and professions.* Clifton, NJ: Humana.

Kant, I. 1964 [1785]. *Groundwork of the metaphysic of morals.* Translated by H. J. Paton. New York: Harper Torchbooks.

Kantor, P. 1988. *The dependent city.* Glenview, IL: Scott, Foresman.

Kaufman, J. 1978. The planner as interventionist in public policy issues. In Burchell, R. and Sternlieb, G., eds. *Planning theory in the 1980s.* New Brunswick, NJ: Center for Urban Policy Research, Rutgers University.

———. 1986. Making planners more effective. In Checkoway, B., ed. *Strategic perspectives on planning practice.* Lexington, MA: Lexington Books.

———. 1987. Hamlethics in planning: to do or not to do. *Business and Professional Ethics Journal* 6:3, 67–77.

Klosterman, R. 1980. A public interest criterion. *Journal of the American Planning Association* 46:3, 323–333.

Kohlberg, L. 1971. From is to ought: how to commit the naturalistic fallacy and get away with it in the study of moral development. In Mischel, T., ed. *Cognitive development and epistemology.* New York: Academic Press.

———. 1977. The future of liberalism as the dominant ideology of the Western world. *Proceedings of the Annenberg conference on the future of the West.* Los Angeles: Center for the Study of the American Experience.

———. 1987. Indoctrination versus relativity in value education. In Sher, G., ed. *Moral philosophy: selected readings.* San Diego, CA: Harcourt Brace Jovanovich.

Kraushaar, R. 1988. Outside the whale: progressive planning and the dilemmas of radical reform. *Journal of the American Planning Association* 54:1, 91–100.

Krumholz, N. and Forester, J. 1990. *Making equity planning work.* Philadelphia: Temple University Press.

Kultgen, J. 1988. *Ethics and professionalism.* Philadelphia: University of Pennsylvania Press.

Lang, R. and Hendler, S. 1986. Right or wrong: planners respond. *Ontario Planning Journal* 1:6, 13–15.

Larson, M. S. 1977. *The rise of professionalism: a sociological analysis.* Berkeley: University of California Press.

Leopold, A. 1968 [1949]. *A Sand County almanac, and sketches here and there.* New York: Oxford University Press.

Leys, W. and Perry, C. M. 1959. *Philosophy and the public interest.* Madison, WI: Symposium of the Western Division of the American Philosophical Association.

McConnell, G. 1966. *Private power and American democracy.* New York: Vintage Books.

McHarg, I. 1969. *Design with nature.* Garden City, NY: Natural History Press.

Marcuse, P. 1976. Professional ethics and beyond: values in planning. *Journal of the American Institute of Planners* 42:3, 264–74.

Martin, M. 1981. Rights and the meth-ethics of professional morality. *Ethics* 91, 619–625.

Martin, R. and Nickel, J. 1980. Recent work on the concept of rights. *American Philosophical Quarterly* 17:3, 165–180.

Martin, S. O. 1989. Above reproach. *Planning* 55:10, 18–21.

May, J. 1976. *Professionals and clients: a constitutional struggle.* Beverly Hills, CA: Sage Professional Papers in Administrative and Policy Studies Series 03–036.

Mayo, J. 1982. Sources of job dissatisfaction: ideals versus realities in planning. *Journal of the American Planning Association* 48:4, 481–498.

Meyer, W. 1975. *The public good and political authority: a pragmatic proposal.* Port Washington, NY: Kennikat Press.

Meyerson, M. and Banfield, E. 1955. *Politics, planning and the public interest.* New York: Free Press.

Miles, M. and Huberman, A. M. 1984. *Qualitative data analysis.* Beverly Hills, CA: Sage Publications.

Mill, J. S. 1985 [1865]. *Utilitarianism.* New York: Macmillan.

Mitchell, R. 1979. National environmental lobbies and the apparent illogic of collective action. In Russell, C., ed. *Collective decision-making.* Baltimore: Johns Hopkins University Press.

Moore, M. 1981. Realms of obligation and virtue. In Fleishman, J., Liebman, L., and Moore, M., eds. *Public duties: the moral obligations of government officials.* Cambridge, MA: Harvard University Press.

Nagel, T. 1978. Ruthlessness in public life. In Hampshire, S., ed. *Public and private morality.* Cambridge: Cambridge University Press.

Needleman, M. and Needleman, C. 1974. *Guerrillas in the bureaucracy.* New York: John Wiley and Sons.

Nigro, L. and Richardson, W. 1990. Between citizen and administrator: administrative ethics and PAR. *Public Administration Review* 50:6, 623–636.

Olson, M. 1965. *The logic of collective action.* Cambridge, MA: Harvard University Press.

Peterson, P. 1981. *City limits.* Chicago: University of Chicago Press.

Rabinovitz, F. 1967. Politics, personality, and planning. *Public Administration Review* 27:1, 18–24.

———. 1969. *City politics and planning.* New York: Atherton Press.

———. 1989. The role of negotiation in planning, management and policy analysis. *Journal of Planning Education and Research* 8:2, 87–96.

Rawls, J. 1955. Two concepts of rules. *Philosophical Review* 64:1, 3–32.

Sagoff, M. 1988. *The economy of the earth*. Cambridge: Cambridge University Press.

Schiesl, M. 1977. *The politics of efficiency: municipal administration and reform in America, 1880–1920*. Berkeley: University of California Press.

Schubert, G. 1957. The public interest in administrative decision-making. *American Political Science Review* 51, 346–368.

———. 1960. *The public interest: a critique of the theory of a political concept*. Glencoe, IL: Free Press.

———. 1967. Is there a public interest theory? In Friedrich, C., ed. *Nomos V: the public interest*. New York: Atherton Press.

Scott, J. 1972. *Comparative political corruption*. Englewood Cliffs, NJ: Prentice Hall.

Sorauf, F. 1957. The public interest reconsidered. *Journal of Politics* 19:4, 616–639.

———. 1967. The conceptual muddle. In Friedrich, C., ed. *Nomos V: the public interest*. New York: Atherton Press.

Strauss, A. 1987. *Qualitative analysis for social scientists*. Cambridge: Cambridge University Press.

Susskind, L. and Ozawa, C. 1984. Mediated negotiation in the public sector: the planner as mediator. *Journal of Planning Education and Research* 4:1, 5–15.

Taylor, P., ed. 1972. *Problems of moral philosophy*. 2d ed. Encino, CA: Dickenson Publishing.

Tillock, H. and Morrison, D. 1979. Group size and contributions to collective action: an examination of Olson's theory using data from zero population growth research. In Kreisberg, L., ed. *Research on social movements, conflict and change*. Vol. 2. Greenwich, CT: JAI Press.

Toulmin, S. 1950. *An examination of the place of reason in ethics*. Cambridge: Cambridge University Press.

Urmson, J. O. 1953. The interpretation of the moral philosophy of J. S. Mill. *Philosophical Quarterly* 3, 33–39.

Vasu, M. L. 1979. *Politics and planning: a national study of American planners*. Chapel Hill, NC: University of North Carolina Press.

Verba, S. and Nie, N. 1972. *Participation in America: political democracy and social equality*. New York: Harper and Row.

Wachs, M. 1982. Ethical dilemmas in forecasting for public policy. *Public Administration Review* 42:2, 562–567.

Walker, R. 1950. *The planning function in urban government*. Chicago: University of Chicago Press.

Walsh, E. and Warland, R. 1983. Social movement involvement in the wake of a nuclear accident. *American Sociological Review* 48:6, 764–780.

Walzer, M. 1973. Political action: the problem of dirty hands. *Philosophy and Public Affairs* 2:2, 160–180.

Warnock, M. 1978. *Ethics since 1900*. Oxford: Oxford University Press.

Weber, M. 1947. *The theory of social and economic organization*. Translated by A. M. Henderson and T. Parsons, ed. Talcott Parsons. Oxford: Oxford University Press.

Weisband, E. and Franck, T. 1975 *Resignation in protest*. New York: Viking Press.

Where do you draw the line? an ethics game. 1977. Del Mar, CA: Simile II.

Wilson, W. 1887. The study of administration. *Political Science Quarterly* 2:2, 197–222.

Index